# THE ONLY TRADITION

SUNY Series in Western Esoteric Traditions
David Appelbaum, editor

# THE ONLY TRADITION

William W. Quinn, Jr.

*State University of New York Press*

BF
1595
.Q35
1997

Permission to include the listed materials from the following persons or organizations is gratefully acknowledged. To David Johns for photo reproduction of his painting, *DO'TSOH (The Holy Spirit)*, in the cover design, and to Jerry Jacka for the photograph of the painting; to the University of Chicago Press for permission to quote from Mircea Eliade's "Some Notes on *Theosophia perennis:* Ananda K. Coomaraswamy and Henry Corbin" in *History of Religions*, Vol. 19, No. 2 (1979). © Copyright 1979 by the University of Chicago; to the Johns Hopkins University Press for permission to quote from Charles B. Schmitt's "Perennial Philosophy: From Agostino Steuco to Leibniz" in *Journal of the History of Ideas*, Vol. 27, No. 4 (1966). Reprinted by permission of the Johns Hopkins University Press; to Cambridge University Press for permission to quote from Edward Shils's "Tradition" in *Comparative Studies in Society and History*, Vol. 13, No. 2 (1971). © Copyright 1971 by The Society for the Comparative Study of Society and History. Reprinted with the permission of Cambridge University Press; to Renée Weber for permission to quote from "The Reluctant Tradition" in *Main Currents in Modern Thought*, Vol. 31, No. 4 (1975); to Theodore Roszak for permission to quote from "Ethics, Ecstasy, and the Study of New Religions" in Jacob Needleman and George Baker, eds., *Understanding the New Religions*, New York: Seabury Press, 1978; to James Wetmore of Sophia Perennis et Universalis for permission to quote from Marco Pallis's "A Fateful Meeting of Minds: A. K. Coomaraswamy and R. Guénon" in *Studies in Comparative Religion*, Vol. 12, Nos. 3 & 4 (1978); and to *Parabola* magazine for permission to quote from Seyyed H. Nasr's "Progress and Evolution: A Reappraisal from the Traditional Perspective" in *Parabola*, Vol. VI, No. 2 (Spring 1981).

Published by
State University of New York Press, Albany

© 1997 State University of New York

For information, address State University of New York Press,
State University Plaza, Albany, N.Y., 12246

Production by Kay Bolton
Marketing by Theresa Abad Swierzowski

**Library of Congress Cataloging-in-Publication Data**

Quinn, William W., 1947–
    The only tradition / William W. Quinn, Jr.
        p.   cm. — (SUNY series in Western esoteric traditions)
    Includes bibliographical references and index.
    ISBN 0-7914-3213-0 (hc : alk. paper). — ISBN 0-7914-3214-9 (pb : alk. paper)
    1. Hermetism—History—20th century.  2. Coomaraswamy, Ananda Kentish, 1877–1947.  3. Guénon, René.  4. Schuon, Frithjof, 1907– . I. Title.  II. Series.
BF1595.Q35  1997
148—dc21
                          96-42957
                          CIP

10 9 8 7 6 5 4 3 2 1

*For Mircea Eliade*

*CREDE UT INTELLIGAS.*
*INTELLIGE UT CREDAS.*

# CONTENTS

# PREFACE

Most thinking people in the modern West are generally anxious, if not actually frightened or depressed, about both the present and the future. People are encouraged, simply by contrast with what predominates, to learn of acts of kindness and selflessness by individuals or groups, and by sincere expressions of beauty in its various forms. Moreover, it cannot be denied that everyone experiences periods of joy, of happiness, moments of pleasure, and even occasional optimism. But these are typically transitory in the times in which we live and eventually fade when peoples' attentions are once again turned to the overbearing, relentless problems associated with modernity of the twentieth century—whose problems *are* unique in history—and of surviving in it on a daily basis.

In the landscape of modernity, these people look around them and see a sustained decline of values, morals, and ethical conduct in the daily lives of the populace. They see the predominance of materialism and secularism and the comparative absence of the sacred. They see both their private corporate and public institutions, including their leaders and legislators, driven by a relentless and sometimes ruthless quest for money and power, insuring benefits for special interests that often sacrifice what is best for society as a whole. They see—and experience as confusion and frustration—the growth of complexity to extremes in these institutions along with the commensurate rise of specialization. They witness an explosion of gratuitous sex both as entertainment and as a universal marketing device. They see random and senseless violence everywhere. They see excessive crime rates, exacerbated by a failure of judicial systems to respond. They see the strain and breakdown of relations between men and women; they see the virtual collapse of the nuclear family and family cohesion and extrapolate about its ultimate effects on society's cohesion. They worry about the impending fate of their children and their grandchildren. They see the appearance of new and the reappearance of old diseases, deadly bacteria, and exotic viruses; they see widespread substance abuse and addiction, and watch the parallel and steady rise in suicide rates. They learn

with a numbing repetition about increasing and horrific acts of terrorism; of anarchy and savage massacres in regional wars, and of "ethnic
cleansing." They see not the demise but the rise in racial bigotry and
religious fanaticism. They see the drastic effects of rapid global overpopulation and the famine, homelessness, and irreversible over-exploi-
tation of natural resources and entropy that occur in its wake. They
witness the physical pollution of their local environments and lament
the steady destruction of the world's rain forests, fisheries, and biosphere. And they still believe in the possibility, if not probability, of
regional nuclear conflict triggering global nuclear conflict and the
advent of mutually assured destruction.

     These same thinking people also sense that history is not merely
repeating itself, but that our times are unique in that these problems are
all interrelated and with each year have gotten a little worse, not better,
with no foreseeable way out except perhaps by some massive, sobering,
apocalyptic event of global dimensions that could occur through one of
several possible alternatives. They seek with little success answers to
their questions and solutions for their problems in popular psychology
or in their churches, which, in these times, offer only rationalistic and
thus confused theology. They further seek meaning, order, purpose, and
orientation to bring serenity to the anxiety, foreboding, and moral relativism brought about by the cumulative and exponential effects of all
these debilitating conditions. They seek relief from a profound malaise
of the spirit.

     One may wonder, and legitimately so, whether reading a book
predicated in part upon such a dire and pessimistic view of the human
condition is worthwhile; whether it would not be more productive to
consume uplifting fare as an antidote to the spiritual, social, and material desolation of modernity. A response to this is provided by Huston
Smith, who writes in *The Religions of Man* that "An observer's depiction of man's current condition may be as dark as can be drawn; the
question of pessimism does not arise until he speaks to whether it can
be improved."

     Therefore one asks: Are there, in fact, answers to these questions
that will provide solutions to these problems? Is there a way out short of
systemic breakdown or annihilation? Is it too late to salvage, or can the
current condition of humanity be improved? Ananda Coomaraswamy
and René Guénon answered affirmatively to these questions. The
answers, they would say, do exist and are there at the peak of the moun-

tain but are accessible only for those who have made or who are willing to make the difficult trek to the summit. The way is not easy. There is no dogma to accept, no organization to join that will ensure success. One must prepare, and train, and study, and persevere. The short answer to these questions is simply stated: All that is wrong with the modern West, indeed, the modern world, can be ameliorated by *an affirmative application of first principles to contingent circumstances*. But what does this mean? Many thinking people of the modern West also suffer from the proclivity for instant gratification: they want bullet answers to everything immediately, and some cryptic, enigmatic affirmation about metaphysical "first principles" will not suffice.

A percentage of these people will read the book in order to clarify this statement, and of those who do some may find it ponderous and difficult. To the extent that this reflects the author's shortcomings in attempting to set forth the central ideas, principles, and worldview of the Tradition as professed by Coomaraswamy and Guénon, he apologizes. But the material itself is not easy, especially insofar as the modern Western mentality typically operates on an empirical and exclusively rational level that will tend to regard the first principles of the Tradition—upon initial encounter—as inscrutable at best, irrational at worst, and unacceptable in either case. For the reader whose heart and mind do not yet resonate to the full meaning of the italicized statement above, but who nonetheless feels compelled to try, unpacking this statement fully will require determination and toil. Yet, one must remember that nothing worthwhile comes easy.

So saying, the author takes no credit for anything worthwhile in this book. Whatever may be worthwhile in these pages is a consequence of the power—in fact, the brilliance—of the exposition of Coomaraswamy and Guénon. Moreover, this book should be viewed by the reader first as simply a *précis* of the Tradition as elucidated by these two men and, second, as an invitation to go directly to their published works. And if, having done this, the reader still fails to intuit and to begin to understand, he or she ought not give up, but should reread, and in addition read the works of others like Frithjof Schuon and Seyyed Hossein Nasr.

This book is not meant exclusively for the academic or the specialist. It has been reorganized in a way that does not presuppose years of learning in the field, and for this reason contains perhaps more prefatory and definitional material than normal. This is what might make the book ponderous to some. But the author hoped by this method to include a wider audience of men and women of intelligence who are impelled to seek answers to the perennial questions that involve not only personal spiritual development but a corresponding cultural equilibrium, and the reciprocity between these.

Strictly speaking, this book contains no "argument" apropos of the current fashion within the academic milieu whereby such monographs are expected to contain advocation of a particular agenda in addition to a thesis or conclusion predicated upon existing and/or new data. Moreover, this book hardly contains a thesis, unless it be that recorded history evidences the existence of an esoteric, primordial Tradition based upon a set of a priori and immutable first principles, true now as always, which in all places and in all times have had expositors, and that the two greatest of such Western expositors in the first half of the twentieth century were Coomaraswamy and Guénon. Less than a thesis, to those already students of the Tradition the proposition just stated is simply a straightforward and self-evident declaration of an objective truth. However, to those for whom the notion of such a Tradition, the only Tradition, is one of first impression, this proposition may be a monumental thesis depending upon the degree of intellectual intuition with which they assimilate it or, to be more precise, "recollect" it.

In a real sense, this book is devoted to the latter and not the former category of reader. Naturally, the author hopes that his efforts will be of some practical use and benefit to those who are now students of the Tradition. But the greater hope is that this book will serve as an introduction to and guide for those who are setting out to acquire knowledge of this most recent, and most brilliant, exposition of the Tradition by Coomaraswamy and Guénon. *Intellige ut credas.* One hopes that these readers—to repeat—will use this work as a tool for reconnaissance and, once having done this, will go directly to the original works of Coomaraswamy and Guénon. From these works, they will be further directed to the study of certain classic texts of the Tradition from all the world's religions and premodern philosophies and to their study in the original languages.

This book also contains various themes or subtheses that are inextricable from the exposition of Tradition in the writings of Coomaraswamy and Guénon. These are more fully developed throughout the book, but briefly they are that the first principles of the Tradition—the *philosophia perennis*—are essential, and that substance proceeds from essence; that Traditional societies were those wholly informed by these first principles and thereby unanimous and substantively reflective of the essential principles; that a key characteristic of Traditional culture is the absence of bifurcation, or alternatively the fusion, of sacred and secular; that the description "Traditional" encompasses both premodern nonliterate or tribal societies and literate civilizations; and that due to the inexorable cycles in duration the modern world is at present virtually entirely secular and therefore the antithesis of Traditional. There is a demonstrable sequence and even reciprocity among these themes or subtheses that this book attempts to clarify for those already students of the Tradition and to reveal to those newly come to its study.

As a an afterthought to the notion of themes and subtheses, the author has two admissions to make. First, the discussions in this book of modern philosophy and medieval Christendom are marginal in the sense that, while the author's familiarity with these areas is adequate, he is by no means a specialist in either. Indeed, they, in addition to Parts 2 and 3 generally, could be the subjects of books of equal size to this one. These areas are painted in very broad strokes in order to accomplish the larger purpose of putting the Traditional material in context. Second, there is a preponderant use of the masculine gender throughout. There are several reasons for this which need not detain us here, but the author recognizes the issue and wishes to state that in all cases not specifically discussing the principle of gender where specific use of "he" and "she" is required, the masculine gender is meant to be inclusive and is not used thoughtlessly or to give offense to anyone.

Finally, the author wishes to make an observation about the life and works of Frithjof Schuon. The reader will discover that relatively little is said about Schuon within the text of this book, nor is there much citation from his considerable corpus of published writings on Traditional principles. This is so because it seemed best to take an historical approach and to begin at the beginning with Coomaraswamy and Guénon, and concentrate, metaphorically speaking, on Boaz and Jachin, the two strong and upright pillars upon which the contemporary structure or school of Traditional thought is established. At the same time, my opinion is that Schuon, who published his greatest works in the second half of the twentieth century, can be viewed as an equal to Coomaraswamy and Guénon in his own right, different from the former as the former were from each other. I encourage those unfamiliar with his published corpus to read and assimilate it, and can suggest no better place to start than with Seyyed Hossein Nasr's compilation of *The Essential Writings of Frithjof Schuon.* I concur with Professor Nasr's remark in that book that Schuon "is the premier living expositor of that *sophia perennis* which lies at the heart of all revelations."

# ACKNOWLEDGMENTS

The author's appreciation for the contributions of others in the production of this book extends across a wide range of individuals, and back nearly two decades to its beginnings. By way of explanation, this book is essentially a revised and updated dissertation submitted in candidacy for the Ph.D. at the University of Chicago in 1981.

The first and most heartfelt expression of gratitude must go to my teacher, the late Professor Mircea Eliade, who first introduced me to the writings of Coomaraswamy and Guénon during the time I was a student in the Divinity School and who oversaw my thesis for Master of Arts, subsequently revised and published as "Ananda K. Coomaraswamy on the Philosophia Perennis." It was Professor Eliade, more than any other, who directed my education in the scholarly research and exposition of such principles as are the subject of this book, and who, during memorable talks in his office at the Meadville-Lombard Theological Seminary, brought me some distance along the path of understanding throughout my years at the university.

How fortunate I was to have three such distinguished scholars on my dissertation committee is equal to my indebtedness to them for what was finally produced. Professor Eliade's role was, in a real sense, cultivating the spirit of this work. Professor Martin Marty oversaw both the organization and logistics and always encouraged me in his typically kind and magnanimous way. Finally, Professor Wendy Doniger's instructive skepticism compelled me to substantiate and justify everything, which, I am now convinced, improved the work immeasurably. I owe these three, together with my Committee Chair Professor Karl Wientraub, much more than these few lines acknowledging my appreciation.

During the intervening years since my studies at Chicago, revisions were made to the dissertation/manuscript in bits and pieces, mostly in terms of updating and of adding to the bibliography as new materials were published. One may wonder why such a hiatus occurred between its production as a dissertation and its publication as a book. To be candid, attempts were made to publish during those intervening years, all with the same result: a polite letter would arrive from the press, containing an avowal of the editor's belief in the quality of the work together with a statement lamenting the fact that no market existed for scholarly treatments of esotericism. One is left to speculate whether the dissertation appeared before its time or whether the SUNY Press series in Western Esoteric Traditions began late.

Whatever one concludes with regard to this speculation, the fact is that the answer no longer matters. The book is now a fait accompli, and for this I wish to acknowledge a great debt to William D. Eastman of the Press for his unremitting support of this project from the very first.

I also wish to thank James R. Wetmore for his review of portions of the manuscript dealing with forums of the Traditional perspective and for insights into certain of the Traditional writers whose works are cited in the text or listed in the bibliography. Professor James A. Santucci was kind enough to review portions of the manuscript concerning theosophy and the Theosophical movement in the late nineteenth and early twentieth centuries, and for this I wish to express my appreciation. Finally, I owe a debt of gratitude to Jessie Camenzind for her skillful and assiduous preparation of the manuscript, and to Les and Kay Bolton for their tasteful and thorough professionalism in its production.

Like all authors everywhere, one is influenced by numerous other people in discussions about the subject, whether those discussions are long and serious or short and casual. To any and all who in such fashion may have contributed an idea or valuable feedback along the way, I wish to express my thanks and acknowledge the debt. Finally, translations from the French, Spanish, and German are mine alone, as are any deficiencies they may contain.

# ABBREVIATIONS

BK        *Am I My Brother's Keeper?* (Coomaraswamy)

BUGB-D    "The Bugbear of Democracy, Freedom, and Equality" (Coomaraswamy)

CLW       *Coomaraswamy: His Life and Work* (Lipsey)

COTPA     *Christian and Oriental Philosophy of Art* (Coomaraswamy)

Crise     *Le crise du monde moderne* (Guénon)

Croix     *Le symbolisme de la croix* (Guénon)

De PP     *De Perenni Philosophia* (Steuchus)

ET        *Études Traditionnelles*

FSFT      *Figures of Speech or Figures of Thought* (Coomaraswamy)

GGK       "Sir Gawain and the Green Knight: Indra and Namuci" (Coomaraswamy)

HB        *Hinduism and Buddhism* (Coomaraswamy)

Hindu     *Introduction to the Study of the Hindu Doctrines* (Guénon)

OEO       *Orient et Occident* (Guénon)

PP:ASL    "Perennial Philosophy: From Agostino Steuco to Leibniz" (Schmitt)

Règne     *Le règne de la quantité et les signes des temps* (Guénon)

SD I&II   *The Secret Doctrine* (Volumes I and II) (Blavatsky)

SCR       *Studies in Comparative Religion*

SG        *The Sword of Gnosis* (Needleman)

SL        *Selected Letters* (Coomaraswamy)

SPM       *Selected Papers: Metaphysics* (Coomaraswamy)

SPTAS     *Selected Papers: Traditional Art and Symbolism* (Coomaraswamy)

TNA       *The Transformation of Nature in Art* (Coomaraswamy)

Vedānta   *Man and His Becoming According to the Vedānta* (Guénon)

# PART I

## BACKGROUND AND PREMISES

# 1

## Introductory

The apse mosaic in the north ambulatory of Rome's fourth-century basilica of Sta. Costanza depicts Christ standing on a rock, from which flow the four streams of Paradise. His right hand is raised in benediction; his left contains a scroll that is being handed to St. Peter. This action is the *traditio legis*, the "handing over of the law," and is drawn from a prevalent motif in the classical art of late antiquity. Yet, there is a new element involved in the Sta. Costanza mosaic. Though the *traditio legis* motif is essentially the same as in the Roman imperial depictions, the Christian mosaic shows a new law—a new tradition—being established.

Not too dissimilar from this fourth-century appropriation of a standard mode used to illustrate a new perception is the use of the term *Tradition* in the writings of two twentieth-century metaphysicists:[1] René Guénon and Ananda K. Coomaraswamy. These two men produced a voluminous amount of written material in the general areas of comparative religion and culture, esotericism, and natural metaphysics. They consistently espoused a particular ideology and hermeneutics of the religious and philosophical material they treated throughout. René Guénon (1886–1951) was a Frenchman who adopted Islam and later relocated to Cairo (1930), and Ananda K. Coomaraswamy (1877–1947) was an Anglo-Ceylonese raised and educated in England who emigrated to America in 1917. In their later years, the two became colleagues and frequent correspondents. Their "particular ideology" they labeled Primordial Tradition and Philosophia Perennis, respectively. They each abbreviated and referred to this ideology in their writings as the Tradition—a specific and limited usage of the word not part of the normal definition. Their works, and their views, are not yet widely known, for as Edward Shils observed, "It is rare [in modernity] to encounter persons who pride themselves on the espousal of a tradition, call it that, and regard it as a good thing."[2] Different from the Roman and early Christian usage, this twentieth-century usage changes the verbal noun form *traditio* into the proper noun form Tradition,[3] by which Guénon and Coomaraswamy meant *a group of interdependent metaphysical principles and a concomitant cultural worldview*—these being the primary subjects of investigation in this work.

A useful prologue to the detailed examination of the highly specific and particularized usage of the term Tradition in the writings of Guénon and Coomaraswamy is the examination in Appendix A of etymology, definition, and variants in current conventional usage of the word tradition, especially as it applies to the history of culture, the "social sciences" (namely, sociology and anthropology), and religious studies. The contrast thereby delineated between the conventional usages and the particularized usage will help localize and define the latter within today's general discourse on tradition, which is also among the specific aims of this work.

Tradition is not a long word; neither is it obscure. Although this is expressly a book about the word tradition and its particularized meaning, it is at the same time a book about *culture* and a way of viewing culture as Guénon and Coomaraswamy viewed it. But this is not all, for in addition to explicating a particular perspective of culture, it is equally an explication of natural metaphysics—of the philosophia perennis— and of the first principles of this metaphysic that both inform and consequently define Traditional culture. This is so because, in the larger worldview of Coomaraswamy and Guénon, these elements of the term Tradition are inextricable and cannot be discussed intelligibly unless discussed in reference to each other.

There is a nuance of difference between the relationship of Tradition and culture that occurs in the thought of Coomaraswamy and in that of Guénon, and which should be disclosed at the outset. It is described as a "nuance" here because it is more a matter of placement of emphasis than of any real disagreement between the two men, yet it goes to the heart of a difference in the way certain Traditionalists—those who have followed in the pioneering footsteps of Coomaraswamy and Guénon— perceive the currents of twentieth-century Traditional thought. Coomaraswamy emphasized an absolute integration or fusion of sacred religion and culture in order for any given society to be called Traditional, and in any society such as this the activity of all persons—by virtue of fulfilling their vocations, whether they be sacerdotal or otherwise—was initiatory. While Guénon did not refute this, he emphasized the Traditionality, as it were, of the orthodox elements in major religions and of esoteric initiatic associations within societies both premodern and modern, and believed in the availability of regular initiation in certain surviving lineages within Christian and Buddhist culture, of bona fide *gurus* and their students in Hindu culture, and most especially in Islamic culture of the Sufi *ṭarīqa* of which he and Frithjof Schuon were and are participants.

Other similar nuances of difference exist both between the views of Coomaraswamy and Guénon, and the way in which they are perceived by others. For example, in Part 1 of *Access to Western Esotericism*, Antoine Faivre posits three "paths" of Tradition or esotericism today—purist, historical, and humanist—and lists René Guénon as a "purist." To this purist path or category, fairly accurately described by Professor Faivre, we add Ananda Coomaraswamy. This we do—using Faivre's own criteria—not only because of the similarity between what Coomaraswamy meant by Tradition and what Guénon meant, but also because his express views of modernity paralleled those of Guénon. Faivre's segregation of Guénon from Coomaraswamy points to a further issue that differentiates certain Traditionalists as amongst themselves, and one to which attention should be given at the beginning in order to establish parameters.

The position taken in this treatise is that, notwithstanding their different methods and styles, Coomaraswamy and Guénon were coequal expositors of the Tradition. One significant effect of this position, for example, is the way in which the forums of Traditional perspective are depicted in chapter 4. This position can be described as the *historical* analysis of the Traditional perspective, and is based on (1) the fact that the two men were close contemporaries, and (2) the fundamental similarity of the metaphysical content of their works.

The other principal position involves the life and work of Frithjof Schuon, and holds that Guénon and he were successive "continuators" of the Tradition, while Coomaraswamy was a "complementor." This position, which can be described as the *initiatic* analysis of the Traditional perspective, primarily involves a strong Sufi or orthodox Islamic influence, insofar as Guénon and Schuon were both regularly initiated into Sufi *ṭarīqas* or spiritual fraternities as were a number of other later Traditional writers, whereas Coomaraswamy was a Hindu and by comparison with the former was neither a specialist in Arabic nor Islamic metaphysics.

Where, as here, the objective is to begin at the beginning to describe Traditional exposition in the twentieth century within a comprehensive framework, the historical analysis is necessary since it alone accommodates the biographical and historical data. Schuon, for example, published his first major doctrinal book in 1948, a year after Coomaraswamy's death and only three years prior to Guénon's death, and so could not be considered a pioneer in the same sense as Coomaraswamy and Guénon. On the other hand, Coomaraswamy differed from both Guénon and Schuon by virtue of his academic credentials and his target audience of academicians. This fact, taken together with the active participation in the Sufi *ṭarīqas* held in common by Guénon and Schuon, does lend viability to the initiatic analysis, but still cannot raise Schuon to the level of a founder of twentieth-century Traditional exposition in the historical sense.

There are, in addition, certain other minority views within the greater Traditional school that can be described as permutations of these two principal positions—for example, Schuon as the culmination of work only partially introduced by Guénon and/or Coomaraswamy, or the various "Guénonian" spin-off groups in France devoted to some particular aspect of the teacher's writings. The point is that it is necessary to clarify and articulate one's premise. Whichever position one begins with will affect the outcome: for the author, it will affect the organization and exposition of the subject; for the reader, it will affect his or her understanding or judgment of the book.

Brief biographies of Coomaraswamy and Guénon will, from here, begin Part 1, followed by an examination of currents or "forums" within modern Traditional exposition, the hermeneutical method of those in the Traditional school, and the basal notions of *quality* and *quantity* that are central to the Traditional worldview. Part 2 discusses briefly, and from several sides, the term and concept of philosophia perennis, followed by a similarly brief discussion of both ancient *theosophia* and modern Theosophy, whose late nineteenth-century dissemination by H. P. Blavatsky is most relevant due to its direct influence on both Coomaraswamy and Guénon, and ending with an enumeration of the first principles of Tradition that contrasts the latter with those principles as found in modern Theosophy. Part 3, which could be called the heart of the book, examines Traditional culture—both tribal, or "primitive," and developed—compares them, and seeks to identify the elements of Tradition in medieval Christendom as viewed by Coomaraswamy and Guénon in order to prepare for the contrast between Traditional Western culture and modern (non-Traditional) Western culture, which is the subject of Part 4. Finally, Part 4 makes the comparison just mentioned and, using the basic notions of culture as revealed in the writings of Guénon and Coomaraswamy, extrapolates about a possible if not inevitable development of a new form of planetary Traditional culture in future millenia based on the first principles of Tradition. Wherever possible, and as much as possible, the views of Coomaraswamy and Guénon are set forth in their own words throughout this treatise.

# 2

## The Tradition

In contrast to the colloquial, religious, social scientific, artistic, and philosophic usages of the term *tradition* and its derivatives, and regardless of any overlapping of meaning that may exist, is Coomaraswamy's and Guénon's usage. Neither Guénon nor Coomaraswamy can be liable to an allegation of fostering a narrow sectarianism that occasionally occurs among metaphysical groups. Nonetheless, the observation of J. S. Judah can be applied to both men and the Traditional school as a whole: Judah asserts that "Most metaphysical groups have a belief in an inner meaning of words beyond their dictionary definition—a meaning that cannot be discovered empirically from the standpoint of usage or etymology, but that is revealed intuitively."[4] Though even what each of them meant by Tradition was not exactly the same, their meanings, when compared to usages in the various fields mentioned in Appendix A, and even within the greater esoteric milieu, form a contrast great enough to ally their meanings and make them almost entirely synonymous. This synonymy is sufficiently complete to allow reference to a single usage of Tradition by both men.

Requisite to understanding their usage of Tradition is understanding the men themselves. For that purpose at least a brief biographical account of each man is necessary.

### ANANDA K. COOMARASWAMY

Ananda Kentish Coomaraswamy was born in Ceylon in August of 1877, the son of an English lady (Elizabeth Clay Beeby) and a prominent Tamil barrister, Sir Mutu Coomaraswamy. Early in 1879, Mrs. Coomaraswamy took Ananda to England where they were to be joined by Sir Mutu later that spring; the reunion never occurred owing to the unexpected death of Sir Mutu in May. Mrs. Coomaraswamy found a cottage in Kent and, with the help of her mother and sister, raised

Ananda. She never remarried or returned to Ceylon, according to Roger Lipsey.[5] At the age of twelve, Ananda entered a preparatory school—Wycliffe College in Gloucestershire—which he attended for eight years. He did exceedingly well academically, with a particular interest in the sciences, especially geology. In 1897, at the age of twenty, he was admitted to University College, London University, where he received a B.Sc. in Geology and Botany with First Class Honors in 1900. In 1903 he was named a Fellow of University College, having continued his education in graduate studies.

During this period, Coomaraswamy's life began a change that was to eventuate in a radical intellectual and vocational shift of direction. Feeling a need to familiarize himself—immerse himself—in the culture and worldview of his father, his geological interests were consequently, perhaps inevitably, obverted toward Ceylon and Ceylonese culture. In 1903 he was appointed Director of the Mineralogical Survey of Ceylon, and his final report for the survey was submitted in 1906, the same year he was awarded the Doctorate (D.Sc.) in Geology from London University. Concurrent with his scientific investigations into the geological phenomena of Ceylon, Coomaraswamy's interest began turning to the culture of the Sinhalese people; an interest stimulated by their graphic arts, architecture, customs, and religion.[6] Within the space of two or three years, his geological researches were completely replaced by his interest in the resuscitation of Ceylonese culture, an interest that later spread further to his involvement in India's *swadeshi* movement. Frequent trips between Ceylon and India in the East and England in the West during the period of 1906–1917 prompted more comparisons of the arts and crafts of both cultures and of the philosophy inherent in them.

In 1917 Coomaraswamy emigrated to the United States and took a position with the Boston Museum of Fine Arts as curator of the Indian and Asian section. His emigration resulted from his status of conscientious objector and his resistance to the British conscription established to provide troops for the battlefields of World War I. The first years in America, until around 1932, were ones of public and social involvement for Coomaraswamy, usually related to his expertise in the arts of Asia. His knowledge and familiarity with the art world in general was reflected by the savoir faire in his writing and speaking engagements. Under his supervision, the Asian section of the museum was built into one of the finest in the West, and his indefatigable efforts in the acquisition and subsequent exegesis of Eastern art and artistic motifs never ceased. In 1932, at the age of fifty-five and with both a new marriage and baby son, his life began to change—a change into a mode that would remain more or less constant until his death fifteen years later. It was at this point that his considerable intellectual energy became directed toward the scholarly exposition of the *philosophia perennis et universalis*; this occupied the central concern of his oeuvre from 1932 until his death in 1947. "There is no doubt that Ananda Coomaraswamy was one of the most learned and creative scholars of the century."[7] His legacy to posterity contains approximately 1,000 published books, essays, and monographs on everything from geology, art, dance, culture, and philology to religion, iconography, mythology, and the philosophia perennis—the sacred Tradition.[8]

## RENÉ GUÉNON

René Guénon (baptized René-Jean-Marie-Joseph) was born in central France in the town of Blois in November of 1886; he was nine years the junior of Coomaraswamy. His parents—and family—were strict Catholics, and thus the strong sense of tradition found in late nineteenth-century French Catholicism was ingrained in Guénon at the earliest and most formative years and was to affect his perspective throughout his life. As a boy, and again throughout his life, he was afflicted with *santé fort délicate*—to the degree that at one point in his graduate school career it prevented him from attending classes. His father was an architect; thus Guénon was raised in a home environment where mathematics and geometry were prominent.

Guénon's early education was in Jesuit-run institutions. At the age of twelve he was enrolled in Notre-Dame des Aydes and remained there until 1901, when he was transferred by his father to Collége Augustin-Thierry. His academic record throughout these years, again like Coomaraswamy's, was exceptionally good; he won several prizes, among them two for physics and Latin. In 1902 he received his baccalaureate and in the following year received his Bachelor of Philosophy with honors. In 1904 Guénon arrived in Paris and enrolled in Collége Rollin; his field was advanced mathematics, and he was studying to prepare for the *license de mathematique*. After two years, however, he withdrew from the university for reasons that are unclear, though one of his biographers, Paul Sérant, speculates that it was due either to ill health or "the seductions of the intellectual life that the capital could offer a provincial youth."[9]

Regardless of the reasons for his withdrawal from the university, this action proved to be a decisive one in Guénon's life, since it was at this point, in 1906, that he began in earnest to pursue a course of study to which he had been introduced only shortly before: the study of occultism. Throughout these years, 1906 to 1922, Guénon both participated in and carried out research in occult groups and esoteric religious doctrines. It was also in this period that he adopted Islam and was accepted as a pupil by Sheikh Abder-Rahman Elish el-Kebir for preparation and initiation into a Sufi sect. His life was shared between Blois and Paris, except for a short interim during 1917 and 1918 when he was appointed instructor of philosophy at Setif, Algeria. He tried, and failed, to earn a *docteur-es-lettres* from the Sorbonne following his short stay in Algeria. In 1922 Guénon ceased his investigation and interest in occultism and spiritualism and began to concentrate solely on that area for which he was to become renowned: metaphysics, *la Tradition primordiale*.

In 1930 Guénon relocated to Cairo, where he remained until his death in 1951. There he perfected his Arabic and became, in effect, an Egyptian Sufi. In 1933 Guénon met Sheikh Muhammad Ibrahim, an elderly lawyer whom he visited often. The following year he married his second wife, the Sheikh's daughter, Fatma, and they moved to Doki, a suburb of Cairo. Two daughters were born to them in 1944 and 1947; a third child—a son—was born in 1949, and another son was born four months after Guénon's death in 1951. In 1948 he officially became a naturalized Egyptian citizen, but throughout his expatriation, Guénon always kept abreast of the intellectual and political climate of France (and the West). His writings remained constant and prolific as they had been before his departure from France, yet during this period they focused more on the process of attaining *effective* metaphysical insight, though still under the same genre of the Tradition, or sophia perennis.[10]

## TRADITION AS THE PHILOSOPHIA PERENNIS

For Coomaraswamy, the terms Tradition and philosophia perennis were practically interchangeable. The difference in their usage lay in their application: use of Tradition was almost always associated with a culture, while philosophia perennis was employed to stand for a group of interdependent metaphysical principles that could be elucidated either without reference to a particular Traditional culture or with reference to them all. Similarly, for Guénon, Tradition or the primordial Tradition was equivalent to the sophia perennis, a term once again entirely synonymous to philosophia perennis. Guénon's reference to sophia perennis was reflective of his repugnance toward modern Western analytical philosophy, which he took to be an aberration of Plato's art, or genuine metaphysics. Regarding Guénon's view of the term philosophia perennis, Lipsey points out that "Guénon himself once questioned the term in the course of a resume of an essay by Coomaraswamy; he suggested that *Sophia Perennis* made more sense than Philosophia Perennis."[11]

The fact that Coomaraswamy's use of Tradition conforms to Guénon's usage is corroborated by more than the syllogism that if philosophia perennis is Tradition and sophia perennis is Tradition then philosophia perennis is sophia perennis. The corroboration lies in their oeuvre; in the fact that for the last decades of their lives, the two men concentrated almost exclusively on the expatiation and promulgation of their common Traditional views. Further, S. H. Nasr, speaking of Frithjof Schuon's work, says that the "unique expression of the *philosophia perennis* which is also the *sophia perennis* [is] meant to guide the man of today out of the labyrinth of ignorance in which the modern world finds itself."[12] But their styles were vastly different in their promulgation of Traditional views. Guénon attacked the problem head on, directly, without equivocation, while Coomaraswamy, the master weaver, employed texts in the four ancient languages he knew perfectly (Latin, Greek, Sanskrit, and Pāli) and weaved into his disquisitions excerpts from relevant passages that he viewed as illustrative of the Traditional worldview. Thus, Coomaraswamy, in Lipsey's words, "devoted no single essay to the idea of Tradition," while Guénon, on the other hand, wrote papers like "Tradition et traditionalism" (*ET*, October 1936), "Les contrefaçons de l'idée Traditionnelle" (*ET*, November and December 1936), and "Tradition et Transmission" (*ET*, January 1937), to name a few.

The lack of singular treatment of the idea of Tradition in Coomaraswamy's work, however, is not to be seen as an indication that Tradition and the philosophia perennis were not consanguineous in his view, or that they were not the principles of primary concern in his later years. The strands of affirmation are to be found throughout his work on religion, art, culture, and the other areas in which he had familiarity. In the introduction to *Hinduism and Buddhism*, he clearly equates the two ideas: "The Indian tradition is one of the forms of the Philosophia Perennis, and as such, embodies those universal truths to which no one people or age can make exclusive claim."[13] Moreover, Coomaraswamy did include Tradition and Traditional in the titles of several of his published works—for example, "The Vedanta and Western Tradition," "On the Indian and Traditional Psychology, or Rather Pneumatology," "The Traditional Conception of Ideal Portraiture," and "The Flood in Hindu Tradition." Still, the only way to see the entire fabric of Coomaraswamy's Tradition, unlike Guénon's, is to extricate carefully each strand, each sentence, or short passage that explicates this idea, and reassemble them into a reintegrated whole. With remarkable consistency, Coomaraswamy's later writings never deviate from this pattern and from his overriding concern with these "first principles." In one rather long excerpt (long by his own standards), Coomaraswamy succinctly formulates the essentials of the modality of the philosophia perennis in an unusually nontechnical style, and indicates some sympathy for Guénon's distaste for the term *philosophy:*

> For if we leave out of account the "modernistic" and individual philosophies of today, and consider only the great tradition of the magnanimous philosophers, whose philosophy was also a religion that had to be lived if it was to be understood, it will soon be found that the distinctions of cultures in East and West, or for that matter North and South, are comparable only to those of dialects; all are speaking what is essentially one and the same spiritual language, employing different words, but expressing the same ideas, and very often by means of identical idioms. Otherwise stated, there is a universally intelligible language, not only verbal but also visual, of the fundamental ideas on which the different civilizations have been founded.[14]

Guénon echoes the same thought: "If Religion is necessarily one with Truth, then religions can only be but deviations of the primordial doctrine."[15] Primordial doctrine here means, of course, the primordial Tradition; the difference in terms is only stylistic, not substantive. Gabriel Asfar, in a lengthy dissertation on Guénon's thought, makes this evident in declaring that "the word 'tradition' taken of course in the context of what Guénon understood by 'la Tradition primordiale'—[is] the unity of thought and action which, transcending the arbitrary rule of culture and society, serves as the one common denominator between men and leads them to an awareness of Unity, supreme and indivisible."[16] Nonetheless, it is true that Guénon seldom used the actual terms philosophia perennis or sophia perennis in his writings; his main term of reference for those first principles was either the Primordial Tradition, usually in uppercase first letters, by which he meant sophia/ philosophia perennis, or simply "metaphysics." Coomaraswamy himself refers to Guénon's "expositions of the traditional philosophy, sometimes called the *Philosophia Perennis*," and Asfar asserts that "the *philosophia perennis*, or Primordial Tradition, whose language Guénon and his friends were looking for was a unifying, self-explanatory revelation of man's wholeness."[17] There is no doubt, therefore, that to Coomaraswamy the Tradition and to Guénon the Primordial Tradition are the same; that these terms are used almost interchangeably with sophia and philosophia perennis; that the essence of what was meant by them was comprised of a group of interdependent "first principles" in which a unique source common to all religions can be intelligibly perceived. As Livingston has defined it in his glossary, Tradition is "(a) The perennial metaphysic. (b) Any human activity based upon conscious application of the principles of the perennial metaphysic to contingent circumstances."[18]

METAPHYSICS VERSUS RELIGIOUS STUDIES<br>AND THE SOCIAL SCIENCES

One of the characteristics of style that readers of the works of Guénon and Coomaraswamy—and those of their school—often notice first is the use of the definite article preceding the word tradition. To these two metaphysicists and their followers, the distinction was between *a* tradition and *the* Tradition. It was more often the definite article instead of the indefinite article. Exceptions to this usage do occur in their writings, but usually with the condition that Tradition would be preceded by a proper adjective, like the Hindu tradition, and so be "a" tradition among the various manifestations of "the" Tradition. Capitalization was another distinguishing feature of their usage as compared to usage of the term in the various other fields or in the colloquial usage.

Guénon frequently capitalized his favorite term *Primordial Tradition*;
with Coomaraswamy it was somewhat less evident, though the capitalization of tradition and traditional did occasionally occur in his work.
Thus, for these two and their protégés it was either Tradition or the Tradition, a term whose usage was also usually in the singular, not the plural, whose first letter was often capitalized, whose article was definite
or deleted, and by which a particular set of principles was meant.

It must now be evident that this usage is radically different from
those of the social sciences, religious studies, and the arts. *A* tradition
can easily exist within these fields—that is, one of the rights of passage
in tribal cultures, or a particular ecclesiastical ritual act, a particular
method of doctrinal exegesis, the concept that in a novel the protagonist
undergoes a significant change, and so on. These and many others are
traditions in the plural; each is a specific tradition existing within a
complex of various traditions, whose amalgamation comprises simply
"tradition" as a whole in Shils's sense, and observed by the social scientists or historians of religions and theologians. Within these milieux,
*the* tradition (lower case "t") would refer to the particular tradition
under discussion or observation.

As has been noted, however, some areas of usage overlap between
Guénon's and Coomaraswamy's usage and the specific fields' usages
and, for that matter, the vernacular usage. The points of commonality
are a hoary and often undeterminable etiology, a continuity within a
given culture or cultures—that is, the ancestor-to-posterity characteristic, and the actual fact of transmission, written or oral. The point of
great dissimilarity is in the object or content of transmission itself; in
contrast to *a* tradition within the special fields as outlined above, *the*
Tradition is, as has been stated, a group of interdependent principles,
"first principles," whose content and definitions shall be examined in
detail in the following Part.

We saw that Coomaraswamy, unlike Guénon, never addressed the
problem of the definition of Tradition directly—that most references to
it were oblique, that is, short lines or passages woven into the text of an
explanation of a principle or artistic motif. As Shils might have said of
Coomaraswamy, he never addressed Traditionality directly. Conversely, Guénon not only addressed Traditionality, he established something of a morphology of Tradition within his own cadre of perceptions
and even contrasted it to normative religious and sociological usages,
though briefly. In 1921 Guénon published *Introduction générale à*

*l'étude des doctrines hindoues*; the book was revised in a second edition in 1932 and again in 1945 when it was translated in English as *Introduction to the Study of the Hindu Doctrines*. As such—that is, in its final revision and English translation—it can be viewed as Guénon's latest and thus most developed statement on Tradition.[19] Chapter 3 of the book is titled "What Is Meant by Tradition," and in it Guénon discursively enumerates the problems surrounding the use of the term and the points at which he is at variance with the normative usages. He first draws a distinction between oral and written tradition—"tradition, whether it be religious in form or otherwise, consists everywhere of two complementary branches, written and oral"—and seems to imply that religious scholars regard tradition as exclusively oral. Guénon then eschews the definition of "certain sociologists," namely, Edmond Doutté et al., regarding the term tradition. Next, Guénon makes a significant bifurcation between East and West relative to their Traditional elements: he states, "Every Eastern civilization, taken as a whole, may be seen to be essentially traditional," but "As for Western civilization, we have shown that it is on the contrary devoid of any traditional character, with the exception of the religious element, which alone has retained it."[20] He then provides us with his views on the relative Traditionality of Islam, medieval Europe (Gothic Christendom), India (Hinduism), and China, which he further divides into a social tradition (Confucianism) and the Primordial Tradition (Taoism).

Guénon also comments on the misuse of the term tradition. In chapter 31 of *Le règne de la Quantité et les signes des temps*, entitled "Tradition et traditionalisme," he points to the French proclivity for confusing the counterrevolutionary notion of traditionalism with the Tradition and assigns to supporters of the former idea the label "traditionalist," a term he did not like applied to himself. He denounces as "mental confusion" the designations "human tradition," "national tradition," and political, scientific, and philosophical "traditions." He even speculates there, in a somewhat facetious tone, that "It would not be surprising, under these conditions, if people one day began talking about 'Protestant tradition,' or even a 'lay tradition' or 'revolutionary tradition'." He summarizes the whole problem of different and misuses of the word tradition in one terse passage:

> All the misuses of the word "tradition" can, to one degree or another, serve this same purpose, commencing with the

most popular of all by which it is made synonymous with
"custom" or "usage," thus creating a confusion of tradition
with things that are on the lower human level and are completely deficient in profundity. But there are other and more
subtle deformations, and because of this all the more dangerous; all have as a common characteristic, moreover, the
bringing down of the idea of tradition to a purely human
level, whereas, on the contrary, there is and can be nothing
truly traditional that does not contain some element of a
superhuman order.[21]

The similarities and dissimilarities of the metaphysical or primordial Tradition to the social science and religious (and artistic) tradition(s)
and to the vernacular meaning of the term are indicative of the habitual
difficulty of word usage and semantic variants. Since no detailed examination or didactic explanation of this difference in usage has previously
been made, readers who first come across the works of Guénon, Coomaraswamy, or works of the core of later writers who contributed to *Studies
in Comparative Religion* or *Études Traditionnelles* on a regular basis, or
even books like Huston Smith's *Forgotten Truth: The Primordial Tradition* and Ray Livingston's *The Traditional Theory of Literature*, may
find themselves applying a social science, religious, artistic, or simply
vernacular definition to Tradition or Traditional when what is meant is
something "wholly other," to improvise Rudolph Otto's succinct phrase.

# 3

## Hermeneutics of The Tradition

One finds in the writings of Guénon and Coomaraswamy a system of hermeneutics, the science of interpretation, which is as particularized as their use of Tradition, and one which most historians of religion and theologians vehemently criticize. The hermeneutic is applied to certain religious and philosophical texts and, as might be expected, is directed at the elucidation of principles of the philosophia perennis. The obloquies of its critics claim it is reductionistic, fails to acknowledge the integrity of the particular religion or tradition in question, minimizes historicity and phenomenology, and lends itself to the construction of a specious "universal religion." The proponents of the Traditional hermeneutic are not unaware of these criticisms; however, they are considered primarily rationalistic and/or empirical criticisms, and subordinate to the quintessential and *effective* spiritual meaning embodied in the texts and oral teachings, and accessible, in the Traditional view, only to the intellectual intuition.

### ESOTERICISM IN WORLD RELIGIONS

The esoteric and exoteric properties of the world's religions (and some philosophies, e.g., Plato, Boethius, Plotinus) have been widely and interminably discussed among academicians and theologians, though no permanent or definitive conclusions have ever been reached. Though neither Coomaraswamy nor Guénon was unapprised of the criticism of their exegesis as doctrinaire, neither of them ever abandoned his esoteric approach to the world's profound texts. Coomaraswamy, like Origen and like the Hellenistic Gnostics with their categories of *hylic*, *psychic*, and *pneumatic*, also held the view that canonical religious and premodern philosophical texts and systems could be interpreted variously; that is, that meanings were multivalent and directly commensurate to the perceptive ability of the interpreter.

19

Moreover, despite the variety of exoteric or external religious or philosophical manifestations, one immutable essence underlies them all.
Thus, Coomaraswamy states metaphorically:

> There are many paths that lead to the summit of one and the
> same mountain; their difference will be the more apparent
> the lower down we are, but they vanish at the peak; each will
> naturally take the one that starts from the point at which he
> finds himself; he who goes around the mountain looking for
> another is not climbing.[22]

This is essentially Guénon's view as well, with the qualification that
he viewed the "living Tradition" to be alive only in the East; specifically in Chinese Taoism, Hinduism, and Sufism. The West had effectively lost its Traditional element according to Guénon, and that meant
that one previous path to the summit had fallen into desuetude. Like so
many mammals with different habitational modalities—such as
aquatic, terrestrial, avian, each sharing an isomorphic mammalian
skeleton—the world's great faiths and "magnanimous philosophers,"
no matter how apparently dissimilar, all have an underlying similitude
in the Traditional perspective, and their respective scriptures, when
studied in their most pristine and primary etymological forms, admit
of this commonality. "Literally hundreds of texts," wrote Coomaraswamy, "could be cited from Christian and Islamic, Vedic, Taoist,
and other scriptures and their patristic expositions, in close and sometimes literally verbal agreement."[23]

Because Guénon and Coomaraswamy chose an esoteric hermeneutic to interpret texts does not necessarily imply that they held other
hermeneutical methods to be fallacious, as do, for example, fundamental Christians who believe in the inerrancy of the Bible and hold exclusively to a literal/moral exegesis. In a letter to the orientalist A.
Berriedale Keith, Coomaraswamy once remarked:

> Just as in mediaeval exegesis the possibility of an interpre-
> tation on at least four levels of reference (literal, moral, alle-
> gorical, anagogic) is always recognized, so I think one can
> approach the Indian texts from different points of view each
> of which is legitimate, so long as one is perfectly conscious
> of what one is doing at the time.[24]

However, the esoteric or anagogic exegesis would be the only one in which the Traditional principles might be extracted from a given text, and for this reason, both Guénon and Coomaraswamy focused on the esoteric interpretation. In his formal, pedagogic writing Coomaraswamy seldom dwelt on the esoteric/exoteric dichotomy and, when he did, it was usually brief and in passing. Guénon, on the other hand, dealt with the problem directly, as he did with the concept of Tradition and its definition and usages. In his *Introduction to the Study of the Hindu Doctrines* is a section on "esoteric and exoteric" qua dichotomy, in which he concisely states his views; that is, that exoteric and esoteric have correspondences relative to written and oral teaching, and that they have specific distinguishing features.

> Exoterism, comprising the more elementary and easily understandable part of the teaching, which was consequently more readily brought within everybody's reach, is the only aspect to be expressed through the writings that have come down to us in a more or less complete form. Esoterism, being more profound and of a higher order, addressed itself as such only to regular disciples of the school who were specially prepared to receive it, and was the subject of a purely oral teaching, concerning which it has obviously not been possible to preserve very precise indications.[25]

Asfar, in commenting upon the principle, concludes that in Guénon's view "both [esoteric and exoteric] are degrees of teaching or revelation, and can in no way, Guénon believes, be opposed or contradictory; indeed, they are complementaries, for esoterism, giving a deeper sense to the exoteric mode, develops and completes it."[26] Coomaraswamy's anagogic exegesis and Guénon's esoteric exegesis, by the application of one's "intellectual intuition" to the particular principle in question, results in the same hermeneutic; that in which the Tradition, the philosophia perennis, is brought to light. In the execution of this method, it was Coomaraswamy's style always and everywhere to *compare*, to cross reference, to establish consistency, while it was Guénon's style to seek the principial heart of the matter and expound upon its metaphysical qualities and significance. Marco Pallis writes that "in terms of their respective dialectical styles contrast between these two authors could hardly have been greater; if they agreed about their main conclusions, as indeed they did, one can yet describe them as temperamentally poles apart."[27] The results of this hermeneutical method as applied by these two metaphysicists are essentially identical, resting entirely on an esoteric/anagogic perception.

HIERARCHIZATION

Coomaraswamy, in his letter to Professor Keith, referred to four levels of "mediaeval exegesis." *Levels* of exegesis necessarily presupposes the notion of a hierarchy of exegesis, a hierarchy of understanding. While the idea of hierarchy, in a qualitative sense, is crucial to both the understanding and structure of the philosophia perennis—and concomitantly to the Traditional hermeneutic—it carries with it a stiff resistance to its acceptance as a functional principle, or even hypothesis, within modern Western culture. Arthur Lovejoy, for example, in most of *The Great Chain of Being* (Cambridge, 1936) strove to show that hierarchy, or "unilinear gradation" as he referred to it, had been unequivocally proven fallacious by the meliorative march of Western analytical philosophy since Plato. In this process, the principle of hierarchy has been either misunderstood, attacked, or both by those whose worldview relies solely on either a dualistic or quantitative foundation.[28]

The principle of hierarchy for Guénon and Coomaraswamy applies to far more than hermeneutics; it is applicable to the most vertiginous macrocosmological concepts of which human cognition and *intellection* are capable, thus it permeates both life in general and the universe as an axial constituent. "In the first place, it must be understood that the terms of the hierarchical classifications are applicable not merely to human beings but *in divinis* and throughout the universe."[29] This short quote by Coomaraswamy encapsulates an entire book by Guénon on the subject: *Les états multiple de l'être* (Paris, 1932). Hierarchy is, for example, tied up in the "symbolism of the cross" (the title of another of Guénon's doctrinal works), in that the cross contains both a horizontal and *vertical* axis, the latter of which symbolizes the quality/hierarchy principle.

With regard to textual (or oral) exegesis, Guénon and Coomaraswamy were both adamant about the absolute and inexorable necessity of using the "intellectual intuition," and this intuition inevitably functions to varying degrees of ability in different people. To Guénon, this intuition had nothing to do with contemporary "intuitionism" of an "exclusively sensitive and 'vital' order" such as is found in the philosophy of Henri Bergson. To Coomaraswamy, the idea of intuition was linked with the Platonic conception of anamnesis; it is thus "by the indwelling Spirit, that we know and understand the thing to which words can only refer us; that which is audibly or otherwise sensed does not in itself inform us, but merely provides the occasion and opportunity to *recognize* [italics mine] the matter to which the external signs have referred us."[30] The approaches to intuition taken by Guénon and Coomaraswamy were different; each man emphasized somewhat different aspects of intuition, but similarly each man arrived at approximately the same notion of it, based on the divine intellection function of the "indwelling Spirit," the Intellect comprising both the *jñāna* or "eye of *gnosis*" (γνῶσις) and the *manas* or *nous* (νους).

The intellectual intuition, therefore, is applied to the Traditional hermeneutic—the esoteric or anagogic. It is toward the top of the hierarchy or vertical axis relative to other forms of exegesis, like rungs on a ladder. Regardless of accusations of elitism, Guénon and Coomaraswamy never ceased to maintain this fact: there always are, and historically have been, fewer individuals with the capacity or ability to exegete the first principles in the Traditional hermeneutic than those subscribing to a literal, moral, or allegorical hermeneutic—that is, fewer individuals at any given time with a sufficiently sensitive and developed spiritual or intellectual intuition than the majority without these same attributes. This notion and that of the downward motion of the etiologic principles on the vertical axis—which Henry Corbin has treated so well and fully in *The Man of Light in Iranian Sufism*, in chapters 1 and 3 on "Orientation" and "Midnight Sun and Celestial Pole"— are discussed together in a long but illuminating passage in Guénon's *La crise du monde moderne:*

A real [understanding] can operate only from above [working downwards] and not from below [working upwards], and this is true in a double sense: the understanding must begin from what is highest, that is to say from the principles, and descend gradually through the diverse orders of application, continuously and rigorously observing the hierarchical dependence that exists between these orders; and this work, by its very nature, can only be the work of an elite, using the word in its truest and most complete sense: we are speaking exclusively of an intellectual elite, since, in our view, no other kind of elite is possible, for all exterior social distinctions are of no importance from the point of view which concerns us here.[31]

Those familiar with Western philosophy will no doubt recognize a Platonic influence here, as with Coomaraswamy. It is this hierarchically vertical axis with its qualitative, intuitive elements that stands as the foundation for the Traditional hermeneutic. It is a priori by nature, deductive in method, and diametrically opposed to the quantitative, a posteriori, inductive method that holds sway in Western thought and that utterly rejects the intuitive and valuational mode of Traditional perspectives (as applied to exegesis or anything else). It was just this quantitative approach to man, the world, and the universe (sensory or supersensory) that led Coomaraswamy to repeat often in his writings one statement by Professor A. Berriedale Keith of Edinburgh that must have struck him forcefully, judging from the number of times one encounters it in his works: referring to it as "an almost classical confession of the limitations of the 'scientific' position," Coomaraswamy cites Keith's infamous line: "such knowledge as is not empirical is meaningless to us and should not be described as knowledge."[32]

It is easy to see that working under the implications of Keith's hypothesis, one could hardly hope to arrive at an anagogic or esoteric exegesis of any text; perhaps because Coomaraswamy found it in the introduction to Keith's translation of the *Aitareya Āraṇyaka* (Oxford, 1909), a text he often cited in his writings and considered among the classical texts of the Tradition, this statement elicited such a strong reaction from him. It was *truth* that lay at the end of the labors of exegesis, and insight. The truly perspicacious could only attain it, moreover, by the use of the intellectual intuition since it is not mere *factuality* but truth in its most profound and principial state. "It can only be realized by each one for himself," wrote Coomaraswamy, "all that can be effected by initiation is the communication of an impulse and an awakening of latent potentialities; the work must be done by the initiate himself," since "whatever can be said *of* it, the secret remains inviolable, guarded by its own essential incommunicability."[33] Only on the hierarchical high end of the vertical scale can be found those who, in interpreting ancient texts and Traditional teaching, "know and understand the thing to which words can only refer us."

## "KNOWING" AND "KNOWING ABOUT"

Implicit in the percept of hierarchy, and as applied in this present case to the Traditional hermeneutic, are different levels of understanding depending on the locus of the "knower" on the vertical axis. The relative position of the knower on this axis points to a subtle yet profound distinction that hinges on a thought expressed by Coomaraswamy: "In the sense that we are what we know, and that *to be and to know are the same* . . . recollection is life itself, and forgetfulness a lethal draught."[34] We cannot separate, in other words, what we are and what we know, any more than we can separate what we are and what we believe, since our beliefs help define our being and vice versa.

If one is a materialist, an empiricist, it is only because one holds beliefs that can be so categorized. Such a person, with respect to religious or metaphysical texts, would either eschew them altogether or interpret them literally, according to his beliefs—that is, according to what he *was*. Seen from a Traditional perspective that includes the principle of hierarchy, such a person would not "know" the content of what he was reading or hearing; he would not be able to "know and understand the thing to which words" referred him. Such a person, regardless of his knowledge *of* the text, language, or historical environment in which the principle under consideration appeared, would not really "know" the principle, though he might "know about" it. On the other hand, the gnostic, following Coomaraswamy's use of *gnosis* in the same sense as Guénon's use of "intellectual intuition," because he *was* a gnostic and thus in a hermeneutic sense on the hierarchically high end of esoteric exegesis, would in fact "know and understand the thing to which the words" referred him.

Thus, for Guénon and Coomaraswamy, it was an absolute and indispensable requisite to believe a profound religious or metaphysical doctrine or principle in order to understand it. And this belief is inextricably bound with one's being, the most quintessential element of which is the "indwelling Spirit." To allow oneself to *be* is to allow belief, being, and true knowledge to merge at the celestial polar zenith of the hierarchical "tree of Jesse," the top of the *axis mundi* or Jacob's ladder. And at the chthonic pole of the axis where "such knowledge as is not empirical is meaningless," where the exclusively material approach to life reigns and once appeared to the early-twentieth-century world through the media of Karl Marx, Sigmund Freud, and Emile Durkheim,and to the late twentieth-century world through B. F. Skinner, E. O. Wilson, and Carl Sagan, are to be found the *apologia* of those who promulgate exclusive rational or discursive knowledge.

Hierarchy is therefore crucial in the axiology of Coomaraswamy and Guénon, and implicit in this axiology is the notion of substantial and essential knowledge—the latter requiring "identification with its object." Coomaraswamy comments upon a hierarchic range in his paper on *Parokṣa*, where he writes that *parokṣa* and *pratyakṣa* "in their degrees represent a hierarchy of types of consciousness extending from animal to deity, and according to which one and the same individual may function upon different occasions."[35] Guénon makes this point repeatedly, and leaves nothing equivocal in his statements:

> It is evident that [action] belongs entirely to the world of change, of "becoming"; only knowledge permits escape from this world and from its inherent limitations, and when it attains to the immutable, as in the case of principial or metaphysical knowledge—which is knowledge *par excellence*—it becomes itself possessed of immutability, since all true knowledge is essentially identification with its object.[36]

Thus, becoming one with the object of knowledge might be said to be the very highest form of belief, since, at such a stage, being, belief, and knowledge are inseparable. But this is rare today, as Guénon states, because modern thought in the West is not only opposed to this approach to exegesis (or learning) in the sense of polarities; it is inimical to it. Continuing the same quote, Guénon goes on to say that

> It is exactly this of which modern Westerners are ignorant, for they envisage no knowledge superior to rational and discursive knowledge, thus indirect and imperfect [knowledge], being what one could describe as reflected knowledge; and even this lower knowledge they come to appreciate more and more only to the measure that it can be made to serve immediate practical ends; engaged in action to the point of repudiating everything beyond it, they do not perceive that this

action itself degenerates, from the absence of principle to an agitation as vain as it is sterile.

It was therefore in the field of textual translation, commentary, and exegesis that Guénon and Coomaraswamy most diligently applied their Traditional hermeneutic, and where they saw the most problematic effects from those whose knowledge was secular or "profane." Coomaraswamy, in fact, devoted a whole book to the subject: *A New Approach to the Vedas: An Essay in Translation and Exegesis* (London, 1933). In the introduction he states, "It is very evident that for an understanding of the Vedas, a knowledge of Sanskrit, *however profound*, is insufficient" (p. vii). Similarly, Guénon, in a section of *Introduction to the Study of the Hindu Doctrines* entitled "Official Orientalism," without being vitriolic decries the lack of ability of scholar-specialists to perceive metaphysical truths, since he contests "their competence in respect of anything that lies outside the field of pure erudition." Because to Coomaraswamy "there can be no real knowledge of a thing from which one holds aloof and cannot love," he was inevitably to hold a depreciative opinion of modern scholarship and epistemology with respect to its mundane hermeneutic of Traditional texts; this opinion was reflected in one of his strongest indictments:

> We maintain, accordingly, that it is an indispensable condition of true scholarship to "believe in order to understand" (*crede ut intelligas*), and to "understand in order to believe" (*intellige ut credas*), not, indeed, as distinct and consecutive acts of the will and of the intellect, but as the single activity of both. . . . We venture to propound that it is precisely the divorce of intellect and will in the supposed interest of objectivity that primarily explains the relative infirmity of the modern approach.[37]

This theme is taken up by Frithjof Schuon in an article entitled "Understanding and Believing," illustrating that this is a theme of primacy in the Traditional hermeneutic. The thought is echoed in a statement of Guénon's: "There is only one really profitable way of studying doctrines: in order to be understood they must be studied so to speak 'from the inside,' whereas the orientalists have always confined themselves to an investigation from the outside."[38] Closely allied with the problem of translation and exegesis is the use, or rather choice, of words in the modern language into which the older texts are translated. Both Guénon and Coomaraswamy abhorred the sloppy use of language and terms, due in great part to their philological expertise. They believed the ancient languages like Greek and Sanskrit were specifically adapted to the expatiation of metaphysical principles, while modern vernaculars were less fit for the purpose. Guénon, in lamenting the misuses of the word tradition, points to a larger problem: "this particular abuse of a word is again very significant of the real tendencies of this falsification of language, of which the perversion of the word 'tradition' [is an example]."[39] This thought is restated by Coomaraswamy: "It is not without good reason that both Plato and Mencius asserted that the misuse of words is the outward sign of a sickness of the soul."[40] These issues are, in turn, integral to Coomaraswamy's repeated insistence that in order to be truly understood, the sacred texts of the world's religions must be studied in their original languages.[41]

### INTEGRITY OF TRADITIONS AND "RELIGIOUS ESPERANTO"

The most frequent and, in fact, the "classical" criticism of the philosophia perennis, its expositors, and here specifically the Traditional hermeneutic, is the accusation that they destroy the uniqueness, the integrity of the particular cultural/religious system in which the principles are found—a sort of sacrifice of the particular to the general. While Guénon was acutely aware of this problem, and Coomaraswamy, whose specific expertise lay in the arts, was similarly sensitive to this accusation, both were impelled to make simple denials to refute the criticism. Coomaraswamy was an artist and an art historian with far too much empathy and sensitivity for creative, individual expression to reduce the beauty and variety of the depiction of the "one truth" to its barest, skeletal structure with disregard for the rest. He enjoyed the personality and originality of all the multifarious expressions, and saw behind or *within* them the unifying and constant principles of the Tradition in their immutable and generative roles, couched in the languages and religious metaphors congruent, contemporaneous, and peculiar to the cultures in which they were found. This he states unequivocally: "the development of a single universally acceptable syncretic faith embodying all that is 'best' [Traditional] in every faith; such a 'faith' as this would be a mechanical and lifeless monstrosity, by no means a stream of living water, but a sort of religious Esperanto."[42]

As we saw in the outline of Guénon's "What Is Meant by Tradition," he also drew sharp distinctions between the various expressions or Traditions that contained the still-living metaphysics and in no way conflated the texts or built a structure of one religion, one Tradition, one expression. Guénon was particularly concerned with both integrity and variety among all genuine Traditions; he admonished his readers to study Eastern traditions, specifically, in their own right and integrity, avoiding speculative comparisons. The Eastern traditions, he said, "must be studied as the Orientals themselves study them, and one must certainly not indulge in more or less hypothetical interpretations, which may sometimes be quite imaginary."[43] And in a whole section of *Orient et Occident* devoted to this single idea and entitled "Entente et non fusion," Guénon disparages both "borrowing" and eclecticism." Thus, to Guénon and Coomaraswamy, the method of Traditional hermeneutics, while it depends entirely on the *gnosis* or intellectual intuition, cannot legitimately be separated from the culture or Tradition in which the "first principle" in question was found. It can be compared, certainly, and the principle can be said to have an immemorial generation and be perennial in its nature, but it still constitutes a central portion of the Tradition in which it was found, without which that Tradition would be less than whole and thus partial. Traditional hermeneutics, therefore, undertakes to exegete a principle or doctrine in the context of all the other principles and doctrines that form the whole, regardless of the universality or perenniality of the principle, and only then to compare it with other cultural expressions of that principle or doctrine.

# 4

## Forums of the Traditional Perspective

In a strict sense, there is only one "forum" of the Traditional perspective, since the Tradition cannot be confined to spacio-temporal parameters. There were, however, in the first half of the twentieth century, two principal centers where Traditional activities were concentrated due to the influence of Guénon and Coomaraswamy; in the second half of the twentieth century, centers of the Traditional perspective appeared in new locations. These early centers or forums of the Traditional perspective were not organized in any functional way, and for this reason it is probably more accurate to speak of the forums and *individuals* of the Traditional perspective than solely of the forums.

The two earliest and principal centers of the Traditional perspective were in France and England. This was due in part to the fact that Guénon wrote predominantly in French and Coomaraswamy in English, and in part to the existing hospitable environment for Traditional ideas in those countries. Guénon lived and worked in Paris during the 1910s and 1920s within a milieu of esotericism, and Coomaraswamy was closely associated with the traditionalist pre-Raphaelite movement in England prior to his immigration to the United States in 1917. These early centers were loose aggregations of like-minded thinkers who espoused the same or very similar ideas to those of Guénon and Coomaraswamy, who came to rely on the works of these two as authoritative exegesis of Traditional sacred principles, and who gathered to discuss and/or publish these ideas. Curiously, in the case of both men, the countries of their youth first bore the fruit of their labors as centers of their thought; even though Guénon and Coomaraswamy carried on their Traditional writings and a wide correspondence from their chosen residences of Cairo and Boston, neither of those cities became a center of Traditional activity compared, for example, to Paris.

In addition to the direct impact of Guénon and Coomaraswamy on their followers, who can be said to belong to the universal forum of Traditional perspective, a rather wide diffusion of their ideas has occurred, and one finds the names of Guénon and Coomaraswamy in bibliographies and indices of the most diverse sources, from Stella Kramrisch's *The Art of India* to R. C. Zaehner's *Mysticism: Sacred and Profane* to Joseph Campbell's *The Masks of God*. Some of the individuals were users of Tradition with a capital T, while others were simply influenced by the ideas of Guénon and Coomaraswamy. Some of the members of the forum were epigones in the sense that their abilities—and perspicacity—were not as fluent as those of their preceptors, yet whether they were members of the forum or "unaffiliated" individuals who were attracted to the essential principles of the Tradition, the common denominator was a certain resonance of response to the writings of Guénon and Coomaraswamy.

FRANCE

When Coomaraswamy was sixteen, a student at Wycliffe College, and Guénon was seven years old, there began in Paris a periodical entitled *Le Voile d'Isis* for the purpose of fostering "études ésoteriques, psychiques et divinatoires."[44] As Lipsey points out, the journal's title, in addition to the field of inquiry for which it came into being, was taken from H. P. Blavatsky's massive work *Isis Unveiled* (New York, 1877), a datum whose significance will be explored in greater detail in the following chapter. By April of 1925, the month of his first article published in *Le Voile d'Isis*, Guénon was already an established French writer and had contributed to a number of different journals, notably *la Gnose, le Symbolisme*, and *La France Anti-maçonnique*. But the beginnings of his submission of articles to *Le Voile d'Isis* marked an important point for Guénon, for by the year 1928 Guénon had begun using *Le Voile d'Isis* almost exclusively as the vehicle for his publications. Asfar describes his involvement with the journal when, in 1928, just a year after the death of his first wife Berthe, Guénon

> . . . was offered an associate editorship in *Le Voile d'Isis*, a journal of esoteric studies published by [Paul] Chacornac, who wished to give his publication ". . . une ligne doctrinale directement inspirée des écrits de René Guénon." During the two years before Guénon left France for good (1928–1930), *Le Voile d'Isis* became, to all intents and purposes, a

review of his thoughts and teachings. In 1935, its name was changed to *Études Traditionnelles*.[45]

It was this renamed journal, *Études Traditionnelles*, which served as both the core or nexus of the Traditional forum in France and its principal organ of expression. Even after Guénon's expatriation, he continued to submit articles to the journal as did an extensive new circle of Traditional writers, including Coomaraswamy. "A school of thought had come into existence," writes Lipsey of this period, "sometimes militantly, sometimes compassionately at odds with the greater part of academic thought on its specialized subjects: traditional thought and its application to all aspects of human life."[46] The force of this French school made its impact felt on the thought of France in the period between the World Wars, from esotericists like Jean Thamar to scholars like Gilbert Durand and Antoine Faivre; from renowned writers like André Gide, Antonin Artaud, and André Breton to members of the surrealist Grand Jeu movement, like René Daumal and André Rolland de Reneville.[47]

ENGLAND

Some of the regular contributors to the French *Études Traditionnelles* decided to establish a journal of Traditional studies in English. What resulted from this decision was a journal that became the leading medium of Traditional views in English, *Studies in Comparative Religion*. This name the journal received in 1967, taking over what was previously called *Tomorrow*, a journal that was begun in 1941, shortly after the outbreak of World War II. *Studies in Comparative Religion* was closely associated with Perennial Books, Ltd., a bookshop/publisher in Middlesex, England. Though a number of this forum were English and lived in England, and though the locus of activity was primarily in London and Middlesex, the "English forum" of the Traditional perspective was actually the English-speaking world. Since the demise of *Studies in Comparative Religion* in 1987, the focus of the English-speaking Traditional perspective shifted from England to the United States. Closely allied with both this shift, and with the vitality of the British forum of Tradition during the early 1980s, was the journal *Temenos,* centered around the energies of Kathleen Raine and devoted to creating a record of the "Perennial Wisdom." Published in thirteen numbers from 1981 to

1992, *Temenos* was somewhat broader in scope than *Studies in Comparative Religion,* but frequently carried articles and essays by the same pool of Traditional writiers who sustained the latter journal.

In a book edited by Jacob Needleman entitled *The Sword of Gnosis* (Baltimore, 1974) one finds many of the original English forum of Traditional exposition together with those who wrote in English; some of those included in this group, whose articles appear in the book, are Frithjof Schuon, Marco Pallis, Titus Burckhardt, Seyyed Hossein Nasr, Leo Schaya, Martin Lings, and Whitall Perry, among others. These names, along with those of Guénon, Coomaraswamy, and a small circle of one-time and occasional contributors (Henry Corbin, Thomas Merton, Gershom Scholem, et al.) are found most frequently in the pages of *Studies in Comparative Religion* (and occasionally in *Études Traditionnelles,* as well) and in the catalog of books published by Perennial Books, Ltd. This forum had, by far, the greatest role in the dissemination of Guénon's thought in the English-speaking world, for not only do their names frequently recur on Guénon's works as translators, but their numerous references to the works of Guénon and Coomaraswamy have introduced many people to their ideas.[48] Coomaraswamy once noted, relative to his regard for Guénon and the central figures of this forum in whom he saw "more than philologues and to whom their knowledge of the great tradition has been a vital and transforming experience," that "At the present moment [1945] I can think of only two or three of this kind: René Guénon, Frithiof [*sic*] Schuon, Marco Pallis; one cannot consider from this point of view those who know only the West or only the East, however well."[49] This British forum with its *Studies in Comparative Religion* was for England and the English-speaking world what Paris with *Études Traditionnelles* was for France. It constituted the essential core of Traditional thought in Great Britain during the early and middle parts of the twentieth century.

NORTH AMERICA

In terms of influence or popularity in the United States and Canada with regard to the exposition and dissemination of the Tradition, Coomaraswamy exceeded Guénon during the 1930s and 1940s. Writing in America, Asfar laments "the intellectual presence of a great thinker who remains practically unknown in this country," regardless of the fact that by the time of that writing (1972), about a half dozen of

Guénon's major works had been translated into English. The reason for Coomaraswamy's hegemony of the Traditional worldview in North America and in academia is best illustrated by the difference in approach that they each took toward it. Coomaraswamy's interest was in Tradition via scholarship—that is, the researching of authors and the translation of ancient texts that exemplified Traditional principles. Since Coomaraswamy lived in the Boston area for thirty years, his influence in the many universities of the area was strong. Had Guénon written in English and had he lived in the United States, his influence would likely have been greater, especially since his was a more popu- lar—rather, less technical—style than Coomaraswamy's. Coomar- aswamy had a continual stream of writing and lecturing invitations from Eastern American and Canadian universities and academic jour- nals. In a letter to Marco Pallis (1944), Coomaraswamy declared:

> It isn't my primary function (dharma) to write "readable" books or articles; this is just where my function differs from Guénon's. All my willing writing is addressed to the profes- sors and specialists, those who have undermined our sense of values in recent times, but whose vaunted "scholarship" is really so superficial. I feel that rectification must begin at the reputed "top," and only so will find its way into schools and text books and encyclopedias.[50]

Perhaps an inverse analogy suitable for the understanding of their respective roles in North America and France is the comparison of Guénon and Coomaraswamy and their Tradition to Henry Corbin and Pir Vilayat Khan and their Sufism. Corbin the Frenchman like Cooma- raswamy the American was highly esteemed in the academic world internationally, while Guénon and Khan share the role of profound popularizers whose influence is primarily confined to their respective milieux—France and America. The essential difference in the two forums of Traditional thought as symbolized by Guénon and Coomar- aswamy, such as in France and in America, was one whose determi- nant was scholarship.

"Respectable" North American scholars who would not have dared to reference Guénon's work were blatantly solicitous of Cooma- raswamy and his approbation of their views on Eastern artistic and philosophical expressions. Coomaraswamy carried on an extended correspondence with many accomplished scholars in a variety of fields such as art, theology, philology, metaphysics, and culture.[51] Though these scholars could not be said to comprise either an American or scholarly "forum" of Traditional thought, Coomaraswamy's Traditional perspective did have an effect on them: he wrote specifically of Traditional principles to Hermann Goetz, Walter Andrae, Paul Mus, Mircea Eliade, Stella Kramrisch, Meyer Schapiro, Heinrich Zimmer, and Joseph Epes Brown. In his dealings with artists, equally extensive, he wrote of Traditional artistic conceptions to authors like Aldous Huxley, Gerald Heard, and Rabindranath Tagore, and to plastic artists like Eric Gill, Albert Gleizes, Georgia O'Keeffe, and Morris Graves.

Originally, the North American forum of the Tradition was not really a forum as those of England or France might be described, since it was the scholarship of Coomaraswamy that dominated virtually all expressions of Tradition in North America in the 1930s and 1940s and encompassed a group of scholars and artists that was international. However, if considered within the context of "one school of thought" concerned with the espousal of Traditional principles, Coomaraswamy could accurately be viewed as carrying the North American counterpart to the European effort, the former reflecting his erudite method.

During the 1980s and 1990s, a new North American forum of the Traditional perspective has assumed a position of centrality within the English-speaking world, no doubt due in part to the demise of *Studies in Comparative Religion* in England. During that time the Foundation for Traditional Studies was established, whose members include scholars and students of Traditional principles. Located near Washington, D.C., the Foundation publishes *Sophia*, a quarterly journal devoted to Traditional issues, and also publishes books based on Traditional subjects. In addition, within this same period Frithjof Schuon, whom most regard as the greatest expositor of the Tradition after Guénon and Coomaraswamy, relocated from Europe to Bloomington, Indiana, where his followers publish his writings through World Wisdom Books. Finally, and also within this same period, a sales/publishing operation began in Ghent, New York, under the name *Sophia Perennis et Universalis*, which sells and publishes both new titles and translations of Traditional works. Taken together, these activities, which are all loosely interrelated, indicate the gradually increasing popularity of Traditional themes in *fin de millennium* North America, and comprise a new American forum of the Traditional perspective.

IRAN

It was perhaps no coincidence that Henry Corbin, a specialist on Iranian Islamic theosophy (his term), spent several months of his year at the University of Teheran and the remainder at the University of Paris. Through a series of outstanding works explicating a neglected area of Iranian *Shī'a* esotericism,[52] Corbin prepared a fertile ground for the implantation of Guénon's interpretation of esoteric Islam in Teheran. Though Corbin eschewed Guénon's Traditional hermeneutic, criticizing Guénon's assumption that Ibn 'Arabī was a master of the Tradition ("to affect to believe that such masters are nothing more than representatives of a certain 'tradition' is to forget their considerable personal contribution"),[53] he is nonetheless regarded in high esteem by one Iranian—Seyyed Hossein Nasr. Nasr exhibits exiguous praise for most Islamicists, but fairly points to the "sympathetic and often penetrating studies of such men as L. Massignon and H. Corbin . . . which border in some cases on actual participation in the world of Sufism and which include excellent translations by men like B. de Sacy, R. S. Nicholson, and A. J. Arberry." Nasr goes on to assert, on the same page, that "Finally there are the truly authentic expositions of Sufism emanating from genuine teachings, such as those of R. Guénon, M. Lings, J. L. Michon, L. Schaya, and especially F. Schuon and T. Burckhardt."[54]

With the *Shī'a* gnosis brought to the attention of Western orientalists by Corbin, with Guénon's persistent interest in Islamic esotericism, and with Nasr's association with the Traditional worldview and those who espouse it, it is easy to see why, as President of the Imperial Iranian Academy of Philosophy in Teheran, Nasr would have sponsored the Academy's journal, entitled *Sophia Perennis*. Peter Wilson, the last editor of the journal, states, "*Sophia Perennis* is indeed related to the thought of Guénon and Coomaraswamy; in fact, you might say it's founded on it."[55] This pocket of the Traditional perspective, the ephemeral Iranian forum, came to its end with the ascent to power of the Ayatollah Khomeini.

ONE UNIVERSAL FORUM

If one employs an essential criterion of the Tradition—that is, "No culture, people, or age can lay claim to any private property in the Philosophia Perennis"[56]—one is forced to admit that in reality there are today no forums in the plural, but only one forum of Traditional thought, international though it may be, whose various expressions, modalities, and methods vary only with respect to particular emphases. The content of the one Tradition remains immutable and perpetual according to its proponents. In the words of Marco Pallis,

> A French periodical [*Études Traditionnelles*] to which Guénon was a frequent contributor . . . was found to contain a continual stream of articles from Coomaraswamy's pen which, as I soon perceived, matched those of Guénon both on the critical side of things and in their most telling exposition of metaphysical doctrine, in which Gita and Upanishads, Plato and Meister Eckhardt's complemented one another in a never ending synthesis.[57]

Guénon and Coomaraswamy, who from the historical analysis must be credited with the establishment of the forum that continues their thought and who, it should be added, never intended to "establish" anything but their views of the probity and integrity of the Tradition in religious and metaphysical contexts, were too close in their beliefs to have allowed the existence of more than one forum or school of Traditional thought. Disparate methods they might have had, but they shared the same belief structure that is the *conditio sine qua non* of Traditional perspective. For that reason, "Coomaraswamy was not a lesser Guénon, nor vice versa; their thought was complementary."[58]

Many of Guénon's and Coomaraswamy's books are still in print and undergoing reissue; *Études Traditionnelles*, *Sophia Perennis*, and *Studies in Comparative Religion* are collected and highly valued by students of the Tradition; journals like *Re-Vision*, *Sophia*, and *Parabola* (the latter published by the Society for the Study of Myth and Tradition) have appeared as media for Traditional thought; Guénon's life and work have never ceased to be a matter of interest and investigation to French thinkers, as indicated by a continual flow of works;[59] and Lipsey's compilation of Coomaraswamy's papers and his biography seems to have been the catalyst for something of a *renaissance* of Coomaraswamy's works since their publication in 1977. In fact, the Indira Gandhi National Centre for the Arts in New Delhi has undertaken to publish the complete works of Coomaraswamy, and has so far produced ten volumes in that series.

The one universal forum of the Tradition, given the evidence available, appears to be flourishing. By this is not meant that it will necessarily become an intellectual or "cultural fashion" in Mircea Eliade's sense of the term, of which he gives as examples Freudianism and structuralism. The inherent hierarchical nature of gnosis or intellectual intuition would preclude this. Rather, what is meant is that for the twentieth century, the forum of Tradition is a viable and critical medium for the dissemination of the *philosophia perennis et universalis*, and that the latter is in a state of relative prosperity and accessibility.

### THE INDIVIDUALS INFLUENCED

There exist (and existed) many individuals who were to varying degrees affected by the thought of Guénon and Coomaraswamy, but who are or were not part of the central core of the Traditional school per se. To trace the writers and scholars who cited either metaphysicist in his or her writings would be impossible; the mission here is to give a brief account of those who were either significantly affected by the Traditional worldview or who responded affirmatively to the writings of Guénon and Coomaraswamy.

In Europe, two figures stand out prominently: Julius Evola in Italy and André Gide in France. Gide was a literary critic, a man of letters whose works were less in the arena of metaphysical speculation and disputation than in poetry and prose. Yet in his *Journal (1942–1949)* Gide confesses that "These books of Guénon are remarkable and have taught me much, if only by reaction." Pondering the fact that he only began reading Guénon in 1943, he speculates: "What would have become of me if I had encountered them [the books of Guénon] in the time of my youth, when I was plunged into *Method for Achieving the Blessed Life* and was listening to the lessons of Fichte in the most receptive possible way? But, in those times, Guénon's books had not yet been written."[60] Certainly, Guénon had a wider impact on French literature than the affirmative response to Gide to Guénon's works just cited. Others, like André Breton, Romain Rolland, Henri Bosco, and Antonin Artaud, were also influenced by the writings of Guénon; it was Gide, however, who enjoyed the most international recognition.

The Italian Julius Evola (1898–1974) was Guénon's spokesman for the Tradition in Italy. Evola had been a spokesman for his own particular theories of political philosophy, one of which he referred to as "pagan imperialism," the title of one of his books (1928). But, in 1930, Evola abandoned his exclusive profession of pagan imperialism and turned to the concepts of Tradition and Traditional cultures as espoused by Guénon. This was, of course, the same year Guénon left France for Cairo, but it marked a significant turning point in Evola's philosophy.[61] According to Pierre Pascal:

> It was during the same period that Julius Evola underwent, in part, a fascination with the ideas of René Guénon, which included the fundamental theme that would thereafter complete the system of his ideas: the notion of Tradition. Evola would therefore become, in 1937, the Italian translator of *La crise du monde moderne*.[62]

From this basic foundation, Evola began his assiduous critiques of liberalism, Marxism, nationalism, and even Christianity, which gained him the reputation—at least in Italy—of being a *maître à penser*.

Among the more reputable and renowned scholars in the United States who have been significantly influenced by Coomaraswamy's work—and to some extent Guénon's—are Huston Smith and Jacob Needleman. Others, like Roger Lipsey, Ray Livingston, and Joseph Epes Brown, are more directly identified within the "school" of Traditional thought per se, based on the content and the views expressed in their works. Jacob Needleman's works genuinely reflect familiarity with an exposition of the Tradition, though in a somewhat modified form. In *A Sense of the Cosmos: The Encounter of Modern Science and Ancient Truth*, for example, he states that "From one point of view . . . sacred tradition can even be defined as the science of transmitting truth by degrees so that it can enter correctly and harmoniously into the human psyche."[63] Though he is cautious not to rely too heavily on Guénon and Coomaraswamy in his writings—such as with regard to citations—the fact that he relies on their perspectives is perhaps most evident in the fact that he edited the Metaphysical Library series for Penguin Books that includes *The Sword of Gnosis* (for which he wrote the introduction explaining, among other things, the notion of Tradition) referred to earlier and containing a collection of reprinted essays by Guénon and members of the English school. The series also contains the translation of Guénon's *The Reign of Quantity and the Signs of the Times* in addition to books by Joseph Epes Brown, Titus Burckhardt, and Frithjof Schuon.

Huston Smith, more than Jacob Needleman, expressly incorporates the works of Guénon and Coomaraswamy, whom he cited in his publications. In *Forgotten Truth: The Primordial Tradition*, published in 1976, Professor Smith was careful to avoid the loaded terms of Tradition and philosophia perennis (in Latin or English), and used instead "the primordial philosophy" and similar constructions. He nonetheless made perfectly clear to whom he was indebted and what constitutes, for him, the primordial tradition. In speaking of the symbolism of the cross, for example, he states that "René Guénon's *Symbolism of the Cross* must be credited for much that we are about to say."[64] Warning the reader that he "will recognize the affinity of this thesis with what has been called 'the perennial philosophy,'" Smith sets forth his thesis:

> Twenty years ago I wrote a book, *The Religions of Man*, which presented the world's enduring traditions in their individuality and variety. It has taken me until now to see how they converge. The outlooks of individual men and women . . . are too varied even to classify, but when they gather in collectivities—the outlook of tribes, societies, civilizations, and at the deepest level of the world's great religions—these collective outlooks admit of overview. What then emerges is a remarkable unity underlying the surface variety.[65]

This is a concise and apposite definition of the Tradition—the "remarkable unity" of which Smith speaks revealed at the "deepest levels" of the world's religions. It is just such a remarkable unity that characterizes all expressions, forums, and individual expositors of the Tradition itself, the philosophia perennis or "primordial philosophy of tradition." Regardless of the "surface variety," whether French, Iranian, Italian, North American, British, the effects of Guénon and Coomaraswamy and their one universal forum on current tendencies of thought and discourse show a constant and intransigent underlying theme. These effects are pondered by Marco Pallis who, presumably, is among the "thoughtful minority" (i.e., the Traditional school) that he describes in his analysis of the influence this school has achieved:

> Since the years when Guénon and Coomaraswamy were both writing, the climate of Western thought and feelings

has undergone a noticeable change, of which those who are watching events from an easterly vantage point might profitably take stock. Though the official ideology in Europe and America is still geared to the dogmas of "progress," that is to say of an optimistically slanted evolutionary process with Utopia . . . at the end of the road, many of the previously confident assumptions that go with such an ideology are now being seriously called into question by a thoughtful minority and more especially among the young.[66]

The influence of Guénon and Coomaraswamy, whether effected directly or through those who followed them in the Traditionalist forum, has continued to spread since the first half of the twentieth century. Those who openly attribute that their expressions were wholly or partially shaped by the Traditional perspective may be said to be within the Traditional forum. Others may not acknowledge the influence but nonetheless infuse it in their oeuvre.

Those in this latter category range in scope from poets like T. S. Eliot and Kathleen Raine to scholars like Mircea Eliade and Henry Corbin to mendicants like Swami Ramdas and Thomas Merton. Many more could be added to this list, but it must be left to another to trace further in detail the emanations of pervading influence of the Tradition as espoused by Guénon and Coomaraswamy. Like the ripples radiating outward from a stone that breaks the surface of a still pond, the combined effect of the life's work of Guénon and Coomaraswamy, who each had an instructive and reciprocal affect on the other, continues to influence minds in earnest search of clarity and meaning as we enter a new century and a new millennium.[67]

# 5

## The *Complexio Oppositorum* of Quantity and Quality

In 1945, René Guénon published *Le règne de la quantité et les signes des temps*, described by Pallis as "perhaps the most brilliantly original among his books," and further described by Roger Lipsey as "the best introduction to his thought." What was treated by Guénon in more than three hundred pages obviously cannot be treated in detail here. What is relevant in this context is to outline the fundamental, principial nature of both quantity and quality, to show their interrelationship, and to show the centrality of the terms and the various accompanying ideas implicit in them to the overall primordial Tradition. As lengthy as Guénon's book is, the idea of the complexio oppositorum—in this case exemplified by quantity and quality—can be expanded to infinity and correlated interminably to other polarities, for as Guénon himself describes it in his book, the complementary poles of quantity and quality represent "the first of all cosmic dualities," since this complement "is at the very principle of existence or of universal manifestation."[68] Not surprisingly, Guénon proceeds to correlate the two principles to metaphysics—that is, to Essence and Substance:

> We are able to speak of the essence and the substance of our world, that is to say of the world which is the domain of the individual human, and we can say that, in conformity with the conditions which define particularly this world, these two principles appear in it under the aspects of quality and quantity respectively.[69]

As in the case of Tradition, esoteric and exoteric, hierarchy, and quantity and quality, Guénon spoke directly to the problem, Coomaraswamy obliquely. As has been mentioned, their styles and methods

43

were different. Therefore, while it may appear that Guénon was the sole spokesman for certain of these principles, in fact each man spoke more or less equally about the same principles in signally different ways. Again, this can be seen in the case of quality and quantity, to which Guénon devoted an entire book, and to which Coomaraswamy devoted intermittent but poignant strands within the complete fabric of his oeuvre.

## THE NATURE OF QUANTITY

No such differences as exist between the colloquial and Guénon/ Coomaraswamy usage of Tradition exist in the latters' usage of quantity (and quality). Though the metaphysical correlations to the terms might appear distinctive in their respective writings, the central meanings of the terms are synonymous in both realms. Nonetheless, for the particular coloring of the terms within the current Traditional worldview, Guénon supplies us with some definitions—in this case for quantity. "Quantity," he writes, "is one of the self-same conditions of existence within the sensible or corporeal world; it is the one, among these conditions, that is most exclusively suited to that world." In the following sentence, he continues:

> One can say that quantity, properly constituting the substantial side of our world, can thus be said to be its "basic" or fundamental condition; but caution must be used not to give it an importance of an order higher than it truly has, and particularly not to try to elicit from it an explanation for this world.[70]

This tendency toward *reductio ad quantitatem* was a major target for both Guénon and Coomaraswamy in their writings, especially as it applied to Western culture and thought. Both men rejected this reduction in favor of the reality of metaphysics—that is, in favor of unmeasurable essence.

In the Traditional perspective, the correlation of opposed or complementary polarities to the notion of quantity and its representatives, in a wide range of dualities, is predictable. Epistemologically, quantity would correlate to discursive ratiocination, as opposed to gnosis or intellectual intuition; symbolically, quantity would correlate to the horizontal axis in the two-dimensional symbolism of the cross, as opposed to the vertical axis; empirically, quantity would correlate to that which is measurable or numerical, as opposed to that which is unmeasurable; metaphysically, quantity would correlate to substance or phenomena, as opposed to essence or noumena; sociologically quantity would correlate to democratization or the "mean average," as opposed to a spiritually informed hierarchization of the social order; theologically, quantity would correlate to the flesh, as opposed to the spirit; the examples are endless.

In examining the writings of Guénon and Coomaraswamy, however, we must always return to metaphysics, since each man believed essence precedes substance, the lower proceeds from the higher, and ontologically, quantity correlates to the sensible, as opposed to the intelligible. In a footnote to his essay "Measures of Fire," Coomaraswamy asserts:

> *Mātrā* (like μέτρον) is etymologically "matter," not in the sense of "That which is solid," but in the proper sense of "that which is quantitative" and has a position in the world (*loka-locus*). Whatever is thus in the world can be named and perceived (*nāma-rūpa*) and is accessible to a physical and statistical science; the unmeasured being the proper domain of metaphysics.[71]

The domain of quantity is therefore the material, the empirical, the literal. The academically fashionable literal or historical exoteric exegesis of ancient religious texts and the writings of the magnanimous philosophers can be said to be a quantitative one, in the Traditional sense. Similarly, the so-called scientific method, or historical method by which as Coomaraswamy once wryly remarked, "the reality is more obscured than illuminated," is also primarily quantitative in approach, placing the superlative value on statistical data and the measurable. Thus, from the point of view of the Tradition's expositors, the quantitative approach was best summed up, to iterate A. B. Keith's infamous line, in the phrase "such knowledge as is not empirical is meaningless to us and should not be described as knowledge."

It should be made perfectly clear, however, that to Guénon and Coomaraswamy the enemy was not quantity or the quantitative approach per se; we live in the physical world inhabiting corporeal bod-

ies, and for this we need quantity, substance, materiality. The enemy
was for them rather the reduction—the *reductio ad quantitatem*—an
apodictic denial of the reality of the intelligible realm, the specious and
at times dangerous conclusions reached by those who held an exclusively quantitative worldview—for example, the proclivity to deraci-
nate the process of intellectual intuition in metaphysics and the results
thereby achieved from the "respectable and relevant" academic milieu.
Quantity, in the Traditional view, is a complement to quality, not an
irreconcilable antithesis; under the right conditions the *complexio
oppositorum* becomes a *coincidentia oppositorum*.

## THE NATURE OF QUALITY

Fewer of Guénon's dicta regarding quality and qualitative
approach are found in *Le règne de la quantité et les signes des temps*
than those regarding quantity, which is the principal subject of the
book. Nonetheless, he treats the idea of quality, and gives us insight into
its meaning as he perceives it. He writes that

> Quality, envisaged as the content of essence, if it is allow-
> able to so express it, is not confined exclusively to our
> world, but is susceptible to a transposition that universalizes
> its significance. Moreover, it should be no surprise that, in
> this context, (essence) represents the superior principle.[72]

"Superior" here is a valuation—that is, a qualitative assessment.
Exactly the same valuation, though on a different subject, is found in
Coomaraswamy's writings: "Our boasted [Western] standard of living
is qualitatively beneath contempt, however quantitatively magnificent."[73]

Just as Plato's "Good" (τὸ ἀγαθόν) implies valuation, so the Traditional worldview of Guénon and Coomaraswamy contains this valuation, which is based upon the same standard or criterion of assessment
as Plato's: its position relative to the vertical axis; its proximity to the
apex from which all manifestations proceeds. Those qualities are good
that are superior to (above) the horizontal axis; those qualities are not
good that are inferior to (below) it, all insofar as these valuations apply
to the contingent realms. The positions of the qualities on the vertical
axis are determined by intellectual intuition, not by the "scientific

method," since their positions are unmeasurable in quantitative terms. "The vertical sense represents the hierarchy," wrote Guénon, "and also for the reason is it indefinite, of the multiple states, each of which, seen in its complete integrality, is one of these groups of possibilities corresponding to the 'worlds' or degrees which comprise the total synthesis of 'Universal Man'."[74]

That the notions of quality and hierarchy are indissolubly bound together in the Traditional worldview we have seen; where these two ideas most often become manifest in the writings of Guénon and Coomaraswamy are in the areas of consciousness and the social order of Traditional cultures. Regarding the latter, Guénon's observation of the necessity of a qualitative spiritual elite in a Traditional (or any) culture reflects Coomaraswamy's understanding of the original Hindu caste system. In contrast with Louis Dumont's later observations of the Hindu hierarchical social order,[75] and perhaps anticipating Georges Dumézil's thesis, which he published in its final form as *L'Idéologie tripartite des indo-européens* (Brussels, 1958), Coomaraswamy wrote metaphorically that *everyman*—Guénon's "Homme Universel"—is constituted of a hierarchy with a sacerdotal element, royal and administrative elements, and an element "consisting of the physical organs of sense and action, that handle the raw material or 'food' to be prepared for all"; and that everyman represented a microcosm governed by "one and the same law" that governs the macrocosmic social order.[76]

Quality and the qualitative approach are thus inextricably linked to hierarchy, and represent the vertical axis of the cross. Quality is noumenal, essential, unmeasurable, and determined by intellectual intuition, the degree or efficacy of which is in turn determined by the individual's axiological insight or development, and differing in each individual. In Traditional metaphysics, quantitative would most closely approximate the description "rational," while qualitative would most closely approximate the description "suprarational."[77] Quality is the nemesis of scientism and the staple of Tradition. The concept of quality lies at the heart of Traditional hermeneutics, and sounds a silent chord of affirmative response in those whose spiritual tendencies direct them toward the dynamic expositors of Traditional metaphysics. Huston Smith's description of quality is a fitting summary:

This [quality] is basic to the lot, for it is the qualitative ingredient in values, meanings, and purposes that accounts for

their power. Certain qualities (such as colors) are connected
with quantifiable substrates (lightwaves of given lengths),
but quality itself is unmeasurable. Either it is perceived for
what it is or it is not, and nothing can convey its nature to
anyone who cannot perceive it directly.[78]

INTERRELATIONSHIP OF QUANTITY AND QUALITY

Regardless of the fact that quantity and quality are opposed concepts in the Traditional view, they are not *contrary* but rather *complementary*. Contraries, like truth and falsehood, are fundamentally
irreconcilable; complements, on the other hand, while they may be different, retain the potential for union, at the point of their conjunction,
intersection, coincidence. The cross, for example, with its vertical and
horizontal axes, intersects; the Taoist symbol of yin/yang is two complements (which can also be seen as opposites) conjoined within a
greater sphere, and so on. The principle is thus twofold, involving (a)
the union of complements, and (b) the coincidence or resolution of
opposites. Chapters 6 and 7 of Guénon's *Le symbolisme de la croix*
entitled "L'union des complementaires" and "La resolution des oppositions," respectively, give a detailed metaphysical explication of the
principle. Huston Smith diagrammatically uses the degrees of the
angles formed by the intersection of the two-dimensional cross to illustrate the union of complements (90° between the horizontal and vertical
axes at their point of intersection) and the resolution of opposites (180°
between polar extremes or opposites of the same axis—horizontal or
vertical) that "resolves" itself at the point of intersection.

It is true that Guénon spoke of a three-dimensional cross in *Le
Symbolisme de la croix*; for our purposes, however, the two-dimensional cross is more relevant, since what is under discussion is a polar
dyad, a biune whole. A concept as utterly profound as the coincidence
of opposites, the *coincidentia oppositorum*, was necessarily discussed
at length by Guénon and Coomaraswamy; by its very proposal the criticism that Guénon and Coomaraswamy entirely rejected the whole
realm of the quantitative is precluded, since both poles or axes—quantitative and qualitative—are requisite for achieving this union. Parallel
to the "quantity: horizontal:: quality: vertical" equation is the percept of
Carl Jung regarding the necessity of the *quaternio* for wholeness, such
as the cross in the circle. Jung wrote that

Often the polarity is arranged as a quaternio (quaternity), with the two opposites crossing one another, as for instance the four elements or the four qualities (moist, dry, cold, warm), or the four directions or seasons, thus producing the cross as an emblem of the four elements and symbol of the sublunary physical world.[79]

Elsewhere he states, "The quaternity of Christ . . . is exemplified by the cross symbol, the *rex gloriae*, and Christ as the year.[80] This powerful and recurrent motif in Jung's writings, which ultimately led him to posit the idea of individuation as the goal of analytical psychology, was most evident in his appreciation of the Hellenistic Gnostic texts, especially in the androgyne and in particular in Christ as androgyne.

By this route, we are led full circle back to the union or intersection of quality and quantity as vertical and horizontal axes of the cross, respectively. This union or intersection occurs naturally among complements; seen as opposites, however, a synthesis that the fifteenth-century bishop Nicholas of Cusa first terms the *coincidentia oppositorum* is precisely the *hieros gamos* (sacred union) of various cosmogonies in mythology, and is further exemplified by the mystical "ceremony of the bridal chamber" of the Hellenistic Gnostics and the *maithuna* of the Vajrayāna Buddhists. It is the center, the point of balance and equilibrium, the *restitutio ad integram*, and the resolution of opposites, all of which serve as referents for the same metaphysical process. This process was indicated by Coomaraswamy, when he declared that it is "precisely from these 'pairs' that liberation must be won, from their conflict that we must escape, if we are to be freed from our mortality and to be as and when we will."[81] Thus these dualistic oppositions are only ostensibly irreconcilable; in a higher level of reference they are ultimately synthetic, and their apprehension as such depends upon the insight of the perceiver. Guénon writes that

> The principal unity demands in effect that there can be no irreductible oppositions;\* therefore, while it is true that opposition between two terms can exist in appearance and possess a relative reality at a certain level of existence, this opposition must disappear as such and be harmoniously resolved, by synthesis or integration, when it passes to a higher level.[82]

The asterisk refers to one of Guénon's footnotes, too significant to omit. He states there that "Consequently, all 'dualism,' whether it is of the theological order such as that attributed to the Manicheans, or of the philosophical order such as that of Descartes, is a radically false conception." Quantity and quality are therefore parts of a reducible dualism, and their union or intersection symbolizes one of the most central and profound doctrines of the Tradition, whose detailed examination will be undertaken in the next Part.

## QUALITY AND THE TRADITION

By their relentless denigration of quantitative Western culture, one might assume Guénon and Coomaraswamy were guilty of seeking to promote only the notion of quality and abandoning that of quantity. The reality is that in their view, the extent of corruption of Western culture was so egregious that the remedy, the prescription for awakening, had to be commensurate to the profundity of the "sleep." They therefore concentrated on the remedy, that is, on trying to establish the necessity and integrity of the qualitative, hierarchical, vertical axis of the cross and what it represented—the Tradition or philosophia perennis. For if, in modernity, the Traditional notion of quality has been lost, then it must follow that any synthesis between the two axes is unattainable.

And this is precisely the predicament of the West, as they saw it. Coomaraswamy saw the necessity of a return to first principles, and Guénon saw the necessity of an intellectually intuitive spiritual elite to take these principles and presumably direct their application to the culture in which they lived. Certain regions of the East, where during their lives one found the only living Traditions left, had survived in this sense, though these surviving Traditions were in sore need of defending themselves from the encroachment of the exclusively quantitative worldview of the industrial West. In the second half of the twentieth century, this struggle for survival has all but been lost.

The idea of quality is closely associated with the Tradition itself—with its essential principles and its cultural (and educational) worldview. Regarding education, both Guénon and Coomaraswamy were on record as favoring the Traditional system of education, where emphasis was on qualitative knowledge, where the first principles were taught via transmission to those who had "ears to hear," and where the various disciplines of mathematics, science, language, and so forth, were conjoined with Traditional doctrines. In such a system, the criterion of "learning" or being "learned" was the qualitative degree to which one was able to understand the subtler and more profound doctrines, as opposed to the quantitative criterion of how much diverse or even specialized knowledge one commanded. "Where the Western world proceeds on the assumption that education is primarily in knowledge, the [Traditional] Indian assumption is that education should be in understanding."[83] Modern Western education they disliked for the reason that the qualitative element was almost entirely missing.

Coomaraswamy's criticisms of modern education are as numerous as Guénon's: he wrote that "The [Traditional] point of view is unwelcome to a democratic age of pathetic belief in the efficacy of indiscriminate 'education'" and, elsewhere, that "The greater part of what is nowadays called 'knowledge' is based on nothing better than statistics, and its 'facts' are only what we 'make' of these; the greater part of modern education, therefore, has little or nothing to do with man's last end, *s'eternar*."[84] Guénon's criticism was even harder in describing what was left after the late medieval period:

> There was, thus, only to be left philosophy and "profane" science; that is to say, the negation of true intellectuality, the limitation of knowledge to its lowest order, an empirical and analytical study of facts separated from any principle, a dispersion into an indefinite multitude of insignificant details, an accumulation of hypotheses without foundation which incessantly undermine each other, and of fragmentary views which cannot lead to anything except practical applications of the type which constitute the sole effective superiority of modern civilization.[85]

In short, the qualitative is missing in modernity; the quantitative alone remains. It should be added that the observation of the loss of quality is not confined to those who promulgate the Tradition; it is widespread throughout the humanities in modern education, and the absence of quality is deprecated by several scholars who have become conspicuous for it. In the field of the history of religions, for example, that represents a unique blend of subjective religious principles and objective "social sciences," Gilford Dudley states, "The hard approach is the empiricist, or data-bound, school of thought; the soft approach relies

on the intuition of essences in religious phenomena." Revolving
around this opposition, he then asks, "Is the humanistic impulse in an
academic field to be avoided because it is subjective and unscientific
to assess knowledge by how much it enriches human experience?"[86]
Theodore Roszak, another scholar and a sort of latter-day Guénon qua
critic of modernity, also laments the paucity of the qualitative in modern thought and education:

> Over the past two centuries, the secular consensus has
> offered us many readings of human nature: Darwinism,
> Marxism, Freudianism, Behaviorism, positivism, existen-
> tialism, sociobiology. We have been told that we are "naked
> apes" and "meat machines," creatures "beyond freedom and
> dignity," governed by neural feedback or the reflex arc, by
> class interest or sexual appetite, by economic self interest or
> genetic programming, by cultural conditioning or historical
> necessity. Curious, is it not, how all these images seem
> determined to root out our deep intuition of freedom and
> higher purpose—how none does justice to our yearning for
> completion at some higher level of being. None waters the
> seed within us that longs for cultivation.[87]

That the notion of quality is a presupposition of the Tradition and
its concomitant cultural and educational worldviews is clear. That the
resistance to the idea of quality within the "secular consensus" of
modernity is tenacious is also clear. What is not clear in the writings of
Guénon and Coomaraswamy is an optimism that the modern quantitative West can have restored to it the idea of quality. Both Guénon and
Coomaraswamy claim that a restoration of quality is possible; the probability is what is in question. "What possibility of regeneration, if any,"
asks Coomaraswamy, "can be envisaged for the West?" His answer is
that "The possibility exists only in the event of a return to first principles and to the normal ways of living that proceed from the application
of first principles to contingent circumstances."[88] Guénon's answer is
that

> Either the West will find within itself the necessary means,
> by a direct return to its own tradition, a return that would
> amount to a sort of spontaneous reawakening of latent pos-

sibilities, or else certain Western elements will accomplish this work of restoration with the aid of a certain knowledge of Oriental doctrines.[89]

The desacralization or degeneration of the West from the viewpoint of the Tradition and its possible resuscitation will be examined in greater detail in Part 4. It has been the purpose of this present section to illustrate the relationship of quality and quantity and to show the great emphasis that was placed by expositors of the Tradition on the idea of quality, as applied to principles, culture, and education—that is, to the notion of *Weltanschauung* in general.

The term tradition and its semantic variants have been discussed and contrasted to the particularized metaphysical meaning of Guénon and Coomaraswamy; the hermeneutical method of the tradition was examined; the forums of the Tradition have been described; and the *oppositorum* between quantity and quality has been related to the idea of Tradition. Attention will now be turned to a more detailed examination of the first principles of the Tradition of Guénon and Coomaraswamy, and these principles will be contrasted with other manifestations of the philosophia perennis, notably that of H. P. Blavatsky and the theosophical movement that began in 1875.

# NOTES TO PART I

1. While it is true that "metaphysician" has been the accepted and conventional epithet for one who studies or promulgates metaphysics, it nonetheless conveys a medieval definition of the learned person or doctor of physics (nature). Since in our own times a "physician" generally refers to an allopathic practitioner of the medical science, and since a "physicist" in the company of Plank, Einstein, Bohr, Heisenberg, et al., is one who studies the intricate properties of forces, energies, and materiality in the universe, it follows that one who studies that which lies beyond "known" (i.e., empirical, measurable) physical laws and substances must more accurately be termed a "metaphysicist." The term is, therefore, a perfectly justified neologism, and will be used in this sense throughout, notwithstanding Guénon's professed aversion to "unnecessary" neologisms.

2. Shils, *Tradition*, p. 3.

3. In order to avoid confusion, and to allow the use of the words *tradition* and *traditional* in their conventional meanings, the reader is advised that the capitalization of these words hereafter refers specifically to the particularized Guénon-Coomaraswamy usage, following the lead (in some of their works) of both these writers and those like Roger Lipsey and Ray Livingston who wrote commentaries of the Traditional perspective. The uppercase format of these two terms admittedly appears awkward and reminiscent of nineteenth-century style; it nonetheless remains the most efficient determinant.

4. Judah, *The History and Philosophy of the Metaphysical Movements in America*, p. 17.

5. In *Coomaraswamy: His Life and Work*, Roger Lipsey states in reference to Elizabeth Beeby Coomaraswamy that after her return to England in 1879, "The young widow never returned to Ceylon and never remarried" (p. 10). James Crouch, in a bibliographical essay entitled "Ananda Coomaraswamy in Ceylon: A Bibliography" (*Ceylon Journal of Social and Historical Studies*), 1973 (3:2, 55–56) contradicts Lipsey, claiming that "in the pursuit of his geological interests Coomaraswamy made nearly annual visits to Ceylon, usually accompanied by his mother, the first taking place perhaps as early as 1896." Rama P. Coomaraswamy, Ananda's son, states, "I suspect Lipsey is right but don't know how it could be proved" (personal communication with the author in a letter dated October 25, 1980).

6. In this Coomaraswamy viewed himself the heir of his father's sustained interest in the Sinhalese culture and Buddhism, notwithstanding Sir Mutu's Tamil heritage and Westernization. Sir Mutu, in fact, had translated from the Pāli certain Buddhist sutras that were published as *Suttanipāta: Dialogue and Discourses of Gotama Buddha*. London: Trubner, 1874.

7. Eliade, "Some Notes on *Theosophia perennis*," p. 171.

8. Until 1977, the centennial of his birth, a scholarly full-length biography of Coomaraswamy did not exist. In that year, Moni Bagchee published *Ananda Coomaraswamy: A Study* (Varanasi: Bharata Manisha, 1977) that only satisfied the latter qualification—that is, full length. The same year, Vishwanath S. Naravane published *Ananda K. Coomaraswamy* (Boston: Twayne Publishers). Before 1977 most biographical material had to be found either in articles, within anthologies, or as prefaces or appendices to studies on Coomaraswamy's thought. The most prolific biographer of the Coomaraswamy family (both Ananda and Sir Mutu) was S. Durai Raja Singam who edited *Homage to Ananda Coomaraswamy: A Garland of Tributes* (Kuala Lumpur, 1948), following it with two subsequent (enlarged) editions in 1952 and 1974, the last edition being retitled *Ananda Coomaraswamy: Remembering and Remembering Again and Again*. Singam also released a biography of his own on Coomaraswamy in two parts or supplements, entitled *Ananda Coomaraswamy: Study of a Scholar-Colosus* (Kuala Lumpur, 1977, 1981). There are short biographical sections on Coomaraswamy in Ray Livingston's *The Traditional Theory of Literature* and P. S. Sastri's *Ananda K. Coomaraswamy*. There are scattered articles as well: specifically, Doña Luisa Coomaraswamy's "Some Recollections and References to Dr. Ananda Coomaraswamy" in *Kalamanjari* (1:1, 1950–1951) 20; Sharon Thomas's "Coomaraswamy: A Vision of Unity" in *The Theosophist* (99:3, 1977) 84; Roger Lipsey's "The Two Selves: Coomaraswamy as Man and Metaphysician" in *SCR* (6:4, 1972) 199; and Whitall N. Perry's "Coomaraswamy: The Man, Myth, and History" in *SCR* (11:3, 1977) 159. Finally, there is Roger Lipsey's outstanding and sensitive biography, *Coomaraswamy: His Life and Work*, which remains to date the "last word" in biographical literature on Coomaraswamy.

9. Sérant, *René Guénon*, p. 8. Waterfield ascribes his withdrawal to ill health and "homesickness," yet Guénon did not return to Blois after his withdrawal but rather moved to a flat at 51 Rue St. Louis in Paris. *René Guénon and the Future of the West*, p. 28.

10. The full-length biographies on Guénon, and other studies that contain much biographical material, include Paul Chacornac's *La vie simple de René Guénon* (Paris: Éditions Traditionnelles, 1958); Jean-Pierre Laurent's

*Le sens caché dans l'oeuvre de René Guénon*; Jacques Maricireau's *René Guénon et son oeuvre* (Potiers: J. Maricireau, 1946); Lucien Meroz's *René Guénon ou la Sagesse initaitique* (Paris: Plon, 1962); Paul Sérant's *René Guénon*; Jean Tourniac's *Propos sur René Guénon* (Paris: Dervy-Livres, 1973); and Robin Waterfield's *René Guénon and the Future of the West* (London: Crucible, 1987). Gabriel Asfar's unpublished Ph.D. dissertation at Princeton University, *René Guénon: A Chapter of French Symbolist Thought in the Twentieth Century* (1972) contains a biographical section on Guénon, as does Marilyn Gustin's unpublished Ph.D. dissertation at Berkeley's Graduate Theological Union, "The Nature, Role and Interpretation of Symbol in the Thought of René Guénon" (1987). Additionally, there are two "special issues" of French journals devoted wholly to Guénon: *Études Traditionnelles* (1951) and *Planète* (1970). Single articles in French journals are more numerous than these biographies and studies; the material here, however, should be sufficient for the reader interested in pursuing Guénon's biography.

11. Lipsey, loc. cit., p. 277. Cf., Schuon, "The Perennial Philosophy," in Fernando, ed., *The Unanimous Tradition*, p. 21.

12. In Schuon, *Islam and the Perennial Philosophy*, p. viii.

13. Coomaraswamy, *HB*, p. 4.

14. Coomaraswamy, *BK*, p. 66. Cf. *SPTAS*, p. 43. "We must not, of course, confuse 'traditional' with 'academic': fashions change with time and place, while the tradition or 'handing on' of which we are speaking is an Eternal Philosophy."

15. Guénon, *La France Anti-maçonnique* (July, 1913). Cited in Asfar, loc. cit., p. 178. See Needleman, *SG*, p. 11.

16. Asfar, loc. cit., p. 175. See Waterfield, loc. cit., p. 91: "Tradition was essentially that body of knowledge and self-understanding which is common to all men of all ages and nationalities. . . . It is supratemporal in origin, the link which unites man as manifestation to his unmanifest origin."

17. Ibid., p. 177.

18. Livingston, *The Traditional Theory of Literature*, p. 179.

19. For this reason, quotations from this book will be in the English of the translators. Marco Pallis, who did these revisions with Richard Nicholson beginning in 1939, was concerned about Guénon's view of Buddhism. With Coomaraswamy's persuasion, Pallis got Guénon's permission to make corrections not only in this book, but "corrections in other texts if and when we came to translate them; for this purpose he [Guénon] supplied a number of reworded passages." Further, throughout the course of this work, use of Tra-

dition in the writings of Guénon and Coomaraswamy is always in its *most developed sense*. Each man grew or evolved into his developed and full meaning of Tradition via a long and complex path, and only in their last decades did the two employ Tradition in its fullest sense—that is, as an interchangeable term with sophia/philosophia perennis. To trace the development of each man arriving at this full sense of the word is beyond the scope of this work; moreover, it would be a duplication of effort, since the job has been admirably done by Lipsey for Coomaraswamy and Asfar for Guénon. The interested reader is referred to their works, already cited, to elicit the details of this development.

20. Guénon, *Hindu*, p. 89. This bifurcated stance between "East and West" is the central thesis of his book by that title (*Orient et Occident*), and shows itself again in an important essay entitled "Oriental Metaphysics" in *SG*, in a most terse statement: "For us, the outstanding difference between the East and West (which means in this case the modern West), the only difference that is really essential (for all others are derivative), is on the one side the preservation of tradition, with all that this implies, and on the other side the forgetting and loss of this same tradition" (p. 55).

21. Guénon, *Règne*, pp. 283, 281.

22. Coomaraswamy, *BK*, p. 50.

23. Coomaraswamy, *SPM*, p. 37.

24. Coomaraswamy, *SL*, p. 108.

25. Guénon, *Hindu*, p. 133. Cf. Asfar, loc. cit., p. 324.

26. Asfar, loc. cit., p. 324. In the modern world, esoteric and exoteric both as concepts and social manifestations are increasingly and often opposed, due primarily to the rise of intransigent and violent fundamentalist groups as substrata of the exoteric aspects of the religions these groups purport to represent.

27. Pallis, "A Fateful Meeting of Minds: A. K. Coomaraswamy and R. Guénon," p. 178. Cf. Lipsey, op cit., p. 272. See, Eaton, *The Richest Vein*, p. 201, "It is chiefly on account of his greater interest in the conditions of life of the men and women around him that Coomaraswamy's work seems more straightforward than Guénon's, rather than an account of any difference of belief between the two men."

28. See above, page 43, where the question of quality and quantity is treated in detail. It is necessary to mention briefly at this point the relationship between "quality" and "hierarchy," since they are principles that are equally codeterminant and inextricable. On hierarchical "chains" see Coomara-

swamy, *SPM*, p. 368: "The traditional and orthodox doctrine is a recognition of the causal chain by which all events are linked in a phenomenal succession, but of their intrinsic and not extrinsic operations." See also Huston Smith's article entitled "Hierarchy Essential to Religion: The Great Chain of Being Reaffirmed Against Scientistic, Modernist, and Postmodernist Atttacks" in *Contemporary Philosophy* 13, No. 8 (1991): 3–9. This entire issue is devoted to the principle of hierarchy, and contains some interesting contributions.

29. Coomaraswamy, BUGB-D, p. 142.

30. Coomaraswamy, *SPM*, p. 51.

31. Guénon, *Crise*, p. 52. Cf., *Les États Multiples de L'Être*, p. 59.

32. Coomaraswamy, *BK*, p. 55.

33. Coomaraswamy, *SPM*, p. 214.

34. Ibid., p. 56. Italics mine.

35. Coomaraswamy, *TNA*, p. 133.

36. Guénon, *Crise*, pp. 52, 53.

37. Coomaraswamy, *SPM*, p. 219.

38. Guénon, *Hindu*, p. 67.

39. Guénon, *Règne*, p. 285.

40. Coomaraswamy, *SPM*, p. 422.

41. Coomaraswamy, *SL*, pp. 128, 140, 159, et passim. "I do feel that one ought not to speak at all of other religions than one's own unless one has a knowledge of their scriptures comparable to that which one has of one's own."

42. Coomaraswamy, *SPM*, p. 40.

43. Guénon, "Oriental Metaphysics," in *SG*, p. 40.

44. Cited in Lipsey, *CLW*, p. 271. For a brief historical account of the journal, whose name and mandate have changed several times, see the relevant section in Michel Valsân's introduction to Guénon's *Symbols fondamentaux de la science sacrée* (Paris, 1962).

45. Asfar, op. cit., p. 203.

46. Lipsey, *CLW*, pp. 271–72.

47. Jean Borella gives a detailed account of the origin of the French school in chapter 12 of *Modern Esoteric Spirituality*, "René Guénon and the Traditionalist School," p. 330.

48. *SCR*, for instance, ran a special number in 1977 in commemoration of Coomaraswamy's centenary, to which several members of the Traditional school submitted articles. One should also mention, at this juncture, the invaluable work of Lester Kanefsky who, under the aegis of Prologos Books in the London suburb of Berwick-on-Tweed, has edited, compiled, and sold the English literature on Tradition for many years, and has served as a clearinghouse for the English forum since the demise of *SCR*.

49. Coomaraswamy, *BK*, p. 67.

50. Coomaraswamy, *SL*, p. 26. Clearly Guénon did not see himself as a "popularizer." He states in *Man and His Becoming According to the Vedānta*, for example, that "we believe it necessary to expound certain ideas for the benefit of those who are capable of assimilating them, without however modifying or simplifying them after the fashion of the 'popularizers,' which would be in flat contradiction with our avowed intentions" (p. 11).

51. Much of this correspondence was preserved and now appears in *Selected Letters of Ananda Coomaraswamy*, ed. Alvin Moore, Jr., and Rama Coomaraswamy (Delhi: Oxford University Press, 1988).

52. The books in question are literally paradigms of superlative scholarship, much like Coomaraswamy's works. They are, in chronological order, *Avicenne et le récit visionnaire*, 2 vols. (Paris, 1954); *L'Imagination créatrice dans le soufisme d'Ibn-Arabī* (Paris, 1958); *Terre céleste et corps de résurrection: De l'Iran mazdéen à l'Iran shi'ite* (Paris, 1961); *L'homme de lumiere dans le soufisme iranien* (Sisteron, 1971); and finally, *En Islam iranien: Aspects spirituele et philosophiques* (Paris, 1973). All these works, except the last, which is in four volumes, are available in English translations. A collection of Corbin's lectures was published as *Cyclical Time and Ismaili Gnosis* (London 1983).

53. Corbin, *Creative Imagination in the Sufism of Ibn 'Arabi*, p. 5.

54. Nasr, *Sufi Essays*, p. 15. This further points to the centrality of Sufism and esoteric Islam with the European schools of the Tradition. As an interesting aside, S. H. Nasr and Martin Lings also wrote an introduction and preface, respectively, for the Theosophical Publishing House's reprints of Jami's *Lawā'ih* (1906) and Ibn 'Arabī's *Tarjumán Al-Ashwáq* (1911).

55. Cited from personal correspondence with the author in a letter from Wilson, dated February 27, 1978.

56. Coomaraswamy, *SPM*, p. 165.

57. Pallis, loc. cit., p. 177.

58. Lipsey, *CLW*, p. 171. Their thought was complementary, their *beliefs* the same, yet their perceptions were not always the same. A case in point is their regard of twentieth-century Neo-Thomism which, though strongly parallel to Traditional thought in many ways, could not legitimately be placed under the aegis of Tradition or classified as one of its "schools." Though Guénon knew Jacques Maritain personally (Coomaraswamy met him once briefly), and both he and Coomaraswamy were thoroughly acquainted with the works of Étienne Gilson and the others representing Neo-Scholasticism, Guénon, possibly because of his "apostasy" and adoption of Islam, basically disagreed with their views. Maritain tried to get Noële Boulet, with whom he was collaborating on a review of Guénon's *Introduction générale à l'étude des doctrines hindoues* in 1922, to see that "la métaphysique de Guénon est radicalement inconcilable avec la foi." Conversely, Coomaraswamy quotes both Gilson and Maritain in his writings in addition to leaning heavily on the medieval Scholastics, especially Aquinas, Eckhart, and Bonaventure. See Étienne Gilson's *The Unity of Philosophical Experience* (New York: Scribner's, 1937) and the Traditional critique by Urban in his *Beyond Realism and Idealism*, p. 244.

59. The principal books have been Sérant's *René Guénon (1953); Chacornac's La vie simple de René Guénon* (1958); Meroz's *René Guénon ou la Sagesse initiatique* (1962); Pawels et al.'s *René Guénon: l'Homme et son Message* (1980), a special issue of *Planète* devoted to Guénon (April 1970); and Laurent's *Le sens caché dans l'oeuvre de René Guénon* (1975). Barella lists twelve separate book-length studies of Guénon and his work in *Modern Esoteric Spirituality*, p. 357. Papers in journals and periodicals are too numerous to list in their entirety, though Barella does list some, idem. at 356.

60. Gide, *Journal (1942–1949)*, pp. 195–96.

61. Evola, in fact, wrote an encomium for Guénon, translated and published as a pamphlet, *René Guénon: A Teacher for Modern Times* (Edmonds, Wash.: Sure Fire, 1994).

62. Mabire, *Julius Evola*, p. 15.

63. Needleman, *A Sense of the Cosmos*, p. 8. Cf. Needleman, *Sacred Tradition and Present Need*, p. 12, where he states that "We may surmise that the external conditions of traditional society contained factors to remind men of what they lose through their egoism . . . [though] he was not without the help of a cosmic, universal scale by which to taste directly his insignificance and dependence."

64. Smith, *Forgotten Truth*, p. 23.

65. Ibid., p. ix. Since the appearance of *Forgotten Truth*, Professor Smith has become less reticent about his endorsements of the Tradition. See, especially, "Perennial Philosophy, Primordial Tradition" in *Beyond the Post-Modern Mind* (Wheaton, Ill.: Theosophical Publishing House, 1984), and "Two Traditions—and Philosophy" in *Religion of the Heart* (Washington, D.C.: Foundation for Traditional Studies, 1991).

66. Pallis, op. cit., p. 184.

67. See Whitall Perry's "The Revival of Interest in Tradition," in *The Unanimous Tradition*, p. 3, which discusses this issue in greater detail.

68. Guénon, *Règne*, p. 21.

69. Ibid., p. 23.

70. Ibid., pp. 32–33.

71. Coomaraswamy, *SPM*, p. 164.

72. Guénon, *Règne*, p. 24.

73. Coomaraswamy, *SPTAS*, p. 317.

74. Guénon, *Croix*, p. 74.

75. Dumont, *Homo Hierarchicus*, pp. 65–92.

76. Coomaraswamy, *HB*, pp. 26, 27. For a more recent discussion of the principle of hierarchy in academic philosophical discourse, see *Contemporary Philosophy* 13, No. 8, 1991, which issue was devoted to the subject and contains contributions from Seyyed H. Nasr and Huston Smith.

77. In the realm of metaphysics and mysticism, one constantly confronts the term *irrational* used by skeptics to describe mystical or metaphysical states of consciousness and realizations. While "rational" applies to the normative realm of spatio-temporality, this does not imply that the higher mystical and/or metaphysical states are by any means "irrational"—they emphatically are not. They rather *transcend* the realm of spatio-temporality and thus of ratiocination; consequently, they are "suprarational" due to their transcendental nature. Irration is a failure of the legitimate rational process within its own locus and by its own criteria—that is, a misuse or abuse of the rational method. Cf. Guénon, *Hindu*, p. 116: "we are dealing with the supraindividual order, which does not in any way mean the irrational; metaphysics cannot contradict reason, but it stands above reason."

78. Smith, op. cit., p. 16.

79. Jung, *Mysterium Coniunctionis*, p. 3. We use Jung's material

guardedly for the reason that Coomaraswamy was ambivalent, at best, about Jung's views. See *SL*, pp. 137, 157. Guénon did not allow any compromises, and spoke of the "subtle confusion" promulgated by Jung. Guénon, *Symboles fundamentaux de la Science Sacrée*, p. 64. I, like Coomaraswamy, cite Jung "because the college man has so much faith in him." *SL*, p. 5.

80. Jung, *Aion*, p. 204.

81. Coomaraswamy, *SPTAS*, pp. 542–43.

82. Guénon, *Croix*, p. 35.

83. Coomaraswamy, "Indian Education" in the *Encyclopedia of Modern Education*.

84. Coomaraswamy, *SPM*, pp. 215 fn, 366n.

85. Guénon, *Crise*, p 30.

86. Dudley, *Religion on Trial*, pp. 3–4. In his provocative book *The Closing of the American Mind*, the renowned professor and commentator on American education Allan Bloom discusses this in detail. See text and notes in the section on "Terminological and Educational Confusion," chapter 14 above.

87. Roszak, "Ethics, Ecstasy, and the Study of New Religions," in Needleman, ed., *Understanding the New Religions*. New York: Seabury, 1978. p. 56.

88. Coomaraswamy, *BK*, p. 62.

89. Guénon, *Crise*, p. 174.

# PART II

## PRINCIPLES AND PARALLELS

# 6

## The *Philosophia Perennis*

Like tradition, philosophia perennis has a somewhat different meaning in the writings of Guénon and Coomaraswamy—and in those of the Traditional school—than it has in modern philosophy. That a sharp contrast between Traditional philosophy and "modern" or "profane" philosophy existed in the perceptions of Guénon and Coomaraswamy has been established. This contrast is pivotal in understanding the difference between what is meant by philosophia perennis in the discipline of modern academic philosophy and in the writings of the twentieth-century expositors of the Tradition. A comparison between these two trends of regarding the philosophia perennis exhibits, on the side of the academic or modern philosophers, an almost total ignorance or disregard of the Traditional usage of the term. The promulgators of Tradition acknowledge the modern philosophical apperception of philosophia perennis, but predictably they reject it. The various reasons for this rejection will be elucidated presently, but first we must try to establish some order in the innumerable problematic cross-currents that beset our perception of and relationship to the philosophia perennis.

First, there are those who can be called perennial philosophers because of their promulgation of the philosophia perennis (though none actually calls himself, to my knowledge, a "perennial philosopher"). These individuals who promulgate the philosophia perennis per se (like Guénon, Coomaraswamy, Wilbur Urban, and others) must be distinguished from (a) those who promulgate the same or similar principles without using the specific term philosophia perennis (e.g., Carl Jung, J. J. Poortman, Huston Smith) and from (b) those who do not promulgate but merely write *about* or discuss the principles as having existed or existing—for example, modern philosophers and/or academic historians of philosophy (the two are different but not exclusive) like Franz Sawicki, Charles B. Schmitt, and James Collins. Second, it follows from these categorizations that differences exist as to what these vari-

ous individuals say the philosophia perennis is: how it is to be seen
against the background of philosophy since philosophical treatises
began being recorded (i.e., 1500 B.C. or so); what principles specifically
constitute philosophia perennis, if any; the epistemological mode of
perceiving these principles; its relevance, probity, unity, ontological
quality or genuineness; its relation to other world philosophical and
mythological systems past and present; the degree to which it is dogmatic or immutable, and so on. These questions will be sorted out and
discussed in this Part in order to bring Traditional views on the subject
into focus.

The case for the Traditional view is summarized by Seyyed
Hossein Nasr, who wrote the preface for Frithjof Schuon's *Islam and
the Perennial Philosophy*:

> But the reality of the perennial philosophy remained
> eclipsed for a long time by the more dominant current of
> profane philosophy in the West based on the idea of the evo-
> lution of thought and "progress" towards the truth. It is only
> during this century—thanks to the rediscovery of tradition
> in the West and the blinding evidence of the presence of a
> metaphysical doctrine at the heart of all authentic traditions,
> which is at once perennial and universal—the key concept
> of perennial philosophy has once again come to the fore . . .
> in the writings of Frithjof Schuon, which, following closely
> upon the work initiated by René Guénon and the Ananda
> Coomaraswamy, may be said to be the most noble and com-
> plete expression of the philosophia perennis available in the
> contemporary world.[1]

It could therefore be said that the Traditional perspective of the
philosophia perennis runs parallel to the modern philosophical one or,
to employ the diction of the Tradition, that the former represents a
philosophically esoteric understanding of the concept, while the latter
represents an exoteric understanding. But in actuality the Traditional
parallel is culturally and academically a subterranean one, based in
large degree on the fact that few of the current proponents of the Tradition, Guénon and Coomaraswamy included, held "credentials" from
academic institutions in the field of philosophy. It is for this reason
that only in the last breath of the few commentators of philosophia

perennis among modern philosophers—almost as an afterthought—
does one find the name of Aldous Huxley mentioned in reference to
the book he produced under the title *The Perennial Philosophy* (New
York, 1944). But while one finds Huxley often mentioned by historians of philosophy in this way, and usually described as an uncritical
popularizer, one never sees the names of Coomaraswamy, Guénon,
Schuon, et al.

   We have seen that Coomaraswamy, unlike Guénon, often used the
term philosophia perennis in his writings. Guénon, consistent with his
distaste for modern "profane" philosophy, more often used Primordial
Tradition or simply "metaphysic." But what Guénon meant by metaphysic, while it shared many of the concerns normally attributed to the
pursuit of metaphysical principles, was again different from normative
usage of the term. Chapter 5 of Guénon's *Introduction to the Study of
the Hindu Doctrines* is entitled "Essential Characteristics of Metaphysic." He says there that "metaphysic in itself remains fundamentally
and unalterably the same, for its object is one in its essence, or to be
more exact 'without duality,' as the Hindus put it, and that object, again
by the fact that it lies 'beyond nature' is also beyond all change" and,
further, that "that which modern philosophical thought is sometimes
content to label as metaphysic bears no relation whatsoever to the conception just put forward."[2] Guénon, however, was not alone in his deprecation of modern philosophy's normal usage of the term *metaphysic:*
Coomaraswamy also shared Guénon's attitude in this regard, and often
used "metaphysics" interchangeably with philosophia perennis. For
example, in an essay entitled "Some Pāli Words," Coomaraswamy, in
speaking of symbolism, states, "This use of symbolisms which are contrary in their literal but unanimous in their spiritual sense very well
illustrates the nature of metaphysics itself, which is not, like a 'philosophy,' systematic, but is always consistent."[3] Elsewhere, he tell us, "The
metaphysical 'philosophy' is called 'perennial' because of its eternity,
universality, and immutability; it is Augustine's 'Wisdom uncreate, the
same now as it ever was and ever will be.'"[4]

   The separation that exists between the Traditional conception of
the philosophia perennis and that held by modern philosophy is not an
innocent division in attitude. Rather, it is characterized by an ignorance
or disregard of Tradition by modern philosophers and by both an objection to and rejection of modern philosophy by those of the Traditional
school. This is a repeated motif in the writings of both Guénon and

Coomaraswamy, as we have seen. Guénon, for example, regretted the conditions that conduced "the birth of what can be described as 'profane' philosophy, that is to say a putative wisdom of a purely human type and therefore simply of the rational order, taking the place of the true traditional, suprarational, and nonhuman wisdom." The inevitable result of the establishment of Western postmedieval profane philosophy was the repudiation of the Primordial Tradition inherent in genuine philosophy, according to Guénon, since "For the 'profane' philosophy to be definitely constituted as such, it was necessary that only exoterism should survive and that it should become purely and simply the negation of all esoterism."[5]

Coomaraswamy took the objection a step further. Not only did he object to modern empirical or systematic philosophies, he objected to their wholesale dissemination by academics. In an essay titled "On the Indian and Traditional Psychology, or Rather Pneumatology," he speaks of the Royal Road or Way as expressed in the Upaniṣadic literature, saying of it that "The Way is that of the Philosophia Perennis, both in theory and practice: a metaphysics that must not be confused with the empirical and systematic 'philosophy' . . . and not at all the same as the 'primary philosophy' or 'theology' . . . now usually taught in our universities, or with the 'philosophies' of individual 'thinkers'." He adds that "The distinction of the traditional from modern 'philosophies' is of fundamental importance."[6] The general rejection of modern philosophy is thus implicit in the specific objections to it by Guénon, Coomaraswamy, and the other writers within the Traditional school.[7]

In the sea of modern philosophical speculation, the expositors of Tradition represent one of two prevalent currents—so far unconnected or unrelated—in recognizing and perceiving the philosophia perennis. With the "philosophical establishment" the Traditional perspective shares some of the principles of the philosophia perennis. There is less divergence of definition concerning the term philosophia perennis when contrasting Tradition and modern philosophy than there is concerning the term tradition when contrasting the Traditional usage and those of the special fields, such as social sciences, religious studies, the arts, and the colloquial usage. To state the idea inversely, Tradition and modern philosophy share far more in their definitions of philosophia perennis than Tradition and the special fields share in the term tradition. But this fact should not be allowed to minimize the dissimilarities, for in reality there are two prevalent but unrelated currents of definition of philosophia

perennis in the twentieth century. And in order to help clarify the divergence, it will first be necessary to show what is meant by the term within
modern philosophy and, in fact, to trace historically both the concept and
the term from their inceptions. Having done this, we can proceed to a more
intelligible examination of the Traditional view of philosophia perennis,
ultimately correlating the latter to the parallel nexus of thought in Western
civilization since early antiquity, *theosophia.*

THE CONCEPT OF PHILOSOPHIA PERENNIS<br>IN MODERN PHILOSOPHY

The concept of the philosophia perennis is as old as the history of
ideas itself. The origins of the concept, before it was labeled as such, are
obscure; often one sees the name of Pythagoras mentioned in connection
with its etiology in the West. Franz Sawicki, in an article entitled "Die
Geschichtsphilosophie als Philosophia Perennis," conservatively places
its origins with the Academy at Athens, "Just as in the other disciplines,
so also in the history of philosophy the philosophia perennis can be said
to connect with Plato and Aristotle."[8] Charles B. Schmitt, a historian of
philosophy who has written more extensively on the philosophia perennis than any other contemporary scholar, describes another view of its
origins. Citing Marsilio Ficino (1433–1499) and using in place of the
term philosophia perennis—which had not yet been coined—the term
*prisca theologica,* Schmitt synopsizes the theory:

> One of the most important facts with regard to Ficino's
> revival of Platonism was his conception of the Platonic tra-
> dition with a supposedly earlier tradition of "pre-Platonism"
> to which he gave the name, *prisca theologica.* According to
> him, the legitimate strand of true knowledge goes back to a
> long tradition before Plato: that is, wisdom did not start with
> the Greeks, but can be traced to very ancient Egyptian and
> Near and Middle Eastern sources, which were themselves
> later taken into Greece and became the foundations for the
> development of Greek philosophy. At the root of Ficino's
> concept lie several writings attributed to pre-Greek authors,
> especially Zoroaster, Hermes Trismegistus, and Orpheus,
> which according to his interpretation were transmitted to
> Plato by Pythagoras and Aglaophemus.[9]

To date there have been no substantiations of this theory by conventional means—neither archeology, textual citations and/or redaction criticism, epigraphic inscriptions, or the like. Thus it cannot be empirically proved either way that a continuous, unbroken tradition did or did not exist in pre-Socratic Greek philosophy identical in concept to the philosophia perennis. An examination and a correlation of the principles espoused, however, are the methods most often applied in support of this theory. Renée Weber, a modern scholar of philosophy who "promulgates the same or very similar principles" as the Traditionalists, addresses the "culture-diffusion" theory of what she calls the "esoteric tradition":

> The literature [of the esoteric tradition] makes clear the weakness of the culture-diffusion theory, which holds that the remarkable identity of doctrine and practice found in numerous communities throughout the world is but the result of the natural spread of social dealings among people. The available data suggest, on the contrary, that the esoteric doctrines are in fact the formulation of basic, universal laws of nature that a few geniuses in every culture have been able to discover and preserve.[10]

Regardless of the origins of the concept of the philosophia perennis and the inchoate attempts at its description or systematization, one aspect of it is incontestible—its continuity throughout Western (and Eastern) thought. James H. Ryan, for example, in a section of his work entitled "Is There a Philosophia Perennis?" states that "beneath the ever-changing current of opinion there flows a steady stream of truth which, if we look below the surface of our disagreements, we can see."[11] This equates the philosophia perennis with a "steady stream of truth," a description that would have sat very well with Guénon and Coomaraswamy. Such an equation points to one agreement of perspective between the modern philosophers and the Traditional philosophers, in addition to the accepted notion in modern philosophy of a continuity for the philosophia perennis. And others besides historians and scholars of Western philosophy are occupied with this idea; the creative philosophers themselves have dealt with it, the best example being, among twentieth-century academic philosophers, Karl Jaspers. In his book entitled *The Perennial Scope of Philosophy* he addresses the percept of continuity: "Through all the change in human circumstances and the tasks of practical life, through all the progress of the sciences, all the development of the categories and methods of thought, it [philosophy] is forever concerned with apprehending the one eternal truth under new conditions."[12] Once again the equation of "one eternal truth" to philosophia perennis appears—in the work of Jaspers—to reinforce the idea of a continuity (perenniality) in philosophy—for example, Ryan's "*steady* stream" of eternal truth.

It is commonly held among philosophers, following Plato, that an unexamined or uncritical life is not worth living, and this presupposes the asking of questions. If there is one eternal truth, continuous and ever present, should not the most relevant and profound questions have been asked by now and their answers discovered? Should not, in Schmitt's words, the task of separating "the perennial elements of philosophical knowledge and the lasting truths from the merely transitory and temporally relative ones" have been accomplished? Or, to construct the interrogative in another fashion, is there within the empyrean of "eternal truth" (philosophia perennis) a deposit of questions unresolvable by conventional philosophic methods—for example, dialectic, reason, logic? If so, are these unresolvable perennial questions impervious to, as phrased above, the "meliorative march" of Western philosophy with its tacit dogma of irreversible "progress"? Modern philosophy seems split on the answer. Jaspers utterly rejects this notion of progress in philosophy as, it might be added, did those of the Traditional school. Progressivism in philosophy is an entirely fatuous notion to them; Jaspers claims that "philosophy proper must, among other things, reject the idea of progress, which is sound for the sciences and the implements of philosophy."[13] Immediately following this assertion, he states that "In this conception [progressivism] the new as such is mistaken for the true." Finally, in a lengthy but astute polemic against the advocates of philosophical progressivism, Jaspers indicts a list of his predecessors:

> Over and over again they believed that they had transcended the whole past by means of something utterly new, and that thereby the time had finally come to inaugurate the true philosophy. This was the case with Descartes; in all modesty and with the most justification Kant held this same belief; it was held in arrogance by the so-called German idealists, Fichte, Hegel, Schelling; and then again by Nietzsche. And tragedy was followed by Satyric drama. The publication in

1910, in the first fascile of *Logos*, of Husserl's article on philosophy as an exact science, in which, speaking as the most important, because supremely consistent representative of his department, he proclaimed that the definitive principles of philosophy were at last securely established.[14]

With a few others, Jaspers spoke out against these claims and advocated a return "to the traditional quest for eternal truth, which is the essence of philosophy." In other words, committed to the idea of continuity in the philosophia perennis, Jaspers claimed the actuality of rationally unresolvable perennial questions that have accompanied the thought of humankind since time immemorial—unresolvable, at least, via the conventional methods of philosophic endeavor as stated above.

The supposed unresolvability of these perennial questions is intimately tied up with the standard methods of modern philosophy: dialectic, reason, and logic. This exclusive reliance on dialectic and reason within the discipline of modern philosophy is repeatedly emphasized in the writings of both the historians of philosophy and the creative philosophers themselves, and accounts for what may be described as perhaps the greatest difference in perspective between modern and Traditional philosophy. Schmitt, for example, obediently consistent with the assumptions of modern philosophy, declares that "The *philosophia perennis* has an epistemology in which God is knowable by human reason; it is a religious philosophy which induces piety and a desire for the contemplation of God."[15] James Ryan, presumably looking ahead to the day when mankind reaches empirical omniscience, describes a "philosophical synthesis" in which "the highest and truest vision of the universe of which man, through the unaided light of human reason, is capable."[16] Human reason is incapable, according to the Traditional view, of resolving the higher metaphysical (perennial) problems: it is precisely the exclusive reliance upon reason that precludes their resolution by it and other conventional techniques of modern philosophy. Guénon declares, for example, that

This [rationalism] amounts to the negation of metaphysical knowledge which is of the superrational order, and which is pure intellectual knowledge, superlative knowledge; modern philosophy cannot admit the existence of true metaphysics without its own self-destruction, and as for the "pseudometaphysics" which it incorporates, it is nothing but a more or less clever assemblage of exclusively rational hypotheses, and thus in reality only scientific and not generally based on anything too serious.[17]

Beyond the first barrier of the methodological problem, Tradition affirms a second barrier concerning the ability to intuit intellectually, which inhibits modern philosophers from piercing, underneath the "merely transitory and temporally relative" truths, the perennial questions that await resolution by each individual. But questions are different from answers or principles, and here again we observe another distinction between Traditional philosophy and modern philosophy. The rational, critical mind of the modern philosopher asks questions of enduring magnitude, but refuses to relinquish an exclusively rational method to discover the answer. The Traditional metaphysicist has at hand the immutable principles of the philosophia perennis; he sees his task as *understanding* them more fully. For this reason the concept of the philosophia perennis in the thought of most academic modern philosophers is more closely connected to interrogation, the dialectic of discovery—that is, rationalism, the "quest for eternal truth," in Jaspers's words—than it is to a group of interdependent first principles comprising a complete and holistic cosmology.

With the advent of the European Renaissance and the post-Enlightenment period, modern philosophy, if anything, has been taking a more and more empirical, positivistic, and rational course.[18] For this reason it might appear surprising to find a revival or resurgence of the concept of philosophia perennis in modern philosophical speculation, but according to more than one historian of philosophy, this is nonetheless what is happening. Beyond the growing interest in the writings of Guénon and Coomaraswamy and the Traditional school, the concept of the philosophia perennis is being considered by an increasing number of modern philosophers and schools of philosophy. Schmitt writes, for example, "particularly during the past seventy years [from 1966] has 'perennial philosophy' become a popular term," and elsewhere that

It seems to have been the Neo-Thomists who first revived the term *philosophia perennis* early in the present century, applying it *par excellence* to their own philosophical tradition and emphasizing the timelessness of the truths to be

found therein. It was not long, however, before other philosophical schools appropriated the term and by the middle of
the century it had been used in many contexts and given
numerous definitions.[19]

Besides the Neo-Thomists, the concept of philosophia perennis appears
in axiomatic positions and favorable lights in the writings of a number
of modern philosophers. Among them are Johannes Hirschberger and
John Hermann Randall; we have seen that Karl Jaspers was a proponent of this idea, and there will be cause to examine in more detail the
extensive writings of Wilbur Marshall Urban on the philosophia perennis. Additionally, the Swiss philosopher Paul Häberlin and Randall, for
example, are more conventional modern philosophers, holding the
view that the philosophia perennis is essentially the deposit of perennially unresolvable questions allied to several uncategorized perennial
principles. Urban and Radhakrishnan, on the other hand, are far closer
to the Traditional views of Guénon and Coomaraswamy, overtly relying on gnosis or intellectual intuition to perceive an omnipresent body
of metaphysical truths.

THE TERM PHILOSOPHIA PERENNIS IN WESTERN PHILOSOPHY

The *concept* of the philosophia perennis has existed in Western
thought far longer than the actual *term*. As to the history of the term—
that is, its origin—it was long believed that "philosophia perennis" was
the creation of Gottfried Leibniz. Aldous Huxley, for example, casually
relates its natal history: "Philosophia Perennis—the phrase was coined
by Leibniz; but the thing . . . is immemorial and universal."[20] A Spanish
commentator, Marcos Manzanedo, declares, "This philosophia perennis, the ideal goal to which Gottfried Leibniz and other thinkers aspired,
is encountered in its germinal and seed state in universal paroemiol-
ogy."[21] The "other thinkers" are not listed.

Leibniz was not, in fact, the originator of "philosophia perennis."
The credit for this must go to the sixteenth-century Italian bishop,
Augustinus Steuchus (alternately Agostino Steuco). Schmitt, who is the
Steuchus authority par excellence, distills the problem in one passage.

It has often been thought that the concept of perennial philosophy originated with Leibniz, who uses the term in a fre-

quently quoted letter to [Nicolas] Rémond, date August 26, 1714. But careful research reveals that *"philosophia peren-nis"* was used much earlier than Leibniz; indeed it was the title of a treatise published in 1540 by the Italian Augustinian, Agostino Steuco (1497–1548).[22]

The actual title of Steuchus's treatise is *De perenni philosophia*; it is a massive book of some five hundred pages, written in Latin, which Schmitt describes as, among other things, "a veritable goldmine of the occult and esoteric lore which was so widespread and influential in the sixteenth and seventeenth centuries."[23] The confusion over the origination of the term is somewhat difficult to understand since, in the first place, Schmitt claims for *De perenni philosophia* that it "has been one of the most widely quoted of all book titles," known throughout Europe during the two hundred years between 1540 and 1740, and, in the second place, Leibniz never used the term in any of his formal treatises, but mentioned it only in letters, and then not extensively.[24] Leibniz is, of course, far more renowned in European history than Steuchus, since his published legacy has been more carefully scrutinized. And, distinguishing between the term and the concept, Leibniz can be said to have pursued the latter more vigorously than to have employed the former. Rudolph Meyer, in a paper entitled "Leibniz und die Philosophia Perennis," claims, "The question about the 'veritable unity' is, therefore, systematic and biographical, and was the reason and purpose of Leibniz's searching—'perennis quaedam philosophia'."[25] Furthermore, it is clear that Leibniz was indebted to Steuchus in his appropriation of the term, since in a letter written to his friend Simon Foucher in 1687, twenty-seven years prior to his letter to Nicolas Rémond, he mentions both Steuchus and *De perenni philosophia* by name.[26]

    If 1540 was the date at which the term philosophia perennis was first established in Western thought, the concept preceded this date by millennia. The question naturally arises, then, as to what this venerable metaphysical tradition, this set of "enduring and lasting truths," was called prior to 1540. In other words, what synonyms of philosophia perennis were used in the writings of the predecessors of Steuchus and, equally as interesting, what synonyms have been used since? The most direct influences on Steuchus regarding this tradition were Marsilio Ficino and even more, Giovanni Pico della Mirandola. In fact, Steuchus

served as librarian for four years (1525–29) at the library of Cardinal
Demenico Grimani of Venice, whose holdings contained the enormous
library of Pico, and was thus enabled to utilize the opportunity to familiarize himself with the foundations of the famous Hermeticist's worldview. In the vast writings expressing this worldview, Steuchus came
across the terms *prisca sapientia* and *prisca theologia*. Of the former,
Schmitt writes that it is "a very high level of wisdom (*prisca sapientia*)"; of the latter he states the following, relating it to Steuchus's view
of the philosophia perennis:

> We are now in a better position to understand Steuco's con-
> ception of perennial philosophy. It turns out to be little more
> than *prisca theologia* in slightly novel dress. Plato, Plutarch,
> Plotinus, Jamblichus, Proclus, Psellus, Pletho, Cusanus,
> Ficino, Pico, Champier, and Giorgio are Steuco's predeces-
> sors. The word *priscus*, probably best translated as "venera-
> ble," is one which recurs often in Steuco.[27]

Frances Yates has described the *prisca theologia* as "the pristine fount
of illumination flowing from the Divine *Mens*," and attributes to Ficino
the notion that its origin can be traced to Mercurius Trismegistus. In his
translation of the Corpus Hermeticum, Ficino states in the argumentum
or dedication, "Hence there is one ancient theology (prisca theologia) . . .
taking its origin in Mercurius and culminating in the Divine Plato."[28] The
synonymy of *prisca theologia* to philosophia perennis cannot be
doubted: "The thread of truth runs through history, preserved most fully,
as we shall see, in the tradition of the *prisca theologia*."[29]

　　The list of synonyms to philosophia perennis, in the final analysis,
is limited only by the various languages in which the concept is expressed.
Wilbur Urban refers to it as the "Great Tradition," much like the usage
of Guénon and Coomaraswamy. Schmitt stretches the meanings of both
philosophia perennis and "syncretism" to form a synonym, since he
views the term *syncretic* as the "best general term to designate this tendency," i.e., the philosophia perennis. Guénon, and sometimes Coomaraswamy, use what they consider the pristine etymological sense of
"metaphysics" to designate the concept (and Sophia Perennis infrequently), though this is admittedly outside the arena of modern philosophical usage. For the Eastern or Sanskrit term, Radhakrishnan employs
*sanātana-dharma*, though one could argue that this is more a translation

than a synonym, regardless of its seniority to Latin. Finally, another term has traditionally been used in Western thought, though seldom employed by modern philosophers despite its genuine historical application in Neo-Platonism, to signify these eternal truths: the term *theosophia*. Examination of the intricate relationship between theosophia and philosophia perennis must wait, however, until the meaning or content of the philosophia perennis in modern philosophy has been examined.

THE MEANING OF PHILOSOPHIA PERENNIS
IN MODERN PHILOSOPHY

"And what is the philosophia perennis?" asks Manzanedo. He answers that "In the strict sense philosophia perennis is the collation of truths of a natural order commonly acknowledged by man throughout history. It is a substantial and universal philosophy, ever present and permanent (distinct from special 'philosophies,' characterized by particular times, authors, and systems)."[30] This succinct and fairly representative description would probably have few critics in the sphere of modern philosophy or, for that matter, in the sphere of Traditional philosophy. Yet when the issue of methodology appears, this "collation of truths of a natural order" would likely have applied to it by modern philosophers the interrogative process of dialectic, based predominantly on logic and ratiocination. In the modern philosophical view, then, one senses that the philosophia perennis resembles a residue of perennially unresolvable questions more than a complete and holistic formulation of first principles.

No doubt some of the latter exist in the modern philosophical conception of philosophia perennis, though this conception would be entirely dependent upon the particular modern philosopher whose thought happens to be under examination. This "residue," is what is left once the sifting process, undertaken to "separate the perennial elements" from the "transitory and temporally relative ones," is completed. The questions sifted out are those that pertain to phenomenology, deontology, philology, and so forth. The questions that remain, which comprise the "residue," would pertain to ontology, epistemology, pneumatology, and axiology. Sample questions of the latter might be Is there a One, a God, a Unity; if so, what is its nature? Is reality and/or truth absolute or relative? What is the purpose of existence; how are we to know it? and What is a person's proper relation to the One, and to humanity? Other questions might relate to individual eschatology or soteriology, the synthesis of opposites, intuition and intellect, cosmic teleology, being and nonbeing, essence and substance—in other words, a whole range of rationally unresolvable problems, accompanied by a very few universally accepted axioms that modern philosophy is content to call the philosophia perennis. Thus in Collins's words, "It is not a speculative premise from which any conclusions follow about the nature of being and the content of metaphysics."[31] It is, for most modern philosophers, the leftover, the residue of profundities that has remained with *homo rationis* since he ceased using his knuckles for support in walking. In the view of modern philosophy, the meaning of the philosophia perennis is necessarily equated to its being a posteriori—a conception radically different, as we shall see, from the Traditional view, which regards it as both a priori and sui generis.

The difficulty in apperceiving any core principles or fundamental, absolute truths of the philosophia perennis within modern philosophy's conception of it lies in the fact that so many different systems and expressions of philosophical speculation exist—and have existed—in Western civilization. Little cohesion or commonality can possibly exist between such divergent and often antithetical systems like Thomism and secular existentialism, Marxism and fascism, nominalism and realism, empiricism and metaphysics, and so forth. One is truly on dangerous ground in generalizing too much about core principles, but in the face of plethoric and heterogeneous philosophical systems, the alternatives are generalization or silence. In order to make any cognizant sense out of the confusion, the former option, however problematic, is indispensable. Thus, one may posit that it seems the most illimitable, universal principle to which most modern philosophers, regardless of "creed," would be willing to concede is the existence of one truth/reality, though it is by no means evident that the various levels from which they might perceive this one truth/reality align. Another point of concession would have to be the actual divergence and plurality of the systems that, in the oeuvre of William James, is skillfully kneaded into something of a philosophical system itself—"pragmatism"—though this is something entirely different from a philosophia perennis. Collins addresses himself to this idea:

> Hence philosophy is essentially a perennial process and is not subject to the law of temporal displacement. But precisely because philosophical inquiry is directed toward God,

the one encompassing reality, it can never express the absolute truth in any single system or in a completely universal way. By the very nature of our finite minds, there must be a plurality of limited manifestations of philosophical truth. Philosophy in its essence is one, but in its actual human development, it subsists in and through a multiplicity of particular expressions.[32]

We shall presently see that this concept of a multiplicity of expressions in philosophy is roughly analogous to the notion, in the Traditional perspective, of the one truth of philosophia perennis being expressed in different cultures and eras via different languages and cultural metaphors. But what we are able to conclude about the meaning of the philosophia perennis in modern philosophy, based on the writings of the various philosophers mentioned here, is at once limited and tenuous. First is the apparent consensus that the quest (or question) is more perennial than any group of principles; second, that one truth and/or reality does in fact exist but is incapable of being fully expressed by means of any one system (or plurality of systems); third, that this truth and the quest to apprehend it penetrate atemporality; fourth, and as a general postulate, that implicated in the concept of philosophia perennis are both a detemporalization and despatialization of ontological predicates.[33]

What might be considered an epiphenomenon to the philosophia perennis is cultural or folk apothegms—"folk wisdom uncreate." The timeless truths of folk wisdom are something to which most modern philosophers would subscribe, and are truths to which Coomaraswamy and others of the Traditional perspective do subscribe. This is the main subject and certainly the strength of Manzanedo's paper, and it is not surprising that such a thesis would have sprung from a culture so rich in folk wisdom as the Castellian. Using Miguel de Cervantes as his cultural paradigm, but including other Spanish authors, Manzanedo supports his philosophia perennis qua folk apothegms thesis with scores of *refranes* or sententious sayings that contain perennial truisms. The content of most of these apothegms or proverbs usually has more to do with human experience than with metaphysical verities, but their sagacity and perenniality cannot be denied, as Manzanedo asserts:

Proverbs and sayings (of all times and places) offer (properly chosen and expurged) both a quarry of riches for systemati-

zation and a precious outline for the philosophia perennis. In
effect, the universality in time and space—of many sayings
and proverbs—is a sure guarantee of their perennial value and
truth. Because of this they are able to constitute a solid foundation for scientific edification (systematic and reasoned) on
higher levels. The sayings are reflections and expressions of
an immense human experience.[34]

At once a correlation to the Traditional perspective becomes apparent:
Coomaraswamy, in speaking of "folklore"—folk tales and proverbs—
states: "The 'catchwords' of folklore are, in fact, the signs and symbols of the Philosophia Perennis."[35] It is doubtful whether modern philosophers would extend themselves en masse—or even individuals
among them—to a point of intersection or agreement with Coomaraswamy's position. Nonetheless, the thesis of folk wisdom and
mythology qua philosophia perennis is certainly a legitimate aspect of
the problem as a whole, and has a rightful place in its investigation.
    The modern philosophers who have discussed philosophia peren-
nis tend to be as indefinite about the relationship between it and metaphysics as they are about the basic principles just enumerated, with one
salient exception: Wilbur M. Urban. Urban set himself the task, in his
three major works,[36] of showing what Sawicki claims—that "The
philosophia perennis affirms the metaphysical idea."[37] Urban could be
described as representing a synthesis between modern philosophy and
the Traditional one, since he is at once a "credentialed" philosopher and
one who takes a philosophical or metaphysical position relatively close
to the position found in the writings of Guénon and Coomaraswamy.
His position is somewhat liminal relative to both views in that, like
most of his professional colleagues, he does not mention Traditional
writers nor would he necessarily have favored their strong religious or
hieratically oriented views. On the other hand, he heaps obloquies on
the trend in modern philosophy that rejects or does not take into account
the *intelligible* (as opposed to the sensible). Urban uses "natural metaphysics" interchangeably with both philosophia perennis and the Great
Tradition. His use of the Great Tradition is, of course, a startling parallel to the particularized usage of Guénon and Coomaraswamy. By
extrapolation, these terms can be equated to intelligibility and truth. He
states, for example, in *Language and Reality* that "in the ultimate metaphysical context truth and intelligibility are one, and metaphysical truth

is immanent in intelligible discourse. But the point here is that it is upon this foundation that the entire symbolic form or structure of philosophia perennis rests. It is, indeed, this that makes it natural metaphysic" (p. 716). Elsewhere, he treats "the thesis that there *has* been a *philosophia perennis*, and that this philosophy is identical with natural metaphysic in our sense of the term" (p. 686).

The possible citations to be extracted from Urban's writings are endless, as the concept, the term, and meaning of the philosophia perennis occupy a position of centrality in his thought. And among the ministers of modern philosophy, Urban is the outspoken champion of the philosophia perennis. His works on the concept philosophia perennis alone provide sufficient material for a complete study, but that task must be left to posterity. It only remains to establish the close connection between Urban's views of "natural metaphysic," to which even the lithic Guénon with his belief that "metaphysic alone embraces the knowledge of the Universal" would mostly agree, and his philosophia perennis, to which Coomaraswamy *had* agreed. Coomaraswamy was, in fact, familiar with Urban's work, and in a paper entitled "Does 'Socrates Is Old' Imply that 'Socrates Is'?" states that "since I am at variance with him on this one point [the nature of ambiguity] I should like to say that I am in full agreement with nearly everything else in his book [*Language and Reality*], and notably with the conclusion that 'metaphysical idiom of the Great Tradition is the only language that is really intelligible.'"[38] Moreover, the two Traditional writers would have found themselves in equally "full agreement" with Urban's axiological premise that "The inseparability of value and reality is the one constant character of the intelligible world, and a world in which they were divorced would no longer be intelligible." In considering Guénon's and Coomaraswamy's views of modern Western civilization and the demise of valuation in detail in Part 4 we will have an opportunity to reintroduce Urban's corroborative thoughts. Out of the miasma surrounding the notion of philosophia perennis in modern philosophy, with its often conflicting and sometimes unintelligible views on the concept, Urban stands as a beacon of clarity, and it is appropriate to end the discussion of the philosophia perennis in modern philosophy with a cogent quote from Urban's writings:

> *Philosophia perennis*, the Great Tradition, as we have called it, contains the *form* of an intelligible world. It is this form, this essential structure—of which the fundamental lines

remain even when certain parts have fallen—that constitutes
the ultimate goal of our interest and endeavor. But we must
first realize that back of this form, this structure, lies a conception or ideal of intelligibility which gives this form its
meaning and its truth.[39]

## PHILOSOPHIA PERENNIS:
### MODERN PHILOSOPHY AND THE TRADITIONAL PERSPECTIVE

The most useful analogical symbol to engage in order to illustrate
the difference between the conceptions of modern philosophy and the
Traditional perspective relative to the philosophia perennis is Jacob's
ladder—one of several symbols for the vertical axis. The lower rungs
represent the rudimentary and relatively few principles of consensus
upon which the modern philosophers would unite; the uppermost rungs
represent the relatively developed and more numerous principles upon
which the Traditional writers tend to concentrate in their discussions of
the philosophia perennis. Irrespective of methodology and etiology,
which do indicate genuine dissimilarities between the two conceptions,
one must not lose sight of the fact that the ladder itself is one, that its
"top" depends upon its "base." Moreover, as between writers of the
Traditional perspective and those of other schools of esotericism, there
can be said to exist, in a general or overall sense, more agreement than
disagreement regarding the components of philosophia perennis.
    The interchangeability of the terms Tradition, philosophia peren-
nis, and metaphysic among the Traditional writers, however, with
Urban being virtually their sole representative within modern philosophy, points to the first of several dissimilarities between modern and
Traditional philosophy with regard to the concept signified by these
terms. Specifically, the first dissimilarity is the contention—and stren-
uous endeavor to show, on the part of Coomaraswamy—that a more or
less complete group of axioms (interdependent first principles) is to be
found among all the world's orthodox traditions and in the works of the
"magnanimous philosophers." Coomaraswamy claims that "there are
scarcely any, if any, of the fundamental doctrines of any orthodox tradition that cannot as well be supported by the authority of many or all
of the other orthodox traditions, or, in other words, by the unanimous
tradition of the Philosophia Perennis et Universalis."[40] This, of course,
presupposes the Traditional hermeneutic in the process of exegesis of

the texts and writings of these orthodox traditions, and further the *belief* in the efficacy and veracity of the philosophia perennis. These propositions taken together would appear to be begging the question, or to be circular logic, but in fact they have nothing to do with logic. "All that I have tried to show," writes Coomaraswamy, explaining the complete *raison d' etre* for all his later writings, "is that the axioms of this [perennial] philosophy, by whomsoever enunciated, can often be explained and clarified or emphasized by a correlation with the parallel texts of other traditions."[41]

A second area not so much of dissimilarity but of separation between modern and Traditional conceptions is how the Traditional school perceives modern philosophy and how modern philosophy perceives itself (i.e., as not perennial), especially on the question of secularization or, more accurately, secularization of philosophy. The Tradition *is* the philosophia perennis according to Guénon and Coomaraswamy; modern philosophy cannot be so described. The Tradition maintains a sacred element from which it cannot be separated, and is the very antithesis of secular. Conversely, modern philosophy, and even its metaphysical branch, is essentially secular: accordingly, it perceives the philosophia perennis as primarily categorical and secular. Schmitt, for example, recognizes the problem in his own discipline, and describes the philosophia perennis as "an undercurrent in early modern philosophy and one which does not fit in very well with many generalizations which we read concerning the Enlightenment, atheism, the rise of 'modern science,' and the secularization of philosophy during the XVIth, XVIIth, and XVIIIth centuries."[42] Urban, not surprisingly, is almost an echo of Guénon in his deprecation of the loss of intelligibility (sacrality) in modern philosophy: "The real interest, the divine *libido* of philosophy," he asserts, "has indeed been drained off from its natural movement and forced to consume itself in fruitless circular movements about phantom problems."[43] In contrast to modern secular philosophy, "It [philosophia perennis] takes God, not man, as its starting point; being, not sensation, as its initial option."[44] More than just entirely secular, modern philosoph(ies) are "closed systems" in Coomaraswamy's view. "Modern philosophies are closed systems, employing the method of dialectics, and taking for granted that opposites are mutually exclusive."[45] Guénon's view of modern philosophy as "profane"—that is, secular—has been discussed. To add just another of his many calumnies against modern philosophy, he speaks of it in terms of a "perversion of meaning," and criticizes the attempt to "substitute philosophy for wisdom, which implies the forgetting or failing to recognize the true nature of the latter."[46] The idea of sacrality, then, is a wedge that fundamentally separates the two perspectives, beyond the list of other dissimilar doctrinal points.

A crucial dissimilarity between the Traditional and modern philosophical apperceptions of philosophia perennis centers around its cultural origins and age. With regard to the cultural or spatial aspect, there seems to be an implicit assumption by Western academic philosophers that the concept—not the term—of philosophia perennis is Western. Almost without exception, most modern Western philosophers and/or historians of philosophy labor under the gratuitous assumption that the concept is limited to civilizations west of the Indus River Valley. They often cite Zoroastrian/Assyrian and other Near Eastern "influences," but the tacit presupposition is that philosophia perennis is a congenitally Western phenomenon. Modern philosophers have failed to utilize Rudolph Otto's comparison, showing the profound similarity of Eastern and Western medieval metaphysics as elucidated in *Mysticism East and West* (New York, 1932), perhaps because Otto was a theologian and used an anathema, "mysticism," in his title. Eastern modern philosophers tend to be less ethnocentristic and more universal in their approach to the concept of philosophia perennis. Consistent with the Traditional view, Radhakrishnan writes:

> This is the teaching not only of the Upaniṣads and of Buddhism but also of the Greek systems and Platonism, of Islam and of the Gospels and the schools of Gnosticism. This is the perennial philosophy, the *sanātana-dharma* of which Plotinus said: "This doctrine is not new; it was professed from the most ancient times though without being developed explicitly; we wish only to be interpreters of the ancient sages, and to show by the evidence of Plato himself that they had the same opinions as ourselves."[47]

Not only does this statement regard the elements of sacrality, atemporality, and alocality as essential characteristics of the philosophia perennis, it also stands in contradistinction to most Western modern philosophical commentators on the concept. Urban never mentions Eastern manifestations of the philosophia perennis, and Häberlin, whose book *Philosophia Perennis: Eine Zusammenfassung* (Berlin,

1952) could be seen as an index of great philosophers commenting on ontology, cosmology, anthropology, aesthetics, logic, and ethics (his chapter headings, in fact) never strays farther East than Mani, though his list of philosophers covers the period from fifth-century B.C. Eleatic Parmenides to Nicolai Hartmann (1882–1950). Against this assumed Western hegemony of the philosophia perennis stands the Tradition, and those like Radhakrishnan and Otto, who reject the idea of a specific venue for the concept. In this vein, it is worth repeating Coomaraswamy's terse assertion: "No culture, people, or age can lay claim to any private property in the Philosophia Perennis."

What *does* have historicity, Coomaraswamy concedes, are the various contingent expressions or adaptations of the first principles of the philosophia perennis: "Of these explications and adaptations a history is possible."[48] The doctrine itself has no history—it is universal, immutable, eternal—and with no history the doctrine cannot be attributed to any particular locus or explained by the diffusion theory. Thus, with historicity applicable to only the various Eastern and Western expressions of the doctrine, and not the doctrine itself, the second or temporal aspect of philosophia perennis allows a basis for comparison between the two perspectives. And here we find more agreement than with its cultural or spatial genesis. Despite attitudes represented in modern philosophy by Sawicki's statement that "The philosophia perennis speaks about a *sense of history*,"[49] most metaphysical modern philosophers disclaim any temporality (i.e., the empirical construct that quantifies duration) in metaphysics and the philosophia perennis. The metaphysical doctrine, the philosophia perennis, cannot have any historicity, since the doctrine itself is ultimately inseparable from atemporal essence. Jaspers, for example, affirms that "In our temporal transience we know the actuality and simultaneity of essential truth, of the *philosophia perennis* which at all times effaces time."[50] In the "natural metaphysic" of Urban, "A timeless present is a present which is not a present, for a present is that which is localized in time."[51] The modern philosophy camp is thus divided, with a majority of modern metaphysicists essentially agreeing with the Traditional view of the atemporality of philosophia perennis, and the comparatively dissimilar modern "historical" and minority view perceiving the philosophia perennis as simply historically recurrent and unresolvable problems.

A nearly total reliance on reason within the sphere of modern philosophy is in distinct contrast to the primary reliance on intuition within

the sphere of the Tradition as regards the principal method of understanding the philosophia perennis. Certainly no dissimilarity between
the two conceptions is as significant, and the battlelines can be consistently drawn between the two factions using a *ratio versus intuitio*
model. The conscription of intellectual intuition (gnosis) by the Traditional philosophers to pierce the higher and subtler principles of the doctrine is unanimous. On the side of modern philosophy the reluctance to
relinquish reason as the primary methodological tool for the perception
of these same principles is nearly as unanimous, with one notable exception. Urban, as might have been expected, confesses his apostasy in this
regard: "An intellectual intuition can be only of ideas or essences, and
this is the very heart of idealism in the traditional sense; only an ideal
world is ultimately intelligible."[52] "Invention, or intuition," Coomaraswamy explains, "is the discovery or uncovering of particular applications of first principles, all of which applications are implicitly contained
in these principles, only awaiting the occasion for their explication."[53]
Guénon, in commenting on this "discovery or uncovering" process,
evinces the contrast between the two perspectives with bitter clarity:

> But the moderns, who are cognizant of nothing superior to
> reason within the intellectual order, cannot even conceive of
> the possibility of intellectual intuition, whereas the doc-
> trines of antiquity and the Middle Ages, even when they
> were simply philosophical in character and, consequently,
> unable to effectively call upon this intuition, nonetheless
> expressly recognized both its existence and its supremacy
> over all the other faculties.[54]

In the view of the those who propound the Tradition, reason as the primary
methodological tool for understanding natural metaphysics is simply
inapplicable, due to the circumstance of despatialized and detemporalized ontological predicates. Reason, to them, is fine in its sphere—that
is, the empirical, sensible realm and that of abstract propositions based
on logical premises. But in the sphere of essential intelligibility, it is inop-
erable, and can lead to no demonstrable or sensible conclusions. Because
the first principles of the philosophia perennis subsist in essential intelligibility, exclusive reason is not functional as a means to their apprehension. Frithjof Schuon's *Logic and Transcendence* explores this issue
in detail and explicates the Traditionalist's position.

Having so far described the concept, term, and meaning of philosophia perennis in modern philosophy, and having shown similarities and dissimilarities in perceptions of the few modern philosophers and the Traditional writers who have addressed the problem, only one further area remains to be examined before a detailed investigation of the first principles themselves is made. In discussing the various synonyms of philosophia perennis above, the term *theosophia* was mentioned. It is to this area that our attention will now be turned, for many if not all of the first principles of Tradition and/or the philosophia perennis will be seen to have their parallels in the theosophic worldview.

# 7

## *Theosophia*

An interesting and significant connection between philosophia perennis and theosophia has been made by Professor Karl von Fritz, a lexicologist, in *Paulys Real-Encyclopäedie der Classichen Altertumswissenschaft* (Stuttgart, 1934). There he states in a two-and-one-half-page explication under the heading *Theosophia* (Θεοσοφία):

> Certain fragments from this excerpt can be found, furthermore, in various other mss. as well as in the one of Laur. 32.16 and related mss., and in the 1540 published work of Bishop Agostino Steuco, de perenni philosophia, prior to the time that K. I. Neumann discovered the complete excerpt in the Tübingen ms.; this was published by G. Wolff in the supplement to his issuance of Fragments of Porphyry (Berlin 1856) de philosophia ex oraculis haurienda.

To have found a single sentence in which the fragment alluded to (viz., "jetzt meistems zitiert als, 'Tübinger Theosophie'"), Steuchus's *De perenni philosophia*, and Porphyry were each mentioned is certainly fortuitous. But the connection between the terms cannot rest solely on the strength of one citation. Rather, a closer examination of the substantive content of the terms is needed.

Regarding both the concept and the term *theosophy*, one finds two very distinct notions, more often confused than not by those who are only vaguely aware of what the term and concept signify. The confusion stems from indiscrimination between the pristine, etymological usage and the later, sectarian usage that equates the term to the doctrines disseminated by leaders of the Theosophical Society, established in 1875. Hastings's *Encyclopedia of Religions and Ethics* serves as a good example to illustrate this difference and/or confusion in usage: it contains *two* entries under "Theosophy." The first is written by Annie

Besant, then international president of the Theosophical Society, and
the second and more scholarly entry was written by Paul Oltramare,
professor of the History of Religions at the University of Geneva. Furthermore, the entry for Theosophy in the *Encyclopedia Britannica*
(1979), written by Professor Carl T. Jackson, contains a succinct formulation of this problem:

> Confusion may be avoided by a recognition of two usages of
> the word. In modern times it has been widely identified with
> the doctrines promoted by the Russian-born religious mys-
> tic Mme. Helena Petrovna Blavatsky (1831–91) through the
> Theosophical Society, founded by her and others in 1875.
> The term may also be employed in a more general sense to
> refer to a certain strain of mystical thought to be found in
> such thinkers as . . . [here a long descriptive list follows,
> which includes the names of Pythagoras, Plato, Valentinus,
> Plotinus, Proclus, Eckhart, Cusanus, Paracelsus, Bruno,
> Böhme, et al.].

Most indicative of all, with regard to this dual application of the term theosophy, is Webster's definition. It is indicative because of Webster's
wide use and accessibility and the fact that the second edition is a descriptive—as opposed to prescriptive—dictionary. There it lists two meanings. The first is the generic usage: "1. any of various philosophies or
religious systems that propose to establish direct, mystical contact with
divine principle through contemplation, revelation, etc." The second is
the specific or sectarian usage: "2. often T—the doctrines and beliefs of
a modern sect (Theosophical Society) of this nature that incorporates elements of Buddhism and Brahmanism." Thus we have in the generic
sense the *theosophia antiqua*, and in the sectarian sense "modern Theosophy." The two are, however, not wholly distinct and separate in
meaning. The latter is simply the latest doctrinal reformulation of the
former with its own culturolinguistic idiosyncrasies and ideological permutations.[55] This distinction is not lost to modern Theosophists either:
in a book entitled *Modern Theosophy* (Adyar, 1952), Hugh Shearman
points directly to the distinction in his introduction, and then devotes the
book to an examination of modern Theosophy.

One can today legitimately speak of "theosophy" without necessarily or particularly referring to the doctrines promulgated by the

renowned expositors of the Theosophical Society, just as one can speak of the Tradition, metaphysics, or the philosophia perennis without referring to these expositors. With regard to the philosophia perennis, however, there exists a greater similarity between it and theosophy (both antique and modern) than is normally supposed, and so, by correlation, between theosophy and the Tradition as well. This assertion would no doubt have met with stiff resistance by Coomaraswamy and particularly Guénon, as we shall see, but to borrow the metaphysical terminology of the latter, it is the objective of what follows to show that the differences between theosophy and the philosophia (sophia) perennis are more "substantial" than "essential."

## I: *THEOSOPHIA ANTIQUA*

### *The Concept*

The distinction between *concept* and *term* that we observed in relation to the philosophia perennis applies equally to *theosophia*. Jackson states that "The beginnings of theosophical speculation may be traced back at least to Pythagoras in the sixth century B.C." Noting the universality of the concept, he further states, "it may be traced from the earliest Vedas . . . through the *Upaniṣads* . . . and the *Bhagavadgītā*."[56] Thus, in West and East, the *concept* of theosophy, by which we mean the *content* of its definition as distinct from the term that now defines that content, goes back to the earliest records of speculative thought and, allowing a similar detemporalization and despatialization of ontological predicates for theosophy as for metaphysical principles, theosophists conclude that it also has no distinct historical etiology, that it is immemorial. However, its expressions, as Coomaraswamy observed about the philosophia perennis, do admit of historicity, so that historically we may say that theosophy had its beginnings in the West with Pythagoras and in the East with the *Vedas*.

Yet, depending upon the exegesis of the fragments remaining to us from antiquity, among other factors, there arise differences of opinion about both the origins and various expressions of theosophy. "Writers have generally fixed the time of the development of the Eclectic theosophical system during the third century of the Christian era." So wrote Professor Alexander Wilder in 1869, six years prior to the formation of the Theosophical Society, in a treatise titled *New Platonism and Alchemy*. But this is disclaimed in his following sentence: "It appears to have had a beginning much earlier, and, indeed, is traced by Diogenes Laertius to an Egyptian prophet or priest named Pot-Amun, who flourished in the earlier years of the dynasty of the Ptolemies."[57] Regardless of when the "theosophical system" just described by Wilder was first developed in the West, the point most relevant is that like the philosophia perennis, the concept of theosophy is far older than the term, the neologism. The "mystical contact with divine principle" has existed in recorded forms since protohistory. The concept of theosophy, though perhaps ill formulated and amorphous in structure in its earliest known manifestation, has no empirically traceable history prior to the early Mediterranean, Near Eastern, and South Asian records, according to theosophists.

Theosophy has a close relationship to what is commonly referred to as the "mysteries" or the "ancient mysteries." Various "mystery schools" or mystery religions flourished in the Near East and the Levant literally for millennia, going far back into antiquity with the Orphic and Mithraic mysteries, the Eleusinian mysteries, and those of the Kabeiroi, the cults of Osiris and Serapis, and extending up to the Ophitic schools of late antiquity; namely, those within the Gnostic worldview. Paul Schmitt, for example, in a paper entitled "Ancient Mysteries and Their Transformation," refers to the cult of Serapis as the "universal mystery religion," and claims that it, along with others in the late Hellenistic era, had undergone a major transformation: "This Alexandrian, late Hellenistic, late Roman theosophy (as we may call this kind of wisdom or *sophia*) embraced—and so annulled—all things; a mystical philosophy had gradually become the content of the mysteries."[58] Hugo Rahner, in a paper entitled "The Christian Mystery and the Pagan Mysteries," also connects theosophy with the mysteries:

> We need only think of the systems of philosophy that in this period [first century C.E.] grew out of the work of Posidonius, all of them tending to become a substitute for religion, a consolation for this life, promising a life beyond the grave: theosophy and Neopythagorean theurgy, *sominum Scipionis*. The actual mysteries of the period, however, were still limited to particular circles and localities.[59]

Oltramare, on the other hand, spends almost all of his lengthy contribution to Hastings's *Encyclopaedia of Religion and Ethics* discussing the Eastern expressions of theosophy. He says there that "The theosophical spirit has left a very deep mark upon Indian thought," and proposes to trace the development of this thought in "Brahmanism (the *Upaniṣads* and the Vedānta, the Sāṅkhya, and the Yoga)" in addition to showing "the transformation of theosophy into religion (into Jainism and Buddhism)."

Finally, with regard to the concept of theosophy, the vast areas between East and West proper have had their expressions, such as the Islamic expressions of the Middle East. Henry Corbin's use of the concept and the translated term has already been noted; in Islamic studies it is almost always associated with various synonyms in Arabic or Persian found within the texts and treatises of Sufism. In English works and translations, Annemarie Schimmel's landmark work on Sufism, *Mystical Dimensions of Islam*, contains a chapter heading entitled "Theosophical Sufism," and A. J. Arberry, in his work entitled *Sufism: An Account of the Mystics of Islam*, has a chapter heading called "The Theosophy of Islamic Mysticism." Even Seyyed Hossein Nasr, a proponent of the works of Guénon and Schuon, uses the concept and term theosophy in *Sufi Essays*. Specifically, in reference to the teachings of Ibn 'Arabī in the Eastern periphery of the Islamic surge, Nasr asserts that "It was here that his doctrines not only transformed the language of doctrinal Sufism but also penetrated into theology and *theosophy or traditional philosophy* (*hikmah*)."[60] It is thus appropriate to conclude that the concept of theosophy is both ancient (perennial) and universally widespread, and substituting theosophia for philosophia in Coomaraswamy's favorite formula, one might as accurately make reference to the "theosophia perennis et universalis."

*The Term*

"The origin of the term *theosophia*," writes Jean-Louis Siémons, "is unknown, but certainly posterior to the classical period of Grecian literature." Professor Siémons adds that the origin of the term "will perhaps remain unknown to us," yet also cites what he believes to be a doubtful reference—the earliest alleged use—to the employment of the term by Apollodorus in the second century B.C. that appears in the University of California's *Thesaurus Linguae Graecae.*[61] What *is* known of the term is that it was first used in a systematic way by Porphyry (*ca.* 234–305 A.D.), a student of Plotinus in the Neo-Platonic school of Ammonius Saccas, in the late third century. Diachronically, the three principal expressions of the term, all essentially related, were the Neo-Platonist, the Christian (as used by the Renaissance "German theoso-phists"), and the modern or late nineteenth- and twentieth-century theo-sophical movement.

With regard to the first of these expressions, the Neo-Platonic, the use of *theosophia* was within the context of classical Greek (sacred) philosophy, and its major proponents after Porphyry were Iamblicus, Proclus, and Damascius. A major pivot from Greek to Christian theos-ophy allied to this school was the writing of Pseudo-Dionysius or Dionysius the Areopagite, regarded as a Christian disciple of Proclus, whose work inspired both later generations of Christian mystics of the *via negativa* and the Renaissance European theosophists. Of the latter, or the second historic expression of theosophy as a central term, the most renown were Paracelsus, Böhme, Gichtel, Swedenborg, Eckhart-shausen, and Saint-Martin. Of note here are Jacob Böhme's publication in 1620 of *Sex Puncta Theosophica* and the foundation, in 1783, of the Swedenborgian "Theosophical Society" in London, among whose members were John Flaxman, William Sharpe, and F. H. Barthelemon. Finally, the modern expression of *theosophia* began with the writings of H. P. Blavatsky, who cofounded The Theosophical Society in 1875. This latter expression is noteworthy for establishing the ubiquity of theosophic principles, drawing as it did in equal measure on classical Buddhist, Hindu, and other non-Western esoteric traditions, as exem-plified in the writings of theosophists like T. Subba Row and Bhagavan Das. It should be added that the modern theosophical movement did not spring into existence in a single leap from the Renaissance, but that a transitional period from the second to the third major expression appears in the historic record and has been well elucidated by Joscelyn Godwin in *The Theosophical Enlightenment* (Albany, 1994).

For the present, etymological origins of the term theosophy remain obscure; one is safe in attributing its origin to the Greek of late antiquity. It is certain that the term was not used by Plato or Aris-totle or any of their predecessors, at least based on what survives of them. Among the published sources for tracing the origin of the term is Liddell and Scott's *A Greek-English Lexicon*. There it gives the first appearances of the nominative term θεοσοφία as being in the *de Abstenentia* of Porphyrius Tyrius, the famous student of Plotinus and scribe of his Enneads, and in an anonymous Hermetic tract now called the *Leiden Magical Papyrus W* whose date is uncertain, though estimated to be somewhere in the late third century (or early fourth century) C.E.[62] The term θεοσοφία also appears in succession chronologically in the *de Mysteriis* of Iamblicus (260?–330?), the *Theologica Platonica* of Proclus (412–485), and the *de Principiis* of Damascius (485?–545?), but the text in which the term first appears as a neologism must be chosen from the first two mentioned. The Hermetic/Neoplatonic flavor of the term is obvious and helps clarify the reasons for which the term is often found in connection with later theosophists, from the early Renaissance to the present, who have relied heavily on the Neoplatonic system.

The aura of sacrality in the term theosophy is explicit in its etymology. The *theos* (θεός) part of the term is that which helps distinguish it from philosophy and, more particularly, from the philosophia perennis of modern philosophy. In this it shares far more similitude with the Tradition: theosophy is the "innate Religion" described by Schuon in his description of philosophia perennis. And J. J. Poortman, who was Professor of Metaphysics in the Spirit of Theosophy at the University of Leiden, discusses this connection, though he avoids using the term philosophia perennis:

> If one does not have in mind modern theosophy, dating from 1875, but the older historic theosophy, then one can observe that this connection between theosophy and profound philosophical thought has often existed. One may think, for instance, of Plotinus' philosophizing about the One: Plotinus who, on the other hand, also knew religious ecstasies. Jacob Boehme, too, used to ponder on the paradoxes in the relationship of God and the creation of multiplicity, concerning, as he called it, "the contrarium in God."[63]

The temporal division between this "older historic theosophy" as Poortman describes it and the modern Theosophy that began with Blavatsky's works is also made by the unassociated phenomenologists. Most modern Theosophists—those at least who are aware of the historical roots of their principles—are for practical reasons proponents of the latest formulation of theosophia perennis, but typically make no distinction between the earlier and later parts of the principial nexus. To them the term covers the whole development of this thought, from prior protohistory to the present. Their detractors see it differently, and thus resist using the term theosophy at all, due to the strong cultural or popular association between the term and the particular worldview commonly found within the Theosophical Society. This, we believe, explains the reluctance of Guénon and Coomaraswamy ever to employ the term, which is a perfectly functional and descriptive one. They were, consequently, obliged to find suitable synonymous terms and phrases, like Primordial Tradition, philosophia perennis, and so on. Furthermore, they were compelled to reintroduce into their terms the element or connotation of sacrality, which the term theosophy has "built in," so to speak.

In the Avant-Propos of his book *Le Théosophisme: Histoire d'une pseudo-religion*, Guénon distinguishes between "Théosophie et Théosophisme," claiming that his creation of the latter term was necessary to describe the doctrines of the modern Theosophists, due to their having desecrated the former term by misuse and misrepresentation. And the renowned Orientalist, Professor Max Müller, in the preface to his book entitled *Theosophy, or Psychological Religion*, indignantly flouts the then (1893) popular conception of the term with the following "explanation":

> It seems to me that this venerable name [theosophy], so well known among early Christian thinkers, as expressing the highest conception of God within the reach of the human mind, has of late been so greatly misappropriated that it was high time to restore it to its proper function. It should be known once for all that one may call oneself a theosophist, without being suspected of believing in spirit-rappings, table-turnings, or any other occult sciences and black arts.[64]

Müller grossly exaggerates the issue in this passage, since he was aware that (a) Blavatsky, who was alone in the production of paranormal phenomena, had ceased this activity years prior to this writing, and (b) the publication of Blavatsky's *The Secret Doctrine*, which was anything but a treatise on spiritualism and "black arts," was primarily religio-philosophical or metaphysical in content.[65] But, regardless of the hyperbole, Müller's—and Guénon's—apologetics in using the term theosophy points to both this dichotomous "historic" and "modern" meaning, and the reluctance of scholars and writers to use the term for fear their readers might confuse the former generic meaning with the popular conception of the latter sectarian meaning.

*Historical Succession of Theosophists and Theosophic Expression*

If one accepts the proposition that theosophy, like its twin the philosophia perennis, is centered within a detemporalized ontological predicate, then it follows that its proponents regard it as ever present; that is, that no period of history or era is without it. To this proposition theosophists would generally agree, with the exception that it tends to be a matter of degree—that certain periods of history are found to contain more effulgent flowerings of the theosophic worldview than others. Robert Ellwood alludes to these various "flowerings":

> The ideal of powerful cosmic harmony attained by interior illuminative breakthrough born of wonder was well known in antiquity by gnostics, neoplatonists, and mystery teachers. It was heard again in the mouths of Renaissance savants and kabbalists like Ficino, Mirandola, Agrippa, and Paracelsus, before it was fairly drowned out by the voices of the Reformation and modern science and technology. Occasionally the cosmic wonder tradition has emerged again, always in new guise, whether in New England transcendentalism, or in the strange tales through the centuries of European fellowships of Rosicrucians and Illuminati.[66]

If we were to extend the definition of theosophy to include its other Western siblings—for example, metaphysics, Kabbalism, philosophia perennis, Hermetcism, and Primordial Tradition—a chain of continuity much stronger than the one Professor Ellwood mentions could be shown, and it would not necessarily be an alternative to the Christian tradition, but rather at times confluent with it. Such a list of individuals, known to us by their extant writings, would include theosophist-metaphysicist-perennial philosophers from Heraclitus to Frithjof Schuon, though by no means would they all be comfortable with each other's company. Plotinus wrote against the great Gnostics, for instance; and Augustine wrote against the Neoplatonists; Blavatsky wrote against Swedenborg; and Guénon, as we have seen, wrote against Blavatsky. Yet in the compilation of such a list, one thing must always be kept uppermost in mind: the essential similarities of the fundamental principles espoused by them all outweigh the externalities of their contingent expression—that is, the admitted permutations that do create actual and undeniable differences.

Others could no doubt be included, but the major luminaries in this list from early and late antiquity in the West would be Pythagoras, Thales, Heraclitus, Plato, Mencius, Philo, Clement, Ammonius Saccas, Origen, Valentinus, Plotinus, Iamblicus, Dionysius the Areopagite, Augustine, Proclus, and Boethius. From the medieval period to the present, and excluding the great Islamic doctors who influenced Western thought like Avicenna and Ibn 'Arabī, the list resumes with Eckhart, Psellus, Ficino, Pico, Steuchus, Bruno, Cusanus, Paracelsus, Boehme, Nostradamus, Fludd, Bacon, Law, Swedenborg, St. Martin, Blavatsky, Mead, Waite, Steiner, Coomaraswamy, Guénon, and Schuon. These individuals may, at first glance, appear to be "strange bedfellows," as the cliché has it. Yet what they all have in common, to greater and lesser degrees, is that they see certain sublime principles as perennial: they all subscribe to a certain set of interdependent "first principles," though this set may be of somewhat differing arrangement and emphasis. Moreover, it could be argued that certain of the great schoolmen—Ockham, Bernard, Abelard, Duns Scotus, Albertus Magnus, Thomas Aquinas, Eckhart, Bonaventure, et al.—could be included in this group, as well as the long roster of Christian mystics since Dionysius and the Cappadocian Fathers of whom Dean Inge and Evelyn Underhill have written so extensively, or the similarly profound line of European Jewish Kabbalists of whom Gershom Scholem has written. But the first genus listed above is sufficient to show that hardly two centuries in Western history have elapsed without the presence of a renowned theosophist, metaphysicist, or "magnanimous philosopher." Thus the theosophia/philosophia perennis can be said to have an almost unbroken continuity of expression from the beginnings of Western thought. The latest and most comprehensive historical treatment of this unbroken continuity to date is Antoine Faivre's *Access to Western Esotericism* (Albany, 1994).

Notwithstanding the attempts of some less articulate theosophists to establish historical hypotheses by ahistorical means (e.g., Édouard Schuré's *Les Grands Initiés* [Paris, 1889]), the abundance of extant tracts and codices of theosophic content from the past allows scholars to testify to this continuity, rendering such efforts as

Schuré's unnecessary. Until the last half of the twentieth century, any treatments of the historical continuity of theosophists and theosophic expression seems by a de facto ignorance to have fallen under the aegis of modern Theosophists themselves. In recent years, however, this situation has changed. Mircea Eliade, in a review article entitled "Some Notes on *Theosophia Perennis:* Ananda K. Coomaraswamy and Henry Corbin," defines terms and encapsulates the problematic study of esoterism in academia: "The *philosophia perennis*," he writes, is "the primordial and universal tradition present in every authentic nonacculturated civilization."[67] The scholarly study of these esoterica, the theosophia perennis, has slowly been gaining acceptability in the past five decades, and associations have been formed for this purpose among academicians. J. J. Poortman describes G. R. S. Mead's "Quest Society" as a forerunner to the Eranos conferences: "His further work in his society and magazine, both called *The Quest*, is continued to a certain extent, also chronologically, in the *Eranos-Conferences* of Ascona, Switzerland."[68] In addition to these groups just mentioned is another begun in 1974 by Henry Corbin and other European scholars, which they call the Centre International de Recherche Spirituelle Comparée. The lectures delivered at this annual conference are also published—just as those of the Eranos conferences found in the *Eranos Jahrbuch*—under the title of *Cahiers de l'Université Saint Jean de Jérusalem*. Most recently, the American Academy of Religion instituted a five-year seminar on Theosophy and Theosophic Thought, reflecting the influence of a growing number of professors and scholars who are teaching and/or writing about theosophy within academia.

Somehow, age legitimizes, so that what may be deemed spurious to contemporary thought becomes the subject of legitimate historical concern after it has aged a century or so. Thus, modern Theosophy is no longer so modern, and particularly is H. P. Blavatsky proper material for historical investigation. In the historical succession of theosophists and theosophic expression, both *theosophia antiqua* and modern Theosophy have found sufficient researchers in the current academic environment, to indicate another greater "flowering" of theosophic expression for our own *fin de siècle*. "We should also point out," writes Eliade, "that in the last decade a number of chairs in French universities have been devoted to the study of esoteric traditions."[69] And in a boldly fatidic statement, he further claims:

What interests the historian of religions the most is the resurgence of a certain esoteric tradition among a number of European scholars and thinkers who represent many illustrious universities. One is reminded of analogous events in the scholarly and academic milieux of the seventeenth and eighteenth centuries.[70]

## II: MODERN THEOSOPHY

Sydney Ahlstrom writes, "Theosophy took shape in America as a specific organized religion in 1875, with the founding of the Theosophical Society in New York."[71] This is, from the point of view of modern Theosophists, a mistake: they assert that modern Theosophy is not a religion, despite the common proclivity of scholars to stuff it into such a comfortable pigeonhole. From the very beginning of the Theosophical Society, repeated declarations from its leaders have restated this fact: Modern Theosophy is not a religion. Blavatsky, on the first page of her *Key to Theosophy*, in fact the first line on the page, declares that theosophy is not a religion. "Enquirer: Theosophy and its doctrines are often referred to as a newfangled religion. Is it a religion? Theosophist: It is not. Theosophy is Divine Knowledge or Science." And H. S. Olcott, in his inaugural address as the first president of the Society in 1875, claims it was a "noncommittal society of investigation," a body of "investigators, of earnest purpose and unbiased mind, who study all things, prove all things, and hold fast to that which is good," as opposed to religions that have "dogmas to impart, which under our by-laws we have not." Each international president has asserted the same fact, the latest being no exception: One–hundred five years and six presidents after Olcott, Radha Burnier, the latest in this company, stated in her first inaugural address, "The Theosophical Society is neither a church nor a sect. It has no belief to offer, no opinions or authority to impose."[72]

Yet, in the face of these repeated and unambiguous assertions to the contrary by modern Theosophists, scholars of religious studies still persist in labeling the Theosophical Society a religion, perhaps for the reason that it is something of an anomaly within religious studies and too difficult to "categorize" in any other way. The modern Theosophical Society is in fact comprised of the religious from every major world faith, with no exceptions. The Society's records show Christians, Parsis, Jews, Hindus, Buddhists, Taoists, and Muslims; these are in addition to agnostics, pure scientists, and holders of a variety of philosophical perspectives with no avowed "religious" overtones. The single requisite for membership in the modern Theosophical Society is sympathy with—and not belief in—the Society's three declared objects,[73] which hardly comprises in their view sufficient foundation for a religion in the normal or accepted sense.

However, the Theosophical Society can be studied as a religion, though this does not make it one. This appears to be where sociologists of religion, especially, get matters confused. One can point to certain of Paul Tillich's criteria for religion—"ultimate concern" for example—and apply them to the Theosophical Society; one can see various forms of ritual or quasi-ritual behavior (Robert Ellwood, for instance, sees the theosophical lecture as ritual); one can observe specific modes of personal (sociological) interaction among members, and so on. These and similar criteria, it should be pointed out, apply as well to the Cousteau Society or Common Cause, but do not make them religions. The perspectives that might be brought to bear on the Theosophical Society from the Max Weber-Ernst Troeltsch-Joachim Wach line of thought regarding the study of *religions* are highly problematic, due to the continuous and insistent claims of modern Theosophists themselves, the inclusive and "open forum" structure of the organization, and by the heterogeneity and antidogmatic nature of the membership. Even by the currently popular definition of religion that Clifford Geertz has established, modern Theosophy is not a religion. In Geertz's "Religion as a Cultural System,"[74] the very first of the five-point definition—a religion is "a system of symbols"—at once precludes Theosophy, since no "*system* of symbols" exists in it, but rather all hieratic symbols everywhere in all cultures at all times.

Few would disagree that modern Theosophy as it appears via the medium of the Theosophical Society began with Helena P. Blavatsky (1831–91). She was the impetus of the whole movement, and her books and collected writings, which comprise around eighteen tomes, serve as the doctrinal core of modern Theosophy. About her life there is much divergence of opinion, and much is unclear. Referring to the period 1849–1872, Bruce Campbell correctly states, "There is no reliable account of the next twenty-five years of Helena Blavatsky's life.[75] As interesting as are the details and questions of Blavatsky's life and antecedents, the problem has been thoroughly treated elsewhere and more than once. Furthermore, it is only tangential at best to the thesis under consideration here, so for these reasons it must be bypassed. What is germane to the issue here are two data: First, that which has already been stated; that is, Blavatsky was the prime mover in the creation of the Theosophical Society and consequently modern Theosophy as a restatement of theosophia via her published doctrinal corpus and commitment to the movement. Second, her use of the terms *occult* and *occultism* is significant. And this usage is significant for reasons beyond the fact that this work deals with questions of terminology. Blavatsky has been severely criticized in the past for promulgating "occultism," but what she meant by the term and what her detractors understood by it were usually two different things altogether.

The popular conception of the occult and occultism is miasmic, a murky stew of black magic, witchcraft, Satanism, horror movies, fortune telling, and the like. Of these arts Blavatsky was the severe critic par excellence, and more vituperous, ironically, than her critics were of her for promulgating "occultism." To Blavatsky, "Occultism embraces the whole range of psychological, physiological, cosmical, physical, and spiritual phenomena. From the word *occultus*, hidden or secret."[76] Her perspectives did admit to the "dark" side of the "Occult Sciences," just as she divided magic into *theurgia* and *göetia*, "white" and "black" magic, respectively. But more often than not in her writings, Blavatsky capitalized the term and used it in its theosophical or spiritual sense. She repeatedly distinguished between Occultism and Occult Sciences using precisely those terms; the former was solely benign, and the latter was dual, containing a positive and negative expression, as did magic.

In a book entitled *Practical Occultism*, Blavatsky's definition of Occultism becomes unequivocally clear. She writes there that "Occultism differs from Magic and other secret sciences as the glorious sun does from a rush-light, as the immutable and immortal Spirit of Man— the reflection of the absolute, causeless and unknowable ALL—differs from the mortal clay—the human body." If this somewhat overstated simile leads one to suspect a synonymy of Occultism with theosophy, the second citation confirms the suspicion: "Let them know at once and remember always, that *true Occultism or Theosophy* is the 'Great Renunciation of SELF,' unconditionally and absolutely, in thought as in action."[77] Thus another term is added to the list of synonyms: Guénon means by metaphysic and Primordial Tradition what Coomaraswamy means by philosophia perennis what Blavatsky means by Theosophy and Occultism—an interdependent group of absolute and essential first principles. Unquestionably each meant something more, and the arrangement or order of the first principles would not necessarily have been agreed to by these three, but the overriding factor that allows synonymy is the content of these principles, whose examination will follow presently.

Neither the biography of Blavatsky nor the detailed history of the Theosophical movement since 1875 has any place in this work. Both have been treated in a huge corpus of material, which includes accounts from the extremely tendentious to the extremely calumnious, and some in between. In fact, it would be more helpful to the interested student of this history to list the significant bibliographies rather than attempt a list of single works.[78] Nonetheless, for the sake of convenience and for those who are totally unfamiliar with the history of the movement, the chronological high points of the Society's history follow:

1874:    Blavatsky and Henry Olcott (cofounder of the Society and president from 1875 to his death in 1907) meet in Chittendon, Vermont, while investigating the paranormal phenomena at the Eddy farm.

1875:    With Blavatsky, Olcott, and William Q. Judge as principal catalysts, the Theosophical Society is founded on November 17 after a series of lectures and meetings on Occultism.

1878:    Two principal founders, Blavatsky and Olcott, after deciding to reestablish in India, depart for Bombay.

1882:    The Society purchases a small estate in Adyar, a suburb of Madras, for their international headquarters, where it is still located.

1885:    Publication of the "Hodgson report"—*Proceedings of the Society for Psychical Research*, Volume II, 1885, pp. 201–400—under the title "Report of Phenomena Connected with Theosophy." This report, based on questionable evidence, ostensibly confirms allegations of fraud by Blavatsky instigated by Emma Coulomb and the Madras Christian College, and seriously afflicted the reputations of both Blavatsky and the Society.

1888 (1): Blavatsky, having left India for good, publishes *The Secret Doctrine*, her magnum opus.

1888 (2):   On October 9, the "Esoteric School of Theosophy" is formed, an event whose significance is usually underrated by historians of the movement but one which is to set the tone of the Society's activity until the second half of the twentieth century.

1891:       H. P. Blavatsky dies on May 8, an event that begins a series of internal disputes and reverberations destined to shake the foundations of the Society.

1895:       One of these disputes leads to the secession of the American Section, under William Q. Judge, from the parent Adyar Society—first and most profound of the splinter movements.

1907:       H. S. Olcott dies and Annie Besant is elected the new international president of the Society.

1912:       C. W. Leadbeater discovers Jeddu Krishnamurti, a South Indian Brahmin boy of twelve, and alleges that he is to become a new World Teacher—that is, Messiah. In the wake of this discovery the whole trend of modern Theosophy is bent—primarily by Besant—toward this new Teacher. Because the Theosophical Society per se had by its own bylaws to remain neutral, the Order of the Star in the East (OSE) is formed as the vehicle for the dissemination of his teachings. Not all agreed, however; Rudolf Steiner was ousted as president of the German Section of the Society over the issue, and eventually began his own Anthroposophical Society.

1925:       In my view, perhaps the darkest hour in the Society's history, when G. S. Arundale—who would become the next international president after Besant—and his colleagues announce the list of chosen "apostles" for the new Messiah of whom most are members of this clíque, and proclaim these revelations at Huizen, the site of a theosophical center in Holland.

1929:       J. Krishnamurti renounces his role as the new Messiah, disbands the OSE, and in so doing literally shatters the seventeen-year crescendo of expectation for the new Messiah and disorients the aged Annie Besant and a huge portion of the Society's membership.

1933:    Annie Besant dies, followed by C. W. Leadbeater several
months later, and George Arundale is elected president of a
Society considerably different from the one begun by Blavatsky and Olcott—one whose existence is marked by more
devotion and also moderation, with little of the notoriety, or
interaction and disputation with the avant garde of scholars
and thinkers, of the early days.

It should be noted that the history of modern Theosophy comprises more than the history of the Theosophical Society in the Olcott,
Besant, Arundale, et al. succession. The Theosophical movement
begun by Blavatsky split several times, forming splinter groups,
among them the Point Loma group and the United Lodge of Theosophists, each of which has its own unique history. Beyond this "splinter-
ing" process, though, were other existing groups and trends of thought
that were heavily influenced by the Theosophical movement. Ancillary
organizations to the Theosophical Society, like the Liberal Catholic
Church and the Co-Masonic Order, were results of the usurpation of
the preexisting doctrines of these groups by the Theosophical worldview. The Irish literary renaissance was influenced by Theosophists
William Butler Yeats and A. E. (George W. Russell). Ambrose Bierce
believed modern Theosophy was significant enough a force to lam-
poon in his *The Devil's Dictionary* (1906), describing it as "An ancient
faith having all the certitude of religion and all the mystery of science."
The world of science had its members in the early years of the movement in Thomas A. Edison, Camille Flammarion, Alfred R. Wallace,
Sir William Crookes, and C. C. Massey. In the arts and music the influ-
ence was felt via the works of Piet Mondrian, Wassily Kandinsky, and
Paul Klee; the music world had a Theosophical analogue in Aleksandr
Scriabin. Among other spiritual and metaphysical groups the impact of
the Theosophical movement was even greater: The Arcane School of
Alice Bailey, the Anthroposophical Society of Rudolf Steiner, the "I
Am" movement of the Ballards, the Rosicrucian Fellowship of Max
Heindel, the Astara Foundation of the Chaneys, and the "nonorganiza-
tion" or teachings of Krishnamurti all had direct and intimate involvement with the Theosophical movement prior to their own autonomous
developments.
    To the extent that the modern Theosophical movement helped
introduce and popularize Oriental religion and philosophy to the West,

the influence is at once inestimable and agreed upon, as the early Orientalist Max Müller points out. With regard to its impact or influence on the arts and sciences, on culture and world thought, modern Theosophy has been far more effective than might be indicated by the members claimed for it within the various groups that espoused its principles. To this assertion even the impartial historians agree: J. Stillson Judah claims a large influence for modern Theosophy, and observes that "it is not quite correct to regard their force as that of many small, unimportant, individualistic sects or cults, but rather as that of one movement with many expressions.[79] Campbell states that "Indeed, the theosophical Society . . . was to have significant effects both East and West on religion, politics, culture, and society."[80] Ellwood declares simply that "Theosophy has had a significant general influence on this century."[81] And, speaking of the tendency of some historians to omit the "context and conditions" of their subjects, Santucci asserts that "To a degree, such omission has minimalized the impact of the Theosophical Society on popular culture, the arts, and political activism."[82]

### COOMARASWAMY AND MODERN THEOSOPHY

It often surprises people familiar with his writings to discover that Ananda Coomaraswamy was a member of the Theosophical Society. Roger Lipsey devotes a paragraph in his biography to Coomaraswamy's involvement with some of the leaders of the Society, but does not mention the fact that he was a member. One wonders if Lipsey did not know, or if he knew and did not say. He committed himself only to saying that "The serious concern of Theosophists with Indian religion, as well as their nationalist activity, attracted Coomaraswamy at this time, although in later years he mistrusted Theosophy and insisted on the necessity of learning directly from the sources of religious knowledge."[83]

Coomaraswamy joined the Society in 1907 at the age of twenty-nine years; his diploma of membership is dated January 20 of that year, and his membership was sponsored by Annie Besant and W. A. English, the latter being a worker with Henry S. Olcott for the revivification of Buddhism and Buddhist education in Ceylon. A little over a year prior to joining the Society, Coomaraswamy had helped form and become president of the Ceylon Reform Society, whose function was to encourage Sinhalese culture in Ceylon relative to the arts, dress, custom, and so on. This venture, was, in fact, part of the broad revitalization begun by Olcott in 1880 when he was invited to the island by the chief monks to help restore Sinhalese Buddhism and Buddhist education. It was almost customary for members of the old Buddhist families of the island, by the year 1900, to become members of the Theosophical Society, since so much of the work of reestablishing Sinhalese Buddhism and Buddhist education was carried out under the auspices of Theosophical Society auxiliary groups. Coomaraswamy no doubt felt himself compelled to support the Theosophical Society since under its aegis Olcott had done so much for Ceylonese culture and religion. But his reasons for joining were obviously for more than supportive reciprocity: it was in the milieu of modern Theosophy that he (like Guénon) had his first glimpse of metaphysics, since his time previous to that had been occupied with geology. It was thus in the Theosophical Society that he got his metaphysical "start," and throughout the course of his life he was never able to denounce completely or condemn the Society—as Guénon did—though he disagreed with some of what he described as "caricatures" of Eastern thought that he believed the Society disseminated.

Coomaraswamy's involvement in the Ceylon Reform Society was only the beginning of his lifelong struggle to bring the integrity and beauty of Eastern art and culture to the attention not only of Western peoples, but to the modernized Easterners as well. This struggle led him into the national *swadeshi* movement in India where he became an intimate part of the Tagore circle and worked in collaboration with Western admirers of Eastern art, like E. B. Havell, Sir William Rothenstein, Roger Fry, and W. R. Lethaby. Additionally, he published two significant works in this area at that time: *Essays in National Idealism* appeared in Ceylon in 1909, and *Art and Swadeshi* appeared in India in 1911. But this activity was not unconnected with modern Theosophy. Lipsey writes that in 1907 "He met the leaders of the Theosophical Society in Benares and Madras—at least Annie Besant and Bhagavan Das, who concerned themselves with Indian religious thought but were also extremely active in the nationalist movement.[84] Bhagavan Das remained a friend of Coomaraswamy's, and in 1916, when Coomaraswamy was faced with leaving England, he tried through Das to obtain an appointment on the faculty of Benares Hindu University, founded by Annie Besant some years earlier. Bhagavan Das writes that "He [Coomaraswamy] came to Benares again in 1916, I believe. He wanted very much to get a post in the Benares Hindu University as Professor of Indian Art and Culture. But it was not possible to get him one. So he went back to U.S.A. where he had already been appointed as curator at the Boston Museum."[85] Beyond his membership, friendships, and *swadeshi* associations with the Theosophical Society, Coomaraswamy also published in Theosophical journals and presses. In the years 1909 and 1910, he published several short articles in *The Theosophist*; in 1923 he published a book through the Theosophical Publishing House at Adyar entitled *An Introduction to Indian Art*; in the Summer 1946 number of *Main Currents in Modern Thought* he published a paper entitled "Gradation, Evolution, and Reincarnation."[86]

In a footnote to "Gradation, Evolution, and Reincarnation," Coomaraswamy claims the paper "summarizes a position" outlined in his more scholarly work entitled "On the One and Only Transmigrant." This summarization in *Main Currents in Modern Thought* epitomizes his relation or association to the Theosophical movement in his later years. He stood strongly against what he perceived to be the conception of Theosophists on the idea of reincarnation, and seldom mentioned Theosophy other than in this context of disagreement on reincarnation. But unlike Guénon, his criticisms were gentle, even patiently didactic. He spoke, for example, of the problematic interpretation of Indian religions through "theosophists by whom the doctrines have been caricatured with the best intentions and perhaps even worse results," and elsewhere of reincarnation specifically, lamenting that "the belief of modern scholars and theosophists is the result of an equally naive and uninformed interpretation of texts."[87] It was largely for these reasons that he—and Guénon—avoided using the term theosophy, and substituted philosophia perennis or primordial Tradition. Regardless of terminology, it seems evident that the first principles of Blavatsky's Theosophy inspired Coomaraswamy's own first principles of philosophia perennis, and that he is indebted to modern Theosophy for the early formulation of his own metaphysical worldview. Other scholars have noted the similarity—and indebtedness—as well. Professor Floyd H. Ross, for instance, writes, "Theosophists generally have always claimed to find a unity underlying the mystical traditions of mankind," and "so have modern scholars like Ananda K. Coomaraswamy."[88]

GUÉNON AND MODERN THEOSOPHY

"In this century there have been several attempts to make this idea [Traditional wisdom] respectable. Philosophers like René Guénon, students of religion like Mircea Eliade and Henry Corbin, and poets like Kathleen Raine have argued movingly for the transmission of knowledge within closed groups." So writes James Webb in *The Harmonious Circle*. But following this sentence is a more significant one: "What is true is that twentieth-century Traditionalists—whether phony or sincere—rely much more than they like to admit on the revival of occultism which took place during the last quarter of the nineteenth century."[89] One only need examine the esoteric milieu of Paris in 1906 to verify this statement with respect to Guénon. Chapter 2 of Waterfield's *René Guénon and the Future of the West* provides a good account of Guénon's debut into French esotericism by becoming a protégé of Gérard Encausse ("Papus"), who was a co-founder of the Theosophical Society in France and a correspondent of H. P. Blavatsky. Waterfield states there that the modern Theosophical movement was "the main vehicle for the dissemination of the idea that secret wisdom was available from the East, and its teachings were no doubt one element amongst those that led Guénon to study Eastern philosoophy and religion." Guénon was later to split with Papus, as Papus had earlier done with Blavatsky and the Theosopohical Society, but there can be little doubt that Guénon's initial introduction to esotericism through his membership in Papus's Faculté des Sciences Hermétique in 1906 was thoroughly imbued with the theosophical legacy of Blavatsky. Indeed, his professed familiarity with the Theosophical Society would appear to have been more than informal for Guénon to have written such a lengthy book debunking it, as he later did.

Guénon devotes several monographs and sections of books to blasting the Theosophical movement. The major one is *Le Théosophisme: Histoire d'une pseudo-religion*, first published in 1921. That year, relative to works in print, was a busy one for Guénon, as he published *Introduction générale à l'étude des doctrines hindoues* in 1921 as well; its third chapter was entitled "Le Théosophisme." In the January–February and May–June numbers of *la Revue de Philosophie* he again published "le Théosophisme," and in the July number of the same journal he published "Théosophisme et Franc-Maçonnerie," followed by publication of "le Théosophisme" in the November and December

1925 issues of *Le Voile d'Isis*. By that time his fulminations against Theosophy seem to have attrited, though all throughout his later writings he would occasionally take a swipe at the Theosophical movement, seeing in it a totally corrupt expression of perennial first principles. The content and tone of all this writing varies little from the initial barrage of obloquies in his book-length work *Le Théosophisme*.

The essence and whole plan of attack of this work can be distilled to one clause, found on page 302 of *Le Théosophisme*. There he wrote that "we will add that the best means to combat theosophism is, in our opinion, to expose its history just as it is."[90] Hence the "histoire" in the title, which points to a profound inconsistency in Guénon's oeuvre. Guénon repeatedly criticizes the "historical method," as we have seen, as being fatuous and irrelevant, yet he undertakes to refute modern Theosophy not on the merits (or demerits) of the principles that it espouses, but on "son histoire telle qu'elle est" ("its history just as it is"). And in this instance, Guénon should have stuck to his metaphysical or principial method and left the historical method that he eschews to historians. The book is full of historical inaccuracies, and uses assumptions for facts at every turn.[91] This might explain why of Guénon's seventeen book-length works, *Le Théosophisme* is one of the few that has not yet been translated into English, and further why the editors of Éditions Traditionnelles in their 1965 second edition of the book decided to add a full sixty-five pages of (equally problematic) "Notes Additionnelles de la second édition" (pp. 311–376). Guénon was at his best when articulating the profound metaphysical principles of the primordial Tradition in his trenchant style, but he was at his worst when attempting to debunk other esoteric or spiritualist movements and organizations using the historical method which he himself held in such contempt.

One does not have to read very far into the work to find oversights and serious distortions. On the first page of chapter 1, Guénon states that Blavatsky was born in 1831, which is true, but omits the day of birth. The very first "additional" note gives the *day* of her birth because "we were not able to find the exact date at the time of the first edition," the "we" (*nous*) presumably being Guénon. Yet on the very first page in Herbert G. Whyte's biography of Blavatsky, *H. P. Blavatsky: An Outline of Her Life*, published in London in 1909, twelve years prior to Guénon's first edition of *Le Théosophisme*, the day of her birth is given. On the third page, Guénon tries to establish hypocrisy or inconsistency by showing that Mrs. Besant, who propounded esoteric Christianity in her later years, was once quoted as having stated the necessity of "above all to combat Rome and its priests, to fight wheresoever against Christianity and chase God from the skies." This is doubtless true, and Guénon cites the reference as an address to a congress of Free Thinkers in Brussels in 1880. What he fails to mention, however, is that this is a full decade *before* Mrs. Besant ever encountered the Theosophical movement, that she had recently undergone an unsuccessful marriage and subsequent divorce from an Anglican cleric, and that the socialist, Fabian Society, free-thought milieu in which she then found a home, was openly hostile to religions and ecclesiastical bureaucracies. Guénon's implication is that one cannot alter one's view of religion—radically or otherwise—in thirty years' time without being hypocritical or inconsistent, an ironic implication that has some bearing on his own views of Buddhism. One could multiply such examples endlessly.

But this is not intended to be a review of *Le Théosophisme*. The point is that Guénon chose an historical vehicle, and not a principial vehicle, to criticize modern Theosophy. He does give a brief outline of the "essential" doctrines of modern Theosophy in chapter 11 of *Le Théosophisme*—namely, "Principaux points de l'enseignement théosophiste"—but most are points at which he is at variance, and not one single similarity of teaching is shown between his view of Traditional first principles and Theosophic first principles. Moreover, he cites only Blavatsky's *Key to Theosophy*, and never there mentions her *magnum opus, The Secret Doctrine*. Were Guénon to have explicated the essential similarity of principles in both systems, it would have defeated his argument that the doctrines espoused by modern Theosophy were entirely bogus. His repugnance toward modern Theosophy is a blind spot in Guénon's worldview, for while there are certainly misinterpretations and ill formulations of Traditional principles on the part of some Theosophists, the promulgators of modern Theosophy were neither intentionally nor wholly corrupt as he seems to think, and there are innumerably more points of agreement between Tradition and modern Theosophy, as we shall presently see, than he was ever willing to admit.

We have seen that Marco Pallis, in contrasting Guénon to Coomaraswamy, is reluctant to endorse Guénon's capacity for scholarship. Whitall Perry, though an admirer of Guénon, has sufficient objectivity to address Guénon's factual carelessness directly, and discusses the possible causes of this problem: "The factual errors referred to may be an indirect consequences of Guénon's inborn metaphysical wisdom: his certitude about principles left him somewhat careless regarding the pedestrian but inescapable requirements of scholarship."[92] Similarly, Eliade writes that "contrary to René Guénon or other contemporary 'esotericists,' Coomaraswamy developed his exegesis without surrendering the tools and methods of philology, archeology, art history, ethnology, folklore, and history of religions."[93] Curiously, Eliade also asserts, relative to Le Théosophisme, that it is an "erudite and devastating critique," and a "learned and brilliantly written book."[94] With this we cannot agree. Yet one should not, on the basis of one ill-conceived "history," suspect all of Guénon's metaphysical work or thought. Regardless of this one work, the profound metaphysical insight and raw perspicacity of Guénon far outweigh his more problematic material, and the positive effect of his sagacity cannot be overestimated within the sphere of Traditional metaphysics. Elsewhere, Eliade describes Guénon's doctrine as "considerably more rigorous and more cogent than that of the occultists and hermeticists" (e.g., Eliphas Levi, Papus, St. Martin, and others) who preceded him, and with this statement we do agree. It is to the first principles of the primordial Tradition, and to those of the philosophia perennis and theosophy as well, that our attention will now be focused.

# 8

# The First Principles

The notion of "first principles" is neither new nor confined to the philosophia perennis. Origen's *de Principiis* (Περὶ Ἀρχων), usually translated as *On First Principles*, is well known to every student of early Christianity, and lists no less than eight first principles in Book I. The counterstroke of the philosophical metronome provides us with Herbert Spencer's 1880 publication of *First Principles* in which he refers to "a new philosophy" arisen from "the true sphere of all rational investigation," and the first "fundamental and universal principles which science has established within that sphere." There is thus an obvious relativity of usage for the term *first principles*. The aim of this chapter, then, is to circumscribe and define the Traditional usage, designating the Traditional first principles.

Up to this point, our concern has been chiefly with what Guénon would have referred to as secondary or contingent issues—that is, those matters of fact that proceed from the causal first principles. But this has been necessary in order to place the discussion of content, nature, and taxonomy, if this latter term is permitted, of these first principles in their proper setting. The treatment of the philosophia perennis and theosophia has been, therefore, something of a prolegomenon to the first principles, which comprise the nucleus of the primordial, perennial Tradition. In this prolegomenon, notice was taken of the differences between *theosophia antiqua*, modern Theosophy, the primordial Tradition and the variety of religions—extant and extinct—in which its basic principles have been formulated, and the various expropriations of the philosophia perennis, from Coomaraswamy's to the diffusion noted by Schmitt that "a great many philosophers of various persuasions have, as it were, appropriated the conception and so bent it that their own philosophy turns out to be the perennial philosophy." Moreover, as all these expressions or systems[95] of "eternal truths," as Jaspers puts it, will be drawn upon to clarify or add to the complete definition and elucidation of the principles, other salient differences will become apparent.

Yet these differences will not constitute the primary focus of our investigation here. To proceed in this fashion is not necessarily to minimize the importance of the differences, but considerations of time and space (length) impose a choice between a full examination of both the similarities and dissimilarities, or examining and focusing only on one of them within the framework of a chapter. Therefore, the procedure to be followed here is one that is in agreement with a statement made in 1900 by the theosophist G. R. S. Mead, who wrote:

> It has been said by Professor Max Müller that we should not speak of the comparative science of religion, but should rather employ the phrase, comparative science of theology. This is quite true of the work that has so far been done, and done well, by official scholarship; the main effort has been to discover differences, and exaggerate the analysis of details. So far there has been, outside of a small circle of writers, little attempt at synthesis.[96]

What will be attempted here is not so much a "synthesis," but rather a very brief comparison of similarities—an effort to determine which principles are common to the philosophia perennis, the Tradition, and theosophy. By drawing on all the systems to elicit the particular expression of the principles in each, the establishment of the commonality of them to all the systems will be an inevitable concomitant to their definition and explanation.[97] It is necessary to add that natural metaphysics is a vast subject area and not one that can be treated in any detail within the scope of a single chapter. Nor is this our objective here; rather it is simply to point to the commonalities of principles and the symbols and/or language used to explain them by the different expositors whose quotations follow.

Central to the ethonomethodological approach as outlined in Appendix D, one finds the same concept expressed, albeit expressed somewhat differently, in all these systems. Furthermore, one finds that the essential principles are and remain the same, despite considerations of epoch or location—that is, regardless of the fact that the cultural or contingent expressions of these principles constantly change. This notion is consistently restated in the writings of the proponents of Tradition and in those of the theosophists. Schuon, for example, asserts that "The antagonisms between these forms no more affect the one universal Truth than the antagonisms between opposing colours affect the transmission of the one uncolored light."[98] Further affirmation comes from Guénon, who says that "the one who has understood truly will always be able, behind the diversity of expression, to recognize the one truth, and thus this inevitable diversity will never be a cause of disagreement."[99] Blavatsky speaks at length about this notion, specifying the magnanimous philosophers and great religious founders:

> These founders were all *transmitters*, not original teachers. They were authors of new forms and interpretations, while the truths upon which the latter were based were as old as mankind. Selecting one or more of those grand verities— actualities visible only to the eye of the real Sage and Seer— out of many orally revealed to man in the beginning, preserved and perpetuated in the *adyta* of the temples through initiation, during the Mysteries and by personal transmission—they revealed these truths to the masses. Thus every nation received in its turn some of the said truths, under the veil of its own local and special symbolism.[100]

Finally, Coomaraswamy corroborates all of these statements, and adds a nuance regarding this notion that is indicated by Blavatsky in her phrase "some of the said truths"—a nuance that is important to emphasize. He writes that "every tradition is necessarily a partial representation of the truth intended by tradition universally considered; in each tradition something is suppressed, or reserved or obscure which in another may be found more extensively, more logically, or more brilliantly developed."

It is our task here to attempt to elicit the best-expressed principles in the Traditional, theosophic, and perennial philosophic writers for a circumscription of the holistic and symbiotic interdependence of eternal truths in their highest principial expressions, employing the method that is reflected in Coomaraswamy's conclusion: "What is then clear and full in one tradition can be used to develop the meaning of what may be hardly more than alluded to in another."[101] The sources upon which we draw here are different from those Coomaraswamy had in mind—that is, "pure" expressions of first principles as opposed to those found in any given Tradition per se—but the method is the same. Thus, following the reasoning and methods of these esoteric systems in themselves, the attempt here will be to isolate the ubiquitous, immutable, and perennial principles by suspending consideration of the surface variety of their expressions. In this way, their similarities become abundantly clear.

To repeat, one should not seek to minimize this "surface variety"— that is, the differences of expression between esoteric schools—which could be the subject of a large work in itself. They constitute important differences regarding, inter alia, the use of reason; terminological disputes (e.g., "occultism"); the question of the existence of highly developed human beings (*mahātmas, jīvanmuktas,* the spiritual "elite"); differences in attitude regarding philosophy, theology, and religion; the question of paranormal phenomena and *siddhis*; and even more profound doctrinal problems like macro- and microcosmic "evolution," transmigration or reincarnation, and the highly significant perspectives (and use) of symbolism. But our purpose here is different; it is to show that *in principle,* regardless of emphasis or the degree to which a given percept plays in a given metaphysical system as a whole, some expression or treatment of the same percept can also be found in the philosophia perennis, theosophy, and the Tradition as described here. Our treatment is, admittedly, briefer than it ought to be. The method is selective, discriminating, and eclectic, using as much as possible the words of the expositors themselves. But this method is unavoidable if, given the practical constraints of space, one is to extract the essentials, to examine the isomorphic skeletal structure of these first principles in the various systems already delineated, drawing primarily from Western sources.

The first principles comprise the heart and mind of all systems, Traditions, and "sophias" that can be deemed perennial. The enumerated principles that follow, then, constitute both a marshalling and distillation, as it were, of all those expressed in the perspectives of Coomaraswamy, Guénon, Blavatsky, certain of their followers, and one or two of the established modern perennial philosophers. That this group of first principles is interdependent will be shown as each is examined and related to the rest. There is no strict "sequence" inherent within the principles themselves, with the exception that the Absolute must be first, though an inherent sequentiality becomes evident as they are literated. Not everyone will agree that the principles chosen here are the most central. Those which we chose to examine here and elsewhere[102] are different from those, for example, which Coomaraswamy himself chose:

> Every notable Christian doctrine is also explicitly pro-
> pounded in every other dialect of the primordial tradition: I
> refer to such doctrines as those of the eternal and temporal
> births, that of the single essence and two natures, that of the
> Father's impassibility, that of the significance of sacrifice,
> that of transubstantiation, that of the nature of the distinction
> between the contemplative and active lives and of both from
> the life of pleasure, that of eternity from aeviternity and
> time, and so forth.[103]

Respectful of Guénon's caveat, "Plus pas que la metaphysique vraie
ne peut s'enfermer dans les formules d'un systéme ou d'une théorie
particuliére" (see note 95), the following principles are enumerated.

### The Absolute and the One

That the amorphic Absolute of metaphysical monism is inex-
pressible in language—which by its own symbolic nature is delimited
to the conditioned realm of spatio-temporality—or in any other symbol,
is a verity universally acknowledged by both the metaphysics of the
world of modern Western philosophy and by the theosophic metaphysics of the Traditional writers. Nonetheless, some metaphysicists have
attempted an expression of it, though not, in any conscious hope of
achieving success or by laboring under the principle that, in Coomaraswamy's words, "a symbol participates in its referent or archetype."
Rather, these attempts are usually framed in the negative—for example,
Eckhart's *via negativa*—since the Absolute is so utterly transcendent
relative to human cognition or anything else (sensible or intelligible)
that only by framing it in the negative can the student gain any direction
whatsoever. Even these negative attempts, however, have led to a wide
variety of terms that often bewilder the student in their profusion—
terms that are inevitably doomed to failure like arrows shot at the
Sun.[104] This is a fact not unknown to those who shoot these arrows, but
though the arrows cannot participate in the referent (for even the term
*referent* is inapplicable relative to the Absolute), they do indicate direction—the direction of the disciple's quest for liberation.

Direction is essential in this quest, since it is neither the path nor its indicator that should be important to the aspirant, but rather awareness and acknowledgment of the Absolute. This problem is recognized in an old Buddhist proverb about pointing one's finger at the moon, whose rendering in French is "Quand le doigt montre la lune, l'imbécile regarde le doigt." And when there exists a multiplicity of "fingers" or indicators, the probability of confusion is high. Thus statements of any type about the Absolute are best left unsaid. And so they are in the theosophic and Traditional writings too, with only the exceptions that the Absolute is beyond both limitation and nonlimitation—that is, futile to try to conceive or express. In one of very few references to the Absolute in Coomaraswamy's writings, he states that "The Absolute (Para Brahman, Aditi) is also, of course, unintelligible; but in another way, being neither an object, natural or artificial, nor even an intellectual form or idea. The Absolute, being *amūrta* ("formless"), *nirābhāsa* ("unmanifested") not in any likeness, impossible to symbolize because not a form, does not fall to be considered here."[105] Blavatsky established the Absolute as one of the three fundamental propositions of the secret doctrine as:

> An Omnipresent, Eternal, Boundless, and Immutable Principle on which all speculation is impossible, since it transcends the power of human conception and could only be dwarfed by any human expression or similitude. It is beyond the range and reach of thought—in the words of *Mandūkya Upanishad*, "unthinkable and unspeakable." It is of course devoid of all attributes and is essentially without any relation to manifested, finite Being.[106]

Guénon is somewhat more evasive about commenting on the Absolute, and presumably refers to it using different terms in different works—for example, the "Absolute" in *La Métaphysique Orientale*, "Infinity" in *The Multiple States of Being*, the "Supreme Principle" in *L'Homme et son Devenir selon le Vedānta*, and simply the "Principle" in *La Grande Triade*, where he describes it as "being beyond all distinction, not able to be correlated to anything whatsoever." Guénon's various references to it were entirely consistent with those of the metaphysicists just cited, with regard to its "attributes."

More problematic is the relationship between the Absolute and the One, or God, or metaphysical Unity—the same terminological confusion exists relative to both principles. Little treatment other than passing references exists on this relationship: Blavatsky claims simply that "Parabrahman is not 'God,' because It is not *a* God," and further unwraps this seed thought in the Proem of *The Secret Doctrine*. And Frithjof Schuon writes that "It is true that God as creator, revealer and savior is not to be identified with the Absolute as such; it is equally true that God as such, in the full depth of His Reality, is not to be reduced to the creative function."[107] Thus, what is implicit in this metaphysical speculation is that there is a "step-down" process, the mechanics of which—the transition from the Absolute to the One or God—are equally as unknowable or incognizable as the Absolute itself. But once the One manifests, once God or Being appears sui generis, somewhat more metaphysical certitude accompanies it. This is not the One or "One Being" of Parmenides and Plato, which more closely correlates to the Absolute,[108] but rather the next step in a process that involves to the many and evolves back to the One. With the appearance of the One, the contingent or conditioned realms of relativity and axiology follow, and the cycle begins.

Functionally, it is the One that takes a preeminent place in metaphysics, and is the foundational a priori postulate upon which are built the theosophical systems and Traditional systems. This One is, to use a simple analogy of finite dimension, the zenith of a pyramid from which all creation graduates in reverse, as it were. To use another geometric analogy, it can be likened to the intangible center point of a sphere of existence that radiates outward but without radial boundary, concurrently superimposed upon the modern physicist's concept of the fluidic nature—owing to its fundamentally atomic or subatomic composition—of the phenomenal universe of matter/motion in which differentiation is due to finite and mutable forms. Mathematically, the number One is both odd and even. The aspect of this manifestation of the One into its separate forms rests on its being the progenitive principle from which all emanates, including the other principles. This aspect is the one that gives so much difficulty to empirically bound thinkers, yet it is the paradoxical aspect that Coomaraswamy expresses as being everywhere "impartite whether transcendent or immanent," or again as "undivided amongst divided things." This is an indispensable key for the understanding of the philosophia perennis, theosophy, the Tradition—truly the "first" of first principles, for it is the task of the seeker to identify with the *Ātman* or *Sanctus Spiritus* within himself, realizing simultaneously his being in the One and the illusion (*māyā*) of thinking himself separate from it.

It is the One, with its inscrutable relation to the Absolute, which can be described as "unity." Guénon writes that "Being is one, or rather it is metaphysical Unity itself, but Unity embraces multiplicity within itself, since it produces it by the mere extension of its possibilities; it is for this reason that even in Being Itself a multiplicity of aspects may be conceived which constitute so many attributes or qualifications of It."[109] These first metaphysical principles of the Absolute and the One (and God, whose attribution to either of the former principles depends on the particular writer in question) and the diaphanous distinction between them are the cornerstones of the Traditional and theosophic systems, since it is from them that all manifestation ultimately proceeds and to them that it ultimately returns.

The timelessness and subsequent polarity of this process point to the interdependence of the principles inherent in it, as will be seen presently, and also to the contingent application of these principles as the promulgation of theosophy and the Tradition in various cultures throughout time. The principial unity of the One, for example, is reflected in the idea of the same principles being found in the historical systems or manifestations of the great religions and in the writings of the magnanimous philosophers. More recently, and relative to the areas now under discussion, this specifc concept is reflected by the Theosophist and Coomaraswamy's friend, Bhagavan Das, writing *The Essential Unity of All Religions* in 1932 and Frithjof Schuon writing *De l'Unite Transcendente de Religions* in 1948.

AEVITERNITY

It is a fact seldom disputed by modern scientists that the quantitative notions of space and time are not only convenient constructs of intellectual origination, but are inextricable notions—that is, time (duration) finds its meaning and existence only within the category of space (dimension). Thus, one often finds the two notions in hyphenated union—for example, spatio-temporality. Yet scientists and those of an empirical orientation do not postulate further, as do the theosophic and Traditional writers, since in their view such postulation constitutes intrusion into the unholy realm of metaphysics. Ever since the discussion of an eternal present by Plato in the *Timaeus* (37d–38c) and Aristotle's ἄτομος νῦν, which Coomaraswamy translates simply as "now-without-duration," the concept of *aeviternity* (from the Latin *aeviternus*, meaning "eternal existence; everlasting immanent duration") has been among the first principles of Western perennial philosophers. Historians of Christianity and Christian theologians meet with the principle in Augustine:

> God is himself in no interval nor extension of place, but in his immutable preeminent all-possibility is both within everything because all things are in him and without everything because he transcends all things. So too he is in no interval nor extension of time, but in his immutable eternity is the principle of all things because he is [metaphysically] prior to all things and the end of all things because the same he is after all things.[110]

Moreover, the Schoolmen dealt with the principle in their writings: Aquinas states that "There is no *before* or *after* to be reckoned with in constant changeless Reality" since "the *now* of time is not time; the *now* of eternity is really the same as eternity."[111] The principle can be found in discussions of other Traditional cultures and worldviews as well. In the third volume of Papers from the Eranos yearbooks entitled *Man and Time*, for instance, Henry Corbin addresses his prefatory remarks to the proclivity of Western "moderns" to "reduce real time to abstract physical time, to the essentially *quantitative* time which is that of the objectivity of mundane calendars from which the signs that gave a sacred qualification to every present have disappeared."[112] This proclivity stands in contradistinction to the theosophic or Traditional perspective that Henri-Charles Puech sees reflected in the worldview of the Hellenistic Gnostics: "Gnostic time is only the consequence and the reflection of the adventures or conflict of transcendent realities, an episodic copy of an atemporal tragedy, and the Gnostic's effort is to transcend time in order to establish himself, as absolutely as possible, in the world of atemporal realities, in a universe that is intelligible and given eternally." Following this paper is one of Mircea Eliade on Indic conceptions of aeviternity in which he claims that in their perspective, "by transcending the Universe, the created world, one also transcends time and achieves stasis, the *eternal intemporal present*."[113]

This "eternal present" or "eternal now" Coomaraswamy refers to in different ways. In "Vedānta and Western Tradition," he refers to it as the "nowever"; but this is a didactic essay, in contrast to his formally pedagogic essays and books in which he generally refers to this principle by the term that stems from its Latin antecedent: *aeviternity*. Coomaraswamy's book, *Time and Eternity*, which treats this theme, contrasts these notions as they are found in Hinduism, Buddhism, Islam, Christianity, ancient Greece, and modernity. There, in perhaps his most succinct statement on the subject, he writes that

> The metaphysical doctrine simply contrasts time as a continuum with the eternity that is not in time and so cannot properly be called *everlasting*, but coincides with the real present or now of which temporal experience is impossible. Here confusion only arises because for any consciousness functioning in terms of time and space, "now" succeeds "now" without interruption, and there seems to be an endless series of nows, collectively adding up to "time." This confusion can be eliminated if we realize that none of these nows has any duration and that, as measures, all alike are zeros, of which a "sum" is unthinkable. It is a matter of relativity; it is "we" who move, while *the* Now is unmoved, and only seems to move—much as the sun only seems to rise and set because the earth revolves.[114]

Further, Coomaraswamy makes a distinction between the principles of eternity and aeviternity: the former denotes time without beginning or end, while the latter includes the former denotation but adds the element of now-ness as encompassing the whole of it. Coomaraswamy's most succinct formulation of aeviternity is found in his essay "Recollection, Indian and Platonic." There he states that "Only from this point of view [temporal omnipresence] can the notion of a 'Providence' be made intelligible, the divine life being uneventful, not in the sense that it knows nothing of what we call events, but inasmuch as all of the events of what are for us past and future times are present to it *now*, and not in succession."[115] With perfect agreement on this point, Guénon follows suit: "metaphysically, it is never a question of 'priority' and of 'posterity' except in the sense of a causal and purely logical chain, which cannot exclude the simultaneity of all things in the 'eternal present'."[116]

The aeviternity of the Traditional writers finds an exact parallel in modern Theosophy. Blavatsky gives a lucid explanation of the essential differences between the empirical illusion of time and "eternal duration":

> Time is only an illusion produced by the succession of our states of consciousness as we travel through eternal duration, and it does not exist where no consciousness exists in which the illusion can be produced, but "lies asleep." The present is only a mathematical line which divides that part of eternal duration which we call the future, from that part which we call the past. Nothing on earth has real duration, for nothing remains without change—or the same—for the billionth part of a second; and the sensation we have of the actuality of the division of "time" known as the present, comes from the blurring of that momentary glimpse, or succession of glimpses, of things that our senses give us, as those things pass from the region of ideals which we call the future, to the region of memories that we name the past.[117]

And the theosophic metaphysicist Poortman is concerned about "theologians as well as philosophers who are conscious of the possibility of experiencing eternity already here and now."[118] This "possibility of experiencing" is one way of saying that it is a matter of metaphysical acuity of the individual to be able to experience this aeviternity, since it is not a principle that is rationally or empirically conceivable. The experience of such a principle is confined to the metaphysical realm of intelligibility. Wilbur Urban refers to the "metaphysical idiom" of the "timeless present," describing it as "The interpenetration which negates the mutual externality of successive moments of time,"[119] or the "succession of glimpses," as Blavatsky phrases it. Aeviternity is thus of the essential, intelligible realm whose center point is the nonspatial, and wherein the etiologic principles of God or the One (when not ascribed to the Absolute) reside. To experience God or the One is to simultaneously experience aeviternity, the latter being the principle in which the ebb and flow of universes occur, and subsuming the principle that is epiphenomenal to it: periodicity.

PERIODICITY

Traditional and theosophic writers sometimes compare the universe to the mammalian heart. With a diastolic and systolic action it appears and disappears, manifestation and nonmanifestation, *manvantāra* and *mahāpralaya* in Sanskrit terminology. Between the mahāpralayas are manvantāras, between nonmanifestations are manifestations, and so on. These periods of manifestation are marked by cycles, smaller within larger, but all following more or less the same pattern of periodicity. One finds that these cyclic patterns exhibit some universal features, one prominent of which is that they contain a quaternity that equates, as we had occasion to observe earlier, to *wholeness*. This wholeness is often symbolized by the circle, and the *quaternio* within by the cross, whose intersection forms four quadrants of the circle-whole. Additionally, to indicate that the eternity-periodicity process is not static, it is often symbolized by the circular *uroboros*.

Traditional Indian metaphysics has developed an elaborate structure of principial periodicity, an intricate cycles-within-cycles cosmology encompassing billions of terrestrial years. "The essential element in this avalanche of figures is the cyclical character of cosmic Time. The same phenomenon (creation-destruction-new creation), foreshadowed in each *yuga* (dawn and dusk) but fully realized in a *mahāyuga*, is repeated over and over."[120] Forming a quaternio, there are four *yugas* in a *mahāyuga: Kṛta Yuga, Tretā Yuga, Dvāpara Yuga*, and *Kali Yuga*.

Guénon dispassionately asserts that his whole perspective of the loss of Tradition in the West and the decline of Tradition in the East is in fact due to the vicissitudes of the *Kali Yuga*, the *yuga* in which the twentieth century C.E is currently situated—that is, the last quarter of the cyclic progression of the *mahāyuga*. Chapter 1 of *La crise du monde moderne*, for instance, is titled "L'âge sombre," at the beginning of which he writes:

We are presently in the fourth age, the "Kali Yuga" or "dark age," and have been there . . . since an epoch much earlier than all those which are known to "classical" history. Since then, the truths which were formerly accessible to all mankind have become more and more hidden and difficult to attain; those who possess access to them have become fewer and fewer in number, and if the treasure of "nonhuman" wisdom prior to all the ages can never be lost, it nonetheless becomes enveloped in veils more and more impenetrable, which hide it from view and under which it is extremely difficult to discover.[121]

Were this statement alone in Guénon's writings regarding periodicity, which it is not, it would nonetheless be enough to deduce that central to and inherent in his works is the underlying principle of periodicity. In a posthumous publication entitled *Formes traditionnelles et cycles cosmique* (Paris, 1970) there appears one of Guénon's essays entitled "Remarques sur la doctrine des cycles cosmiques." He states there that "Moreover, by virtue of the law of correspondence upon which all things in universal Existence rely, there is always and necessarily a certain analogy either between the different cycles of the same order, or between the principal cycles and their secondary divisions."[122] This relates not only to the cycles-within-cycles principle on the one hand, but to another profound principle on the other; namely, the so-called hermetic axiom found in the *Tabula Smagardina* that is commonly rendered "As above, so below." This principle, which Guénon variously refers to as the "law of correspondence" or the "law of harmony," is central to both the theosophic and the Traditional writers, and pervades not just the notion of periodicity but all the first principles under discussion here.

Coomaraswamy was more reluctant to advertise "yuga" periodicity as a fundamental axiom of his faith, as did Guénon, but his writings are nonetheless replete with the principle of cycles. In one of the most illustrative essays dealing with this topic, "The Flood in Hindu Tradition," he equates the various flood myths "incidentally noted" to the Hindu flood myth, the others being Sumerian, Semitic, and Eddaic. He states there that "'Floods' are a normal and recurrent feature of the cosmic cycle, i.e., the period (*para*) of a Brahma's life, amounting to 36,000 *kalpas*, or 'days' of Angelic time."[123] He explicates the whole notion of cosmic ebb and flow from the standpoint of these several different linguistic and Traditional systems, and observes that the close of periods of cosmic manifestation are "essentially resolutions of manifested existences into their undetermined potentiality."

Blavatsky's commentary on the principle of periodicity is, again, both complementary to the understanding of Coomaraswamy and Guénon, and self-evident. She affirms that

This second assertion of the Secret Doctrine is the absolute universality of that law of periodicity, of flux and reflux, ebb and flow, which physical science has observed and recorded in all departments of nature. An alternation such as that of Day and Night, Life and Death, Sleeping and Waking, is a fact so common, so perfectly universal and without exception, that it is easy to comprehend that in it we see one of the absolutely fundamental laws of the universe.[124]

The Theosophical perspective of periodicity as a first principle is perfectly consistent with the Traditional perspective of Guénon and Coomaraswamy, and it is important to remember the historical fact that the latter perspective follows in the wake of the former, as Webb notes. Yet the principle of periodicity has several ancillary principles, which bring to mind what Guénon previously refers to as "the law of correspondence upon which all things in universal Existence rely." The macrocosmic first principle of periodicity must necessarily include within it by the law of correspondence the microcosmic cycle of human reincarnation or transmigration, together with the notion of "evolution."

It must be stated unequivocally at this point that the *perception* that Guénon and Coomaraswamy held of how modern Theosophy regarded reincarnation is divorced from the *actuality* of its views. This divorce is evident in Coomaraswamy's and especially Guénon's criticisms of the "principal points of teaching" of modern Theosophy, and is due to the fact that the erudition and open attitudes characteristic of the early days of the Theosophical movement (1875–1895) had undergone a change by the time Guénon and Coomaraswamy came under its influence. It was further due to the facts that Eric Hoffer's "true believer" syndrome—in a spiritual mode—had infiltrated the Theosophical movement by the 1920s, and that some (though still not all) of the allegations of misinterpreting or oversimplifying recondite metaphysical principles did occur on the part of some Theosophists. It seems lost to Guénon and Coomaraswamy, however, that Blavatsky had earlier staged pitched battles with segments of the Spiritualist movement regarding the individual's morphology in postmortem states; that she took an essentially Buddhist approach: "It [the Pilgrim] is the only immortal and eternal principle in us," she writes in *The Secret Doctrine*, "being an indivisible part of the integral whole—the Universal Spirit—

from which it emanates, and into which it is absorbed at the end of the cycle."[125] It is this "Pilgrim," elsewhere referred to as the "Monad (the two in one)," which undergoes the "long series of metempsychoses and reincarnation." The central point of misunderstanding concerns the perception of the Traditional writers that the superessential and indivisible divine element together with surviving "personality" (an aggregation of emotions, mind, and personal memories) was thought by Theosophists to incarnate in successive corporeal forms—a notion that Blavatsky did not promulgate. For Coomaraswamy, in the reincarnation process, "Only the 'intellectual virtues' survive. This is not the survival of a 'personality' (that was a property bequeathed when we departed); it is the continued being of the very person So-and-so, no longer encumbered by the grossest of So-and-so's former definitions." He concludes in complete agreement with Blavatsky that "In this way, by a succession of deaths and rebirths, all of the fences may be crossed."[126]

The second ancillary principle to be mentioned under the rubric of periodicity is that of "evolution," and with it the idea of the helix, since they are inseparable. Guénon writes that

> We know that a horizontal plane represents one state of being, each modality of which corresponds to a spiral turn that we have merged with a circumference; on the other hand, in reality the extremities of the turn do not lie in the plane of the curve, but rather in two immediately adjacent planes, for this curve, envisaged in the vertical cylindrical systems, is a "spiral, a function of the helix," whose thread is infinitesimal.[127]

Coomaraswamy refers less specifically to the helix, but describes "a spiral having for its center the vertical axis of the universe," and the helico-evolution of individual reincarnation. "Two directions of motion," he writes of this process, "one circumferential and determinate, the other centripetal and free, have been distinguished; but I have not made it clear that their resultant can be properly indicated only by a spiral."[128] Blavatsky agrees: "This tracing of 'Spiral lines' refers to the evolution of man's as well as Nature's principles; an evolution which takes place gradually . . . as does everything else in nature."[129] The ideas of "helix" and "evolution" in the Theosophical and Traditional writings have little to do with the normative meaning or definition of evolution à la Darwin and the origin of species. For some unknown reason, modern Theosophy has often been singled out as containing an evolutionistic worldview in a sense parallel to Darwin's. Mircea Eliade, for instance, writes that "Mme Blavatsky presented a theory of indefinite spiritual evolution through metempsychosis and progressive initiation. . . . But I must interrupt at this point to observe that if there is anything characteristic of all Eastern traditions, it is precisely an antievolutionistic conception of the spiritual life."[130] Yet, Coomaraswamy, in describing this "succession of deaths and rebirths," states that "For us, then, there is an alternation of evolution and involution. But for the central Spectator there is no succession of events."[131] And Guénon echoes this thought: "Etymologically indeed these terms 'evolution' and 'involution' signify nothing more nor less than 'development' and 'envelopment,'* but we are well aware that in modern language the world 'evolution' has acquired quite a different meaning, which has almost converted it into a synonym for 'progress'."[132] The asterisk alludes to a rather significant footnote where Guénon agrees to use the term as he does in his chapter heading, "Posthumous Evolution": "In this sense, but only in this sense, it would be possible to apply these terms to the two phases that are distinguishable in every cycle of manifestation." One might ask whether Blavatsky's usage of evolution was different from these. The answer is, decidedly not: "The Darwinian theory," she writes, "of the transmission of acquired faculties, is neither taught nor accepted in Occultism. Evolution, in it, proceeds on quite other lines."[133] In a thought almost encapsulating the entire argument here, Blavatsky writes elsewhere that "Before we can approach the evolution of physical and *divine* man, we have first to master the idea of cyclic evolution."[134]

Finally, one last point needs to be made that could be described as a transition between periodicity and polarity, the next principle to be considered. This is a phenomenon regarding the dynamic of periodicity and polarity, which is that the seed forms or archetypes of the opposite pole of the axis within the cycle reside in the one presently occurring. So, when the *mahāpralaya* or "flood" destroys the antediluvian world, the "seeds" or archetypes of the next manifestation or *manvantāra* survive as possibilities. "In each case," writes Coomaraswamy, "the seeds, ideas, or images of the future manifestation persist during the interval of inter-Time of resolution on a higher plane of existence, unaffected by the destruction of manifested forms."[135]

There are terms for this dynamic, referred to as the "compensation theory" and *enantiodromia* that operate in tandem to ensure the viability of continuity or survival from one cycle (or phase of a cycle) to another. Carl Jung discusses this dynamic at length in his works, describing enantiodromia as "the regulative function of opposites," and a "running contrariwise, by which he [Heraclitus] meant that sooner or later everything runs into its opposite."[136] The most useful symbol for the comprehension of this dynamic—though the symbol itself is static—is the Chinese *yin-yang* symbol, which contains the white seed or nucleus in the black half and the black seed or nucleus in the white half. In Jung's most succinct statement on the compensation/enantiodromia dynamic (which Guénon describes in similar terms, referring to it as "reinstatement") he writes:

Of these [*yin* and *yang*] it is said that always when one principle reaches the height of its power, the counterprinciple is stirring within it like a germ. This is another, particularly graphic formulation of the psychological law of compensation by an inner opposite. Whenever a civilization reaches its highest point, sooner or later a period of decay sets in. But the apparently meaningless and hopeless collapse into a disorder without aim or purpose . . . nevertheless contains within its darkness the germ of a new light.[137]

The incessant interplay between these forces is only another way of perceiving the spiralling process of periodic evolution in which the notion of polarity plays such a significant part.

POLARITY, DUALITY, *COINCIDENTIA OPPOSITORUM*

The concept of polarity and the synthesis of its poles was already discussed—though not in great detail—above in the chapter entitled "The *Complexio Oppositorum* of Quantity and Quality" with specific reference to those concepts. It serves no purpose to repeat here what was said there but, keeping the former in mind, our purpose now is to extend the dimensions of the principle of polarity (or duality) and its synthesis to the macrocosmic proportions of metaphysics, and in turn to examine how, by the law of correspondence, theosophists and Traditionalists apply this principle to a microcosm—that is, to humankind.

Blavatsky, like Coomaraswamy and Guénon, often addresses the principle of polarity, or contrasts, or opposites, and in reference to various phenomena. Among her most succinct statements, and one which does a perfect job in corresponding the macroprinciple with the microsubject, is the following:

> Esoteric philosophy admits neither good nor evil per se, as existing independently in nature. The cause for both is found, as regards the Kosmos, in the necessity of contraries or contrasts, and with respect to man, in his human nature, his ignorance and passions. There is no *devil* or the utterly depraved, as there are no Angels absolutely perfect, though there may be spirits of Light and Darkness; thus Lucifer— the spirit of Intellectual Enlightenment and Freedom of Thought—is metaphorically the guiding beacon, which helps man to find his way through the rocks [symplegades?] and sandbanks of Life, for Lucifer is the Logos in his highest, and the "adversary" in his lowest—both of which are reflected in our *Ego*.[138]

Guénon treats the same subject at length both in *Le symbolisme de la croix*, particularly in chapters 6 and 7, entitled respectively "L'union des complémentaires" and "La résolution des oppositions," and in *La Grande Triade*, his principal treatise on Taoism. But as the poles or bases of all manifestation, Guénon looks to Indian thought, and expresses this principle via the notions of purusha and prakriti: "The correlative of *Purusha* is then *Prakriti*, the undifferentiated primordial substance; it is the passive principle, which is represented as feminine, while *Purusha*, also called *Pumas*, is the active principle represented as masculine; and these two are the poles of all manifestation, though remaining unmanifested themselves."[139]

It is undeniable, as we have seen, that the first principle of polarity is central to both Blavatsky and Guénon; with Coomaraswamy it is almost a *leitmotiv*. Few themes within the philosophia perennis intrigue Coomaraswamy as much as polarity, both in the macrocosmic principles of metaphysics, and in the human condition, where the incidence of opposites and their synthesis provide Coomaraswamy with his most favored (and meaningful) material. It is reflected in the numerous references and, indeed, whole essays like "Symplegades" and "The Tantric

Doctrine of Divine Biunity," in which he treats the subject. In "The Darker Side of Dawn," he asserts the paradoxical inversion of the duality-unity principle, declaring, "every [Traditional] ontological formulation affirms the duality of Unity as well as the unity of Duality." Religious scripture and associated historical literature both abound in references to this principle, the most visible of which are found in the Taoist, Tantric (both Buddhist and Hindu), Manichean, and Hellenistic Gnostic expressions, but which are recognized nonetheless in all the major religious traditions. Moreover, this principle was a central element of pre-Socratic thought, as evidenced by the "table of [ten] opposites" formulated by Pythagoras, and preserved by way of Aristotle in his *Metaphysics* (Bk. I, Ch. 5). Coomaraswamy saw the principle of polarity or duality, and concomitantly the *coincidentia oppositorum*, everywhere and in every manifested operation; it led him to write that

> However the ultimate truth of "dualism" may be repudiated, a kind of dualism is logically unavoidable for all practical purposes, because any world in time and space, or that could be described in words or by mathematical symbols, must be one of contraries, both quantitative and qualitative, for example, long and short, good and evil; and even if it could be otherwise, a world without these opposites would be one from which all potentiality to act, would be excluded, not a world that could be inhabited by human beings such as we.[140]

There is, perhaps most importantly, the human perspective—the perspective of divinity—in which these two opposites are in a constant state of intercourse, striving for resolution or reconciliation. In his *Selected Letters*, Coomaraswamy makes repeated reference to Aquinas's formulation of *duo sunt in homine* (literally, "two there are in man"), further illustrating the centrality of this principle in his thought. The two sides are allied with their correlatives, as Blavatsky points out: God, Spirit, light, or consciousness versus Satan, Soul, darkness, and the unconscious.

The correspondences of the principle of polarities, such as the various polarities of manifestation, are numerous and cannot all be treated here. Carl Jung, in *Mysterium Coniunctionis*, a work devoted to this principle of polarity/duality and its synthesis, gives an elaborate list:

To begin with they form a dualism; for instance the opposites are *humidum* (moist)/*siccum* (dry), *frigidum* (cold)/ *calidum* (warm), *superiora* (upper, higher)/*inferiora* (lower), *spiritus-anima* (spirit-soul)/*corpus* (body), *coelum* (heaven)/*terra* (earth) [and so on, for eleven more "opposites" in this particular list].[141]

One interesting latter-day example of duality-as-complements is the work being done in neurology regarding the dual cerebral hemispheres theory of the brain and the effects this has on prevailing notions of human cognition. The right and left hemispheres of the brain conjoined by the *corpus callosum* have been found to control entirely different cognitive functions, and this is having significant effects on the scientific approach to epistemology. The interest of this theory to metaphysics is that, if correct, it serves as a superlative example of the law of correspondence—that is, the principle of polarity applied directly to the substance of cognition.

However interesting and multifarious the correspondences of polarity may be in the sensible realm, they are still contingent, and still only point to the supreme aspect of polarity—its resolution or synthesis, the duad into a monad. This resolution is the *coincidentia oppositorum*; further descriptions of it here would be repetitious. It is sufficient to note one or two other passages from Traditional sources: Guénon writes that "Complementarism itself, which is still duality, must, at a certain degree, disappear before unity, its two terms sort of equilibrizing and neutralizing themselves when uniting to indissolubly fuse in the primordial indifferentiation."[142] This two-subsumed-in-one is the final goal of human endeavor, the *ens perfectissimum* of Western metaphysics, total liberation, *mokṣa*, *nirvāṇa*; it is identity with unconditioned Being, since "Liberation differs from all human or posthuman states that being may have traversed in order to realize it, inasmuch as it is the realization of the ultimate and unconditioned state."[143]

It is, in short, the most sublime and sacred theme of the Tradition and theosophy, alluded to in the various religio-philosophical and mystical systems as total enlightenment, transformation, or God-realization—terms peculiar to specific doctrines but which convey the same meaning. Stated in terms of the only Tradition, it is complete synthesis or *coincidentia oppositorum*, each pole transubstantiated into the other forming one of the two. This goal has been symbolized mythologically by the androgyne in many cultures, and esoterically in the late medieval alchemical material of the West upon which Jung drew so heavily. Further, it is the *hieros gamos* or secret "sacred marriage" in all mystery traditions from time immemorial, of complete absorption of the self into the Self of the neophyte, who from that point begins to "live with God." A consistent and highly evident strain in Coomaraswamy's writings, this concept of the syzygies-as-one appears in many concise statements, such as, in reference to the "two selves," "Their marriage, consummated in the heart, is the *hieros Gamos, Davan Mithunam*, and those in whom it has been perfected are no longer anyone, but as He is 'who has never been anyone.'"[144]

CAUSE AND EFFECT

One way to describe the interplay or tension between two poles, which occurs inevitably whenever polarity exists, is action (*karma*). The term *karma* is certainly much abused as it appears increasingly in the modern vocabulary of the West; it is given an unwarranted etiologic character, or it is used frequently as an excuse for the immediate results of personal stupidity. No less infrequently, karma is misapplied to a principle to which it is genuinely related: transmigration. These abuses and misapplications of the term are thought by Traditional writers to have largely been the handiwork of modern Theosophists, since one so often encounters the principles of "karma and reincarnation" in the worldview of modern Theosophy as an *ensemble*. And perhaps to a certain degree, with regard to the later developments of the Theosophical movement (1910–1950), some of these accusations may be justified. But like the case of reincarnation and evolution, the perception of the original modern Theosophical view of karma is divorced from the reality, especially when applied to Blavatsky's treatment of the term. The pristine dissemination of modern Theosophy is consistent with the precepts of the Tradition regarding both causality and action (karma).

Coomaraswamy provides a passage that conveniently incorporates three of these first principles under discussion here: periodicity, aeviternity, and causality. He writes:

In other words, the *pitryāna* [the "Patriarchal Voyage" of the "Pilgrim"] is a symbolic representation of what is now called the doctrine of reincarnation, and is bound up with the

notion of latent (*adṛṣṭa* or *apūrva*) causality. The purely
symbolic character of the whole conception is made all the
more apparent when we reflect that from the standpoint of
very Truth, and in the absolute Present, there can be no distinctions made of cause and effect; and that what is often
spoken of as the "destruction of *karma*," or more correctly
as a destruction of the latent effects of Works, effected by
Understanding and implied with *mukti*, is not really a
destruction of valid causes . . . but simply a Realization of
the identity of "cause" and "effect."[145]

In this quote, Coomaraswamy gives a definition of karma that extends
beyond its merely etymological sense—from which Guénon seems
reluctant to stray at all—of "action"; karma, in this passage, is equated
to "the latent effects of Works." It was Guénon's fidelity to prescriptive etymological usage of terms, perhaps, that precluded him from
expanding the definition of karma beyond "action." He had, as has
been noted, lamented sloppy use of language and the evisceration of
metaphysical terms in modernity. He more often mentions what karma
is not than what it is, except for his references to its being "simply"
action: "le mot 'karma,' en effet, signifie tout simplement 'action,' et
rien d'autre" [the word *karma*, in effect, simply means "action" and
nothing more]." But this reluctance did not stop Guénon's colleagues
in the Tradition from expanding its use. Marco Pallis, in an essay entitled "Living One's Karma," adds the inevitable corollary to action:
"cosmic flux, together with its parallel conception of karma, 'concordant action and reaction,' as the determinant of each being's part in
that flux, is an essential feature of all the traditions directly or indi-
rectly deriving from India."[146] Karma, therefore, as Pallis correctly
observes, covers *both* action and reaction, for reaction, though it is
contingent upon ingenerate action, is nonetheless action itself. This
principle of the essential realm applies subsequently, by the law of
correspondence, to the substantial realm. With regard to the latter, the
homology can be observed in the first part of Isaac Newton's third law
of motion, published in *Principia* in 1686: "To every action there is
always opposed an equal reaction: or, the mutual actions of two bodies
upon each other are always equal, and directed to contrary parts." It
should be made clear, however, that this homologue cannot imply causality, but only, in Pallis's words, "concordant action and reaction,"

and that reference to "bodies" in Newton's formulation is relative strictly to the physical world.

The question of causality relative to the concept of karma is as much a semantic one as a metaphysical one. The equation "action: cause:: reaction: effect" is certainly not a dyslogical proposition. Therefore, if one accepts this equation as valid, the concept of karma must necessarily include cause and effect—for example, Coomaraswamy's "latent effects of Works." As to the correlation between the understanding of the term by Traditionalists and modern Theosophists, there is nothing fatalistic or deterministic in Blavatsky's definition of karma. Rather, the following quote demonstrates that her's is consistent with Coomaraswamy's—and Pallis's—understanding:

> This Law [karma]—whether conscious or unconscious—predestines nothing and no one. It exists from and in Eternity, truly, for it is Eternity itself; and as such, since no act can be coequal with eternity, it cannot be said to act, for it is Action itself. . . . Karma creates nothing, nor does it design. It is the man who plans and creates causes, and Karmic law adjusts the effects; which adjustment is not an act, but universal harmony, tending ever to resume its original position, like a bough, which bent down too forcibly, rebounds with corresponding vigor. . . . Karma is an Absolute and Eternal law in the world of manifestation; and as there can only be one Absolute, as One eternal ever-present Cause, believers in Karma cannot be regarded as Atheists or materialists—still less as fatalists: for karma is one with the unknowable, of which it is an aspect in its effects in the phenomenal world.[147]

In the final analysis, there can be said to be only one Cause, whose Effect is manifestation. But to invoke again the aid of the law of correspondence, like cycles-within-cycles, there are microcauses too—or at least what appear to be microcauses. The real cause is the causeless cause, the Absolute, and all micro- or contingent causes, and thus all micro- or contingent effects, proceed from the first cause. This is not a tautology; it is a metaphysical first principle, interdependent with the others, and beyond the powers of reason to apprehend. One can only "construct" absolute causality and relative causality, the latter being

frequently expressed as the proverbial "chicken and the egg" argument. But the concept of karma would inhere in both aspects of causality. Karma, or action, is therefore the "action of linking" or the
"linking process" in the Traditional and theosophic perception of causality, restated here by Coomaraswamy: "The traditional and orthodox
doctrine is a recognition of the causal chain by which all events are
*linked* in a phenomenal succession, but of their intrinsic and not
extrinsic operation."[148] In other words, viewed from *instasis* or inherent unity and wholeness (via gnosis), this process is seen as one giant,
universal cause, with one giant universal effect; viewed from *extasis*
or apparent multiplicity and differentiation, this process is seen as
innumerable causes with innumerable effects. And karma, or action,
adjusts and so pervades the entire process, regardless of how it is perceived.

GNOSEOLOGY

The last of the first principles to be considered here, by which the
intricacies of the former ones are apprehended, constitutes the great
dividing line between modern Western philosophy and the Tradition.
Like the *coincidentia oppositorium*, this principle of gnosis, *prajñā*, or
intellectual intuition was briefly discussed in the preceding section. In
addition to the process and/or human faculty of intellectual intuition,
gnosis is also used to refer to the ancient wisdom or Tradition itself, but
it is the process-faculty usage of the inclusive term that is under discussion as gnoseology.

Whatever may be said about the variations in the approaches to
gnosis as a process among the Traditional and Theosophical writers,
one thing is certain: all of them unequivocally held to an intuitive
method for the comprehension of recondite metaphysical issues and for
the apprehension of metaphysical (first) principles. The precision for
which Guénon strives in this definition of the faculty gives us a better
insight into its nature:

> To be more precise, it should be said that the faculty we are
> now referring to is intellectual intuition, the reality of which
> has been consistently denied by modern philosophy, which
> has failed to grasp its real nature whenever it has not preferred
> simply to ignore it; this faculty can also be called the pure

intellect, following the practice of Aristotle and his Scholastic successors, for to them the intellect was in fact that faculty which possessed a direct knowledge of principle.[149]

Schuon, following Guénon, states in his book *Gnosis* that this faculty "is our participation in the 'perspective' of the divine Subject." The renowned scholar of Gnosticism, Elaine Pagels, though neither a Traditionalist nor a Theosophist, also speaks of gnosis as intuition: "The name [Gnostic] comes from the Greek word *gnosis*, which can be translated 'knowledge.' It does not mean intellectual or scientific knowledge, but intuitive knowledge. It is like the German *kennen*, as distinct from *wissen*, or the French *connaître*, as distinct from *savoir*."[150] Kelley, citing Eckhart, states that "when Eckhart says that 'nothing is more true than detached intellection grounded in pure Intellect Itself,' he means that it is indefectable from the fact that its knowledge is immediate and because, not being really distinct from its object, it is knowledge through identity."[151]

Coomaraswamy's perception and expressions of the concept of gnosis have already been discussed and shown to be intimately connected to Plato's theory of anamnesis. But he states in one very incisive sentence in a footnote to "*Svayamātṛṇṇā*: Janua Coeli," that "The direction of a lower heaven attainable by merit and a higher attainable only by *gnosis* is one of the basic formulae of the Philosophia Perennis and is strongly emphasized in the Upaniṣads."[152] Blavatsky completes the consensus: "The whole essence of truth *cannot be transmitted from mouth to ear*. Nor can any pen describe it, not even that of the recording Angel, unless man finds the answer in the sanctuary of his own heart, in the innermost depths of his divine intuition."[153] Even the professed "empiricist" Carl Jung states:

> My psychological experience has shown time and again that certain contents issue from a psyche more complete than consciousness. They often contain a superior analysis or insight or knowledge which consciousness has not been able to produce. We have a suitable word for such occurrences—intuition.[154]

The number of possible quotes on this topic is endless. The point is sufficiently made: the intellectual intuition is a fundamental axiom of the Tradition and theosophy, ancient and modern. This assertion is, in fact, the subject of a book by Dan Merkur entitled *Gnosis: An Esoteric Tradition of Mystical Visions and Unions* (Albany, 1993), which traces the principle in Western and Islamic culture, and whose chapter 5 provides a useful definition of the term.

The correlations and ramifications of gnosis are both numerous and profound. More accurately, it should be said that the subjects of gnosis are profound, primarily those of hierarchy and axiology. The notion of hierarchy, symbolized by the vertical *axis mundi* in its multiplicity of forms, in turn implies a hierarchical arrangement of the constituents of each person, one of them being the *nous* or *manas* principle, which Coomaraswamy so consistently refers to, for example, in his essay entitled "Manas." Again, by the law of correspondence, the emanation of the "One Life in a descending and reascending scale of hierarchic degrees," as Blavatsky phrases it, is seen equally in the hierarchic constituents of each individual. These constituents, described as "bodies," "sheaths," "vehicles," "envelopes," and so forth, depending upon the writer, range from the densest corporeality to the finest spiritual or intuitional mode. In G. R. S. Mead's *Doctrine of the Subtle Body*, for example, a sevenfold constitution of man's constituents is outlined, further condensed in a chapter in his *The World-Mystery* entitled "The Vestures of the Soul." J. J. Poortman did for these "vestures" what Mircea Eliade has done for "Religious Ideas" in his four-volume *Vehicles of Consciousness*—that is, drawing from the world's religious texts everything pertaining to these vehicles. In *Man and His Becoming According to the Vedānta*, Guénon outlines "The Envelopes of the 'Self'; the Five Vayus or Vital Function," and elaborates further on this subject in *Les États multiples de l'etre*.

Whatever the system and however many "bodies" are attributed to each person—it usually varies from three to seven, according to the context—the important points are that they are all in essential agreement as to the existence of several denser and subtler bodies as constituting the human individual; that these bodies represent different functions and are arranged hierarchically; and that one of these bodies on the subtlest end of the scale is the seat of the intellectual intuition. Metaphysically, the intelligible realm is perceived via the medium of pure Intellect, and since "The inseparability of value and reality is the one constant character of the intelligible world . . . a world in which they were divorced would no longer be intelligible."[155] Thus, hierarchy and axiology are intrinsically related, and ultimately determinable by intellectual intuition.

Kelley, in discussing Eckhart's views, declares that "The hierarchical relationship holds within each species as well as between species."[156] This notion brings us to the troublesome question of a spiritual *elect* or *elite*, in Guénon's words, and of the "Brotherhood" or "Lodge," as those terms were used by Blavatsky. By reason of its being a logical sequitur, there must be, in the Traditional view, a hierarchy of *homo intuitionis*—a group of those with an irrepressible zetetic impulse who have developed their latent, inherent intuitive capabilities (through yogic disciplines or otherwise) to an extraordinary degree. Such a group would be something like an association of *jīvanmuktas*, like the *pneumatics* of the Hellenistic Gnostics, though not in the ludicrous sense of a corporate organization or association with bylaws, and so on.

Coomaraswamy is mute on the subject, except for an etymological discussion of the term *Mahātmā,* which he published as an essay under that title in 1939. Guénon, however, is not so laconic. On the one hand, he totally rejects the association of Mahātmās to which Blavatsky makes constant reference, saying they did not exist and were her creation alone. On the other hand, he devotes a whole chapter in *Orient et Occident* to discussing the "Constitution et role de l'Élite"—the elite consisting of liberated or near-liberated individuals who act as guides, teachers, and applicators of metaphysical principles to mundane existence. Elsewhere he states that knowledge of "The Language of the Birds" is the "prerogative of a high initiation," and that "degrees of initiation" are part of and identical to "spiritual hierarchies." Guénon did not reject Blavatsky's brotherhood on the grounds that such a brotherhood or elite could not exist in reality; rather he rejected it because he believed Blavatsky to have been a fraud. Thus, none of the Traditional or Theosophical writers discounts either the possibility, feasibility, or indeed, the desirability of such an organization of illuminati who, by virtue of their activated *siddhis* and highly developed intuitions, would act as mediators between the society at large and the sublime and rationally inscrutable first principles of metaphysics. In fact, Guénon adds that this elite—whom he also refers to as "guardians" of the earth's "Sacred Land" or mysteries—currently has a further obligation with respect to this Sacred Land. He writes that "this Sacred Land, defended by guardians who keep it hidden from profane view while assuring nevertheless certain exterior communications, is in effect invisible and inaccessible except for those who possess the requisite qualifications for entry."[157] This statement does not merely approximate Blavatsky's assertion of the fact of such guardians that she made decades before Guénon wrote; it repeats the same fact.

The philosophia perennis, theosophy, and the metaphysical first principles, all as outlined in the preceding pages, is the vocation and purpose and defining essence of this group of illuminati. In the tradition of Socrates, Ammonius Saccas, Plotinus, and Coomaraswamy, they would not advertise themselves, but would, within their circle of students and friends, help "step down" the lofty first principles of the Tradition, thereby making elements of these principles accessible to the culture as a whole. Guénon proposes that "a numerically small but well-established elite would suffice in order to give direction to the mass, which would respond to its suggestions without having the slightest idea of its existence or the means of its function."[158] Thus, lines of communication are established between the intelligible realm of metaphysics and the sensible realm of culture, as has always been the condition in Traditional cultures. These lines of communication can be dysfunctional or nonexistent, and Coomaraswamy and Guénon so perceive them in modern Western culture. They can also be functional and harmonious, as they see them in archaic Traditional cultures and (though in serious decline) in some modern Eastern cultures. In the following Part, attention will be given to this transformation of higher intelligible principles into sensible expression—that is, to how these first principles manifest in human cultures.

# NOTES TO PART II

1. Schuon, *Islam and the Perennial Philosophy*, pp. vii–viii. See p. 534 in Nasr's *The Essential Writings of Frithjof Schuon* on "Sophia Perennis."

2. Guénon, *Hindu*, pp. 113, 119.

3. Coomaraswamy, *SPM*, p. 324.

4. Ibid., p. 7. The reference to Augustine, uncited by Coomaraswamy in this passage, is to his *Confessions*, Book 9, section 10. The Penguin Classics edition, translated by R. S. Pine-Coffin, gives the following sentence: "But that Wisdom is not made: it is as it has always been and as it will be forever—or, rather I should not say that it *has been* or *will be*, for it simply *is*, because eternity is not in the past or in the future" (p. 197).

5. Guénon, *Crise*, pp. 25, 26.

6. Coomaraswamy, *SPM*, p. 344n.

7. See, for example, Huston Smith's "Two Traditions—and Philosophy" in *Religion of the Heart* ed. S. H. Nasr and W. Stoddart; the section in Part 8 of S. H. Nasr's *The Essential Writings of Frithjof Schuon* titled "Criticism of Modern Philosophy."

8. Sawicki, "Die Geschichtsphilosophie als Philosophia Perennis," in Fritz-Joachim von Rintelen (ed.), *Philosophia Perennis*, volume 1, p. 519.

9. Schmitt, *De PP*, p. ix.

10. Weber, "The Reluctant Tradition," p. 99.

11. Ryan, *An Introduction to Philosophy*, p. 381.

12. Jaspers, *The Perennial Scope of Philosophy*, p. 173.

13. Ibid., p. 174.

14. Ibid., pp. 174–75.

15. Schmitt, "PP:ASL," p. 522.

16. Ryan, op. cit., p. 382.

17. Guénon, *OEO*, p. 140. See also F. Schuon's *Logic and Transcendence*, which gives a fuller exposition of Guénon's position.

18. One could doubtless cite many exceptions to this admitted generalization, but we are speaking here of trends and not of individual philosophies. However, even within the category of trends, exceptions to this are possible. It should be noted that other modern trends are to be found in secular existentialism and nihilism, neither of which is progressive or positivistic. One often sees nihilism, for example, referred to as the nadir of philosophy, an apposite representative of the logical conclusion of life in modernity, having its artistic expressions not only in Ivan Turgenev, Feodor Dostoevski and the "Russian school," but in Dada of the 1920s and Punk of the 1980s.

19. Schmitt, *De PP*, p. v.

20. Huxley, *The Perennial Philosophy*, p. vii.

21. Manzanedo, "Los Refranes y la 'Filosofía Perenne,'" p. 426.

22. Schmitt, "PP:ASL," p. 506.

23. Schmitt, *De PP*, p. xiv.

24. The famous letter in question, dated August 26, 1714, and sent to Nicolas Rémond in Paris, contains this frequently cited paragraph: "La vérité est plus répandue qu'on ne pense, mais elle est très souvnet fardée . . . et ce seroit en effect perennis quaedam Philosophia." Taken from C. J. Gerhardt (ed.), *Die philosophischen Schriften von Gottfried Wilhelm Leibniz* (Berlin, 1875–90), volume 3, pp. 624–25.

25. Meyer, "Leibniz und die Philosophia Perennis," p. 244.

26. "J'ai vu Augustinus Steuchus Jugubinus de perenni philosophia, mais son dessein est principalement d'accomoder les anciens au christianisme (ce qui est en effect très beau), plustot que de mettre les pensées de philosophie dans leur jour." Taken from C. J. Gerhardt, op. cit., volume 1, p. 395; q.v. n. 23.

27. Schmitt, "PP:ASL," p. 520.

28. Yates, *Giordano Bruno and the Hermetic Tradition*, pp. 14, 17.

29. Schmitt, "PP:ASL," p. 518.

30. Manzanedo, op. cit., p. 426.

31. Collins, *Three Paths in Philosophy*, p. 278.

32. Ibid., p. 262. Cf. Schmitt, "PP:ASL," p. 505.

33. The tenuousness and limitations of these concluding points are serious. First, the percentage of modern philosophers who even address the question of the philosophia perennis is minuscule, even *with* the condition

that it is more likely than not that some have been overlooked. Thus, the conclusions regarding the philosophia perennis are based on the writings of those cited herein. Second, of these modern philosophers there is no consensus at all as to what it is or what it means—that is, whether the philosophia perennis is immutable, a hybrid, eclectic, syncretic, atavistic, or simply factitious. Third, and finally, there is a general reluctance among most of this exiguous number of "accredited" philosophers to conjecture, to enumerate specifically any fundamental principles they deem inherent in the philosophia perennis. We are therefore compelled to make our own determination of the common denominators and list them accordingly.

34. Manzanedo, op. cit., p. 426.

35. Coomaraswamy, *SPTAS*, p. 539.

36. Urban, who was Professor of Philosophy at Yale University, had three major book-length works that dealt extensively with the philosophia perennis, each separated by a decade. Chronologically listed, they are *The Intelligible World: Metaphysics and Value* (New York, 1929); *Language and Reality* (London, 1939); and *Beyond Realism and Idealism* (London, 1949).

37. Sawicki, op. cit., p. 516. "Die philosophia perennis bejaht die metaphysische Idee."

38. Coomaraswamy, *SPM*, p. 412. Cf. ibid., p. 421, and *SPTAS*, pp. 330, 327–28n.

39. Urban, *The Intelligible World*, pp. 177–78.

40. Coomaraswamy, *SPTAS*, p. 411.

41. Coomaraswamy, *SPM*, p. 165.

42. Schmitt, "PP:ASL," p. 531.

43. Urban, *The Intelligible World*, p. 175.

44. Urban, *Beyond Realism and Idealism*, p. 258.

45. Coomaraswamy, *SPM*, p. 6.

46. Guénon, *Crise*, p. 25. The sacrality of the philosophia perennis in the Traditional view is clearly expressed by Schuon on pp. 194–95 of *Islam and the Perennial Philosophy*. There he states, "The inward and timeless Revelation is still present, but it is hidden away beneath a sheet of ice which necessitates the intervention of outward Revelations; but these cannot have the perfection of what might be termed 'innate Religion' or the immanent *philosophia perennis*."

47. Radhakrishnan, *History of Philosophy, Eastern and Western*, volume 2, p. 447. In discussing certain similarities between Radhakrishnan and the Traditionalists, there is no intention to imply that the former was of the Traditional school. In fact, Coomaraswamy once took Radhakrishnan to task in a review of his *Eastern Religions and Western Thought*, which Coomaraswamy claimed exhibited more of a European than a Hindu mentality.

48. Coomaraswamy, *SPM*, Pp. 7.

49. Sawicki, op. cit., p. 523.

50. Jaspers, op. cit., p. 176.

51. Urban, *Language and Reality*, p. 707.

52. Urban, *Beyond Realism and Idealism*, p. 254.

53. Coomaraswamy, *SPTAS*, p. 49.

54. Guénon, *Crise*, p. 67.

55. Using the same mode followed earlier in distinguishing the Tradition from "a tradition," for the same reason (i.e., the capitalization of the term by those who themselves used it in a particularized way), the capitalized "T" forms of Theosophy and Theosophist will hereinafter refer to the modern reformulation of theosophic principles within the Theosophical Society and to its members respectively. The uncapitalized theosophy or *theosophia* will refer to the more inclusive generic meaning within which such diverse characters as Henry S. Olcott and Professor Max Müller could feel comfortable in referring to themselves "theosophists." Cf. Godwin, *The Theosophical Englightenment*, p. xii.

56. Jackson, "Theosophy," *Encyclopedia Britannica*. Chicago, 1979.

57. Wilder, *New Platonism and Alchemy*, p. 3.

58. Paul Schmitt, "Ancient Mysteries and Their Transformation," in *The Mysteries*, p. 110.

59. Rahner, "The Christian Mystery and the Pagan Mysteries," in ibid., p. 348.

60. Nasr, *Sufi Essays*, p. 97. Italics mine. Schuon also uses the term, in reference to the "German Theosophists," whom he believes were examples of a manifestation of *gnosis*. *Islam and the Perennial Philosophy*, p. 27.

61. Siémons, *Theosophia in Neo-Platonic and Christian Literature*, pp. 4, 24. See also Bruce Campbell, who wrote that "The term theosophy, meaning divine wisdom, had become common in the seventeenth century. It

was used to refer to the strain of occult, mystical speculation associated with the Kabala and with the writings of such occultists as Agrippa, Paracelsus, and Fludd." *Ancient Wisdom Revived*, p. 28.

62. The entire Greek tract of the "Leiden Magical Papyrus W" was redacted and published in full in a book entitled *Abraxas*, a Festschrift for Hermann Usener, ed. A. Dieterich (Leipzig, 1891). Since the exact date of the papyrus is uncertain, there is no way to determine which text—Porphyry's or the magical papyrus—preceded the other.

63. Poortman, *Philosophy, Theosophy, and Parapsychology*, p. 50.

64. Max Müller, *Theosophy, or Psychological Religion*, p. xvi.

65. Müller and H. S. Olcott, president of the Theosophical Society from 1875 to 1907, carried on an amiable correspondence for over twenty years—until Müller's death in 1900. Müller, in fact, had once invited Olcott to visit him at Oxford, which Olcott did. This was in 1889, and Olcott records that Müller had insisted he meet Sir William W. Hunter and Professor E. B. Tylor, which meeting Müller arranged. In Olcott's six-volume memoir, *Old Diary Leaves*, he excerpts a portion of a letter from Müller, stating, "Professor Müller was so kind to say that the Oriental reprinting, translation, and publishing portion of the Society's work was 'noble, and there could be no two opinions about it, nor were there among Orientalists'" (volume 4, p. 60).

66. Ellwood, *Religious and Spiritual Groups in Modern America*, p. xiii. An excellent treatment of seventeenth- and eighteenth-century European theosophical writers, into which a discussion of the conceptual and definitional aspects of the term theosophy is integrated, appears in Antoine Faivre's *Access to Western Esotericism* (Albany 1994), pp. 23–32.

67. Eliade, "Some Notes on *Theosophia Perennis* . . . ," p. 169.

68. Poortman, op cit., p. 54. In this connection, the esoteric or theosophic origins of the Eranos conferences are very literally unequivocal. The conferences were begun under the impetus of Alice Bailey who, in 1924, left her position in the Theosophical Society in America and eventually founded the Arcane School. In collaboration with Dr. Roberto Assagioli, the Italian psychiatrist and founder of Psycho-Synthesis, the two directed activities at Ascona for the first few years. The fact that Bailey was the major impetus for the conferences is one that Joseph Campbell and Olga Fröebe-Kapteyn would apparently like to forget. But Bailey, in her *The Unfinished Autobiography* (New York: Lucis, 1951), records a visit by Olga Fröebe to the Baileys' home in Stanford, Connecticut, in 1930: "She [Olga Fröebe] suggested the idea that with our help she should start a spiritual center at Ascona near Locarno on Lake Maggiore and that it should be undenominational, nonsectarian and

open to esoteric thinkers and occult students of all groups in Europe and else-where" (p. 217). The outcome of this, and the relationship with Dr. Assagioli, is given in another paragraph: "The talks by Dr. Assagioli were outstanding features of the Ascona conferences. He would lecture in French, Italian, and English and the spiritual power that poured through him was the means of stimulating many into renewed consecration in life. For the first two years he and I carried the bulk of the lecture work though there were other able and interesting speakers. The last year we were there (1933) the place was over- run by German professors and the whole tone and quality of the place altered. Some of them were most undesirable and the teaching given shifted from a relatively high spiritual plane to that of academic philosophy and a spurious esotericism" (p. 225).

69. Eliade, op. cit., p. 173.

70. Ibid., p. 176. Cf. Campbell, op. cit., pp. 197–98.

71. Sydney E. Ahlstrom, *A Religious History of the American People*, volume 2. An Image Book. New York: Doubleday, 1975, p. 553.

72. H. S. Olcott, "Inaugural Address," in *Inaugural Addresses of Four Presidents of the Theosophical Society*. Adyar: Theosophical Publishing House, 1946. Radha Burnier, "Inaugural Address," *The Theosophist*, August 1980 (101:11) p. 494.

73. The three declared objects of the Society have a history in them- selves, having changed several times—though they retained essentially the same principles—since the inception of the Society. As they appear today, the objects are: "(1) To form a nucleus of the universal brotherhood of humanity, without distinction of race, creed, sex, caste, or color; (2) to encourage the study of comparative religion, philosophy, and science; and (3) to investigate unexplained laws of nature and the powers latent in man." Recently, some gender-neutral versions of the above using different language have been proffered by individuals who wish to have such a version adopted by the Society.

74. Geertz, "Religion as a Cultural System, p. 4.

75. Campbell, *Ancient Wisdom Revisited: A History of the Theosophi- cal Movement*, p. 4. To date there are approximately eighteen biographies of Blavatsky, depending on whether one accepts "memories of" and "remini- sciences of" as biography, or a mixture of these with some biographical data. Of these eighteen, about half are encomia and half are indictments. The spec- ulations regarding these twenty-three unaccountable years tend to place Blav- atsky in various spiritual retreats learning occult and metaphysical lore on the one hand, or living the high lowlife with profligate excesses on the other. The

latest "definitive" biography, Sylvia Cranston's account entitled *HPB: The Extraordinary Life and Influence of Helena Blavatsky, Founder of the Modern Theosophical Movement* (New York, 1993), leans toward the former speculation. Although her book is punctuated with occasional references to that time, Cranston admits, "After her departure from Russia [1849], HPB's life [to 1872] is not easy to document." p. 42.

76. H. P. Blavatsky, *Theosophical Glossary*. London: The Theosophical Publishing Society, 1892. p. 238.

77. The booklet *Practical Occultism* (Adyar: Theosophical Publishing House, 1972) is actually a posthumous compilation that first appeared in 1948 of two articles that appeared in early numbers of *Lucifer*, under the titles "Practical Occultism" and "Occultism versus the Occult Arts." The first citation is found on page 32 of the booklet, and the second is found on page 43— the italics are Blavatsky's.

78. There are no book-length or separate bibliographies on the history and influence of the Theosophical movement, though there are several histories. The best bibliographies are to be found in James A. Santucci's *Theosophy and the Theosophical Society* (pp. 29–35); Bruce Campbell's *Ancient Wisdom Revived* (pp. 409–514); Robert Ellwood's *Religious and Spiritual Groups in Modern America* (pp. 305–12); Boris de Zirkoff's "Index and Bibliography" to *The Secret Doctrine* (pp. 409–514); Alvin Boyd Kuhn's *Theosophy* (pp. 351–73); and Charles J. Ryan's *H. P. Blavatsky and the Theosophical Movement* (pp. 325–35). One cannot overlook the monumental work of Michael Gomes, *Theosophy in the Nineteenth Century*, an annotated bibliography, but as its title indicates it is limited to the last decades of the nineteenth century. The library at the national headquarters of the Theosophical Society in America prints a lengthy annotated bibliography of its holdings, which includes a short section on the Society's history. Of the histories per se there are Campbell's, Santucci's, and Ryan's just cited, plus Joy Mills's *100 Years of Theosophy: A History of the Theosophical Society in America* (Wheaton, IL: Theosophical Publishing House, 1987) and Michael Gomes's *The Dawning of the Theosophical Movement* (Wheaton, IL: Theosophical Publishing House, 1987). The rest range from somewhat to highly tendentious, and include the anonymous *The Theosophical Movement 1875–1925* (New York: E. P. Dutton, 1925) and *The Theosophical Movement 1875–1950* (Los Angeles: Cunningham, 1951); Josephine Ransom's *A Short History of the Theosophical Society* (Adyar: Theosophical Publishing House, 1938) and *The Seventy-Fifth Anniversary Book of the Theosophical Society* (Adyar: Theosophical Publishing House, 1950); René Guénon's *Le Theosophisme: Histoire d'une pseudo-religion*; and C. Jinarajadasa's *The Golden Book of the Theosophical Society* (Adyar: Theosophical Publishing House,

1925). Other books contain much valuable historical information; among these are J. Stillson Judah's *The History and Philosophy of the Metaphysical Movements in America*; Charles Braden's *These Also Believe: A Study of Modern American Cults and Minority Religious Movements* (New York: Macmillan, 1949); Sven Eek's *Damodar and the Pioneers of the Theosophical Movement* (Adyar: Theosophical Publishing House, 1955); and Henry S. Olcott's six-volume *Old Diary Leaves*.

79. Judah, *The History and Philosophy of the Metaphysical Movements in America*, p. 7.

80. Campbell, op. cit., p. 1.

81. Ellwood, *Alternative Altars*, p. 137.

82. Santucci, *Theosophy and the Theosophical Society*, p. 9.

83. Lipsey, *CLW*, p. 31. Cf. Coomaraswamy, *SL*, p. 127.

84. Ibid. Coomaraswamy respected Bhagavan Das's ability as a Sanskritist, and relied on Das and Besant's translation of the *Bhagavad-Gītā* (1895) in his research. *SL*, p. 78.

85. In Bagchee, *Ananda Coomaraswamy: A Study*, p. 125.

86. In the years 1909 and 1910, Coomaraswamy submitted seven short explanatory pieces on Indian art to *The Theosophist*, which were all published. They are, in chronological order, "Dharmapāla or Bhairava: (31:2) 140; "Sundara Mūrti Svāmi: (31:2) 273: "Raginī Torī" (31:11) 1473; "Shiva's Dance" (31:12) 1619; "Shiva Rātri" (32:1) 140; "Lailā and Majnūn: (32:2) 297; and "Baz Bahādur and Rūpmatī" (32:3) 450. Perhaps *Main Currents in Modern Thought* is a tenuous link qua "theosophical journal," but it was begun in 1940 by Fritz L. Kunz, who was its editor until his death in 1972. Fritz Kunz was a lifelong member of the Theosophical Society, and spent many years in Ceylon continuing the work that Olcott began. He was also a personal friend of Coomaraswamy's. After Fritz Kunz's death, the editorship was assumed by Henry Margenau and Mrs. Emily Sellon, the latter another lifelong member of the Society. As an interesting aside, Fritz's wife, Dora Kunz, was president of the Theosophical Society in America from 1976 to 1986; her vice-president for that tenure was Mrs. Emily Sellon.

87. Coomaraswamy, *SPM*, pp. 6, 16.

88. Floyd H. Ross, unpublished paper, printed and distributed by the Theosophical Society in America. As another interesting aside, Ross was one of three professors on the Supervisory Committee of John Hatfield's dissertation on the Traditional thought of Coomaraswamy.

89. Webb, *The Harmonious Circle*, p. 501.

90. "... nous ajouterons que le meilleur moyen de combattre le theosophisme, c'est, a notre avis, d'exposer son histoire telle qu'elle est."

91. In *Orient et Occident* (p. 13) Guénon gives a short, impuissant defense of his "methode historique": "nous pensons avoir montré ailleurs* [*Le Theosophisme: histoire d'une pseudo-religion], et sans nous mettre le moins du monde en contradiction avec nous-même, que nous sommes capable, lorsqu'il le faut, d'appliquer cette méthode tout aussi bien qu'un autre, et cela devrait suffire à prouver que nous n'avons point de parti pris." ("[W]e think we have shown elsewhere* ... and without in the least contradicting ourselves, that we are just as capable of applying this method as anyone else, and this should be sufficient to prove that we have no prejudice.")

92. Perry, "The Revival of Interest in Tradition," in *The Unanimous Tradition*, p. 11. While Perry confines himself to criticism of Guénon's "historical" method, Frithjof Schuon takes Guénon to task for more fundamental errors. In his contribution to *Les Dossiers H: "René Guénon"* (Pierre-Marie Sigaud, ed. Lausanne: L'Age d'Homme, 1984) entitled "Quelques critiques," Schuon levels some startling broadsides aimed at Guénon, not the least of which is a criticism of Guénon's criticism in *Le Théosophisme* of the Theosophists' views on reincarnation, citing his lack of familiarity with the *manavadharma sastra*.

93. Eliade, op. cit., p. 169.

94. Eliade, *Occultism, Witchcraft, and Cultural Fashion*, pp. 51, 65.

95. Regarding the word *system*, the cliché says it best: It is used "for lack of a better word." Coomaraswamy would have objected: "This consistency of the Philosophia Perennis is indeed good ground for 'faith' ... but as this 'philosophy' is neither a 'system' nor a 'philosophy,' it cannot be argued for or against" (*SPM*, p. 90fn.). Guénon would also have objected: "Pas plus que le métaphysique vraie ne peut s'enfermer dans les formules d'un systéme ou d'une théorie particuliére" (*OEO*, p. 190). (Never can true metaphysic be incarcerated within the formulas of any particular system or theory.) Against their objections, and with reluctance, the term *system* will be used anyway. The "true metaphysic" is one, but its expressions—the various "systems" in which it finds expression—are manifold.

96. Mead, *Fragments of a Faith Forgotten*. London and Benares: Theosophical Publishing Society, 1900. p. 8.

97. I am fully aware that any attempted comparison between the expression of theosophy by Blavatsky and the principles of the Tradition as

professed by Coomaraswamy, Guénon, and the later Traditionalist writers—most notably Schuon—will be enough for many of the Traditional school to dismiss this work as meritless and confused. Others will hold that but for the introduction of Blavatsky into this work, it would have been a valuable contribution, but that the effect of the Blavatsky comparison is fatal. We believe this propensity is due to a lack of personal familiarity with Blavatsky's works that is explained by an established prejudice within the Traditional school against Blavatsky and modern Theosophy since the 1921 publication of *Le Théosophisme* by Guénon that highlighted the later historical excesses of the movement and ignored the metaphysical content, for example, of *The Secret Doctrine*. Moreover, we also believe an honest and objective study of Blavatsky's works by such Traditionalist critics would reveal to them that much of what Guénon alleged initially plus what was repeated uncritically in the later literature—for example, Blavatsky's supposed views about transmigration and evolution—is in fact incorrect.

98. Schuon, *The Transcendent Unity of Religions*, p. 16.

99. Guénon, *OEO*, pp. 167–68.

100. Blavatsky, *SD I*, p. xxxvi.

101. Coomaraswamy, *SPM*, p. 40.

102. See my paper entitled "Ananda Coomaraswamy on the Philosophia Perennis" in *Re-Vision* (2:2) 1979: 18–27.

103. Coomaraswamy, *SPM*, p. 37.

104. The lexicon of metaphysics—and for that matter of mysticism, theosophy, parapsychology, and so on—is a quagmire of confusion. Depending on whom one reads, two different terms may refer to the same principle or, conversely, the same term may refer to two different principles. The situation is, of course, exacerbated in the realm of comparative metaphysics. The terminological problems are less as they apply to one given expression or system such as Plotinus's or Aquinas's or Śaṅkara's. Still, definitional *nuance* can differ within given single systems. The problem is neither new nor unnoticed: Ludwig Wittgenstein devoted his best efforts to making others aware of it in the area of general philosophy, and we have already cited several instances of Coomaraswamy's and Guénon's deprecation of the misuse of language. The additional point that we wish to make here is that beyond "philosophy" per se, metaphysics is more liable to terminological confusion and comparative metaphysics even more so. Thus, for certain "standard" terms in the world's metaphysical systems whose English renderings are Absolute, One, Being, Becoming, Essence, Substance, Intelligible, Sensible, Phenomenal, Noumenal, God, Godhead, and so on, one cannot assume a consensus or

agreement of definition but must clarify and correlate the terms as they are used.

105. Coomaraswamy, *SPTAS*, p. 75n.

106. Blavatsky, *SD I*, p. 14.

107. Schuon, *Islam and the Perennial Philosophy*, p. 97.

108. Here is a good example of terminological disparity as mentioned in n.104. The One is described in Plato's *Parmenides* as if it were the Absolute: "So the one, since is 'is' in no sense whatever, must not possess being or lose or acquire it in any way. Therefore the one which is not, not possessing being in any sense, neither ceases to be nor comes to be" (163d; F. M. Cornford's translation). Cf. Kelley, *Meister Eckhart on Divine Knowledge*, p. 251, n.25: "Only since the sixteenth century has the term 'existence' been commonly used for *esse*, and this unfortunate usage has led to much confusion by actually distorting and restricting the metaphysical significance of *esse*." See also James Olney's learned discussion of this principle generally in chapter 4 of his *The Rhizome and the Flower: The Perennial Philosophy—Yeats and Jung*, and in particular of Parmenides' views on pp. 130–34.

109. Guénon, *Vedānta*, p. 164.

110. Augustine, *De Genesi ad litteram*, p. 8. Translation by B. F. Kelley.

111. Aquinas, *Summa Theologica* I, q 10, a l; a 4; and *Commentarium I Sententiarum* xix, q 11, a 2. Translation by B. F. Kelley.

112. Henry Corbin, "The Time of Eranos," in *Man and Time*, p. xviii.

113. Puech, "Gnosis and Time," p. 83, and Eliade, "Time and Eternity in Indian Thought," p. 187 (italics mine), both in *Man and Time*.

114. Coomaraswamy, *Time and Eternity*, p. 3.

115. Coomaraswamy, *SPM*, p. 60.

116. Guénon, *Croix*, p. 238. ("métaphysiquement, il n'est jamais question d'antériorité' et de 'postériorité' que dans le sens d'un enchaînement causal et purement logique, qui ne saurait exclure la similtanéité de toutes choses dans l'éternal présent.'")

117. Blavatsky, *SD I*, p. 37.

118. Poortman, *Vehicles of Consciousness*, volume 4, p. 231.

119. Urban, *Language and Reality*, p. 707.

120. Eliade, "Time and Eternity in Indian Thought," in *Man and Time*, p. 179.

121. Guénon, *Crise*, p. 16.

122. Guénon, *Formes traditionnelles et cycles cosmique*, p. 14. See also the chapter in *La Grande Triade* titled "La Roue Cosmique" where he discusses the dynamics of the "cycle of manifestation." For an insightful analysis of the relationship between the principle of cycles and their symbols in Guénon's work, see pages 193–96 of Marilyn Gustin's "The Nature, Role and Interpretation of Symbol in the Thought of René Guénon."

123. Coomaraswamy, *SPM*, p. 398.

124. Blavatsky, *SD I*, p. 17.

125. Ibid., p. 16n. Guénon's chapter "Résidus psychiques" in *Règne* is almost *verbatim* the same argument Blavatsky used against the spiritualists some decades earlier.

126. Coomaraswamy, *SPM*, p. 17. Cf. ibid., p. 296.

127. Guénon, *Croix*, p. 236.

128. Coomaraswamy, *SPM*, p. 18.

129. Blavatsky, *SD I*, p. 119.

130. Eliade, *The Quest*, p. 43. In *Yoga: Immortality and Freedom* (Princeton, 1969), Professor Eliade writes: "It is important that we understand the notion of evolution in Sāṃkhya. *Pariṇamā* signifies development of what exists, *in posse*, in the *mahat*. It is not a creation, nor a transcendence, nor the realization of new species of existence, but simply the realization of the potentialities that exist in *prakṛti* (under its living aspect, the *mahat*). To compare 'evolution' in the Indian sense with Western evolutionism is to be guilty of great confusion" (pp. 21–22). This indictment would apply equally for anyone who confused evolution in Blavatsky's sense with "Western evolutionism."

131. Coomaraswamy *SPM*, p. 14.

132. Guénon, *Vedānta*, p. 123. See also *Croix*, chapter 22, first footnote, where he discusses "individual evolution" and repeats his own definition as "the development of a given set of possibilities."

133. Blavatsky, *SD I*, p. 219.

134. Ibid., p. 416. Among the best encapsulations of the Traditional (and we would add theosophic) view of modern evolutionism as a whole is found in Smith's *Forgotten Truth* (pp. 129–39). See also Whitall Perry's full-length treatment titled *The Widening Breach: Evolutionism in the Mirror of Cosmology* (Cambridge: Quinta Essentia, 1995) and Titus Burckhardt's dis-

cussion of "evolutionism" in *Mirror of the Intellect* (p. 32). Nasr, in a stinging *coup d'assommoir*, writes: "Wallace and Darwin did not induce the theory of evolution from their observations. Rather, in a world in which the Divinity had been either denied or relegated to the role of the maker of the clock, and where sapiential wisdom based on the contemplation of the higher states of being had become practically inaccessible in the West, the theory of evolution seemed the best way of providing a background for the study of the amazing diversity of life forms without having to turn to the creative power of God. The theory of evolution soon turned to a dogma, precisely because it rapidly replaced religious faith and provided what appeared to be a 'scientific' crutch for the soul to enable it to forget God. It has therefore survived to this day, not as a theory but as a dogma, among many scientists whose world view would crumble if they were but to take evolution for what it is—namely, a convenient philosophical and rationalistic scheme to enable man to create the illusion of a purely closed Universe around himself. That is also why logical and scientific arguments against it have been treated not at all rationally and scientifically, but with a violence and passion that reveals the pseudoreligious role played by the theory of evolution among its exponents." "Progress and Evolution" in *Parabola* 6:2 (Spring 1981): 50.

135. Coomaraswamy, *SPM*, p. 398.

136. Jung, *Two Essays in Analytical Psychology*, p. 72. Jung understood the principle but incorrectly attributes it to Heraclitus, in whose extant writings the term never appears, though to be fair it is wholly consistent with the emphasis Heraclitus puts on ceaseless change and flux. On Jung's views with respect to this principle and its antecedents, and to his views of cycles and *quaternio* generally, see chapters 3 and 5 of Olney, *The Rhizome and the Flower: The Perennial Philosophy—Yeats and Jung*.

137. Jung, *Civilization in Transition*, p. 143.

138. Blavatsky, *SD II*, p. 162.

139. Guénon, *Vedānta*, p. 46.

140. Coomaraswamy, *SPM*, p. 24.

141. Jung, *Mysterium Coniunctionis*, p. 3.

142. Guénon, *Croix*, p. 114.

143. Kelley, *Meister Eckhart on Divine Knowledge*, p. 110.

144. Coomaraswamy, *SPM*, p. 31.

145. Ibid, p. 403.

146. Pallis, "Living One's Karma," in *SG*, p. 253.

147. Blavatsky, *SD II*, pp. 305–06.

148. Coomaraswamy, *SPM*, p. 368. A very similar expression of this is found in Guénon's *Vedānta*, p. 109, n.1. There he says, "Effects subsist 'eminently' in their causes, as has been said by the Scholastic philosophers, and they are therefore constituents of its nature, since nothing can be found in the effects that was not to be found in the cause first of all; thus the first cause, knowing itself, knows all effects by that very fact, that is to say it knows all things, in an absolutely direct and 'non-distinctive' manner." Elsewhere, in attacking modern Theosophical usages, Guénon writes that karma, which "means 'action,' is regularly used in the sense of 'causality,' which is worse than an inaccuracy." The reader at this point may wonder if, in light of Blavatsky's statement above, this accusation is "worse than an inaccuracy." But polemics aside, the central question is whether the relationship between cause and effect can be described as "active," thus equating to "action" or karma. An affirmative response to this last question seems a small concession indeed in light of the wide variety of uses and meanings for *karma* described by the twelve Indologists whose papers on karma appear in Wendy Doniger O'Flaherty's *Karma and Rebirth in Classical Indian Traditions*. In her introduction, Professor Doniger integrates some of the "various karmic theories" evinced from the Indic traditions themselves by the participating scholars, all of which serves to illustrate that as against the Theosophists, against the expertise of modern scholarship, and against even the later proponents of Tradition, Guénon stood quite alone in his assertion that *karma* means "action et rien d'autre."

149. Guénon, *Hindu*, p. 117.

150. Elaine Pagels, "Gnostic Texts Revive Ancient Controversies." *The Center Magazine* (September/October, 1980), p. 55. Since the discovery of the Gnostic texts at Nag Hammadi in 1946, a huge corpus of material has been published on Gnosticism. Most modern scholars, who no longer view Gnosticism as simply an early Christian heresy, define *gnosis* in terms similar to Pagels. Kurt Rudolph, for example, defines it as not "any ideal philosophical knowledge nor any knowledge of an intellectual or theoretical kind, but a knowledge which had at the same time a liberating and redeeming effect," and further one which has "an esoteric character." *Gnosis: The Nature and History of Gnosticism* (New York, 1987), p. 55.

151. Kelley, op. cit., p. 79.

152. Coomaraswamy, *SPTAS*, p. 518.

153. Blavatsky, *SD II*, p. 516.

154. Jung, *Psychology and Religion*, p. 49.

155. Urban, *The Intelligibile World*, p. 178.

156. Kelley, op. cit., p. 146.

157. Guénon, *Le roi du Monde*, p. 96. Guénon's cryptic reference to continuing "exterior communications" from these guardians is highly suggestive of the communications received, as part of an admitted "experiment," by E. O. Hume and A. P. Sinnett in India during the 1880s from two such guardians whom Blavatsky asserted were her teachers. These communications were later published as *The Mahatma Letters to A. P. Sinnett* (London: Rider, 1923). Controversy about these Mahatmas, beginning with a subsequently repudiated 1885 report of the London Society for Psychical Research, has generated a considerable volume of material among historians of the Theosophical movement, but examination of that issue is beyond the scope of this work. (See, e.g., Harrison in *Journal of the Society for Psychical Research* 53:803 [April 1986]: 286.) It should be noted that K. Paul Johnson, a prodigious researcher of historical data, postulated in *The Masters Revealed* (Albany: SUNY Press, 1994) that these Mahatmas were actual historical persons using pseudonyms, but his conclusions about their historicity are at odds with the fundamental tenets of their worldview as expressed in the writings attributed to them by Blavatsky, Sinnett, Olcott, and many others. Johnson's theses and conclusions were challenged in a review essay by the president of the Theosophical Society in America, John Algeo, which is very probably the consensus opinion of modern Theosophists about Johnson's book. "K. Paul Johnson's *The Masters Revealed*," *Theosophical History* 5, No. 7, 1995: 232–47. See also, Johnson's rebuttal to Algeo's review essay, published as "Response to John Algeo's Review of *The Masters Revealed*," *Theosophical History* 5, No. 8, 1995: 264–69.

158. Guénon, *Crise*, p. 170.

# PART III

## TRADITIONAL CULTURE

# 9

## Primitive Traditional Culture

In the two preceding Parts the focus of attention was directed toward establishing both a lexical and definitive base of terminology to be used cumulatively and subsequently as the reader progressed, and a historical, philosophical (metaphysical) background in which to place the all-important first principles of the Tradition. We now prepare to engage the difficulties presented by the applications of these terms and principles to the concept—and reality—of *culture*[1]—that is, the perspectives that Coomaraswamy, Guénon, and those of the Traditional school hold toward the cultures of humankind. One of the major difficulties, as will be seen, is in sufficiently surrendering our own powerful presuppositions and biases not only about the tacitly or unconsciously presumed superiority of modern Western scientifically industrialized cultures, but also about the similarly presumed inferiority of all the rest, especially the so-called primitive cultures. Recognition of and allowances for these biases have now become standard *modus operandi,* and the whole issue among academic cultural commentators is somewhat passé. Yet, it is worth devoting a short section to the antecedents of the problem since it will serve ultimately to clarify the perceptions of the Traditionalists on non-Western (nonindustrialized) and primitive cultures.

We have alluded in several places to the different emphases given to various aspects of the Traditional worldview by Guénon and Coomaraswamy, with the crucial addendum that their different emphases in no way implied a lack of agreement or unanimity of thought on the Traditional worldview as a whole. Not the least of these differences of emphasis, however, was that regarding the concept and phenomenon of culture. The principal subject matter of Part 3 concerns both primitive and what has been termed "developed" Traditional culture—a usage that will be explained in due course—and is primarily Coomaraswamy's jurisdiction. In the development of the thesis presented in this Part, which concerns the composition of Traditional culture, we will deal with primitive culture and the various lights in which it has been held by moderns, and will attempt to establish a definition of Traditional culture without the aid of any paradigms but drawn exclusively from the writings of the Traditional school. Finally, we will compare primitive and developed Traditional cultures, with a brief examination of certain elements of a developed Traditional culture to which the Traditional writers constantly made reference: medieval Christendom. Part 4, conversely, concerns modern Western or secular culture, and is primarily within the jurisdiction of Guénon. These two succeeding Parts, therefore, can be regarded as approximate mirror images of one another in terms of the emphasis and expertise that were applied to them by Coomaraswamy and Guénon. Moreover, what Guénon did say of primitive and Traditional culture and Coomaraswamy of modern culture is not so exiguous as might appear from what has just been said and, along with the observations of other commentators that are apposite and pertinent, will be incorporated into the argument.

PRIMARY CONSIDERATIONS

Primitive cultures, whether ancient and extinct or current and extant, have been roughly equated to designations normally applied to cultures and "stages of development" of humanity in a chronological sense. Not counting whatever cultures may have been created by *homo habilis* or other such hominids prior to *homo sapiens*, the most primitive (Latin *primus*, or "first") cultures are Paleolithic, followed by Upper Paleolithic, Mesolithic, and Neolithic. The cutoff point for the "Stone Age" (Greek *lithos*, or "stone") is the development of metallurgy, while the pivotal points of separation within the Stone Age taxonomy are fire and stone implements, stone structures, domestication of certain plants and animals, and the plantation of cereals, respectively. Thus, modern anthropologists can speak of the Tasaday of Mindanao, for example, as Paleolithic in development (i.e., "modern primitives") or the Anasazi, Hohokam, and pre-Columbian Pueblo Indians of the American Southwest as Neolithic.

Yet, there inheres in these essentially chronologic classifications a subtle but no less apparent attitude of evolutionism and progressivism based upon the predominantly quantitative standards of modern Western culture. This attitude will be treated in greater detail in the following pages. It is mentioned at this point in order to illustrate the problematic nature of such categorizations, especially in light of the fact that "The recent discoveries of paleontology have it in common that they continually push the beginnings of man and culture backwards in time. Man proves to be more ancient and his psychomental activity more complex than they were thought to be a few decades ago."[2] All evaluation, assessment, and classification requires a standard; that standard may either be quantitative or qualitative in orientation. By the quantitative standard, whose roots are in mathematics and technology, the chronologic taxonomy applied by the archaeologists, anthropologists, and paleontologists grown in the modern West may be justified. By the qualitative standard, whose roots are in values and principles (or axiology and metaphysics), certain conclusions reached by the modern Western social scientist regarding the complexity of primitive man's "psychomental activity," of which Mircea Eliade speaks, may be seriously flawed.

In essence, from the Traditional standpoint the question is not one of degrees of mentality, but of types of mentality. The types of mentality that are under consideration here are quantitative and qualitative or, to translate these types respectively into more utilitarian terms, historical and mythological.[3] History is predicated on factuality and the placment of events within numerical units of rectilinear time, is primarily quantitative, and from it springs the classifications of Paleolithic to Neolithic and so on. Mythology is predicated upon the aeviternal and is thus qualitative, is "true now as always," and deals in archetypes and symbols, many of which are not only highly sophisticated in the (Traditional) esoteric sense, but ironically often beyond the grasp of the quantitatively dominant mind, regardless of the "primitiveness" of the culture from which they derive. Thus, typologically, the mentality of a people indicates the nature of their culture and vice versa. Mentality and culture are therefore coindicative, if not codeterminant. Primitive mentality is primarily mythological in both its ontological predicates and modality, and so are primitive cultures mythological. Labels of "inferior" and its synonyms applied to primitive cultures by historically minded social scientists are, consequently, highly suspect.

The whole question of "primitive mentality" is a multifaceted one, and can be approached from a number of different perspectives, as is evidenced by the tremendous amount of literature on the subject. Notwithstanding the number of possible vantages from which primitive mentality and culture might be viewed, for the purposes of this study the question can be distilled to two basic attitudes, since it is not our intention to treat the whole problem in detail, but rather the preeminent attitudes entertained by the most influential anthropologists and ethnologists who have discussed it in the nineteenth and twentieth centuries. This binary formulation of the basic and contrasting attitudes is referred to in what follows as the "chauvinistic perspective" and the "magnanimous perspective" of primitive culture, applying equally to primitive mentality. Our central concern here is these perspectives within the academic discipline of anthropology, from its beginnings in the mid-nineteenth century through the present. Certainly, one can point to attitudes inherent in numerous earlier journals, letters, travelogues, and similar accounts of European explorers and missionaries who wrote about tribal peoples which, to be honest, were used by certain early anthropologists as data, but such accounts did not reflect the institutional views about tribal societies that grew from the advent of anthropology as a systematic study of the subject.

CHAUVINISTIC PERSPECTIVE OF PRIMITIVE CULTURE

When it comes to the analysis of primitive culture, the so-called eighteenth-century rationalists were by no means confined to the eighteenth century. It was, in fact, in the nineteenth century where the ideas that formed the basis of the chauvinistic perspective had their widest currency. First and most obvious of these ideas is the Darwin/Wallace construct of evolutionism and its inevitable concomitant, progressivism. Evolutionism is the quantitative measuring stick par excellence, based on the temporally rectilinear pole whose polar extremes according to Darwin were pre-cellular amino acids as *première* and the English gentleman as *derrière*. Paul Radin, for example, in a 1957 introduction to E. B. Tylor's *The Origin of Culture*, requests the reader to "make allowances for ... the evolutionary phraseology which he [Tylor] shared with his contemporaries." But it is not the "phraseology" that should be singled out. Rather, it is the attitude of which it is only reflective: the same attitude, that is, which led Tylor to state that "the phenomena of Culture may be classified and arranged, stage by stage, in a probable order of evolution," and elsewhere that "the main tendency of culture from primeval up to modern times has been from savagery towards civilization."[4]

The other anthropological luminary of the late nineteenth century who acquiesced to evolutionism was Sir James G. Frazer. It was he who established the triune category of religio-intellectual evolutionism: "we shall be disposed to conclude that the movement of the higher thought, so far as we can trace it, has on the whole been from magic through religion to science."[5] Magic for the primitive, science for the civilized. This same evolutionistic *schema* was appropriated wholesale by Freud, as clearly evidenced by his statement that "The human race . . . have [*sic*] in the course of ages developed three such systems of thought—three great pictures of the universe: animistic (or mythological), religious and scientific."[6] Freud, however, was not the only holdover from the nineteenth-century rationalists whose perceptions of primitive culture and mentality were molded by evolutionism, and especially social evolutionism. In 1910 Lucien Lévy-Bruhl wrote that

To the primitive mind the mystic properties of things and beings form an integral part of their representation, which is at that moment a synthetic whole. It is at a *later stage of social evolutionism* that what we call a natural phenomenon tends to become the sole content of perception to the exclusion of the other elements, which at first assume the aspect of beliefs, and later become superstitions.[7]

As a concept in itself, though, evolutionism *a seul* did not comprise the whole of the attitude that these "scientists" took toward primitive culture and mentality. Evolutionism served rather as instigator for two other aspects that were components of the syndrome as a whole—progressivism and ethnocentrism.

Whether or not progressivism and ethnocentrism were unconscious elements in the minds of these observers, or however much they might have disclaimed or criticized others who blatantly or arrogantly proclaimed these biases, their tacit acceptance of evolutionism ineluctably implicated them as well by the force of logical necessity. "A blind faith in 'progress' makes it all too easy to accuse the 'backward races' of ignorance or a 'prelogical mentality'."[8] To them it was progress to have evolved from amino acids fortuitously energized in the inchoate seas of early *tellus mater*, up through the long life chain, past the primitive and savage states, to reach the pinnacle of biological form—the civilized and educated European gentleman of the nineteenth (and early twentieth) century. Since they were thus representative of the highest estate then known, it was to their condition of centrality that all life forms on earth aspired by the brute force of evolution. And naturally, since the predominant religious expression of these superlative European cultures was Christianity, it was deemed the highest of religions, and this not only with respect to the primitive tribal religions—often strictly reduced to the classifications of animism or totemism—but to the other major world religions as well (i.e., Buddhism, Hinduism, Islam, etc.). Thus Tylor, discussing some rudimentary principles of "savage religion," seemed somewhat surprised to learn that "these principles prove to be essentially rational, though working in a mental condition of intense and inveterate ignorance."[9] Using this theory as a base, Tylor formulates his progressivism in one succinct statement:

> The thesis that I venture to sustain, within limits, is simply this, that the savage in some measure represents an early condition of mankind, out of which the higher culture has gradually been developed or evolved, by process still in regular operation as of old, the result showing that, on the whole, *progress* has far prevailed over relapse.[10]

More indicative still of this progressivism is the dogmatic belief in the last of the three stages of religio-intellectual evolutionism: scientism. Possibly a prolepsis of the thesis propounded by Freud in his famous (or infamous, depending upon one's perspective) work entitled *Die Zukunft einer Illusion* (Leipzig, 1927), translated as *The Future of an Illusion*, is Sir J. G. Frazer's solemn declaration that "It is probably not too much to say that the hope of progress—moral and intellectual as well as material—in the future is bound up with the fortunes of science, and that every obstacle placed in the way of scientific discovery is a wrong to humanity."[11]

What other conclusion could possibly be drawn using these attitudes than to postulate that the educated, scientifically oriented, European Christian gentleman was the epitome of civilization itself, and therefore the paradigm by which all other people—their mentality, religion, culture, and race—were to be compared? And by so applying this standard to other peoples, what other possible conclusion can be drawn than an implicit ethnocentrism, condescension, and even arrogance will be found in the evaluations of primitive cultures by those in whom these attitudes are manifest? A perfect example is the prolonged resistance of Russian and European ethnologists to admit any genuine religiosity in the ecstatic experiences of Siberian shamans—primitive holy men. "From the time of Krivoshapkin (1861, 1865), V. G. Bogoraz (1910), N. Y. Vitashevsky (1911), and M. A. Czaplicka (1914), the psycho-pathological phenomenology of Siberian shamans has constantly been emphasized."[12] It is obvious that ethnocentrism can take many forms: Tylor's religiocentrism ("The connexion which runs through religion, from its rudest forms up to the status of an enlightened Christianity, may be conveniently treated of with little recourse to dogmatic theology.")[13] is no less virulent than Freud's psychocentrism:

> I am under no illusion that in putting forward these attempted explanations I am laying myself open to the charge of endowing modern savages with a subtlety in their mental activities which exceeds all probability. It seems to me quite possible, however, that the same may be true of our attitude toward the psychology of those races that have remained at the animistic level as is true of our attitude towards the mental life of children, which we adults no longer understand.[14]

Further, Freud can be indicted along with the ethnologists of Siberian shamanism in correlating primitive mentality with psychopathologic aspects of modern mentality. His book *Totum und Tabu* (Vienna, 1913) was a collection of four essays originally published under the title "Über einige Übereinstimmungen in Seelenleben der Wilden und der Neurotiker" ("On Some Points of Agreement between the Mental Lives of Savages and Neurotics"). Perhaps the most devastating stream of protean ethnocentrism was Lévy-Bruhl's ratiocentrism, which evinced from him the theory of "prelogical mentality" as the normative *modus operandi* of primitive thought. This theory was proposed in his 1910 publication whose title is itself a billboard advertisement of ethnocentrism: *Les fonctions mentales dans les sociétés inférieures,* misleadingly translated into English as *How Natives Think* (London, 1926). In his sequel to *How Natives Think*, entitled *Primitive Mentality*, Lévy-Bruhl again encapsulates this theory, using as his standard in this specific case his sacrosanct Aristotelian principle of noncontradiction:

His [primitive man's] thought is not subject to the same logical exigencies as our own. It is governed, in this case as in
many others, by the law of participation [i.e., Lévy-Bruhl's
"law"—*participation mystique*] . . . prelogical mentality is
able to adapt itself to two distinct affirmations at once.[15]

Citing endless examples of this superiority complex is not germane to
our purpose. The problems of this syndrome are sufficiently recognized by modern ethnologists to make extending this exercise unnecessary. In fact, most of the chauvinistic attitudes and theories relating
to primitive culture and mentality have by now been discredited. One
might legitimately ask, then, why any of this was mentioned in the
first place. For what reasons were these dated notions exhumed and
reexamined? First, this is necessary to provide a background for
understanding the change in attitudes that occurred during the first
half of the twentieth century, such as the shift in perspective from
"chauvinistic" to what we have termed "magnanimous." In certain
ways this latter perspective can be viewed as a reaction or response to
the former one, the a priori assumptions of which came to be regarded
as fallacious. Second, it is necessary in terms of serving as a sort of
caveat for contemporary thought, since it can by no means be categor-
ically affirmed that modern ethnologists are entirely free from these
biases and, a fortiori, it is by no means certain this superiority complex
is still not the prevalent cultural attitude of the masses of Western
industrialized nations—those, for example, who view undeveloped
"third world" cultures as backward in all respects. Third, it is necessary to illustrate the complexities and subtle problems attendant to
both the analysis and evaluation of cultures other than one's own, and
to the difficulties involved in how one can either classify or comment
upon other cultures—especially primitive cultures—with the least
possible ethnocentrism, regardless of the phenomenological method,
"ethnoscience," and similar tools. In this regard, Melville Herskovits,
the champion of "cultural relativism" and the antiethnocentristic sentiment, whose major essays stem from his work in the 1950s and 1960s,
might well have agreed with Guénon, who wrote in 1924 that

As long as Westerners imagine that there exists only a single
type of humanity that is the one and only "civilization" at
various degrees of development, no mutual understanding

will be possible. The truth is that there are multiple civilizations developing in different ways, and that that of the modern West, shown by its characteristics, constitutes a very
singular exception. One should never speak of superiority or
inferiority in an absolute way, without clarifying from what
perspective one views the thing to be compared, presuppos-
ing the things are effectively comparable. There is no civilization which is superior to all the others from every
perspective, because man cannot apply equally, and at the
same time, his activity in all directions, and further because
there are ways of development which would appear veritably
incompatible.[16]

Finally, it must in fairness be added that in spite of the evolutionism—and its handmaiden progressivism—and ethnocentrism that characterized much of the thought of nineteenth- and early twentieth-
century culture analysts, all the authors mentioned in connection with
the chauvinistic perspective, with the possible exception of Freud,
were, in contrast to other ethnologists of their milieu, apologists for
primitive culture, and often criticized the more blatant and scurrilous
attempts at relegating primitive culture to a debased and morally, intellectually deficient state. Frazer, for example, invoked the "judge not
lest ye be judged" axiom in chapter 23 of *The Golden Bough*, titled
"Our Debt to the Savage." Tylor was vehemently opposed to Christian
missionary sectarianism that he claimed was "occupied in hating and
despising the beliefs of the heathen" and equally opposed to the utterly
fatuous and superbly ironic claims of J. D. Lang that primitives (Australian aborigines) have no idea of religion or the sacred. And Lévy-
Bruhl's posthumously published *Les Carnets de Lucien Lévy-Bruhl*
(Paris, 1949) indicates a modification or reformulation of his theory of
primitive "prelogical" mentality. The possible abuses of selective
excerpting are too well known to warrant comment, and while it may
appear that the excepts used here were chosen with no other reason than
to denigrate the chauvinistic perspective, the actual intention was to
illustrate how subtle were the deep-seated cultural and intellectual
biases of the writers discussed from which little else but a chauvinistic
attitude—however good the attempts by them to conceal or neutralize
it—could have arisen.

## Magnanimous Perspective of Primitive Culture

Shortly after the turn of the twentieth century at a time when the dominant attitudes regarding primitives (and anthropology in general) were still of racial and social evolutionism, Franz Boas wrote *The Mind of Primitive Man*. He stated there that "The judgment of the mental states of a people is generally guided by the difference between its social status and our own, and the greater the difference between their intellectual, emotional and moral processes and those which are found in our civilization, the harsher our judgment."[17] Thus began a new current among modern ethnologists, antiquarians, historians of culture, and anthropologists with regard to primitives. The *ex fonte* thought of Boas affected the succeeding generations of scholars, and within three decades had revolutionized the attitudes toward primitive culture and mentality. The great differences between "intellectual, emotional and moral process" were seen as less important as criteria of judgment, and the previous chauvinism gradually gave way to magnanimity. The solely quantitative standard—the temporal—implied by evolution and progress was replaced by more qualitative standards. There developed an appreciation for the integrity, the depth, the coherence of the primitives' mythological cosmology and worldview. Wilhelm Schmidt, for instance, argued indefatigably that monotheism was characteristic of primitive mentality and religiosity.

Closer examination and newer ethnological evidence indicated that within primitive societies there could be found a hierarchy of intellectual capability, usually contained within the shamanic and/or healing elements of a given group, though not exclusively. As a consequence, it became evident that primitive peoples ponder various of the perennial questions of cosmic significance in addition to knowing certain processes of an occult nature—the manipulation of natural forces and the techniques of self-mastery and altered states of consciousness, as represented in the ubiquitous myth motifs of mastery over fire, flight, and celestial ascent. Paul Radin's influential work, *Primitive Man as Philosopher* (New York, 1927), was among the first in which this notion was treated as a whole, though relative to primitive mentality in general, not in specific. Radin postulated two basic temperaments of human constitution, a sort of *homo faber*, *homo philosophicus* bifurcation:

No notion of primitive man's concept of the external world, his analysis of himself, of the nature of the godhead, and so on, is possible unless it be recognized that, as among us, there exist, roughly speaking, two general types of temperament: the man of action and the thinker, the type which lives fairly exclusively on what might be called a motor level and the type that demands explanations and derives pleasure from some form of speculative thinking.[18]

In specific, A. P. Elkin took up the same theme and discovered the evidence within the Australian aboriginal societies, the results of which confirmed Radin's notion, and were published as *Aboriginal Men of High Degree* (Sydney, 1946). After it was recognized, therefore, that modern Western social scientists suffered from inherent ethnocentristic biases and that speculative thinking did exist among primitive cultures, it was left to discover the nature and properties of their thought and to rediscover, as it were, the world of primitive man.

The pursuit of this "rediscovery" is inextricably linked to the problem of modes of thought—that is, that which has been presented here as historical (quantitative) and mythological (qualitative). This problem of modality is, however, not incorporated to suggest that primitive man's thought is exclusively qualitative, and that that of modern man is exclusively quantitative: there is, in fact, an overlapping and reciprocity between both modes. The difference in modes appears more subtle and, indeed, can be reduced for the sake of clarity to a question of ontology. The nature of being and reality to both the primitive and the modern thinker appears to be the major dividing line. To frame the problem in terms of Jungian analytical psychology, for example, one might say that the mythological mode of thought for the primitive thinker is analogous to the internal realities of the unconscious (as an autonomous and coequal partner with the conscious psyche) while the modern thinker's mode of thought is analogous to the external realities of the conscious. The epistemic process in each case is equally as rigorous and potentially as capable and sophisticated as the other. Jung himself, like Lévi-Strauss, states in his essay on "Archaic Man" that "As a matter of fact, primitive man is no more logical or illogical than we are. His presuppositions are not the same as ours, and that is what distinguishes him from us."[19] Wilbur Urban might have seen the problem in terms of different ontological predicates and not in any substantive

172 The Only Tradition

epistemological differences. Claude Lévi-Strauss, perhaps the foremost exponent of the magnanimous perceivers next to Mircea Eliade, comes remarkably close to this perception of the problem. He writes that

> Prevalent attempts to explain alleged differences between the so-called primitive mind and scientific thought have resorted to qualitative differences between the working process of the mind in both cases, while assuming the entities which they were studying remained very much the same. If our interpretation is correct, we are led toward a completely different view—namely, that the kind of logic in mythical thought is as rigorous as that of modern science, and that the difference lies, not in the quality of the intellectual process, but in the nature of the things to which it is applied.[20]

Lévi-Strauss encapsulated his theory in a very succinct statement in a later work, *The Savage Mind* (Chicago, 1966) in which he asserts that "Certainly the properties to which the savage mind has access are not the same as those which have commanded the attention of scientists. The physical world is approached from opposite ends in the two cases: one is supremely concrete, the other supremely abstract; one proceeds from the angle of sensible qualities and the other from that of formal properties."[21] What must be kept in mind here, however, is that the difference in ontological predicates that characterizes primitive and modern thought also determines, to some extent, the mode of thought by which these predicates are explicated and made intelligible as far as they are communicable. Moreover, in applying what is at least obvious from the behaviorist's formula, from early childhood both primitive and moderns learn to emulate the mode of thought employed by those around them, which further concretizes modality. And while it is still true that the actual mental processes per se may not be radically different, as Lévi-Strauss suggests, or the potential capability of the primitive mind for assuming the scientific-quantitative-historical mode (or method) exists in most cases (and vice versa), it is not necessarily incorrect to make a distinction between the *modes* of thought as well, based on the "nature of things" to which the mental process is applied. For this reason, one should not view the observations of Lévi-Strauss as mutually exclusive of those of Ernst Cassirer, who wrote in *The Philosophy of Symbolic Forms: Mythical Thought* (vol. 2) (New Haven, 1955) that

To begin with the category of *quantity*, we have already seen how mythical thinking makes no sharp dividing line between the whole and its parts, how the part not only *stands for* the whole but positively *is* the whole. For scientific thought, which takes quantity as a synthetic relational form, every magnitude is a one in many, i.e., unity and multiplicity are equally necessary, strictly correlative factors in it.[22]

Whether one accepts the theory that only the ontological predicates differentiate primitive from modern mentality, whether one accepts that modes of thought are the differentiating factor, or whether one sees these two theories as being inclusive and accepts both—these are not as important to the magnanimous perspective of primitive culture and mentality as is the overriding conclusion that primitive culture is only *different* from modern culture, often severely underestimated, but not necessarily inferior. Indeed, in the magnanimous perspective, primitive mentality and culture can be valuable assets to modern thinkers in terms of helping them more accurately perceive and define their own mentality and culture. In 1926, for example, Malinowski wrote the following in *Myth in Primitive Psychology*: "I do, however, want to emphasize the fact that anthropology should be not only the study of savage custom in the light of our mentality and our culture, but also the study of our own mentality in the distant perspective borrowed from Stone Age man."[23] There is attributed to primitive cultures in the magnanimous perspective a coherence and integrity, even a beauty, of thought and worldview, based in mythology, which only envelop their complexity and depth.

The complexity of the primitive mythological worldview is well known to students of structuralism as postulated by Lévi-Strauss, especially with regard to the multivalencies of myths. Of the various "codes" Lévi-Strauss detects in South American myths, for example, one is cosmological. In a parallel vein, Giorgio de Santillana, discussing the Homeric myths, claims that "Archaic thought is cosmological first and last; it faces the gravest implications of a cosmos in ways which reverberate in later classic philosophy."[24] And Eliade, in *Patterns in Comparative Religion*, discussed "The Complexity of 'Primitive' Religion," (chapter 1, subsection 10), where he states: "One has only to glance through a few ethnological writings . . . to note first, that the religious life of the 'primitive' spreads beyond the sphere one normally allots to religious experience and theory, and second, that that religious life is always complex."[25] Boas gives an example of primitive sociology when he asserts that "There are people, like the Australians, whose material culture is quite poor, but who have a highly complex social organization,"[26] a phenomenon, it should be added, not at all peculiar to the Australians. In the magnanimous view, therefore, the epistemology, philosophy, religion, and sociology of primitive peoples combine to form a whole that is a culture far more complex and in most cases sophisticated than the earlier chauvinists would have dreamed.

By the last half of the twentieth century there appeared ardent spokesmen for the complexity, integrity, and depth of primitive culture. These individuals followed in the wake of the pioneering magnanimous ethnologists and cultural commentators previously cited, among whom one must also include the early classicists, Biblical historians, and philologists discussed by Joseph Campbell in the Prologue to *The Masks of God: Primitive Mythology* (New York, 1969). Regardless of the popular conception (or misconception) of primitive peoples, most specialists in the field have, generally speaking, come to accept the notion of positive, sacred, sophisticated elements of primitive societies and mentality. Adolf Jensen's *Mythos und Kult bei Naturvolkern* appeared in 1951 and dealt with the holdover and residual effects of the chauvinistic perspective still lingering in Western thought as it pertained to primitive culture. *Primitive Views of the World*, edited by Stanley Diamond, was published in 1964 and contains papers by eleven acclaimed ethnologists in defense of aspects of primitive culture and mentality. Marshall Sahlins, in *Stone Age Economics*, turned the tables on a commonly held presupposition that our "advanced" civilization is necessarily materially superior—relative to subsistence commodities—than any primitive or hunter-gatherer (Paleolithic) societies. Stanley Diamond, in the pages of *In Search of the Primitive,* stressed the need for not only an accurate appraisal of the depth and complexity of primitive cultures but for synthesis and integration of ethnologic perspective, showing both sides of modern and primitive culture, and finally bringing some balance to a problem that had nearly been played out—from one extreme to another, and then to the center.

As will presently be seen, the Traditional perspective of primitive culture shared by Coomaraswamy and Guénon approximates most of what has been said by the magnanimous observers, but with certain differences. As a unique transition from the magnanimous to the Traditional perspective of primitive culture stands the work of Mircea Eliade who, as we saw, was influenced by the writings of Coomaraswamy. Specifically, it is Eliade's notion of an "archaic ontology" that allows correlation to the Traditional views. Eliade's most succinct statement on the archaic ontology is, in fact, the first three sentences in his *The Myth of the Eternal Return*. There he writes:

> This book undertakes to study certain aspects of archaic ontology—more precisely, the conceptions of being and reality that can be read from the behavior of the man of the premodern societies. The premodern or "traditional" societies include both the world usually known as "primitive" and the ancient cultures of Asia, Europe, and America. Obviously, the metaphysical concepts of the archaic world were not always formulated in theoretical language; but the symbol, the myth, the rite, express, on different planes and through the means proper to them, a complex system of coherent affirmations about the ultimate reality of things, a system that can be regarded as constituting a metaphysics.[27]

This insight effectively bridges the gap between the magnanimous and the Traditional perspective of primitive mentality, or ontology, and primitive culture as well. For while Eliade was willing to attribute to primitive thinkers a cogent, developed but endemic metaphysics, the Traditional perspective of Coomaraswamy and Guénon *expressly* extends the attributes of primitive thought to another dimension—that of the Tradition itself, with all the implications relating to the philosophia perennis *et universalis* this extension entails.

TRADITIONAL PERSPECTIVE OF PRIMITIVE CULTURE

Coomaraswamy had much to say regarding "primitive" or "savage" mentality and culture. The most indicative statement of his—and Guénon's—views is found in his essay on "Sir Gawain and the Green Knight: Indra and Namuci," where he writes that "the Philosophia Perennis has left its traces everywhere, as well in popular or savage as in more sophisticated environments." The Traditional view of primitive wisdom, while it begins with the notion proposed by Mircea Eliade— "Ultimately, for the man of archaic society, the very fact of *living in the world has a religious value*"[28]—conspicuously expands this idea by adding to it a participation in the Primordial Tradition, the philosophia perennis. One could hardly imagine anything more abhorrent to the modern Western philosophers—those, especially, who have commented on the philosophia perennis—than the Traditional writers' affirmation that the mythological worldviews of savage and primitive peoples bears any resemblance whatsoever to the philosophia perennis.

To Coomaraswamy and Guénon, the establishment of primitive wisdom or mythology qua philosophia perennis was based on perceiving the difference in modes of thought and apperception and, by extension, their ontological predicates. Primitive peoples tended to think in images and symbols, unlike moderns, who are used to empirically based scriptural or graphic abstractions and models by which they adjudge all other forms of thought and expression. In writing, "In order to understand such [primitive] cultures we must learn to think in their terms, not in our own, which are already *pre-judicial*,"[29] Coomaraswamy demonstrates the fact that he recognized the problem of ethnocentrism. In the following quote, he states what "their terms" are:

> I shall only say that unless one learns to think in symbols one might as well not try to understand the so-called primitive mentality, call it "prelogical," and let it go at that. In fact, if we excluded from our theological and metaphysical thinking all those images, symbols, and theories that have come down to us from the Stone Age, our means of communication would be almost wholly limited to the field of empirical observation and the statistical predictions (laws of science) that are based on these observations; the world would have lost its *meaning*.
>
> We are, then, necessarily in agreement with Professor Eliade . . . that "la mémoire collective conserve quelquefois certains détails précis d'une 'théorie' devenue depuis longtemps intelligible . . . des symbols archaiques d'essence purement métaphysique."[30]

In the Traditional perspective, therefore, both primitive mythology and ontology are essentially metaphysical which, by definition, means they are concerned with the first principles. The mythologic mode of expression is imaginative and symbolic, as opposed to dialectic, discursive, or rational, in the Aristotelian sense. It is, in short, *sacred*, and this sacrality is not delimited to the particular mythological formulations of the culture in which it is found, but ties into the eternal, perennial principles that have come to be designated the philosophia perennis. Moreover, the sacred principles of primitive mythologies are inseparable from and inherent in the cultures themselves. In other words, they determine or *inform* the culture, being a priori. But in the transition from essential to substantial—that is, from principial to cultural—the differences in expression are created, which makes each tradition unique. Only the motifs or essential principles remain recognizably universal—those principles and motifs to which Coomaraswamy devoted so much of his energy and which so much of his published writing was designed to clarify—for example, Symplegades, Sundoor, dismemberment and reintegration, and so forth.

Because in the Traditional perspective the first principles or cosmological mythology of a given primitive people cannot be legitimately separated from the morphology and dynamics of that people's culture, it can be safely asserted that the Traditional perception of the informing mythology perfectly equates to the perception of that people's culture. Therefore, in the case of Guénon, whose written legacy contains comparatively little on the topic of primitive culture per se, one is justified in speaking of his perceptions of primitive culture by invoking his comments on primitive shamanism, for example, and applying the rule of coindication of mentality (mythological, in this case) and culture. Guénon wrote:

> If one considers shamanism properly so-called, the existence of a very developed cosmology becomes clear, and one which could indicate correlations with those of other traditions on numerous points. . . . Additionally, shamanism will be found equally to include rites comparable to certain others which belong to traditions of the highest order: some, for example, recall in a striking way the Vedic rites that are themselves among the ones which are clearly derived from the primordial tradition, such as those in which the symbols of the tree and swan play a principal role.[31]

In the Traditional perspective, then, most primitive or savage societies are not ones in which only the major rites of passage are deemed sacred, nor ones in which the people are exclusively "animistic," "totemistic," "prelogical," "childlike," or any other of a range of facile and reductive categorizations. Rather, such societies contain most of what is attributed to primitive culture and mentality by the magnanimous observers, with the added attribute of being wholly within the primordial Tradition. Generally speaking, primitive culture in the Traditional view is one in which *all* activity, regardless of how mundane or banal it is considered in modern Western culture, is sacred, since it has a divine archetype or referent or paradigm in mythology. It is one in which the notions of wholeness and value are preeminent considerations regarding all activity. Far from the chauvinistic perspective, and exceeding the allowances made by the magnanimous ethnologists for primitive peoples, the Traditional perspective of primitive mentality and culture endows them with thinkers having no less an ability to tap into the vertiginous heights of the perennial first principles than sages and philosophers in developed Traditional cultures, and, ironically, perhaps even more of such an ability than the modern philosopher. To Coomaraswamy, "primitive man was far more than we are a metaphysician," due to his ability to think in the images and symbols of his myths, so that

> Bearing in mind, accordingly, that we are speaking not of learning but of an "ancient wisdom," one that the modern world has not originated but scornfully rejects . . . can there be any real objection made to the supposition that, let us say, neolithic man already knew what St. Augustine called the "Wisdom uncreate, the same now that it ever was and ever will be."[32]

Stated simply, and as a general proposition, to Coomaraswamy and Guénon primitive culture was Traditional culture, though not all Traditional cultures were or are primitive.

# 10

## Developed Traditional Culture

It is against the standard of Traditional culture that Guénon and Coomaraswamy compared all culture, especially that of the modern West which they saw as diametrically opposed to the Traditional genre. Without perception and acceptance of first principles there is no Traditional culture, and one cannot presume to explain Coomaraswamy's and Guénon's definition of Traditional culture without first making these principles both indispensable and etiologic. The undeniable necessity of the metaphysical first principles as *fondement* of Traditional culture is expressed repeatedly in the writings of both Coomaraswamy and Guénon. The latter writes:

> What we call a normal civilization[33] is a civilization which is based on principles, in the true sense of the term, and where everything is ordained and hierarchically arranged in conformity with these principles, so that everything there is seen as the application and extension of a doctrine purely intellectual or metaphysical in its essence; this is what we mean also when we speak of a "traditional" civilization.[34]

Built upon such a sacred hierarchical and integrated structure, the principal consequence of Traditional society is *order*: "The distinctive characteristic of a traditional society is order." It is further, Coomaraswamy adds, a society in which "The life of the community as a whole and that of the individual, whatever his special function may be, conforms to recognized patterns, of which no one questions the validity."[35] And because of its metaphysical progenesis, a further characteristic of Traditional culture is that it is entirely sacred, or hieratic. Everything has a place in the cultural or social scheme; the scheme itself is sacred, a mimesis of a metaphysical prototype with which it shares a "referent" relationship; thus everything is sacred, with no "sacred and profane" distinctions being drawn. In short, "For Guénon [and Coomaraswamy], all civilization worthy of the name serves a spiritual function: to act as a channel for the influence of tradition upon every sphere of human life." Jacob Needleman further condenses his statement to one succinct phrase: "traditional civilization is the reflection in the human social order of the entire reach of universal reality."[36]

If, concurring with Roger Lipsey, we may assume that "'Traditional' described cultures that, whatever their historical faults, were founded on an understanding of the spiritual nature of man and the world," the question arises as to which, specifically, were or are Traditional cultures. A partial answer to this question is easily discoverable, since both Guénon and Coomaraswamy made lists of them. Coomaraswamy, in an essay titled "Is Art a Superstition, or a Way of Life?" referred to "the normal and long-enduring types of civilization" as "Indian, Egyptian, early Greek, mediaeval Christian, Chinese, Maori, or American Indian."[37] One can recognize that the Maori and American Indian tribal cultures could be differentiated from the others in this list and might be classified as "primitive" in older anthropological taxonomies, yet Coomaraswamy does not hesitate to include them as Traditional. Guénon, in reference to the *surviving* Traditional cultures (of 1927), spoke broadly of those of "the Far East, represented essentially by the Chinese culture; the Mid-East, by the Hindu culture; the Near East, by the Islamic culture."[38] Most, if not all, of the world's primitive cultures could be included in these lists as well, as was concluded in the preceding chapter. Yet, there do exist some noticeable differences between the so-called primitive cultures and those, for example of Gupta India (320–650 C.E.), Kamakura Japan (1192–1338 C.E.), Sinhalese Sri Lanka (i.e., the Polonnaruva period c. 950–1200 C.E.), Burgundian Christendom (1100–1400 C.E.), Inca Empire (c. 1400–1533 C.E.), T'ang China (618–907 C.E.), and the Baghdad Caliphate of the Abbasids (750–1258 C.E.). These differences, however, will be explored in the following chapter. The task at hand is to determine the morphology and dynamics of developed Traditional culture via an analysis of its essential constituents; that is, to see how, in Coomaraswamy's words, "The politics of the heavenly, social, and individual communities are governed by one and the same law."[39]

## DEVELOPED METAPHYSICS

A Traditional culture is so named because it rests wholly on the Tradition and, as we have seen, Tradition as a term can be used virtually interchangeably with natural metaphysics—that is, philosophia peren-nis. Since the principle of hierarchy is inherent in Traditional metaphys-ics, one must by necessity begin at the "top" when discussing Traditional culture by reaffirming the condition that from the meta-physical first principles proceed all cultural (i.e., contingent) phenom-ena. In an essay on "A Metaphysics of Cultures," Juan A. Vazquez notes that "According to Coomaraswamy, the study of cultures should begin with the recognition that throughout the different local expres-sions there exists the traditional doctrine which points out the reality of one basic principle, the metaphysical foundation of all that exists."[40]

This "metaphysical foundation" or "one basic principle" of which Professor Vazquez speaks is that which the great metaphysicists of all Traditional cultures have discussed in their extant works. Such authors and works could be fully cited in several pages, but of the genre of which we speak here, only a few are necessary to indicate the type: of the Indic tradition, Śaṅkara, Rāmānuja, Buddhaghosa; of the Islamic tradition, Avicenna, Ibn 'Arabī, Jalāludīn Rūmī; of the Jewish tradition, Philo, Maimonides, Moses of Leon; of the early Greek tradition, Hera-clitus, Pythagoras, Plato; of the medieval Christian, Thomas Aquinas, Albertus Magnus, Meister Eckhart; and others. The writings of these men, of course, are too diverse to categorize as exclusively treating the absolute, the One, duality, periodicity, self-realization, and so forth, as have been enumerated above in the chapter on first principles. Nonethe-less, there can be no objection to labeling them "developed metaphys-ics," nor to asserting that their expositions were reflective of particular Traditional societies and cultures (or in the case of the postdiaspora Jewish tradition, culture within cultures). The nexus of reciprocity between these metaphysics and the cultures they informed is to be found in the religious symbols and idioms used as vehicles to convey the principles. Hinduism, Buddhism, Islam, certain periods of Greek religion,[41] Judaism, and Christianity were the principal media for the great metaphysicists just listed, though it must be kept in mind that in the Traditional view a sharp distinction separates the aforementioned expositors from the interminable opera of later theologians.

As a final descriptive of the dynamic interrelationship of natural metaphysics and cultures—which equates to Traditional society—the Traditional view asserts that culture or society is telelogical. Far from having no discernible end or purpose, the human order in its ideal form is a medium for the individual's attainment of release from the human order. This perspective implies the synergy of several of the first prin-

ciples of developed metaphysics already discussed and so often promulgated in the writings of the metaphysicists listed above as
Coomaraswamy has amply shown in his later writings. The homologous percepts of "the peace which passeth understanding," *fanā'*,
*mokṣa*, *nirvāṇa*, and so on, all of which further imply the process of *dai-
van mithunam*, the *hieros gamos*, the inner synthesis of the "two in us,"
all set within the cadre of an ongoing evolutive helico-spiral, and characterized by periodic *manvantāras* and *mahāpralayas*, are the *telos* in
Traditional cultures wherein these developed metaphysics are found.
These are the implicit and underlying prerequisites of Traditional society. In a more explicit manner, Coomaraswamy explains that

> In the unanimous society the way of life is self-imposed in
> the sense that "fate lies in the created causes themselves,"
> and this is one of the many ways in which the order of the
> traditional society conforms to the order of nature: it is in
> the unanimous societies that the possibility of self-realiza-
> tion, that is the possibility of transcending the limitations
> of individuality, is best provided for. It is in fact for the
> sake of such a self-realization that the tradition itself is
> perpetuated.[42]

### SOCIAL STRUCTURE

Nowhere is the metaphysical presupposition of *ordo ab chao*
more reified than in the actual social structure of a Traditional culture.
Always consistent with its teleological character, the Traditional culture is structured upon certain axioms dispositive of Ray Livingston's
assertion that "If divided man is to become whole, he is more likely to
accomplish this in a social order designed to give him maximum guid-
ance and support in an undertaking that even at best has always been
difficult."[43] Foremost among these axioms is that of hierarchy.
"Humanly speaking," wrote Coomaraswamy in reference to the classification of gods in the Hindu pantheon—namely, Sacerdotium, Reg-
num, and Commons—"the hierarchy of the castes is the same. It is not
a hierarchy of races, but of functions and of standards and ways of living."[44] Among Coomaraswamy's most unequivocal statements of the
hierarchical arrangement of society in a Traditional culture is the section of "The Social Order" in *Hinduism and Buddhism*. There, using the

classical Hindu social system of "caste," he declares that "the functional hierarchy of the realm is determined by the requirements of the Sacrifice on which its prosperity depends. The castes are literally 'born of the Sacrifice.'"[45]

But the heuristic value of the classical fourfold Hindu caste system[46] as a paradigm for all Traditional cultures is questionable, just because it is so well defined. There has already been occasion to mention Georges Dumézil's theory of social tripartition among the ancient Indo-European cultures and its proximity to Coomaraswamy's views. It is germane to the point in question to draw a remarkable parallel to Dumézil's theory in a work by Coomaraswamy. One of the major criticisms to the tripartition theory is that it is much less applicable to classical Greek culture than to the other Indo-European cultures to which Dumézil makes reference. In this regard, Coomaraswamy wrote, "Plato's functional order takes account not only of the three 'kinds' of free men in the state, which corresponds to the three upper castes of the Indian system, but of another kind to which he refers as that of the 'servants' διάκονι [*diakono*] comparable to the Indian *Sūdras* and men without caste."[47] It is a matter of personal opinion as to how well Dumézil proved his theory—that is, how exact all the correspondences must be in order for the theory to qualify as true. Nonetheless, what cannot be denied is that a hierarchical *pattern* exists in these cultures and, for Guénon and Coomaraswamy, in all Traditional cultures. The reason for this view was that, assuming the cultures were Traditional, because based on metaphysical first principles, it could not have been otherwise. This is not tautological, but presupposes the consequence of hierarchy in the application of metaphysical principles to culture. As Guénon stated,

> What we call a traditional civilization is a civilization which is based on principles in the true sense of the word, that is to say, one where the intellectual order dominates all others, where everything proceeds from it directly or indirectly, and whether it is a question of science or social institutions, these are not definitive but rather contingent, secondary, and subordinate applications of purely intellectual truths.[48]

By whatever standards the social structure in different Traditional cultures is divided, by whatever criteria the various social castes and their concomitant functions are determined, one fact of developed Traditional culture is inescapable in the Traditional view: the existence of a spiritual elite. This elite is emphasized more by Guénon than by Coomaraswamy, but both agree it is an elite of a purely "intellectual" (Traditional metaphysical) nature. Its equivalent in the classical Hindu system is the Brahmin or "priestly" (Sacerdotium) caste. Its function, in the words of Guénon, is to "direct everything by means of an influence that would be imperceptible to the majority of men," and to "act as guides for the mass," by drawing down the ever-present metaphysical verities, translating them into cultural metaphors and idioms, and, acting as advisers and teachers, directing their application to the needs and exigencies arising from the general operation of society.

It must always be kept in mind that in the Traditional view this elite is ideally a spiritual one—not a materialistic one. To take a "modern" view of this spiritual elite—namely one predicated on control of resources and/or political power as being the highest human aspiration—is fatal to the correct understanding of its role in society. The socialist notion of "exploitation" of the lower by the higher strata, though it may have some probity in modern secular industrialized societies, is simply inapplicable in a truly Traditional culture. In the first place, the hierarchical system inherently provides for the exercise of temporal power by the kingly warrior caste: it is simply not the function of the spiritual elite to control wealth or to rule. In the second place, in a holistic and integrated society, such exploitation would be tantamount to the elite exploiting itself, since to affect the part is to affect the whole.

Guénon's view of the elite and of the hierarchical structure of Traditional culture was almost always phrased in the negative. In his repudiation of the concepts of democracy and equality—the latter being viewed by Coomaraswamy and him as a logical and practical impossibility—are found by reverse implication some of his views and many of his statements on the morphology and dynamics of Traditional culture. Conversely, Coomaraswamy generally presented these definitions in the positive; for him, as stated in an essay on "The Religious Basis of the Forms of Indian Society,"

> A traditional social order, like that of India, is not a haphazard development but imitative of a body of principles or values that are understood to have been revealed and of which the truth is taken for granted. Institutions represent an appli-

cation of metaphysical doctrines to contingent circumstances, and take on a local color accordingly, changing with the times, but maintaining throughout a high degree of stability, comparable to that of a living organism in which, by the repeated process of death and rebirth that we call "becoming" or "life," an existing order preserves a recognizable identity and produces order from order.[49]

## ARTS AND CRAFTS

Like the social order, the arts and crafts of a Traditional society are indissolubly connected to the first principles. Neither art nor craft in a Traditional culture is avocational—both, if a distinction between art and craft needs to be made, are vocational. The arts and crafts, like the culture itself, are sacred, hieratic. Beauty in art, therefore, is measured by the extent to which the objet d'art or artifact is intelligible and fulfills its design as a functional and hieratically symbolic article in daily life. In Traditional societies "Nothing unintelligible could have been thought of as beautiful. Ugliness was the unattractiveness of informality and disorder."[50] Livingston's seminal statement that "All true Traditional arts are imitative of the art of the Divine Artificer,"[51] is carefully unpacked by John T. Hatfield in a doctoral dissertation titled "The Structure and Meaning of Religious Objects: A Study in the Methodology of the History of Religions Based upon the Thought of Ananda Kentish Coomaraswamy" (Claremont Graduate School, 1964). Hatfield states there in chapter 3, "The Work of Art: Use," that Coomaraswamy proposed "As a symbol, a work of art may be made to serve as a *yantra*, a device used in meditation to focus the mind."[52] One wonders if the distinction made here by Hatfield is necessary, since a *yantra* can as easily be described as serving a functional purpose. Regardless of the validity of this distinction, the essential point is that nothing, in the Traditional view, can be legitimately called "art" if it is not principial in motif and as such relective of the sacred Tradition that informs the culture in which it was produced.

Coomaraswamy was renowned for his expertise in art theory and art history, especially in the area of Asian art. Consequently, trying to encapsulate his—and the Traditional—views of art in a brief chapter subsection is not unlike trying to slip "the shining sea into the dewdrop." Well over half of his voluminous written corpus was devoted in some way to the arts; in light of this, the possible quotes on the relevant points of his Traditional art theory are nearly inexhaustible. Nonetheless, our intention here is to outline the central points of the concept of Traditional culture as a whole. As standard for all Traditional art, Coomaraswamy relied upon one passage from the *Sāhitya Darpaṇa*, which he transliterated and rendered as "Vakyaṁ Rasātmakaṁ Kāvyam": "Art is Expression Informed by Ideal Beauty." This was his theory of Traditional art in seed form, and this, along with the explicated notions of its sacrality, function, execution, and symbolic nature formed the basis of his Traditional *Kunsttheorie*.

On the relation between the arts and crafts, Guénon asserts that "If the crafts thus used to entail in some manner the 'arts' properly speaking—for the two were not distinguished by any essential characteristic—it is because their natures were truly qualitative, therefore no one could refuse to recognize the same nature for art, more or less by definition."[53] To this assertion Coomaraswamy agreed: "Actually, there never has been, and never can be agreement as to the point at which art ends and industry [craft] begins," since in a Traditional culture "whoever makes or arranges anything, whatever the material, is an 'artist'."[54] It is just for this reason that Coomaraswamy often reiterated one of his favorite aphorisms in various places throughout his writings: in vocational societies, he said, "the artist is not a special kind of man, but every man a special kind of artist." This was so because every man and woman had a specified place and function in a Traditional society, determined by the organic and hierarchical structure of the whole, and no less applicable, as we have seen, to the social order. The arts and crafts of a Traditional society are contingent upon and inseparable from the first principles of Tradition. Therefore, consistent with the reasoning in these propositions, Coomaraswamy is justified in asking his readers the following: "Do you begin to see now what I meant by saying that works of art consistent with the Philosophia Perennis cannot be divided into the categories of the utilitarian and the spiritual, but pertain to both worlds, functional and significant, physical and metaphysical?"[55]

WORK AND PLAY

When, in the following Part, we begin to contrast the diametrical differences between Traditional and modern cultures, it will be of special value to return to one of these differences—that of the different perspectives of work and play as held by Traditional and modern cultures. The perspective of the Traditional alone concerns us at this point, however, and that is simply, in Coomaraswamy's words, "The indistinction of play and work on a higher level of reference." The inardent Guénon appears not to have discussed the concept of play—or work—per se in any of his published material; he was apparently mute on the subject. Coomaraswamy, on the other hand, wrote several essays treating the subject, among them *"Līlā," "Play and Seriousness,"* and "The Symbolism of Archery."

When Coomaraswamy speaks of a "higher level of reference," in apprehending the distinction of work and play, he is speaking of that of the Pilgrim or Comprehensor, the "higher Self" within each person and not "this man So-and-so" or the "lower self" (personality). Hatfield, commenting on Coomaraswamy's Traditional views, tells us that "For the comprehensor, the creation of life itself is a game (*līlā*)."[56] Conversely, when viewed from the "contingent" perspective of the lower level of reference (the mundane), Coomaraswamy can state that "It is not the personal view of anyone that I shall try to explain, but that doctrine of art which is intrinsic to the Philosophia Perennis and can be recognized wherever it has not been forgotten that 'culture' originates in work and not in play."[57] Yet even in this last sentence, Coomaraswamy does not negate his earlier contention of the indistinction of work and play in Traditional culture. Instead, he is alluding to the "modern" notion that those elements of society that are often deemed "cultural"— for example, arts, sports, customs, leisure activity, and so forth—are usually sharply differentiated from the more serious side of life—work. "We have gone so far as to divorce work from culture, and to think of culture as something to be acquired in hours of leisure; but there can be only a hothouse and unreal culture where work itself is not its means; if culture does not show itself in all we make we are not cultured."[58] Thus, culture, in the Traditional view, does indeed stem from work and not from idle leisure. But this work in the Traditional culture is in fact, as stated above, indistinct from play (*līlā*).

The sharp differentiation of work from play in modern cultures is accountable, in Coomaraswamy's view, by the fact that most modern work is little else than drudgery. He sees no greater condemnation of modernity than "the man at work is no longer doing what he likes best, but rather what he must, and in the general belief that a man can only really be happy when he 'gets away' and is at play."[59] Conversely, in

the Traditional society where art and craft are one and determined by
one's vocational *svadharma* within the holistic social order, work and
play are precisely one since the worker—or Sacrificer—is daily
involved in the sacred process of practicing his potential to the fullest.
The outcome of all these inseparable notions, stated succinctly, is that

> In the sacramental order there is a need and a place for all
> men's work: and there is no more significant consequence
> of the principle, Work is Sacrifice, than the fact that under
> these conditions, and remote as this may be from our secular
> ways of thinking, every function, from that of the priest and
> the king down to that of the potter and scavenger, is literally
> a priesthood and every option a rite.[60]

Moreover, under these conditions, the work, the sacrifice,
becomes the play, just because the law of correspondence demands it.
The creation of the universe is the "play" of God, reflecting the "continuity and universality of the notion of the divine activity thought of as
a kind of game and dalliance." By correspondence, the creation and
maintenance of society and culture is "play." In this sense, Coomaraswamy and, by extension the Traditional perspective, is remarkably
close to the "ludique" element of culture as proposed by Johan Huizinga in his work *Homo Ludens*. With the qualification that Huizinga
makes a conscious bipartition of play from "ordinary life" (i.e., work
and everything that is "not-play"), parallels of the play-culture relation
in the two views are pervasive. Huizinga writes, for example, that "In
culture we find play as a given magnitude existing before culture itself
existed, accompanying it and pervading it from the earliest beginnings
right up to the phase of civilization we are now living in."[61] Elsewhere
he proposes that "Instead of the old saw, 'All is vanity,' the more positive conclusion forces itself upon us that 'all is play.' A cheap metaphor, no doubt, mere impotence of the mind; yet it is the wisdom of
Plato arrived at when he called man the plaything of the Gods."[62] It is
interesting to note here, as well, that both Coomaraswamy and Huizinga invoke the same passage of Plato in their discussion of play;
namely, *Laws* 803. Were Huizinga to have taken a further step and syn-
thesized work and play into a single element of culture, or rather into
culture itself, he would have concurred with the Traditional view
encapsulated here by Coomaraswamy:

The activity of God is called a "game" precisely because it is assumed that *he* has no ends of his own to serve; it is the same sense that our life can be "played," and that insofar as the best part of us is in it, but not of it, our life becomes a game. At this point we no longer distinguish play from work.[63]

## THE PRINCIPLE OF FUSION IN TRADITIONAL CULTURE

If one were forced to choose a single word to describe the preeminent feature of a Traditional culture, the most accurate and inclusive would be *holistic*, or a close synonym. By virtue of the fact that every activity in Traditional society is grounded or connected in a higher metaphysical principle—a first principle—the culture can be seen as a substantive mirror image of the essential principles on which it is established and of which it is reflective. Moreover, a Traditional culture is purposive and teleological in its orderliness so that "Traditional man," as Nasr says, "knew with certainty where he came from, why he lived and whither he was going."[64]

Much has been written on the reciprocal interrelationship between religious or metaphysical principles and architecture. In *The Pivot of the Four Quarters*, Paul Wheatley examined the metaphysical and cosmological implications in the traditional layout, axial orientation, and architecture of the classical Chinese imperial city, using hundreds of crosscultural correlations from the megalithic empires of South and Central America to the *Roma quadrata* and the ancient cities of the Eastern Levant. In a task somewhat more tricky, H. P. L'Orange has traced in his work, *Art Forms and Civic Life in the Late Roman Empire*, the subsequent change in architecture resulting in the great shift in both religious and political paradigms—that is, from the Principate to the Dominate and from Roman mythology to Christianity in the world of late antiquity. The common factor in the cities described in these works is that the patterns of design and layout reflect the hieratic principles of the culture's mythological or metaphysical worldview.

Similar correlations are made by Paul Mus in his *Barabadur*, relating to a Buddhist temple, and by Erwin Panofsky in his famous *Gothic Architecture and Scholasticism*, though it is limited primarily to cathedrals. Panofsky is concerned with showing "a connection between Gothic art and Scholasticism which is more concrete than a mere parallelism," which he claims is "a genuine cause-and-effect relationship" reflective of the medieval Christian "mental habit" and based in the proposition *principium importans ordinem ad actum* ("a principle that regulates the act").[65] And applied to primitive as well as developed Traditional cultures, Eliade has shown a homology between religious principles and, as the title of his essay indicates, "The World, the City, the House" (*Occultism, Witchcraft, and Cultural Fashion*). There, discussing the requisite for order in Traditional cultures in terms of orientation and center—for example, *axis mundi* and *omphalos*—Eliade asserts that "The same cosmological symbolism, formulated in spatial, architectonic terms, informs house, city, and universe."[66] Earlier than any of these theses, Coomaraswamy had written "All traditional architecture, in fact, follows a cosmic pattern. Those who think of their house as only a 'machine to live in' should judge their point of view by that of neolithic man, who also lived in a house, but a house that embodied a cosmology."[67]

The most complete statement on this subject is that of Professor Adrian Snodgrass, as found in his monumental two-volume book titled *Architecture, Time and Eternity: Studies in the Stellar and Temporal Symbolism of Traditional Buildings* (New Delhi, 1990). Snodgrass undertakes an analysis of the relationship between the informing metaphysical first principles of the culture in question with the architectural and architectonic expression as found in Indian, Greek and Roman, Christian, Chinese, and Islamic Traditional cultures. He also discusses the same with regard to the aboriginal cultures of Africa and the Americas. Of particular relevance here is his chapter on "The Doctrine of Correspondences," another first principle of natural metaphysics, in which he quotes Guénon's description of the law of correspondence/ harmony as "a reflection of principial unity in the multiplicity of the manifested world."[68]

As with the architectonic homology of universe, city, temple, and house as sacred space and reflective of the informing principles in Traditional cultures, so with every mode of activity in life. On a cultural level, for example, the cycle of yearly activity or the calendar of rites is based on the religion or mythology of the people. Early on Frazer collected mountains of evidence to support this fact, and regardless of the obviousness that all agricultural societies were ritually oriented around the annual occurrences of equinox and solstice, the essential point with regard to Traditional culture is the supreme importance, the complete unanimity, the holism of this calendrical ritual blueprint in the world-view of the people.

Cycle and wholeness, quaternio and cross are predominate features—and symbols—in Traditional cultures, and are in turn so integrated into the other aspects of culture as to be inseparable. On the vertical axis of the cross, the hierarchy of the social order—including its government—is reflected. While the ruling element is typically not the priestly or higher element, the hieratic bond and responsibility of the rulers are unquestioned, as exemplified by the Chakravarti principle in Traditional Asian monarchies and the Traditional Near Eastern and Western notion the "divine right of kings" where the "right" also included the notion of responsibility. These latter percepts are fully examined in Coomaraswamy's book on the subject, *Spiritual Authority and Temporal Power in the Indian Theory of Government* (New Haven, 1942). The activity of the people as a whole, the "work as play" in all respects, further reflects the essential property of holism with regard to Traditional culture. Guénon wrote that

> In every traditional civilization, as we have often said before, every human activity of whatever sort is always considered as derived essentially from principles. . . . By this attachment to principles human activity might be said to be "transformed," and in place of its being restricted to what it is in itself as a simple external manifestation (this is in its totality the profane point of view), it is integrated with the tradition and constitutes, for those who accomplish it, an effective means of participation in this tradition, and this amounts to saying that it takes on a truly "sacred" and "ritual" character.[69]

Every aspect of Traditional culture, therefore, is integrated with the rest in such a way as to be *fused* into a whole, the whole being sacred and reflective of the Tradition. At this point we would venture to appropriate a model for Traditional culture that Guénon and Coomaraswamy never did, since the concept and term were too little known in the 1930s and 1940s. Traditional culture, in our view, could be described as *holographic*—that is, based on the idea of what is today called the hologram, in which the whole is to be found in its qualitative entirety, though less quantitatively, in all the parts. Two quotes from Coomaraswamy, though he never employed the term *holographic*, are more than adequate to substantiate the applicability of the holographic model for Traditional culture. He writes in "The Bugbear of Democracy, Freedom, and Equality" that

> The parts of a traditional society are not merely aggregated in it, but co-ordinated; its elements are fitted together like the parts of a jigsaw puzzle; and it is only when and where the whole picture can be seen that we can know what we are talking about. Wholes are immanent in *all* their parts; and the parts are intelligible only in the context of the whole.[70]

The holographic model has frequently been applied to consciousness and brain function of late, but not, to date, to culture as a whole. Ken Wilbur, in a paper entitled "Physics, Mysticism, and the New Holographic Paradigm," is concerned precisely with the area of consciousness, but begins his paper with a more general statement: "In order to understand how the new scientific holographic paradigm fits into the overall scheme of things, it is necessary to have an overall scheme of things to begin with. The perennial philosophy has always offered such a scheme."[71] And the Traditionalists can assert similarly that the Tradition "has always offered such a scheme," and one which fits perfectly well onto the morphology of Traditional culture, as well. For this reason, Coomaraswamy believed that in a Traditional culture, "The folk included every class of men, and all that was essential to the common structure inhered in every part of it, so that from any individual activity, whether the edict of a King or the gesture of a dancer, the whole consistent tissue could have been deduced."[72]

It must be left to other others to explore fully the relation of the holographic paradigm and Traditional culture, since such a task is outside the range of the present study. But, regardless of subsequent conclusions based on any future correlations between these ideas, the holographic principle has been an intrinsic feature of the Tradition since the first perception of the One was made. Thus, we may say with Blake in his *Auguries of Innocence* that it falls within the realm of supraindividual perception "to see a World in a Grain of Sand," or with Emerson in his essay "Self-Reliance" that "The universe is represented in every one of its particles. Everything in nature contains all the powers of nature. God reappears with all His parts in every moss and cobweb."

ANOMALOUS ELEMENTS IN TRADITIONAL CULTURE

It might appear from the way in which Traditional cultures have been described by Guénon and Coomaraswamy that the most conspicuous characteristic of their views is a sort of naive utopianism; that they appeared to describe societies or cultures in which no evil exists, everyone conforms to the hieratic framework like automatons, all authority is benign and incorruptible, and so on. Though to some it may appear that way, this is in fact not the case. It is quite true that neither man concentrated on the criminal or anomalous elements in Traditional cultures. Further, their comments on these elements are rare and infrequent in their writings. Yet, they were not unaware that anomalisms and criminality existed in Traditional culture, nor was it ever their intention to camouflage this fact.

Guénon, for example, at one point speaks of the fact that no thing is considered "profane" in a Traditional society except by those "who for one reason or another are outside the tradition and whose case is then a mere anomaly."[73] There do exist, then, from the Traditional perspective, elements of Traditional culture that are nonconformist, iconoclastic, reactionary, or criminal. Coomaraswamy describes the last of these elements as indicating more an ignorance of the norms of social behavior than of an unwillingness to adapt to them. He wrote that in a Traditional society "the criminal is much rather the man who does not *know* how to behave, than a man who is unwilling to behave."[74] Coomaraswamy relies in this explanation on the idea that willingness to behave in society follows a knowledge of or belief in the impeccable order of the Traditional society.

Regardless of the causes of anomalous behavior, it is nonetheless a fact of life. There have always been swindlers, thieves, prostitutes, assassins, and the generally unscrupulous in the world's complex and populous societies, Traditional or not. And corruption in high places seems likewise a universal inevitability: "There have been, of course, good and bad kings there [in the Orient], as everywhere else," wrote Coomaraswamy, addressing himself to this problem. "The whole prosperity of the state depends upon the king's virtue; and just as for Aristotle, the monarch who rules in his own interests is not a king but a tyrant, and may be removed 'like a mad dog.'"[75] And where in Traditional societies there were wars of aggression, or famine and pestilence not attributable to natural disaster but rather to the moral degeneracy of the ruling element, the latter were often so removed.

One must also take into consideration the fact that the first principles of the philosophia perennis were manifest in different ways and
with varying degrees of emphasis in the Traditional cultures of which
Coomaraswamy and Guénon wrote. The different application or even
absence of certain of these principles explains in part the corresponding
substantive differences in Traditional cultures. Furthermore, in the
dynamic fluidity of the cultures themselves, one or more of the foundational first principles will become eclipsed by others or die out altogether as responses to new circumstances, thus throwing off the social
equilibrium and producing more anomalies, in turn foreshadowing the
gradual decline of the Traditional society. It is extremely difficult, from
a purely historical standpoint, to know when a given Traditional culture
ceases to be Traditional by virture of its abandonment of the first principles. The Classic Maya (200–900 C.E.) of Central America, for example, practiced ritual blood sacrifice for centuries as part of their religion,
in which king and queen shed small amounts of their blood (of the penis
and tongue, respectively) to ensure prosperity for the people. Yet in the
later stages of the Maya culture, ritual sacrifice took a macabre turn, in
which hundreds of sacrificial victims annually were brutally dis-
patched. At what point did this degeneration occur, and what caused it?
Such questions are difficult to answer, as we have seen in the descriptions by Coomaraswamy and Guénon of the staggered decline of Western culture since medieval Christendom.

While the inherent structure of Traditional culture may be formally or ideally static, it is never static in manifestation, as has been
said repeatedly. In praxis, Traditional culture is, like all cultures, fluid,
dynamic, and ever changing in response to new circumstances and conditions, though the rates of this dynamism may be different for Traditional and modern cultures. In the general dialectic of cultures, the
combination of the principles of cycles or periodicity—upon which
Guénon wrote extensively—and that of *enantiodromia*, practically
necessitates the appearance of anomalous elements in Traditional culture. These factors, taken in conjunction with Coomaraswamy's view
as expressed in his speaking of "the many ways in which the traditional
society conforms to the order of nature," further combine to make a
strong parallel to the biological discovery of a mutant gene in every
genetic complex or structure through which any necessary adaptive
changes or permutations may gradually occur. Thus, Guénon's and
Coomaraswamy's views of Traditional society were neither utopian

nor naive nor idyllic, since they fully recognized and admitted the exist-ence of anomalous elements within it. They simply chose not to expli-cate these elements; not, we would venture to say, to make Traditional culture look better in contrast to modern culture, but rather that on the hierarchical scale of valuation, the anomalous ranked low, and conse-quently was not "worthy" of detailed or extensive explication.

# 11

## Primitive and Developed Traditional Culture Compared

At the end of chapter 9, "Primitive Culture," it was stated that "primitive culture was Traditional culture, though not all Traditional cultures were or are primitive." This implies that a distinction exists between what Guénon and Coomaraswamy viewed as normative "primitive" or "savage" culture and normative "Traditional" culture in its most developed or complete form. In certain passages in their writings, one can detect allusions to this distinction as, for example, when Coomaraswamy observes that "The metaphysician may, like the primitive, be incurious about the scientific facts" or, elsewhere, that there exists "a distinction of aristocratic and cultivated from folk and primitive art."[76] It is clear that among those Traditional cultures Coomaraswamy and Guénon viewed as "aristocratic and cultivated," that of India was used as the basic paradigm. "For Coomaraswamy," writes Lipsey, "India was the epitome of traditional civilization." Lipsey continues: "A knowledge of Indian thought—metaphysics, spiritual disciplines, iconographic and symbolic repertoire, aesthetics, social theory, and so on—provided him a touchstone when he studied other traditional civilizations, and seems also to have served in this fashion for René Guénon."[77] Lipsey's assertion is easily borne out by an extensive reading of the two men's works.

The task at hand, therefore, is to determine the nature of this distinction between "primitive" Traditional culture and developed or aristocratic Traditional culture. Such a determination is necessary because this may be for some a possible source of confusion, insofar as it might appear that the distinctions to which Guénon and Coomaraswamy allude somehow correlate to the eristic arguments that the chauvinistic ethnologists of the late nineteenth century used to establish their hypothesis that a quantitative gulf separated primitive from a more modern mentality—and thus culture—based on the linear chrono-evolutionistic model that underlay their thought. In fact, in the Traditional perspective the difference between primitive and modern culture, like the difference between developed Traditional and modern culture, is a qualitative difference, like that between essence and substance. But closer examination of these differences must wait for the next Part dealing with modern culture. What necessarily concerns us here is the difference between primitive and developed Traditional culture that, ironically enough, is essentially quantitative. This quantitative distinction, however, shares no similarity with the genetically based dogma of empirical evolutionism, but is based in the incessant process of periodicity, wherein the cyclic rise and fall of Traditional cultures occurs without end like seeds to trees to seeds, but rooted always and inexorably in the ground of first principles.

One difficulty of this undertaking—that is, formulating the fundamental distinctions between primitive and developed Traditional cultures—is that neither Guénon nor Coomaraswamy addressed it directly. Nonetheless, the issue begs clarification, and it is with some trepidation that we undertake to clarify this distinction, based exclusively on passages in their writings that are at once significant of the distinction but oblique and infrequent. That such distinctions existed between primitive and developed Traditional cultures in their views cannot be disputed; the difficulty, to repeat, is determining the exact nature of the distinctions so as to represent accurately the thoughts that Guénon and Coomaraswamy never directly or explicitly set forth.

## "DEGREE" OF DEVELOPMENT AND PERIODIC MANIFESTATION

The difference between a primitive and a developed Traditional culture can be seen metaphorically as the difference between an acorn and an oak tree. In other words, they are not qualitatively or essentially different, since the oak tree exists potentially in every particular in the acorn. The first principles are found, expressed in different modes, in both primitive and developed Traditional cultures. This conception, of course, presupposes the Traditional hermeneutic in the perception of the principles, with the inevitable provision that different emphases and variations occur in the expression of different principles. This is quite a natural and even expected phenomenon in the Traditional view, and in no way precludes any of the cultures in question from being regarded as Traditional, whether primitive or developed since, as was shown in the preceding chapter, the requisites for fulfilling the definition of "Traditional culture" are more pervasive than simply the inclusion of all the first principles equally in the worldview of the people. Thus the primitive (acorn) culture—which may be further correlated in the Traditional perspective to the "popular" or "folk" cultures *within* a developed Traditional culture—does not differ *essentially* from the developed or aristocratic (oak tree) Traditional culture—for example, Gupta India, or any of the other examples given in the preceding chapter. Coomaraswamy exhorts us to recognize the distinction as it applies within a culture:

> The sooner we realize that the popular mysteries are not essentially, but only accidentally to be distinguished from the Greater Mysteries, the nearer we shall come to an understanding of the nature of both. It is a great mistake to suppose that the folk motives are ever "pressed into the service" of the higher thought; they can be used in its service, because they spring from the same source and are of the same essence.[78]

Both primitive and developed Traditional cultures are representative, as it were, of the vertical axis in the symbolism of the cross—that is, the qualitative element,—but naturally occupy different levels of the axis from the standpoint of clarity of detail and extensiveness of expression.

Perhaps the best clue to the distinction between primitive (and folk) culture and developed Traditional culture is that of the modality of expression of the first principles that we had occasion to mention. The mode of the former type of culture (primitive) is primarily, if not exclusively, mythological. The mode of the latter type, or developed Traditional culture, correlates exactly to what was described in the preceding chapter under the subheading "Developed Metaphysics," and which both Guénon and Coomaraswamy have referred to as the "Greater Mysteries." In a vitally important paragraph concerning this distinction, and among the closest that explicitly describes the two modes, Coomaraswamy writes the following in his essay "Primitive Mentality":

> The actual unity of folklore represents on the popular level precisely what the orthodoxy of an elite represents in a rel-

atively learned environment. The relation between the popular and the learned metaphysics is, moreover, analogous to
and partly identical with that of the lesser to the greater mysteries. To a very large extent both employ one and the same
symbols, which are taken more literally in the one case and
in the other understood parabolically: for example, the
"giants" and "heroes" of popular legend are the titans and
gods of the more learned mythology, the seven-leagued
boots of the hero correspond to the strides of an Agni or a
Buddha, and "Tom Thumb" is no other than the Son whom
Eckhart describes as "small, but so puissant." *So long as the
material of folklore is transmitted, so long is the ground
available on which the superstructure of full initiatory
understanding can be built.*[79]

It is clear from this excerpt that oral primitive mythology and popular
folklore were, to Coomaraswamy, the practical modes of expression
for the first principles intrinsic to any given Traditional culture, primitive or sophisticated. His views on mythology, too profound and
extensive to be treated fully here,[80] can be deduced from a few brief
lines, such as "Myth embodies the nearest approach to absolute truth
that can be stated in words"; or "it is by the Myth that our Inner Man is
fed"; or "There have been teachers such as Orpheus, Hermes, Buddha,
Lao-Tzu and Christ, the historicity of whose human existence is
doubtful, and to whom there may be accorded the higher dignity of a
mythical reality"; and so on. The point is that "The student of 'primitive beliefs' and of 'folklore' must be, if he is not to betray his
vocation . . . an accomplished theologian and metaphysician."[81] This
is because there is a perfect correlation between such "primitive
beliefs" (i.e., mythology) and metaphysics, and since the cultural morphology and dynamics depend fundamentally upon these principles in
a Traditional culture, the correlation works similarly between the cultures. In short, the acorn and the oak tree analogy works as equally on
primitive mythology and developed metaphysics as it does on the cultures that manifest from them; while the modes differ, the content
remains essentially the same.

   But primitive cultures do not always remain primitive, nor does
the populace always remain plebeian, nor do, in the final analysis,
developed Traditional cultures always remain at their apices. Cultures,

Traditional or otherwise, are never static, but are incessantly changing. The perception of the change is the crucial factor for our purposes. In the Traditional view, the change is cyclic (seed, tree, seed, etc.), while in the so-called normative or (social) scientific view, heavily influenced as it is by the presumptions of evolutionism, the change is rectilinear and progressive. While both views would repudiate the notion of ineradicable stasis for a given culture, they are nonetheless radically different.

The former view, as the Traditional perspective, is clearly promulgated and explained by Guénon. His views of the process of cosmic duration were evinced during the discussion of his belief in the Hindu *yugas*, and apply no less via the law of correspondence to the cyclic life of a given culture. Despite what would appear as a strong parallel to the cultural theory of Oswald Spengler (the Traditional view—based on the ancient Hindu view—precedes Spengler, whose *Der Untergang des Abendlandes* was released between 1918–22), Spengler's view of time and his "organic form" are still linear from growth to decay, while the Traditional view is exclusively cyclic. In every circle a zenith and nadir can be assigned, as well as the midpoints between them, symbolized by the *quaternio* of the circle and the vertical and horizontal axes of the cross by which it is depicted. Thus, Guénon concludes that

> History shows us in fact, at every epoch, civilizations independent of one another, often quite divergent, of which certain ones are born and develop while others fall into decadence and die, or are quickly annihilated in some cataclysm; and the new civilizations do not always recover the heritage of the old ones."[82]

Therefore, when every classical period of developed, cultivated, aristocratic culture can be found, or where history can find traces of it, there existed before the epoch in which it achieved its height a more primitive but still qualitatively similar precursor. The pre-Aryan Dravidian culture of South India, blended with later extraneous elements, became the seat of a high Indian culture in a later period, just as the Celtic and Visigothic elements of the Europe of late antiquity subsequently became the basis of the culture represented by the medieval centers of Paris and Cologne, and so on. Both these high cultures are now gone, as are the Traditional cultures of Egypt, Greece, and

Rome, which Guénon cites as examples of the process. Acorns to saplings to mighty oaks to wizened giants to humus for the new seeds, ad
infinitum. The difference between any one point in a particular cycle
to any other point is thus a matter of degree, and consequently of
quantitative—not qualitative—difference.

### FUNDAMENTAL DISSIMILARITIES

Ever since—and in some cases before—the discreditation of the
notion of a separate and inferior primitive or "prelogical" mentality,
anthropologists and social scientists in general have sought standards of
measure for their evaluation of primitive and archaic cultures. Among
the most ubiquitous of these standards in modernity (discounting the
questionable meaning of the data elicited by physical anthropology and
the abuses to which it led), and approaching something of a consensus,
is the idea of "advanced" resting upon the sophistication of technologic
and material phenomena of a given culture. Notwithstanding the metaphysical or religious sophistication of the fourteenth-century Andean
Inca empire, for instance, with its capital at Cuzco, hundreds of thousands
of dollars in research grants have been spent solely on archeological
research into their systems of roads, agriculture, food preservation and
storage, accounting methods (*quipus*), building construction, textile
manufacture, and so on. The Incas are generally considered by social scientists to be a relatively advanced culture, and this consideration is based,
for the most part, on the cultural elements just delineated: technologic
and, in terms of the Traditional perspective, "accidental" or contingent.
    Far less is known or apparently sought with regard to the Incas'
religious and metaphysical (mythological) cultural foundation. Yet,
this is the primary measure or standard that, in the Traditional perspective, would determine the distinction between the Incas and their
anthropophagus neighbors to the East in the Amazon basin, or between
the Pallava Dynasts of South India (sixth to tenth centuries) and their
primitive tribal neighbors of the Nilgiri Hills, and so forth. In short, in
the Traditional perspective, the fundamental dissimilarities between
primitive and developed Traditional cultures are not the degrees of
development of technology or similar material criteria, but rather the
degree of development as it relates to the expression of the principles by
which the culture is infused. This development is, as has been noted,
analogous to the growth cycle of a tree, with its potential (germinal)

state and its realized (mature) state. This does not mean, however, that the maturation is by any means inevitable, that all primitive cultures cannot but develop into the "aristocratic and cultivated" Traditional societies of which examples have been given. Saplings disease and die in all stages of development; some are inalterably deformed; still others are felled by natural catastrophes. Yet, all the Traditional cultures so named—extinct and extant—have undergone the same cyclic maturation process, otherwise they would not have developed into what they were; namely, aristocratic and cultivated. It is to what constitutes in visible form the degrees of difference which concerns us here.

The degrees, like the mysteries to which they correlate, are "greater" and "lesser." The primitive man would fight with thunderbolts, put on celestial garments, ride in a chariot of fire, see in his roof the starry sky, and in himself more than "this man So-and-so." For Coomaraswamy, "All of these things belonged to the 'Lesser Mysteries' of the crafts, and to the knowledge of "Companions'."[83] To the lesser mysteries are contrasted the greater, the comprehension of which is done parabolically, with the intellectual intuition brought forth to its fullest potential by the Tradition itself. This is the process within a more developed Traditional culture, in which there exists an organized and initiatory gnostic elite. The greater mysteries are the "higher thought" earlier referred to by Coomaraswamy, and described in these terms:

> It is only one who *has* attained to an immediate Gnosis that can afford to dispense with theology, ritual, and imagery: the Comprehensor has found what the Wayfarer is still in search of. This has too often been misinterpreted to mean that something is deliberately withheld from those who are to depend on means, or even that means are dispensed to them as if with intent to keep them in ignorance; there are those who ask for a sort of universal compulsory education in the mysteries, supposing that a mystery is nothing but a communicable, although hitherto uncommunicated, secret and nothing different in kind from themes of profane instruction. So far from this, it is of the essence of a mystery, and above all of the *mysterium magnum*, that it cannot be communicated, but only realized: all that can be communicated are its external supports or symbolic expressions; the Great Work must be done by everyone for himself.[84]

This "Work" is the essence of the Greater Mysteries reflected in the developed metaphysics of the Traditional cultures, and Guénon has gone further than Coomaraswamy in explicating it. Guénon outlines a threefold process of metaphysical realization that begins with the lesser mysteries and ends with the achievement of the "absolutely unconditioned state." In his essay entitled "Hermes," Guénon writes that "the essential aim and end of Hermeticism, as of the 'Lesser Mysteries' of antiquity, is the restoration of the human 'primordial state'." This correlates exactly with the first of the triune states he outlines in "Oriental Metaphysics," which "is described by all traditions as the restoration of what is called the primordial state."[85]

This first primordial state of the Lesser Mysteries, found in primitive and folk cultures, corresponds to the person who is "freed from time," though "is without effective possession of any supraindividual states." The second phase of metaphysical realization, a transitional one, corresponds to "supraindividual but still conditioned states," and those who manifest these qualities are most likely found in cultivated Traditional societies. Finally, the third and highest state of such realization, and found almost exclusively in Traditional cultures (and in rare exceptions in modern cultures), is the "absolutely unconditioned state," which is "free from all limitation," and to which Guénon gives full vent in chapters 22, 23, and 24 of *Man and His Becoming According to the Vedānta*. This is normally far removed from the oneiric or psychotropic visions of the shaman or the trancing medicine man. This is the *jīvan-mukta* in the Hindu tradition, the true *bodhisattva* in Mahayāna Buddhism, the same as Rūmī's "dead man living" (*Mathnawī* Vi. 744), and Eckhart's "blessed dead, dead and buried in the Godhead." It is never maintained in the Traditional perspective that such release from conditionality (*mokṣa, nirvāṇa, fanā'*) is beyond possibility in primitive culture; only that it is beyond probability.

As Guénon makes a distinction in the different ranges of metaphysical realization varying not only within one particular Traditional culture but also from one to another type of Traditional culture— namely, the "Lesser Mysteries of antiquity"—so Coomaraswamy makes a distinction regarding the variety of Traditional cultures. In Coomaraswamy's view, there exist three such varieties: the primitive or "savage" culture, the "popular" culture of folklore within a developed Traditional culture,[86] and the learned expression of that developed genre that is the high element indicating the existence of a detailed and articulated Traditional metaphysics. The latter constitutes the highest expression of the first principles of the Tradition in their strictly metaphysical mode. The distinction between a tribal primitive culture and a developed Traditional one is more explicit and evident than between the two elements—folk and aristocratic—always found within the developed Traditional society. Coomaraswamy has stated tersely and unequivocally that "The content of folklore is metaphysical." Unpacking this statement, he carefully distinguishes the diaphanous relationship between peasant or folk perspectives and aristocratic perspectives, using their respective arts as an example:

> In traditional and unanimous societies we observe that no hard and fast line can be drawn between the arts that appeal to the peasant and those that appeal to the lord; both live in what is essentially the same way, but on a different scale. The distinctions are of refinement and luxury, but not of content or style; in other words, the differences are measurable in terms of material value, but are neither spiritual nor psychological. The attempt to distinguish aristocratic from popular motifs in traditional literature is fallacious; all traditional art is a folk art in the sense that it is the art of a unanimous people (*jana*).[87]

The fundamental dissimilarity between primitive and developed Traditional cultures is that the former is unanimous in all respects, principially and quantitatively, while the developed Traditional culture contains a dichotomy of the quanitative or material element (folk and aristocratic), though retaining its unanimity of principle and worldview. Moreover, different degrees of metaphysical realization typically characterize primitive and developed Traditional cultures. Care should be taken here not to draw a parallel between the triune states of metaphysical realization postulated by Guénon, and Coomaraswamy's three varieties of Traditional cultural expression: primitive, popular, and aristocratic. Both these fundamental dissimilarities are liable to difference in degree, based on a cyclic dynamic—which naturally includes both progeneration and degeneration—and due to this liability are thus quantitatively different. This cyclic-degree quantifiability is analogous, for example, to the same motifs depicted in the popular and aristocratic arts of a Traditional culture, the only difference of which is, in Coomaraswamy's words, that the media are "measurable in terms of material value." The "refinement," as Coomaraswamy puts it, between the "severe abstraction" of a principial motif in primitive art and the copious detail, for example, of Jan van Eyck's similarly principial or hieratic art is as overtly evident as the increased complexity of the division of labor in the classical Durkheimian formulation[88] between Gupta Indian society and the Arunta of Australia. But these sorts of distinctions are material, contingent, and thus quantitative, generating and degenerating in the wheel of duration without end. They are matters of substantive degree, not of essential indivisibility.

FUNDAMENTAL SIMILARITIES

There was also occasion in chapter 9, "Primitive Culture," to discuss the similarities of primitive and developed Traditional cultures and, indeed, to classify primitive cultures under the general rubric of Traditional. We take the opportunity here simply to present a few addenda regarding some further points of similarity and draw certain parallels indicative of the homogeneity of primitive and developed Traditional cultures.

First, it is prudent at this point, after discussing the quantitative or cyclic difference in degree between primitive and developed Traditional cultures, to reiterate and reaffirm the basic consanguinity of primitive and developed Traditional cultures as basically qualitative in orientation. In this perspective of the Traditional writers, the distinction, difference, the *oppositorum* between Traditional and modern culture is so vast and so prodigious that the verb "contrast" must almost always be used in place of "compare" when examining both simultaneously. The full contrast must wait until Part 4. For the present, one should keep in mind that regardless of any dissimilarities between primitive and developed Traditional cultures, it is crucial never to lose sight of the more significant fact that the essential similarities of primitive and developed Traditional cultures, in contradistinction to modern culture, by far outweigh any dissimilarities, just as the essential similarity of an acorn and an oak tree far outweighs their dissimilarities when each is contrasted, for example, to an automobile.

Second, it is necessary to emphasize the addendum of the essential homogeneity of primitive and developed Traditional cultures, as opposed to the heterogeneity of modern culture or, to use another pair of terms, the unanimity of the former as opposed to the plurality of the latter. Both primitive and developed Traditional cultures share the hallmark of containing a single unified, integrated worldview or cosmology stemming from essential principles to which everyone adheres and in which everything coheres. Certainly, ethnologists and social scientists can point to a variety of documented cases where reciprocity between cultures—Traditional or otherwise—has occurred, where mutual influence is evident, as well as to strictly religious syncretisms and a huge variety of myth variants whose permutations are the results of thematic accretions from other cultures. This sort of work, such documentation, is quite literally endless since, as we have pointed out, cultures are not static but dynamic. But considered in their pristine states and/or the periods of their highest florescence, both primitive and developed Traditional cultures are entirely unanimous.

An objection may be raised at this point that in the more developed, aristocratic, or "complex" of the Traditional societies, one can find philosophical differences representing sectarian biases, as in the case, for example, of the six *darśanas* in the Brahmanic Indian tradition, or the differences reflected in the great *disputatio* between the medieval Dominicans and Franciscans, and so on. Concerning the former, Coomaraswamy, agreeing with Heinrich Zimmer in his *Philosophies of India*, informs us that "the six *darśanas* of the later Sanskrit 'philosophy' are not so many mutually exclusive 'systems' but, as their name implies, so many 'points of view' which are no more mutually contradictory than are, let us say, botany and mathematics."[89] It is true the Hindu *darśanas* are somewhat neatly packaged and cannot explain away the sectarian views found in other cultivated Traditional societies like the medieval Christian and premodern Islamic, Japanese, Sinhalese, and similar cultures. Nonetheless, the idea that the *darśanas* are subsumed into one greater view is heuristically valuable; for whatever case one may make with regard to sectarian heterogeneity in developed Traditional societies, the ultimate fact is that, like the *darśanas*, all such differences are contingent and subsumptive to the larger whole that inhere in not only the religio-philosophical expressions of the culture, but the entire culture as a whole.

Third, and most important, primitive and developed Traditional cultures share a common element that transcends all dissimilarity; that defines them as Traditional; that sets them irreconcilably apart from secular cultures. They are both hieratic and hierarchic in constitution, these two properties being codependent. "In dealing with *any* traditional civilization it must always be realized that no real distinction can be drawn there as of culture from religion or profane from sacred."[90] "To the degree that the hegemony of the Spirit and the just subordination of all elements of the hierarchy are maintained, the social order flourishes."[91] Thus, sacrality of the whole of life, of being in the world, and the connection of gradation or hierarchy from the essence to the substance—from the first principles to their contingent manifestation—both combine to create in its most distilled form the definition of Traditional culture—primitive or folk or aristocratic.

Finally, an equation may serve to illustrate the principial similarity of primitive and developed Traditional culture. The shaman is to the primitive tribe what the metaphysicist is to the cultivated Traditional society. The former uses, in his celestial flights and psychopompic experiences, the rituals intimately connected to the mythology of his tribe. The metaphysicist, on the other hand, uses in his approach of that third state of metaphysical realization that Guénon described as "absolutely unconditioned," the existing corpus of metaphysical doctrine (*Upaniṣads, dharmapiṭaka, summae, ishārāt*, etc.), which is the principial flower of its particular culture. Thus, the trance state of the shaman equates analogically to the intuition or "divine intellection" of the metaphysicist, and the tribal cosmogonic mythology to the higher metaphysics. "Shamans," writes Eliade, "are of the 'elect,' and as such they have access to a region of the sacred inaccessible to other members of the community."[92] So, too, do those metaphysicists involved in the higher states of realization, as Guénon has repeatedly remarked. The same thought is echoed, though he does not use the specific term *metaphysics*, even in the writings of Franz Boas, who stated that "'Mythology,' 'theology' and 'philosophy' are different terms for the same influences which shape the current of human thought, and which determines the character of the attempts of man to explain the phenomena of nature."[93] Guénon addresses the question of this similarity quite explicitly:

> There can be no doubt therefore that it [shamanism] comes from some form that, originally at least, constituted a regular and normal traditional form; moreover that it has retained up to the present epoch a certain "transmission" of the powers necessary to exercise the functions of the shaman.[94]

Acorn to oak, lesser to greater, shaman to metaphysicist, cosmogonic mythology to metaphysics: all these represent the equation or correspondence which indicates the essential and overriding similarity of primitive to developed Traditional cultures. According to the Traditional perspective, Eliade is correct in writing, in connection with this equation, that "there is every likelihood that such words as 'being,' 'nonbeing,' 'real,' 'unreal,' 'becoming,' 'illusory,' are not to be found in the language of the Australians or of the ancient Mesopotamians. But if the word is lacking, the *thing* is present; only it is 'said'—that is, revealed in a coherent fashion—through symbols and myths."[95]

MEDIEVAL CHRISTENDOM (1100–1400)

While it is true that, as Lipsey has pointed out, Guénon and Coomaraswamy used the classical Indian Brahmanic society as their principal paradigm for Traditional culture, other developed or aristocratic cultures also contained most if not all of the elements delineated above as constituting Traditional culture. To these other cultures Guénon and Coomaraswamy made frequent allusions, correlating or contrasting this or that element in order to show the unanimity between them—their principial and structural isomorphism. Among the many to which they alluded was the culture of medieval Christendom.

Since neither Guénon nor Coomaraswamy was particularly tolerant or generally appreciative of history, and in specific of the historical method, neither man was particularly concerned in drawing inviolable chronological or geographical boundaries of medieval Christendom. In their writings on the subject, which amount to far less than those on Asian or Near Eastern cultures and metaphysics, one finds references in passing about certain figures like Eckhart, Thomas Aquinas, or St. Bernard, or about trends of thought and social patterns, such as Panofsky's "mental habits" and Huizinga's "cultural forms." To most medievalists the chronological parameters of the "Middle Ages" begin with the final Gothic incursions into Rome and their ascent to power (476 C.E.) and end with the beginning of the so-called Quattrocénto, or the Italian Renaissance, so well described by Jacob Burckhardt—a period of nearly 1,000 years. Though we choose the dates 1100 to 1400 as being the High Middle Ages arbitrarily, this choice is based on (a) what Charles Homer Haskins has called, regarding the former date, "the Renaissance of the 12th century," a proposition he supports in his book by the same title (Cambridge, 1927), and (b) regarding the latter date, the "rounding off" of a century that began the Renaissance of Europe, and wherein the symptoms of Luther's famous posting of his "95 theses" 117 years later were already beginning to germinate. As to the geographical parameters—they are more equivocal since they shift. Essentially, they include the area of what was established in the Carolingian era as the Holy Roman Empire, taking into consideration the eventual shifts in boundary as the centuries passed, but including primarily north-central France and Burgundy, Flanders, Lombardy, the Alpine regions and the Rhineland, plus the then flowering England.

It would be one thing to contrast the principal Traditional paradigm of Indian culture to modern Western secular culture. It is quite another to contrast two distinct cultural phases—medieval and modern—within the framework of Western civilization, since this entails both an endemic and true, in the Traditional perspective, passing of a Traditional society. The history and dynamics of this passing do not concern us here. It is sufficient to say—moreover, it is incontrovertible—that this passing did in fact occur. Consequently, it is more to our purpose to retain this stark contrast—from the qualitative, hieratic Traditional culture of the thirteenth-century Occident to the quantitative, secular, heterogeneous culture of the twentieth-century Occident, since it is precisely the way in which the contrast was viewed by Guénon, Coomaraswamy, others of the Traditional perspective and, as we shall see, Carl Jung.

Far from being a comprehensive or detailed discussion of the culture of the High Middle Ages, for which we have neither the inclination nor expertise, the intention here is to draw from studies of certain renowned medievalists[96] material that corroborates, point by point, those constituent elements that form the definition of Traditional culture as enumerated in chapter 10. Unquestionably, there is also in the field of medieval scholarship material that tends to refute the ideas as set forth below, not to mention studies that deal with what has been termed "anaomalous elements" within Traditional medieval Christendom—for example, R. I. Moore's *The Formation of a Persecuting Society: Power and Deviance in Western Europe, 950–1250* (Oxford, 1990). Moreover, the scope of this venture into Western medieval culture will be extremely limited since we propose to scan an area that contains numerous lengthy studies, as Barbara Tuchman's *A Distant Mirror* illustrates. Neither is our purpose an examination of the culture in its entirety. Rather, our purpose is specifically an examination of five aspects or elements of this Traditional culture upon which Guénon and Coomaraswamy commented and upon which academic specialists of medieval culture have written in corroboratively similar or parallel terms, resulting in persuasive support for the proposition advanced when considered in the aggregation. This is not undertaken to compare a specific developed Traditional culture—medieval Christendom in this case—to any specific primitive culture, but rather to usher in the discussion of *modern* Western culture, which will immediately follow.

## Developed Metaphysics

The corroboration of the fact that within the culture of medieval Christendom there existed a highly developed metaphysics is made easy by simply listing the outstanding metaphysicists of the era who are universally acknowledged as such. Christian theologians may wish to designate them mystical or sacramental theologians, but this is purely a matter of semantic tastes. In order, these renowned scholastics are St. Anselm (d. 1109), Peter Abelard (d. 1142), Hugh of St. Victor (d. 1142), St. Bernard (d. 1153), Peter Lombard (d. 1160), St. Bonaventure (d. 1274), Thomas Aquinas (d. 1274), Albertus Magnus (d. 1280), Duns Scotus (d. 1308), and Meister Eckhart (d. 1328). This was an era when the *in divinis* intellection or intuition soared upwards on the vertical axis, like the great spires of the Gothic cathedrals; where the intellect predominated, occupied with the perennial questions of first principles and expressing them in Christian idiom. "Probably never before, and perhaps never again, did the Christian view of the world and man play so decisive a role in the life of the mind."[97]

These men and a host of other unnamed medieval doctors, most of whom were holders of the *licentia docendi* and the initiators of the first European universities, were in the bona fide sense the intellectual (spiritual) elite of which Guénon and Coomaraswamy wrote. It was an age in which a growing number of speculative theological and metaphysical systematizations or *summae* were to prefigure the grandest of them all, the *Summa Theologica* of Thomas Aquinas, whose architectonic structure, once referred to as a "cathedral of human thought," is divided and subdivided into *partes*, *quaestiones*, and *articuli*. Panofsky draws a fascinating homology between these *summae* and ecclesiastical architecture in notes 23 and 24 of *Gothic Architecture and Scholasticism*. Some of these figures have been referred to as mystics, notably Eckhart and Bernard. Not surprisingly, these latter were the most often cited by Guénon and Coomaraswamy. Guénon wrote a short monograph on Bernard, in which he describes Bernard's resolution to answer the perennial questions, "the most difficult questions," "by the intellectual intuition, without which no real metaphysics is possible."[98] He further declares that

> In the Middle Ages, Western civilization had a character incontestably traditional; it is difficult to decide whether it was as completely traditional as the Oriental civilizations, particularly when it comes to showing formal proofs one way or the other. To stay within the confines of what is generally known, Western tradition, such as it existed at that time, was a tradition which took a religious form; but this does not mean that there was nothing else there, and that within the milieu of a certain elite the apprehension of a pure intellectuality above all forms was to be necessarily absent.[99]

Coomaraswamy leaned most heavily on St. Thomas, St. Bonaventure, and Eckhart and, regarding the last of these, Carl F. Kelley, the foremost of modern Eckhartian scholars, has described Eckhart as a "great contemplative metaphysician." Further, Kelley states that "Being wholly traditional in the truest sense, and therefore perennial, the doctrine he [Eckhart] expounds will never cease to be contemporary."[100] Such magnanimous scholastic metaphysicists as these, in the Traditional perspective, served as conduits, or more accurately, as transformers to bring down from the empyrean realms the first principles of metaphysics and supply them with Christian vehicles (doctrine, dogma, symbol), thus imbuing the whole of medieval European culture with a hieratic (and hierarchic) light.

An addendum to the notion of a developed metaphysics in medieval Christendom, or more particularly the Christian semiology and symbology by which the culture was saturated, is the question of a psychological reciprocity between such exterior signs and symbols and the interior archetypal contents within the psyche of the individual. Carl Jung has written extensively on this interaction, and specifies a *need* for existing cultural symbols to act as recipients for projected archetypal elements of the unconscious psyche. In Jung's view, where the culture is wholly informed by a sacred myth or religion (or metaphysical doctrine) a special dialogue is achieved—the individual to the collective symbolic system, and back again—via a dynamic reciprocity or mutual influence, and the life of the culture thus achieves a relative stability. With regard, therefore, to the individual of the High Gothic Christian culture, "The whole life of the collective unconscious has been absorbed without remainder, so to speak, in the dogmatic archetypes, and flows like a well-controlled stream in the symbolism of the church calendar."[101]

This control prevailed because the culture had "a richly developed and undamaged world of dogmatic ideas, which provide a worthy receptacle for the plethora of figures in the unconscious and in this way give visible expression to certain vitally important truths with which the conscious mind should keep in touch."[102] At this point a significant correlation appears between Jung's analytical psychological interpretation of signs and symbols, or "dogmatic ideas," and Coomaraswamy's interpretation of Traditional man's "thinking in symbols," with his reluctance to exclude from "metaphysical thinking all those images, symbols," and so on, by which life is given *meaning*. We shall have occasion to examine Jung's theory in greater detail in the following Part, where it will be shown that, like the Traditional thinkers, he saw the transition of medieval to modern Western civilization replete in a pernicious mass "despiritualization," beginning with the Reformation, and the present "mass neurosis" of modern culture in the absence of a structure of signs and symbols that serve as common extant media for the hypostatization of the contents of the unconscious.

*Social Structure*

With reference to the "hierarchic light" mentioned above, Dumézil may have been laconic on the tripartite structure of medieval European society, but others are not. Chapter 3 of Huizinga's *The Waning of the Middle Ages* is titled "The Hierarchic Conception of Society," and there he speaks of the synonomy of "estate" and "order," referring to the three estates of society. "Medieval political speculation," wrote Huizinga, "is imbued to the marrow with the idea of a structure of society based upon distinct orders."[103] Speaking of the writings of Chastellain, the historiographer for the dukes of Burgundy, Huizinga continues: "God, he says, created the common people to till the earth and to procure by trade the commodities necessary for life; he created the clergy for the works of religion; the nobles that they should cultivate virtue and maintain justice."[104] But most indicative of the hieratic nature of the hierarchy in Huizinga's thought is the passage in which he states, "Now, if the degrees of the social edifice are conceived as the lower steps of the throne of the Eternal, the value assigned to each order will not depend on its utility, but on its sanctity—that is to say, its proximity to the highest place."[105] If this be true, then it would follow that, regardless of the consensus of medievalists (barring Duby and Le Goff) who hold that the nobility under the Emperor and the various national monarchs comprised the highest estate, the scholastic theologians (metaphysicists) and subsequently the clergy at large under the Pope would be the highest order or estate, as is the case in the classical Hindu tradition and also in Dumézil's formulation. This thought is not offered as unequivocally the case, but rather as a hypothesis that is thoroughly consistent with the views of several distinguished scholars.

A further point of agreement can be offered in support of this suggestion. In volume three of *The Christian Tradition* (The Growth of Medieval Theology (600–1300)), Jaroslav Pelikan devotes a subsection to "The Celestial and Ecclesiastical Hierarchies," where he discusses the "parallel between the celestial hierarchy and the ecclesiastical hierarchy" that found its first Christian exposition in Pseudo-Dionysius's *The Celestial Hierarchy* (ca. 480 C.E.). Citing also Bonaventure's "concordance of hierarchies" and Thomas's hierarchization of the "entire universe," (*Collations on the Hexaemeron* and *Commentary on the Sentences*, respectively), Pelikan asserts that the medieval scholastic perspective assumed "the ecclesiastical hierarchy was modeled after the celestial."[106] This being the case, the ecclesiastical hierarchy is necessarily in closer proximity, being ostensibly a "mirror image" of the highest order, and by the law of correspondence closer to the highest order than the estate of the nobility.

More important to the thesis here, however, than which estate comes first is the fact that the society is hierarchically arranged. The most detailed study to forward this assertion is Georges Duby's *The Three Orders: Feudal Society Imagined* (Chicago, 1980). There, Duby, acknowledging a debt to Georges Dumézil, seeks to apply the trifunctional theory of social order that he finds in the oeuvre of "Adalbero, bishop of Leon, and Gerard, bishop of Cambrai," both of the third decade of the eleventh century, to "the eleventh and twelfth centuries pursuing it until the allusions to the three social functions, the three orders, proliferate, until it becomes certain that the 'theory' is 'quite widespread,' that the 'model' enjoyed 'a considerable success.'"[107] Characterizing the then prevalent attitudes, Duby writes: "Order comes from above. It is propagated through a hierarchy. The arrangement of ranks, one above the other, ensures that order will spread throughout the whole."

This basic concept is that to which the subsequent explication in Duby's work is devoted, within the time parameters of the eleventh and twelfth centuries and within the geographic boundaries of Poitou, Berry, and Burgundy. Seven points of "the system" are given in the chapter of that title, which correspond in many cases to the Traditional notion. Other chapters, "Hierarchy," "Orders," and "Ternarity," give fuller and more elaborate accounts of the thesis. Corroborating the theosophic law of correspondence, Duby declares that the first aspect of the "system," was a "coherence between heaven and earth, two parts of one homogeneous world, built to a single plan and hence reciprocally related." Elsewhere he observes that "They [Adalbero and Gerard] explicitly linked the three social functions with the exemplary structures of the heavenly Jerusalem."[108] And, he continues, the principle of hierarchy existed *within* the specific orders as well: "Hierarchically arranged within each order were various offices or tasks."[109] Certainly, without more extensive works like Duby's, critical historians would reject the assertion for the unequivocal reality of a trifunctional social order as applied to the Holy Roman Empire and the area under discussion here. But that is not to say that trifunctionality was *not* the case, and even without such detailed and careful studies as Duby's, one can safely say that similar patterns existed in many of the smaller states which, as a combined whole, comprised the European Christendom of that period.

*Arts and Crafts*

At this juncture, the works of Coomaraswamy can be used as authoritative with regard to the medieval conception of art, since this was his academic specialty. It was, in addition, intertwined with his exposition of the Tradition, and both were manifest in the prodigious amount of material he produced on the subject, the more familiar ones being "The Christian and Oriental, or True, Philosophy of Art," "The Nature of Mediaeval Art," "The Traditional Conception of Ideal Portraiture," "The Mediaeval Theory of Beauty," "*Ars sine scientia nihil*,"

"The Meeting of Eyes," and "Meister Eckhart's View of Art," among others. His view was that

> In the twelfth and thirteenth centuries, when Christian art was at its zenith, art [and by extension "crafts"], from the Mediaeval point of view, was a kind of knowledge in accordance with which the artist imagined the form or design of the work to be done, and by which he reproduced this form in the required or available material. The product was not called "art," but an "artefact," a thing "made by art"; the art remains in the artist. Nor was there any distinction of "fine" from "applied" or "pure" from "decorative" art. All art was for "good use" and "adapted to condition." Art could be applied either to noble or to common uses, but was no more or less art in the one case than in the other.[110]

Because it was Traditional it was an art that proceeded from principles, that expressed or signified principle(s). Haskins said of the twelfth century that "Its art is rich and distinctive both in sculpture and architecture, but it is an art of types, not of individuals."[111] Huizinga had far more to say on the subject. In his chapter on "Art and Life" in *The Waning of the Middle Ages*, he states that "Outside ecclesiastical [hieratic] art very little remains"; art "had to be enjoyed as an element of life itself, as the expression of life's significance." Consistent with Coomaraswamy's statement just cited, Huizinga continues: "Consequently, we might venture the paradox that the Middle Ages knew only applied art. They wanted works of art not only to make them subservient to some practical use. Their purpose and their meaning always preponderated over their purely aesthetic value."[112]

In an essay entitled "Initiation and the Crafts," Guénon discusses the relation of these two Traditional concepts within the milieux of Islam and "the Christian civilization of the Middle Ages." Only the briefest précis of his thesis is possible here, and it is that the arts and crafts of these Traditional cultures are to such an extent wholly integrated into the entire fabric of life that the craft of the "artifex" is in fact a means of initiation, since "it is integrated in the tradition and, for the one who performs it, it is a means of effectively participating in this tradition." Similarly, Jacques Maritain, in *Art and Scholasticism* (New York, 1962), asks:

More generally, does it not seem that the happiest conditions for the artist are conditions of peace and spiritual order
within and around him, such that having, we certainly hope,
his soul under control and turned towards its last end, he
have however in addition to this no other concern than to
reveal himself—such as he is—in his work, without giving
a thought to anything else, without pursuing any particular
and determined human end? Was not this precisely how the
artists of the Middle Ages worked?[113]

The unique reciprocity between the artist and the patron was again
reflective of the mental habits of the era, and for this reason, explains
Coomaraswamy, most of the art was left unsigned by the artist, since it
was in favor of the patron to which the art was directed. "Art was subservient to life," wrote Huizinga. "Its social function was to enhance
the importance of a chapel, a donor, a patron, or a festival, but never
that of the artist."[114] This notion of anonymity, as applied to the arts or
to anything else, is an implicit doctrine of medieval scholasticism, and
is intimately connected to the notion of "self-naughting," which
Coomaraswamy has fully expounded in his essay "*Ākiṃcañña*: Self-
Naughting," and one to which Guénon devoted a chapter—"Le double
sens de l'anonymat"—in his *Le règne de la quantité et les signes des
temps*. For "to understand Mediaeval art [and culture] needs more than
a modern 'course in the appreciation of art:' it demands an understanding of the spirit of the Middle Ages, the spirit of Christianity
itself, and in the last analysis the spirit of what has been well named
the 'Philosophia Perennis' or 'Universal Unanimous Tradition'."[115]

*Work and Play*

The corroboration of the Traditional indistinction of work and
play in Traditional culture is one difficult to procure, since the idea is so
wholly foreign to the modern conception, and thus to many modern
medievalists. Further, Coomaraswamy's assertion that such a principle
is usually evinced within a "higher level of reference" must be kept constantly in mind and applied not only with reference to modern medievalists but to the medieval chroniclers and historiographers
themselves—as opposed to the metaphysicians. Nonetheless, in *Homo
Ludens* Huizinga declares that "In fine, the influence of the play-spirit

was extraordinarily great in the Middle Ages, not on the inward structure of its institutions, which was largely classical in origin, but on the ceremonial with which that structure was expressed and embellished."[116] Whether or not one is to view the ceremonial expression of a culture's institutional structures as "work," the Traditional perspective as projected by Coomaraswamy essentially nullifies the distinction since, in his view, in medieval Christendom as in the totality of "traditional societies all those actual games and performances that we now regard as merely secular 'sports' and 'shows' are, strictly speaking, rites, to be participated in only by initiates."[117] "And so extremes meet," he continues, "work becoming play, and play work; to live accordingly is to have seen 'action in inaction, and inaction in action,' to have risen above the battle, as so to remain unaffected by the consequences of action." The pageants, tournaments, and modes of chivalry are too well known in medieval Christendom to require documentation here; that they comprise many of the rites just referred to is evident, since all were done "in the name of the Father," that is, under the auspices of Christian benedictions.

Furthermore, by the law of correspondence, this theme of play manifests in the metaphysics of origination, for example, when Eckhart refers to "this play going on in the Father-nature," "the eternal playing of the Son," and "The playing of the twain is the Holy ghost in whom they both disport themselves and he disports himself in both."[118] In truth it may offend the sensibilities of the modern reader who erects a mental picture of the toiling European serf (technically, *agricolae*) living in thatch-roofed cottage to describe this activity as "play," yet, this offense is taken only via the medium of an exclusively secular worldview, or "lower level of reference"—one perhaps, which views the essential aspect of life as economic, and thus the greatest life determinant as the control of the means of production. To this toiling serf (who, in fact, may have been living a life more akin to what today might be referred to as an "organic" lifestyle—animal husbandry, tilling the soil, and eating the fruits of his own labors), his "estate" was predetermined within the hieratic plan, which can be translated into the Traditional metaphysics as a manifestation of the divine "dalliance" or play.

Jacques Le Goff, in a work entitled *Time, Work and Culture in the Middle Ages* (Chicago, 1980), informs us that "Between the ninth and the thirteenth centuries ... an economic and social revolution took place in the Christian West, of which urban expansion was the most

striking symptom and the division of labor the most important characteristic."[119] It is thus difficult to say anything strictly definitive about
the "third estate"—those who felt the major effects of this revolution.
Yet there were retained in that era of medieval culture what Le Goff
refers to as "Sacred and Prestigious Craftsmen"—metallurgists and
swordsmiths. And within the great cenobitic traditions of the High Middle Ages, Le Goff speaks of the change in attitude with regard to the
"theology of labor": "The concept of penitential labor was supplanted
by the idea of labor as a positive means to salvation."[120] There was thus
a return to a "sublime labor," based on this notion, the new attitude
being that "before penitential labor, which was a consequence of sin
and the Fall, there had been joyful labor, blessed by God, and earthly
labor had kept about it something of the quality of a paradisiacal labor
from before the fall."[121] Whether those of the third estate in the social
hierarchy viewed their work as play in the sense that Coomaraswamy
invokes is questionable, and it is far from our intention to superimpose
the Traditional theory—even in its higher level of reference—on the
historical data without equivocation. What can be said without reserva-
tion, however, is that both the concept and actuality of the indistinction
of work and play can be found in medieval Christendom. The unan-
swerable question remains the pervasiveness or degree to which this
notion was conscious or realized within and throughout the culture as a
whole. From the Traditional perspective, however, we come closest to
finding the answer in the percept of total fusion in Traditional culture.

*Fusion*

The detail within detail within detail of, for example, the "Adora-
tion of the Lamb" by the brothers van Eyck, or the intense and similarly
detailed manuscript illuminations of the brothers Limberg among
whose patrons was the duke of Berry (*Les très riches heures*) may give
us some insight into the holographic nature of medieval Christendom of
1100 to 1400. Thoroughly infused by sacred motifs, paradigms, and
symbols for every conceivable activity, the culture "lived and moved
and had its being" in Christianity. "It should never be forgotten," wrote
Huizinga in his essay "Abelard," "that in the Middle Ages the Church,
besides being the organism of religion, was also by far the most important organism of culture, and the only one capable of holding together
and *fusing* the elements essential to culture and society."[122]

The cultural norm was to imbue and perceive in the most trivial and seemingly insignificant task a link to the sacred whole, "God's plan," thus transforming that task into something significant of the great (hieratic) chain of being (and becoming). Barbara Tuchman writes that "Christianity was the matrix of medieval life: even cooking instructions called for boiling an egg 'during the time wherein you can say a Miserere.' It governed birth, marriage, and death, sex, and eating, made rules for law and medicine, gave philosophy and scholarship their subject matter."[123] While one must concede that the mystic Henry Suso (c. 1295–1365) is an extreme exemplar in this case—that is, not truly representative of the "average" citizen of his time—his pious consumption of an apple and glass of water is nonetheless indicative of the cultural minutiae imbued with sacred referents in the High Middle Ages:

> At table Suso eats three-quarters of an apple in the name of the Trinity and the remaining quarter in commemoration of the "love with which the heavenly Mother gave her tender child Jesus an apple to eat"; and for this reason he eats the last quarter with the paring, as little boys do not peel their apples. After Christmas he does not eat it, for then the infant Jesus was too young to eat apples. He drinks in five draughts because of the five wounds of the Lord, but as blood and water flowed from the side of Christ, he takes his last draught twice.[124]

As a historian of culture, Huizinga disapproves of this tendency, for he views this cultural phenomenon as harboring grave dangers, since "holy things will become too common to be felt." "In the Middle Ages," he laments, "the demarcation of the sphere of religious thought and that of worldly concerns was nearly obliterated."[125]

To Guénon and Coomaraswamy, however, it was not "nearly" obliterated: it was entirely obliterated, and that was precisely what made it a Traditional culture. Guénon holds before us the cultural example of the "Christian civilization of the Middle Ages [where] it is easy to see the 'religious' character which the most ordinary acts of existence assume in it." He continues:

> Religion there is not a thing that holds a place apart and unconnected with everything else as in the case of the mod-

ern Westerners (those at least who still consent to acknowledge a religion); on the contrary, it pervades the whole
existence of the human being; or, it would be better to say,
all that constitutes this existence and the social life particularly, is as if included in its domain, so much so that under
such conditions there cannot really be anything "profane."[126]

Huizinga, though he comes extremely close to the Traditional perspective of complete fusion, still retains the "sacred and profane" dichotomy as applied *within* the culture of the High Middle Ages.

Guénon and Coomaraswamy eschewed this dichotomy, and
viewed the entire culture of medieval Christendom as sacred (Traditional), and the entire culture of the modern West as profane. The reason they held this view was their belief that the people who comprised
these respective cultures—either consciously or subliminally—viewed
their own cultures in these ways; that is, sacred and profane were attitudes intrinsic to these respective cultural eras and comprised the *consensus omnium* in both. If any dichotomy can be said to exist in their
worldview, it is the stark contrast between medieval Traditional culture
and the modern secular culture of the West. The former represented
order, fusion, purpose, and meaning to Guénon and Coomaraswamy;
the latter represented chaos, fission, aimlessness, futility—all on a
descending scale whose bottom was oblivion with the potential yet real
danger of total autoannihilation. It is to a more complete examination of
the Traditional perspective of this latter culture, modern Western secular culture, that our attention will now be turned in the following, and
final, Part.

# NOTES TO PART III

1. What is meant here by the term *culture* is explained in Appendix B. See page 329, passim.

2. Eliade, *A History of Religious Ideas*, vol. 1, p. 22.

3. These two "types" of mentality, while they are often used in tandem, do not represent the only two types in the general areas of consciousness and epistemology. But they do represent the principal types as they are seen from the Traditional viewpoint. Further, they are seen in Professor Eliade's writings. He gives a lengthy explanation and comparison, for example, in *Myth and Reality*, chapter 6, "Mythology, Ontology, and History." See also, inter alia, chapters 3 and 4 of *The Myth of the Eternal Return* and chapter 5 of *The Quest*.

4. Tylor, *The Origins of Culture*, pp. 6, 21.

5. Frazer, *The Golden Bough*, p. 824.

6. Freud, *Totem and Taboo*, p. 77.

7. Lévy-Bruhl, *How Natives Think*, pp. 38–39 (italics mine).

8. Coomaraswamy, *BK*, p. 99.

9. Tylor, op. cit., p. 23.

10. Ibid., p. 37 (italics mine).

11. Frazer, op. cit., p. 825.

12. Eliade, *Shamanism*, p. 24. See Eliade's refutation of this hypothesis on pp. 29–32 of *Shamanism* and pp. 76, 77 of *Myths, Dreams, and Mysteries*. See also Peter T. Furst's discussion of this in "Introduction: An Overview of Shamanism," in Seaman and Day, eds., *Ancient Traditions: Shamanism in Central Asia and the Americas*, pp. 1–28.

13. Tylor, op. cit., p. 23.

14. Freud, op. cit., p. 99.

15. Lévy-Bruhl, *Primitive Mentality*, p. 55. This is just the tip of an ontological iceberg. It has often been said of the "mystic" mentality such as Meister Eckhart that, like the primitive mentality, it also "adapts itself to two

distinct affirmations at once"; namely, the simultaneous immanence and transcendence of God. Fritz Staal, for example, in his learned book *Exploring
Mysticism: A Methodological Essay* (Berkeley, 1975), hammers away at this
problem: "nobody can effectively talk or act without assuming, at least
implicitly, the validity of the law of noncontradiction" (p. 6). And Staal is
entirely correct, insofar as one's approach to mysticism is exclusively an
empirical and rationalistic one. But what of the trans- or suprarational
approach, like the Traditional view that incorporates *intuition* into understanding or cognition? In such a case, this understanding is confined to the
intellectual metaphysicist, who is perfectly able to comprehend "two distinct
affirmations at once," this process being related to the synthesis of the *coincidentia oppositorum*. His advanced comprehension would thus be not pre- but
*post*logical, and similar (ironically enough) to what Lévy-Bruhl claimed for
the primitive mentality. Cf. Bertrand Russell's "Mysticism and Logic" in the
book by that title, where questions are raised but not answered, and Frithjof
Schuon's *Logic and Transcendence*, where such questions are both raised and
answered. More recently, this polemic has been joined and renewed by the
contributors to Robert K. C. Forman's *The Problem of Pure Consciousness*
(New York: Oxford University Press, 1990), who published largely in
response to their empiricist adversary, Steven T. Katz, and his contributors to
*Mysticism and Philosophical Analysis* (New York; Oxford Univeristy Press,
1978).

16. Guénon, *OEO*, p. 8.

17. Boas, *The Mind of Primitive Man*, p. 8. The recognition of this
"difference" must necessarily require a revision of earlier assessments of
primitive culture: "If it can be shown that the thinkers among primitive peoples envisage life in philosophical terms," wrote Radin, "then obviously our
customary treatment of cultural history . . . must be completely revised."
*Primitive Man as Philosopher*, p. 386.

18. Radin, *Primitive Man as Philosopher*, pp. 229–30.

19. Jung, *Modern Man in Search of a Soul*, p. 127.

20. Lévi-Strauss, *Structural Anthropology*, p. 230.

21. Lévi-Strauss, *The Savage Mind*, p. 269.

22. Cassirer, *The Philosophy of Symbolic Forms*, vol. 2, p. 64. Cf.
Charles Long, *Alpha: The Myths of Creation* (New York, 1963), p. 16: "It is
our position that mythic thinking as a specific mode of apprehending the
world is present in many in spite of the particular worldview of his time. The
advent of modern science is not the only important (and some would say, not
the most important) change which has taken place in human history. Myths

and mythological structures have been discarded by man throughout human history whenever new revelations of being and sacredness have been manifested, but it is precisely the mode of apprehension which we have called mythic which allows man to respond to the new and novel manifestation." G. S. Kirk, in his book on myth, accuses Cassirer, when the latter is trying to show "how the 'mythical consciousness' forms its symbols," of falling back "on a modified form of the idea of 'primitive mentality' outlined by Lévi-Bruhl," as if it were necessary to have a "primitive" mentality to form symbols. And this for a classicist (Kirk) for whom "myths are not connected with religion any more by a universal emotional intensity than they are by their subject matter—for, as has been seen, whereas some myths are about gods, others are not."

23. Malinowski, *Myth in Primitive Psychology*, p. 123.

24. de Santillana, *Hamlet's Mill*, p. 56.

25. Eliade, *Patterns in Comparative Religion*, pp. 30–31.

26. Boas, op. cit., p. 197.

27. Eliade, *The Myth of the Eternal Return*, p. 3, and passim regarding "archaic ontology." See Gilford Dudley's treatment of Eliade's archaic ontology in *Religion on Trial: Mircea Eliade and His Critics* (Philadelphia, 1977), pp. 78–81. There Dudley states: "He [Eliade] specifies that ontology as Parmenidean, Platonic, and Indian. It is Parmenidean because it refers to an unchanging, inexhaustible time of infinite duration. It is Platonic because it refers to forms or archetypes, in comparison with which all nonarchetypal or nonparadigmatic phenomena are unreal. . . . The archaic ontology is also Indian and can be observed in both Vedantic thought and in the practice of yoga." Cf. Rennie, *Reconstructing Eliade* (Albany, 1996), pp. 94–95. We will risk another modifier to the three which Dudley has correctly listed: this archaic ontology is also Traditional in the particularized sense of Guénon and Coomaraswamy—though Eliade never publicly professed this—insofar as it is consistent with the same principles of the philosophia perennis.

28. Eliade, *Occultism, Witchcraft, and Cultural Fashion*, p. 21. Cf. Sahlins, *How "Natives" Think*, pp. 6–7. ("Hawaiian [i.e., Traditional] thought does not differ from Western empiricism by an inattention to the world but by the ontological premise that divinity, and more generally subjectivity, can be immanent in it.")

29. Coomaraswamy, GGK, p. 124.

30. Ibid., p. 123. The following is a translation of the French of Eliade cited by Coomaraswamy: "the collective memory sometimes retains certain

precise details of a theory which became intelligible only after a long time . . . of archaic symbols which in essence are purely metaphysical."

31. Guénon, *Règne*, p. 244.

32. Coomaraswamy, GGK, p. 125. In this regard, and adding substantiation to the concluding remarks of n.27 above, Eliade's statement is illuminating: "this 'primitive' ontology has a Platonic structure; and in that case Plato could be regarded as the outstanding philosopher of 'primitive mentality,' that is, as the thinker who succeeded in giving philosophic currency and validity to the modes of life and behavior [culture?] of archaic humanity." *The Myth of the Eternal Return*, p. 34.

33. Guénon does not use the term *culture*, but rather the conventional French *civilization* in its place (see Appendix B). Often employed as synonyms to Traditional, when the latter was used to modify *culture* or *society*, are the terms *normal, unanimous, orthodox,* and *vocational.* These descriptive synonyms were employed both by Guénon and Coomaraswamy.

34. Guénon, *OEO*, p. 236.

35. Coomaraswamy, *FTFS*, p. 218.

36. Needleman, in the Foreword to *SG*, p. 11.

37. Coomaraswamy, *COTPA*, p. 84. In different places in his writings, Coomaraswamy makes other "lists," often with different cultures included. In "The Bugbear of Literacy," for example (*BK*, p. 34), he cites other "traditional cultures (e.g., Gaelic, Indian, Polynesian, American Indian)."

38. Guénon, *Crise*, p. 39. See also *Hindu*, pp. 90, 91.

39. Coomaraswamy, *HB*, p. 26.

40. Vazquez, "A Metaphysics of Culture," in *Remembering and Remembering Again and Again*, p. 225.

41. It can be reasonably argued that the Homeric myths and Greek mythology in general were not the principal media for Socratic/Platonic metaphysics. However, that Greek mythology and the Olympian pantheon combined were the official "state" religion and cultural norm of Attic Greece cannot be disputed. Every reader familiar with the dialogues of Plato knows the extent to which mythology is incorporated in them. Wilbur Urban, for example, states that "Plato . . . follows the light of reason in myth and figure when the dialectic stumbles" (*The Intelligible World*, p. 171); John A. Stewart in *The Myths of Plato* (New York, 1905) asserts, "Myth is an essential element in Plato's philosophical style; and his philosophy cannot be understood apart from it." The famous myth segment in *Phaedo* (107a–114d), for exam-

ple, can be said to contain the heart of Plato's transmigration thesis; Socrates admonishes Meletus, his accuser, for accusing him of being paradoxically "guilty of not believing in the gods, but believing in the gods" (*Apology* 27a). Moreover, there have been several studies done of the use of mythology in Plato beyond Stewart's, among them Francis Cornford's *Greek Religious Thought from Homer to the Age of Alexander* (London: J. M. Dent, 1923); Bruno Snell's *The Discovery of the Mind: The Greek Origins of European Thought* (Oxford: Basil Blackwell, 1953); John P. Anton's *Essays in Ancient Greek Philosophy* (New York: State University of New York Press, 1971).

42. Coomaraswamy, *FTFS*, p. 219.

43. Livingston, *Traditional Theory of Literature*, p. 22.

44. Coomaraswamy, BUGB-D, p. 143.

45. Coomaraswamy, *HB*, p. 27.

46. For those unfamiliar with the caste system, the fourfold classification is: (1) *Brahmana* (priests), (2) *Kṣatriya* (rulers, warriors), (3) *Vaiśya* (farmers, merchants), and (4) *Śūdra* (laborers). The two Sanskrit words for "caste" are *varna* (color) and *jati* (birth) and, as Coomaraswamy notes, "are not synonymous but normally concomitant." The concept of *varna* is often grossly misapplied (see Louis Dumont, section 107 in *Homo Hierarchicus*) to race and skin complexion, when in fact the representative colors are white, red, yellow, and black, respectively, significant of the qualities of brilliance, strength, fertility, and support—all necessary for the operation of a stable and integrated society. The origination of the caste system, like all else in Traditional Indian society, is found in the cosmogonic myths of dismemberment (see especially *Taittirīya Samhitā*, 7.1.1–3 and *Aitareya Brāhmaṇa*, 8.4) wherein the castes derive respectively from the mouth, arms, thighs, and feet of the sacrificed deity.

47. Coomaraswamy, BUGB-D, p. 155.

48. Guénon, *OEO*, p. 163.

49. Coomaraswamy, "The Religious Basis of the Forms of Indian Society," in *East and West and Other Essays*, p. 13.

50. Coomaraswamy, *COTPA*, p. 112.

51. Livingston, *The Traditional Theory of Literature*, p. 29.

52. Hatfield, *The Structure and Meaning of Religious Objects*, p. 77.

53. Guénon, *Règne*, p. 79.

54. Coomaraswamy, *SPTAS*, pp. 51, 73.

55. Coomaraswamy, *COTPA*, p. 33.

56. Hatfield, op. cit., p. 37.

57. Coomaraswamy, *COTPA*, p. 23.

58. Ibid., p. 15.

59. Ibid., p. 26.

60. Coomaraswamy, *HB*, p. 27.

61. Huizinga, *Homo Ludens*, p. 4. Cf. p. 27: "Play consecrated to the Deity, the highest goal of man's endeavor—such was Plato's conception of religion. In following him we in no way abandon the holy mystery, or cease to rate it as the highest attainable expression of that which escapes logical understanding. The ritual act, or an unimportant part of it, will always remain within the play category, but in this seeming subordination the recognition of its holiness is not lost." Huizinga, a philologist and Sanskrit specialist before turning to the history of culture, was no doubt aware of the Indian conception of *līlā*, though it does not appear in *Homo Ludens*. Nonetheless, it does appear incognito in passages such as the one just excerpted.

62. Ibid., p. 212.

63. Coomaraswamy, *SPM*, p. 156.

64. Nasr, *Sufi Essays*, p. 92.

65. Panofsky, *Gothic Architecture and Scholasticism*, pp. 20–21.

66. Eliade, *Occultism, Witchcraft, and Cultural Fashion*, p. 25.

67. Coomaraswamy, *COTPA*, p. 32.

68. Snodgrass, *Architecture, Time and Eternity: Studies in the Stellar and Temporal Symbolism of Traditional Buildings*, p. 40.

69. Guénon, *Règne*, p. 80.

70. Coomaraswamy, BUGB-D, p. 151.

71. Wilbur, "Physics, Mysticism, and the New Holographic Paradigm," p. 43. For the intrepid who wish to pursue the new holographic paradigm further, good background sources are *The American Theosophist*, Fall 1979 Special Issue, "Approaches to Holistic Principles"; Fred Unterseher, ed. *Holographic Handbook* (Berkeley: Ross Books, 1982); Lawrence F. Berley, *Holographic Mind, Holographic Vision: A New Theory of Vision in Art and Physics* (Bensalen, Pa.: Lakstun Press, 1980); Ted Jones, ed. *Holography: A Source Book to Information* (Nashville, Tenn.: New Dimension Studio, 1977); *International Conference on Holography, Correlation Optics, and Recording Materials* (Bellingham: SPIE-International Society for Optical

Engineering, 1993); Graham Saxby, *The Manual of Practical Holography* (Boston: Focal Press, 1991); Philip Heckman, *The Magic of Holography* (New York: Atheneum, 1986). Beyond these is the technical work of scientists like Bohm, Wheeler, Sarfatti, Pribram, and others.

72. Coomaraswamy, "America and India," in *Coomaraswaminana* (unpaginated).

73. Guénon, "Initiation and the Crafts," p. 164.

74. Coomaraswamy, *FTFS*, p. 218. Cf. p. 233 n.12, loc. cit., where he discusses the Traditional notion of sin: "Sin, Skr. *aparāddha*, 'missing the mark,' 'any departure from the order to the end,' is a sort of clumsiness due to want of skill. There is a ritual of life, and what matters in the performance of a rite is that whatever is done should be done correctly, in 'good form.' What is not important is how one *feels* about the work to be done or life to be lived: all such feelings being tendentious and self-referent. But if, over and above the correct performance of the rite or any action, one also understands its form, if all one's actions are conscious and not merely instinctive reactions provoked by pleasure or pain, whether anticipated or felt, this awareness of the underlying principles is immediately dispositive to spiritual freedom. In other words, wherever the action itself is correct, the action itself is symbolic, and provides a discipline, or path, by following which the final goal must be reached: and so on the other hand, whoever acts informally has opinions of his own, and 'knowing what he likes,' is limiting his person to the measure of his individuality."

75. Coomaraswamy, BUGB-D, p. 140. See Guénon's discussion of temporal authority in chapter 1 ("Autorité et Hiérarchié) of *Autorité Spirituelle et Pouvoir Temporel*.

76. Coomaraswamy, *FTFS*, p. 231 and *COTPA*, p. 136.

77. Lipsey, *CLW*, p. 268.

78. Coomaraswamy, GGK, p. 116.

79. Coomaraswamy, *FTFS*, p. 220.

80. Hatfield has done a reasonably good job in explicating Coomaraswamy's views on mythology in chapters 4 and 5 of his unpublished dissertation mentioned above, though concentrating largely on symbols. There remains to be done a thorough study on the subject, and endnote explanations require brevity, so obviously nothing comprehensive can be done here. Briefly, however, Coomaraswamy saw mythology as a germinal and primary expression of the first principles of the Tradition, a rudimentary formulation of the philosophia perennis expressed in symbols and types. Perhaps his

clearest and most succinct statement on myth is found in his essay "Recollection, Indian and Platonic": "All mythology involves a corresponding philosophy; and if there is only one mythology, as there is only one 'Perennial Philosophy,' then that 'the myth is not my own, I had it from my mother' (Euripides) points to a spiritual unity of the human race already predetermined long before the discovery of metals. It may really be true that, as Alfred Jeremias said, the various cultures of mankind are no more than the *dialects* of one and the same spiritual language" (*SPM*, p. 65). Cf. "Literary Symbolism" in *SPTAS*, p. 327. In footnote 4 of "Primitive Mentality," Coomaraswamy states that "One might add, that it [mythology] will exist for ever in the eternal now of the Truth, unaffected by the truth or errors of history. A myth is true now, or never was true at all." From this assertion, it is clear that Coomaraswamy despised the euhemeristic exegesis of mythology, which he openly declares in "The Christian and Oriental, or True, Philosophy of Art": "The vulgarity of humanism appears nakedly and unashamed in all euhemerism." Regarding this latter, empirical approach, one observation by Eliade strikes me as particularly appropriate: in perhaps one of his most profound (but little noticed) insights into mythology, he perceives the basic dynamics of "mytholization" as a "*reduction of events to categories and of individuals to achetypes*" (*The Myth of the Eternal Return*, p. 44). Thus, notwithstanding historicity and "factual data," the *categories* and *archetypes* are the perennial elements, the *patterns* of the dynamics of first principles, the more important and true elements to the mythological mentality, and precisely the reverse of euhemerism. So are the "events of history" translated and/or "recorded" in folk and primitive cultures, which is one explanation for accretions and variants found universally in all myths.

81. Coomaraswamy, *BK*, p. 88.

82. Guénon, *OEO*, p. 28. Cf. Gerard Casey, "There is the *succession* of traditions as well as the archetypal *simultaneity* implied in the 'transcendent unity of religions.' What the perennialists have done so admirably and exhaustively for the perspective of simultaneity remains to be done for that of succession. The cycles begin and end, and there is truth in the 'extremes meet' of the Ouroboros biting its own tail; but circle-upon-circle is not the geometrical symbol of the cosmic drama. The appropriate figure is the spiral: it returns to its starting point, but at a higher level, and this higher level is just what measures the realization of spiritual freedom." From James Wetmore (ed.), "Traditions's Tide: An Interiew with Gerard Casey." *Parabola* 21, No. 2, 1996: 44–51.

83. Coomaraswamy, *COTPA*, p. 32.

84. Coomaraswamy, *SPTAS*, pp. 155–56.

85. The "Hermes" quote is found on p. 375 in *SG*: the "Oriental Meta-physics" quote on p. 49. The remaining quote fragments are all found on pp. 49–51. Regarding this "primordial state" of which Guénon speaks, cf. Coomaraswamy, *FTFS*, p. 228, "We say that what seems to 'us' irrational in the life of 'savages' . . . represents the vestiges of a primordial state of meta-physical understanding."

86. With care not to extend the analogy too far, one can correlate these "popular" or "folk" and "aristocratic" levels of Traditional culture to our own designation of "blue collar" and "white collar" within the modern industrial West. The parallel is that these two basic levels of culture as a whole are dif-ferent in degree but not in kind, since there is always some overlapping and reciprocity between them. In modernity, the criteria that define each level are fewer—for example, education, training, or wealth—and the mobility or exchange between them is greater. Different in kind, and not to be confused with this bipartition above, are so-called subcultures indicative of the great social plurality and heterogeneity of modernity.

87. Coomaraswamy, *COTPA*, p. 136.

88. We are not concerned here with the reasons for nor the modes of the division of labor, but rather employ Durkheim's formulation heuristically; that is, that artificers and craftsmen, as well as priests, laborers, soldiers, and so forth, simply fulfill different functions in a developed Traditional society. Coomaraswamy might have objected to this heuristic application: see *HB*, p. 27: "The caste system differs from the industrial 'division of labor,' with its 'fractioning of human faculty,' in that it presupposes differences in kinds of responsibility but not in degrees of responsibility." We agree with Coomar-aswamy insofar as this applies to modern industrialization, but still employ the term nonetheless, as it remains a useful distinction between primitive and developed Traditional societies relative to "differences in kind of responsibil-ity."

89. Coomaraswamy, *HB*, p. 4. Zimmer's views are found on the first page of Appendix A ("The Six Systems") in his *Philosophies of India*: "Though apparently and even overtly contradictory, they are understood to be complementary projections of the one truth on various planes of conscious-ness, valid intuitions from differing points of view—like the expressions of the seven blind men feeling the elephant, in the popular Buddhist tale."

90. Coomaraswamy, *BK*, p. 99 (italics mine).

91. Livingston, op. cit., p. 23.

92. Eliade, *Shamanism*, p. 8. See also his *Myths, Dreams, and Myster-ies*, pp. 61 and especially 95, where the connection is made: "Thus there

exists a perfect continuity of these metaphysical techniques, from cultures at the paleolithic stage right up to the modern religions. The true meaning[s] . . . indicate the attainment of a known condition of ecstasy, or, upon other cultural levels (in India, for instance), access to a *nonconditioned state of perfect spiritual freedom.*" The italics here are mine, used to draw a parallel to this "nonconditioned state" and the third state of metaphysical realization just described by Guénon.

93. Boas, op. cit., p. 222.

94. Guénon, *Règne*, p. 244.

95. Eliade, *The Myth of the Eternal Return*, p. 3. Cf. Joseph Campbell, "Primitive Man as Metaphysician," in Stanley Diamond's *Primitive Views of the World*, pp. 20–32.

96. There exist, of course, full and lengthy bibliographies on medieval studies, and to attempt any such reproduction here would be useless. However, the specific concern here is medieval *culture*, and more specially, the three-century period of the High Middle Ages (1100–1400) under discussion here. The reader interested in pursuing this area will find a good "select" bibliography of works in English on pages xv, 175, and 350 of David Herlihy's *Mediaeval Culture and Society* (New York: Harper Torchbooks, 1968). To the many books listed there we would add, inter alia, R. W. Southern's *Western Society and the Church in the Middle Ages* (Harmondsworth: Penguin Books, 1970); Carrolly Erickson's *The Mediaeval Vision: Essays in History and Perception* (Oxford: Oxford University Press, 1976); for the High Middle Ages culture in England, Sir Arthur Bryant's second volume of *The Atlantic Saga: The Age of Chivalry* (New York: Doubleday, 1964); and more recently, Georges Duby's *The Three Orders: Feudal Society Imagined* (Chicago: University of Chicago Press, 1980); for a cross section dealing with various aspects of the time, *The Culture of Christendom*, ed. Marc A. Meyer (London: Hambledon Press, 1993); Jacques Le Goff's *Time, Work, and Culture in the Middle Ages* (Chicago: University of Chicago Press, 1980); and Jacques Le Goff's *Medieval Civilization, 400–1500* (Oxford: Blackwell, 1988).

97. Pelikan, *The Christian Tradition: The Growth of Medieval Theology (600–1300)*, vol. 3, p. 268. While we are dealing here specifically with a developed Christian theological metaphysics, which Pelikan outlines in his work, there is still a popular or folk mythology at work in medieval European culture that shares a cultural necessity with the metaphysics. Eliade describes this popular medieval mythology: "In the Middle Ages we witness an upwelling of mythical thought. All the social classes depend on their mythological traditions. Knights, artisans, clerks, peasants, accept an 'origin myth' for their condition and endeavor to imitate an exemplary model. These

mythologies have various sources. The Arthurian cycle and the Grail theme incorporate, under a varnish of Christianity, a number of Celtic beliefs, especially having to do with the Other World." *Myth and Reality*, p. 174.

98. Guénon, *Saint Bernard*, p. 19.

99. Guénon, *OEO*, p. 176.

100. Kelley, *Meister Eckhart on Divine Knowledge*, p. xiv.

101. Jung, *The Integration of the Personality*, p. 60.

102. Jung, *Psychology of Religion: West and East*, p. 192. In a remarkable substantiation of Jung's observations coming from an historical quarter, Le Goff writes: "This was a phenomenon of subjectivization and internalization of the spiritual life, from which introspection and hence the whole of modern Western psychology originated. It is no accident that the all-important spiritual doctrines of the twelfth century may be defined as Christian Socraticisms, whether intellectualist as in Abelard; mystical as in Hugh of Saint-Victor, Hildegard of Bingen, or Saint Bernard; or even the grammatical and scientific humanism of Chartres." *Time, Work, and Culture in the Middle Ages*, p. 114.

103. Huizinga, *The Waning of the Middle Ages*, p. 57.

104. Ibid., p. 59.

105. Ibid., p. 58.

106. Pelikan, op. cit., p. 294.

107. Duby, *The Three Orders*, p. 8. Le Goff also devotes a chapter to this concept in *Time, Work, and Culture in the Middle Ages*, entitled "A Note on Tripartite Society, Monarchic Ideology, and Economic Renewal in Ninth- to Twelfth-Century Christendom."

108. Ibid., p. 109.

109. Ibid., p. 75.

110. Coomaraswamy, *COTPA*, p. 111.

111. Haskins, *The Renaissance of the Twelfth Century*, p. 12.

112. Huizinga, *The Waning of the Middle Ages*, p. 244.

113. Maritain, *Art and Scholasticism*, p. 96.

114. Huizinga, *The Waning of the Middle Ages,* p. 258.

115. Coomaraswamy, *COTPA*, p. 114.

116. Huizinga, *Homo Ludens*, p. 180.

117. Coomaraswamy, *SPM*, p. 151. In the sense he uses the term here, *initiates* does not have to do necessarily with "metaphysical realization," as Guénon usually meant it, but rather initiated by ceremony into a caste or "estate" (knighthood, *bushido* of the *samurai*, *kṣatriya*, etc.) that precluded participation in the "game" or "rite" by any other than just that particular group.

118. Eckhart, in Evans, *Meister Eckhart* (London, 1924–31), p. 148.

119. Le Goff, *Time, Work, and Culture in the Middle Ages*, p. 62.

120. Ibid., p. 115.

121. Ibid., p. 115.

122. Huizinga, "Abelard," in *Men and Ideas*, p. 184.

123. Barbara Tuchman, *A Distant Mirror: The Calamitous Fourteenth Century* (New York: Ballatine Books, 1980), p. 32.

124. Huizinga, *The Waning of the Middle Ages*, p. 152.

125. Ibid., p. 156.

126. Guénon, "Initiation and the Crafts," pp. 163–64.

# PART IV

## MODERN CULTURE

# 12

## Introductory

The degree of invective used by Coomaraswamy and Guénon to describe the Western culture of modernity of the 1930s and 1940s would no doubt have increased had they survived to witness the remarkable progeny of science and technology of only half a century later. Among the most indicative of such progeny are biological cloning, psychocybernetics, recombinant DNA production, laser weaponry, global nuclear proliferation (energy and armaments), manned space exploration, virtual reality, ubiquitous computerization, and so on. Doubtless they would have been among the first to point out the irony of exponents of modern Western positivistic scientism trying to extricate themselves from the terminal effects of the high-entropy, high-pollution lifestyle—after the fashion of a Chinese finger puzzle where the harder one pulls to free the fingers the tighter the grip becomes—by the use of more and greater scientific, technologic permutations whose possible side effects and byproducts are devastating to such a degree as to make the causes for which they were designed to be solutions seem virtually innocuous. "Modern civilization," wrote Coomaraswamy, never having seen these latest of its progeny, "by its divorce from any principle, can be likened to a headless corpse of which the last motions are convulsive and insignificant."[1] Yet, both he and Guénon died before the "last motions" had reached such feverish convulsions, and their being insignificant is a matter for twenty-first-century posterity—if it survives—to decide in retrospect.

The corrosion of the few surviving Traditional cultures by the modern Western culture that Coomaraswamy and Guénon so lamented has, if anything, increased by geometric progression since the era in which they wrote. This period also has seen the intentional genocide of numerous Traditional cultures. The most notorious examples of this are the genocide of the monastic orders and people of Tibet by the secular, Marxist Chinese government and the extermination of rain-forest tribes

in the Amazon basin by Brazilian ranchers and miners with the government's tacit approval. Modern Western culture, quantitative and unprincipled, has metastasized throughout the planet. The Traditional cultures,
their principles, religions, and worldviews, have subsequently died out
altogether or eroded to the edge of extinction by the process of attrition.
The secular, quantitative, industrialized culture of the modern West has
in fact become worldwide, aided and abetted by technologic creations,
and has at least partially supplanted even the endemic cultures of the Orient—for example, South Korea, Japan, China, Taiwan, and Indonesia.

The world is getter smaller, as the cliché has it, and with greater
alacrity due to international telecommunications, satellite technology,
the Internet, jet travel, "development," and relative to world commerce,
the so-called corporate monoliths or international conglomerate cartels
like Mitsubishi, Royal Dutch/Shell Group, Exxon Corporation, Sumit-
omo, General Motors, and so forth.[2] The great steel-concrete-glass
office buildings, like Chicago's Sears Tower and New York's World
Trade Center, whether ten stories or 110, dominate the skylines of the
world's major cities, and attest to the global homogenization of "efficient" architecture.[3] The central downtown sections of Tokyo, Hong
Kong, Sydney, Singapore, Calcutta, Bombay, Teheran, Istanbul, Mos-
cow, Cairo, Cape Town, Rome, Hamburg, Paris, London, Rio, Buenos
Aires, Bogota, Houston, Los Angeles, and Honolulu, inter alia, are fill-
ing up with these buildings and looking more and more alike—or less
and less distinguishable—each time an older building of regional architectural style is razed and an "international glass" building is erected in
its place, the latter statistically proven to be more cost effective. The
products that fill the street-level shops in such buildings and which are
generally to be found in these cities are truly international as well, as are
the fast-food and other franchises that crowd the downtown areas.
Architecture, products, and transportation are virtually all Western in
origin and/or design, as is the concomitant secular lifestyle that normally follows in their wake.

Guénon and Coomaraswamy were concerned with the prevailing
conditions of the first half of the twentieth century. Our concern here is
with the first and last halves, since from a Traditional perspective the last
half can be seen as an era in which conditions of the first half are exacerbated and consequently more devastating. Again the difference in temperament between the two writers makes itself apparent: it is clear that
regarding the morphology and dynamics of both primitive and devel-

oped Traditional cultures, Coomaraswamy was the more outspoken of the two. But of the malaise of modernity, Guénon is the unequalled critic. While this area of criticism is not exclusively Guénon's turf, his twin works, *La crise du monde moderne* and *Le règne de la quantité et les signes des temps*, must be considered the standard and classic Traditional critiques of modernity. Where Coomaraswamy was the sniper, taking occasional well-aimed shots at the modern mentality and its effects, Guénon was the cannoneer, levelling vast areas of modernity's facade—such as scientism and progressivism—and shaking the putative infallibility of its empirical superstructure. All of Guénon's barrages against the modern mentality and culture of the West—now more or less worldwide—were motivated by his observation, most succinctly expressed in a passage in *Orient et Occident*:

The modern world has made an exact reversal of the natural relations of the various orders; once more, it is the desuetude of the intellectual order (and even the absence of pure intellectuality) and exaggeration of the material order and the sentimental order which all combined make the present Western civilization an anomaly, not to say a monstrosity.[4]

It is not by any quantum leap that our examination traverses the first half of the twentieth century—using primarily the writings of Guénon and Coomaraswamy—to the second half; this occurs by a necessary and obvious continuity. Moreover, there is today no lack of commentators and critics who point out the tremendous resultant problems to which our collective empirical and quantitative worldview has subjected us. These contemporary "up daters" are found both in the Traditional school in the works of Frithjof Schuon, Martin Lings, Marco Pallis, Titus Burckhardt, Seyyed Hossein Nasr, et al., and among many non-Traditional intellectuals as well, notably in the works of E. F. Schumacher, Buckminster Fuller, Theodore Roszak, William Irwin Thompson, and Robert Heilbroner, to name but a few. Where Guénon and Coomaraswamy differ from the legion of other critics of modernity, however, is in the fact that they were the first to formulate this Traditional perspective of modernity and, a fortiori, correctly identify its causes. They and later Traditional writers concentrated primarily upon, consistent with their metaphysical assumptions, the causal ideological elements of the worldview of modernity, and only secondarily on the effective economic, ecologic substance of its application throughout the planet. Guénon and Coomaraswamy can thus be described as "theorists" of modern culture; as critic-expositors of its informing and conceptual properties, even though their exposition often amounted to describing modern culture as devoid of all Traditional elements, a sort of *via negativa* or negation of the essence and essential properties of Traditional culture. In this regard, Martin Lings's *The Eleventh Hour: The Spiritual Crisis of the Modern World in the Light of Tradition and Prophecy* (Cambridge, 1987) can be viewed as an update, as it were, of the two principal works on the subject by Guénon.

Guénon and Coomaraswamy, let it be clear, were not the first critics of materialism, industrialization, secularization—in short—of modernization since the post-Enlightenment period of Western culture. Among the more renowned of the earlier critics was William Blake (1757–1827), whose poetry contains frequent allusions to the "problem." In the Luddite rebellion in England (1811–1816), workers in the new wave of factories marking the beginnings of the Industrial revolution "smashed new labor-saving textile machinery in protest against reduced wages and unemployment." Such machinery was labor saving to the owners alone, whose main interests were profit margins; it was "labor losing" to the workers, in addition to being craft-destructive. Even the early sociologists, following Blake and the Luddites, developed their thought in response to "the political and industrial revolutions of modern times": Robert Bellah views the "work of Henri Saint-Simon and Auguste Compte as an effort to reconcile order, which in their view characterized the Middle Ages [an interesting parallel to the Traditional viewpoint] but has since become disrupted."[5] Henry David Thoreau (1817–1862) is another who can be placed squarely in this stream of thought, especially as his views are expressed in *Walden*. Following Thoreau and the sociologists, the work of John Ruskin (1819–1900) in England once again renewed the attack on modernity, focusing on the supercedure of art and craft by industrialization and mass production. Ruskin was to become a model for Coomaraswamy on this point, as was William Morris.[6] One cannot fail to include in this list the outspoken criticism of Friedrich Nietzsche (1844–1900) who, up to the year of his incompetency in 1889, professed a deep contempt for modernity.

With the advent of Guénon and Coomaraswamy, in the philosophical heyday of positivistic scientism, the climax occurs in the fight of quantitative versus qualitative. Too few of the ever-increasing critics of the modern quantitative worldview are aware of the intensity of the indictments in the 1930s and 1940s brought by Guénon and Coomaraswamy against the proponents of empiricism as scientism. As learned and eloquent as they were, their voices on this point were practically ignored, virtually inaudible against the din of triumphant pronouncements heralding the total victory of science, technology, empiricism, evolutionism, positivism—in short, of the quantitative, secular worldview, summed up by A. B. Keith, a true believer, in one of Coomaraswamy's often-cited quotes: "Such knowledge as is not empirical is meaningless to us and should not be described as knowledge."

These few examples of modernity's critics since the inception of the Industrial Revolution and the "Enlightenment" are hardly meant to be comprehensive, but only to show that criticisms of modernity that are philosophically in consonance with those of Guénon and Coomaraswamy can be evinced from its beginnings. Furthermore, Part 4 is not meant to be a detailed description of modernity utilizing the method of the history of culture designed to capture the *Zeitgeist* of the period—the method at which Huizinga was an undisputed master. Detailed descriptions of modern culture are numerous and ever present, and consequently unnecessary here. Our senses are today literally deluged with the sights and sounds of our culture, no little part of which is devoted to the pervasive information dissemination by the various on-line, printed, and audio-visual media. Rather, the aim here is, consistent with the methods of Guénon and Coomaraswamy, to examine the mentality and underlying ideologic presuppositions of modernity,[7] of the modern "individual," particularly in contrast to the Traditional worldview with which the reader should now be adequately familiar. "My interest and conviction," to borrow words of Theodore Roszak, "have been with those dissenting elements who have climbed aboard William Blake's chariot of fire to join his 'mental fight' against the total secularization and scientization of modern culture." And though Roszak does not explicitly include Coomaraswamy and Guénon as major strategists or "dissenting elements" in this "mental fight," the reasons Roszak cites for the struggle are the same as those that motivated Coomaraswamy and Guénon: "For theirs is the struggle to expand our conception of human personhood beyond anything that industrial necessity can tolerate or scientific intellect comprehend."[8]

It is easy enough to see what is absent in the primitive, archaic, and older Traditional cultures in terms of technological hardware and material conveniences and luxuries. A further aim of Part 4 is to see what is absent in modern culture from the point of view of Traditional culture: specifically, what the moral, intellectual, and principial losses have been in the West from the Traditional culture of medieval Christendom to the twenty-first century. In other words, we will use what C. S. Lewis called *The Discarded Image*—that is, the medieval "model of the universe"—as a mirror by which to assess the culture or model of the universe of modernity and to measure its separation from the sacred. Again, we invoke a straightforward bifurcation for the purposes of stark contrast: medieval Christendom between the years 1100 and 1400 C.E. as described in the preceding pages, in contrast to modern Western life of the late twentieth century. By the invocation of this bifurcation, there is no suggestion or implication that the six intervening centuries did not provide a gradual change. As in the preceding Part, our concern is not with the dynamics or process of the change—it is rather with the essential properties of the cultural realities that represent polar extremes of the transition, and by which alone a proper contrast can be made. The desiderata of modern culture will be seen implicitly in an examination of the elemental properties—the mental habits (and their effects) of modernity—and this will be followed by a discussion of solutions to the modern philosophical and cultural malaise offered by Guénon, Coomaraswamy, and others.

As will presently be seen, what is lacking in modernity, in its most succinct formulation, is the principle of wholeness or integrity, the latter in its pristine etymological sense (Latin, *integrare*, "to make whole"). Without wholeness, both in philosophical outlook (first principles) and its cultural expression, there can be no harmony, no value, no meaning. The lack of first principles, the general metaphysical hebetude of modernity that Guénon and Coomaraswamy disparaged, is echoed by Wilbur Urban: "In any case, it is precisely this dissolution of *philosophia perennis* which is the outstanding feature of modern culture. The forces which have led to it have been described as modernism in philosophy and may be directly connected with the Neo-nominalism described in earlier contexts."[9] Not unaware that their views are diametrically antithetical to the cultural *consensus omnium* of modernity that elevates the notion of progress both in philosophy and history, those of the Traditional school—and those doctrinally close to it—never lost sight of the truism that, as Coomaraswamy expressed it, "what the modern terms progress is for the Traditionalist disintegration."[10] The notion of progress and all the other notions within the quantitative worldview of modernity that help comprise it, form the filler needed for the hiatus created by the loss of the principles of periodicity and regeneration, which in their turn are subsumed in the greater theme of wholeness.

With the loss of quality, the remaining standard of value for modernity is quantity, by which the modern meretricious "standard of living" is measured. In the Traditional perspective "It is only when measured in terms of dignity and not merely in terms of comfort that a 'standard of living' can properly be called 'high.'"[11] A lack of wholeness or integrity spells disintegration, and in terms of the worldview of modernity Guénon phrases it almost axiomatically: "Western science is analysis and dispersion; Eastern [traditional] knowledge is synthesis and concentration."[12] What is *lacking* in the modern West—the combined "losses" since the predominance of the holistic medieval Traditional worldview—is mirrored and thereby becomes observable in those assumptions that have come to be predominant in the modern world:

> For example, private ownership of resources, increased centralization of power, the elimination of diversity [i.e., numerical standardization], greater reliance on science and technology, the refusal to set limits on production and consumption, the fragmentation of human labor into separate and autonomous spheres of operation, the reductionist approach to understanding life and the interrelationships between phenomena, and the concept of progress as a process of continually transforming the natural world into a more valuable [through exploitation] and more ordered human-made environment have long been considered as valid pursuits and goals in the modern world.[13]

In such a discussion as this, they would be conspicuous by their absence if any mention of the terms *postmodern* and *postmodernity* were altogether omitted. These terms, while currently en vogue, do not convey any particular meaning that is sufficiently circumscribed to warrant their inclusion and use here. While it is encouraging to think that part, at least, of the philosophical world has responded to Ludwig Wittgenstein's challenge to certainty based on the accepted cerebral tools of modernity, the worlds of artistic critcism, theology, and even architecture now have exclusive—if not competing—definitions of these terms. From our standpoint, the sprawling culture of the West remains strictly modern in all ways, notwithstanding its recent introspective paranoia: postmodernity. While signs may even now indicate a substantial cultural paradigm shift along the lines theorized by Thomas S. Kuhn for science, such a sea change is far from being a fait accompli and, until it is, we must wait for the truly "postmodern" world. Nonetheless, if postmodernity were to be used in this treatise, it would be of the "revisionary" type as described by David Ray Griffin and Huston Smith in *Primordial Truth and Postmodern Theology* (Albany, 1989).

Our initial method, then, is not a simple description of modernity, but rather a contrast of modernity with the last expression of Traditional culture in the West—medieval Christendom. Furthermore, it is not a contrast of details, phenomena, or cultural substance, but rather, following the methods of Guénon and Coomaraswamy, a contrast of principles, mental habits, noumena, and cultural essence. The primary focus will be the principial battle fought on a higher level of reference, the clash between the a priori assumptions and informing principles that characterize the cultural expressions, and of which these cultural expressions are only reflections. The ontological and ideological foundations and frameworks of modernity are called into question here by Guénon and Coomaraswamy, as they contrast to those of the Traditional worldview. It is, in short, a process of examining a quantitative consciousness in contrast to a qualitative consciousness. All phenomena can be said to be defined in their opposites, and this comprises the method assumed here. Guénon has drawn the parameters of this process in one sentence:

> There are some things which cannot be truly defined except by negation: anarchy, in whichever order it may be, is only the negation of hierarchy and is nothing positive; an anarchic or unprincipled civilization—this is the basis of the present Western civilization—is exactly the same thing we express in other terms when we say that, contrary to the Eastern civilizations, it is not a "traditional" civilization.[14]

The comments on the modern mentality made by Guénon and Coomaraswamy will, as always, be the central sources of the views expressed, though corresponding observations of more recent scholars and historians of culture whose remarks pertain specifically to the issues under discussion have also been included.

# 13

## Losses and Gains of the Western Worldview

What follows is the Traditional view of the results of the loss of first principles or Tradition on the worldview of the modern West. In some cases these results are equal to the loss in cultural consciousness of certain of the first principles themselves. In other cases they equate to the loss of certain cultural "forms" and mental habits that are concomitant to the influential presence of the first principles. As nature, and we might add by extension *culture*, "abhors a vacuum," these losses were inevitably replaced by "gains"; gains that in the Traditional view can hardly be described as anything positive in terms of a productive and harmonious interaction between members in the community of humankind with each other and, a fortiori, of each individual with his or her own inner spiritual essence. These "gains," in fact, are in the Traditional view the stigmata of modernity—not in the New Testament sense of sanguine marks signifying the passion of Jesus, but in Nathaniel Hawthorne's sense of Hester Prynne's scarlet letter—translated by the modern mentality into the "advances" made by science and technology as they have swept through modern history by the inexorable force of "progress." The losses are, in short, antinomies of the "gains" that replaced them in modernity.

It should by now be apparent why the mental habits and worldview of medieval Christendom were chosen as paradigms for Traditional culture, as opposed to those of an Oriental Traditional culture. To repeat, the cultural polar extremes had to be kept within one locality—the West—in order to create a meaningful contrast. It was in this Western locality, in Guénon's view, that the "rupture with Tradition" took place—that is, the beginnings of cultural degeneration, which was eventually to colonize and ultimately corrupt all other indigenous Traditional cultures either by conquest or by the latter's imitation and adoption of Western material, technologic supremacy. The first effects of this degeneration were obviously in the West itself, and the pivotal

juncture of these principial losses and empirical "gains" is placed by
Guénon in the fourteenth century:

> Similarly, the Renaissance and the Reformation, which are
> most often regarded as the first great manifestations of the
> modern spirit, completed the rupture with tradition much
> more than they provoked it; for us, the beginning of this rup-
> ture dates from the 14th century, and it is from that moment,
> and not from one or two centuries later, that the beginning of
> modern times ought, in reality, to be dated.[15]

Before proceeding to the losses and gains, a few prefatory
thoughts regarding the process or dynamic of this desacralization or
despiritualization that occurred during the intervening centuries will be
helpful, even though this process does not constitute a central feature of
our discussion. In a booklet entitled *On the Disfiguration of the Image
of Man in the West*, Gilbert Durand addresses this process directly and
specifically, referring to three great "metaphysical catastrophes."[16]
Guénon gives a full page to this process in *Le règne de la quantité et les
signes des temps* that could be described as the most succinct précis of
the thesis of the book he ever wrote.[17] Buckminster Fuller gives his particular views of the process in the first chapters of *Critical Path*. The
reason this process is not treated here is purely practical: it is both complex and would require a work equally as comprehensive and long as
the present one to do the job properly. Of course, one finds many volumes devoted to precisely this task among the resources of the history
of philosophy and ideas, but the Traditional perspective is different
from these, and from a Traditional perspective no such single work
exists. Only these brief treatments just cited, to which the interested
reader is referred, offer a glimpse into the process or dynamic whose
current status incorporates Traditional and modern culture in the West
as polar extremes. These references are given because those in the Traditional school themselves recognize that this is a somewhat forced
bifurcation; that, as Guénon says, "a rupture with the past, however radical it may be, can never be absolutely complete and such that it precludes all continuity."[18] The transitional process from the height of
Gothic Christian metaphysical acuity of the twelfth and thirteenth centuries to the present-day mechanical and technologic acuity is essentially one from sacred to profane worldview, and this is referred to
variously as desacralization or despiritualization.

Many current scholars and cultural observers employ these and similar terms to describe this process, though the simple term often belies the long duration and complexity of the transition. Eliade refers to sacred activities that "have undergone a long process of desacralization and have, in modern societies, become profane"; Jung refers to the "historical process of the despiritualization of the world"; and Huston Smith, apparently referring to the effects of Rudolf Bultmann's lifelong work of *Entmythologisierung* (demythologization), asserts, "In religion modernity demythologizes tradition to accommodate it to its one-story universe."[19] Such quotes could be multiplied extensively. These are given to illustrate that the contrast between the cultural polar extremes is not acknowledged by Traditional writers alone. Other scholars, historians, and observers are cognizant of these extremes and view the process that separates them as a desacralization or, inversely, as a secularization.

LOSS OF THE SACRED, GAIN OF THE SECULAR

There are, of course, elements of the sacred in modernity, as there were elements of the secular as anomalies in Traditional medieval Christendom. But when we speak of the loss of the sacred and the gain of the secular, it is in total terms: terms of societal or cultural magnitude. Shils writes in *Tradition* that "Even in societies in which religious traditions were more pervasive and more intensely possessed than they are at present in most Western societies, secular beliefs were widespread. They existed however in a framework set by religious traditions which hedged them in and dominated them."[20] The worldview of a unanimous Traditional culture as a whole was sacred, and this property has been lost and replaced by a carefully restrained division of sacred and profane in modern culture, further complicated by the plethoric heterogeneity of what constitutes the surviving and fragmented elements of the sacred in modernity. Moreover, this modern fragmented sacred gives way increasingly to what is tantamount to a worship of science and technology, bound up with a sort of soteriological belief in "progress." "The technocracy," as Roszak writes, "is not simply a power structure wielding vast material influence; it is the expression of a grand cultural imperative, a veritable mystique that is deeply endorsed by the populace."[21]

This division of sacred and secular is frequently constitutional, as one find in America—ably documented by Stephen Carter in *The Cul-*

*ture of Disbelief* (New York, 1993)—and consequently ensures the viability of phenomena like institutional atheism, as in the case of American Atheists. Such organizations, though they serve a useful purpose in their own environment as a sort of necessary leavening relative to various strains of bigoted religious fundamentalism, would have served no purpose in a culture whose entire outlook was sacred, from undertaking the minutiae of daily routine to its grandest cosmological formulations. "Today," as Martin Marty writes, regarding modern American religiosity, "transcendent order has disappeared from consciousness. Any new quest by people who have experienced the disappearance of transcendence must take place in the empirical world."[22] And though secularism may pullulate in concentration within urban areas, the modern worldview so prevalent in Harvey Cox's secular city is spread nonetheless throughout all the regions of the Western world so that secularism prevails six and three-quarters days a week and the sacred, if then, during morning of the Sabbath.

One cannot properly speak of secularization without including its basic doctrinal elements, science and technology. These in turn are inseparable from the overall worldview of modernity, which includes as parallel doctrinal elements empiricism and materialism, based on exclusive reason, logic, and the quantification of knowledge. All of these doctrinal elements are both necessary and useful in their respective domains. The trouble occurs, according to the Traditional perspective, when they become reductionistic and deny the existence of metaphysical realities or principles; when, in Guénon's phraseology, the "lesser denies the greater." This scientific reductionism is more properly termed "scientism," and Huston Smith draws the distinction succinctly: "Whereas science is positive, contenting itself with reporting what it discovers, scientism is negative. It goes beyond the actual findings of science to deny that other approaches to knowledge are valid and other truths true."[23]

In the struggle between not *science* and religion—which have no quarrel—but between *scientism* and religion in the modern era, scientism is the clear victor. The victory of scientism over metaphysics and the first principles has been even more resounding. Whereas Tradition was all but obliterated by scientism in modernity, the various branches of the Christian church are still apparent, though they are predominantly social in function and have devolved to spiritually lifeless shells of what the living Traditional expression of the Christianity was in the

Middle Ages. "What secular humanism [as an epiphenomenon of scientism] wants from religion is first and foremost a social gospel. And, having that, it looks no further. For, in truth, it believes that there is nothing more to be found that is of historical and social consequence."[24]

This profanation or secularization of the religious in modernity has manifested beyond the shores of the Western world. During the era of European colonial expansion—and even to the present—it was exported under the guise of modern Christian proselytism to other Traditional cultures in various parts of the non-Western world. Coomaraswamy addressed the Christian missionaries, whom he saw as exporters of a bifurcated worldview, sacred and profane:

> *You* have already reached the point at which culture and religion, utility and meaning, have been divorced and can be considered apart, but this is not true of those people whom you propose to convert, whose religion and culture *are one and the same thing* and none of the functions of whose life are necessarily profane or unprincipled.[25]

Add to this bifurcation a strong "social gospel," and even the sacrality of the sacred element in this dyad is questionable. The gain of modernity here is, at best, a bifurcated worldview, though prodominantly secular, in place of holistic and purely sacred one. "The modern mind," writes Jung in a somewhat facetious tone, "has forgotten those old truths that speak of the death of the old man and of the making of a new one, of the spiritual rebirth and similar old-fashioned 'mystical absurdities.'"[26] Coomaraswamy's precise definition of "secularization," almost dictionary-like in construction ("Secularization: a subtraction of meaning from form, a 'sundering of soul from spirit' not in the scriptural sense but *a l'envers*, a materialization of all values"), serves as the basic standard for the Traditional perspective in measuring what has been lost in the Traditional West and gained in the modern West, and even today exported to and assimilated by different cultures around the planet. One result of this metastasizing secularization and loss of the sacred in Western societies is summarized by Professor Eliade:

> Satisfied with the vertiginous secularization of Western societies, the scientists are inclined to suspect obscurantism or nostalgia in authors who see in the different forms of reli-

gion something other than superstition, ignorance, or, at the most, psychological behavior, social institutions, and rudimentary ideologies fortunately left behind by the progress of scientific thought and the triumph of technology. Such a suspicion does not belong exclusively to the scientists in the strict sense of the term; it is equally shared by a large number of sociologists, anthropologists, and social scientists who conduct themselves, not as humanists, but as naturalists with respect to their object of study.[27]

## LOSS OF VALUE, GAIN OF THE MEAN

The axiological nature of the Traditional principial hierarchy presupposes the absolute constitution of this hierarchy as a standard by which to assign value to all contingent phenomena. The principial hierarchy, as the axis of first principles, does in fact serve a valuational function in Traditional metaphysics and thought. Frequently expressed or translated in the form of religious dicta and ethics through which these principles are often reified in Traditional cultures either in a mythological or intellectual-theological mode, both of which rely on symbols as a primary medium, the first principles are nonetheless considered immutable, not liable to shift or sway, static and intransient. Superior and inferior are therefore assignable to all phases of human activity and character; to all phenomena; to all events, social or natural. And these adjectives of valuation *were* assigned in Traditional cultures, which ultimately gave life its meaning and direction, for without value meaning does not exist. Without absolute value only the existential ebb and flow of a ceaselessly changing morality survives, a protean collective representation of the *consensus gentium* at any given moment in the life of the culture, a chameleon relative value consisting of little more than a collective opinion determined by the statistical "average mean." "The pathetic attempts of modern man to retain his values without the rational structure with which they have been bound up, and to graft them upon an evolutionary naturalism with which they are wholly incompatible, constitutes the intellectual scandal of modern thought."[28] To lose value—and thus meaning—is to lose the qualitative hierarchy and oneness of Tradition, since that "Oneness is revealed to traditional man as an *Order*, a Cosmos, whose spatio-temporal principle is a qualitative hierarchy."[29]

Because value in the Traditional sense cannot be perceived apart from hierarchy, a parallel tension is brought into play in the discussion of Traditional axiology: intellectual intuition or intellection (*gnosis*), and reason. To deem accurately a phenomenon or event superior (or inferior), there must be access to the higher, subtle realms of principial knowledge, and this requires a developed intellectual intuition—reason alone will not work. In modernity, and especially in modern academia, reason is elevated above all modes of perceiving, and intellection is given no credence. So begins an ineluctable chain reaction—since intellection is declaimed, natural metaphysics is ignored; since natural (Traditional) metaphysics is ignored, value and hierarchical valuation are unattainable; since value is unattainable, meaning is lost and modern man is thus cast adrift in a sea of relativism, incessantly changing "average means," and a mass of disconnected facts. And the conditions that provoked Wilbur Urban's caveat come to pass: "A metaphysic which abstracts being from value is not only unnatural but in the end can only lead to meaninglessness and unintelligibility."[30]

Once lost, value was replaced by pragmatic "value free" systems and the *mean* of statistics (which Traditionalists would consider precisely a "standard deviation") in modern Western culture. Traditional values became inverted, and direction, purpose, and meaning were lost. "Values are to such an extent inverted," wrote Coomaraswamy, "that action, properly means to an end, has been made an end in itself, and contemplation, prerequisite to action, has come to be disparaged as an 'escape' from the responsibilities of activity."[31] Science and scientism become the guideposts for value, and though science claims a value-free position, value becomes further inverted when scientism implies that any idea or sentiment nonscientific is inferior, while all those in explicit support of science, reason, the empirical method, and technology are superior. This attitude has even been extended into purely humanistic endeavors, as Eliade just noted, which above all should retain valuation. Presumably it is ratiocination and science which alone can be considered serious academic tools in modernity, and rationalism and scientific inquiry the only serious methods. All this regardless of the Traditional percept that "Values, life meanings, purposes, and qualities slip through science like sea slips through the nets of fishermen. Yet man swims in this sea, so he cannot exclude it from his purview."[32]

This scientific paradigm of the modern mass man is a numerical reduction to the average mean, with no connection to higher states of consciousness, being, or reality via a hierarchical chain: thus is he "value free." From the contemporary perspective the modern person has been "set free" by science, technology, and exclusive reason, and has presumably seen through the miasma of atavistic superstitions, like the values of integrity, dignity, quality, and sacrality, to which he was, like Prometheus, "bound" before the liberating advent of modern thought. He is consequently fungible, dispensable because he is "proven" virtually identical by a numerical, statistical realism with the average mean of the mass. Only his fingerprints and DNA make him unique. Anomie is his "gain," the gain that has replaced the loss of value resulting from the repudiation of intellectual intuition, metaphysics, the concept of hierarchy—that is, Tradition. This "gain" is seen by Guénon in the fact that "it is something like a 'principle' of all modern administration to treat individuals simply like numerical units entirely alike; that is to say to act as if, by hypothesis, the 'ideal' uniformity had already been realized and thus constrained men to adjust themselves, so to speak, to the same 'average' mean."[33]

## LOSS OF ART AND VOCATION, GAIN OF REPRODUCTION AND INDUSTRY

In our examination of work and play in Traditional society, to which we now return to draw points of contrast to these concepts in modern Western industrial societies, the ideas mentioned were that work and play were identical on a "higher level of reference," that every person in Traditional culture had a vocation, an art or craft by which he or she participated in the Tradition of that culture since it served both as a means of Self-expression and initiation, and that in Coomaraswamy's words, "an artist was not a special kind of man, but every man a special kind of artist." Further, the unanimity of perspective of Coomaraswamy and Guénon and those of the Traditional school on art and vocation was shown, especially as it applied to art and craft being proper descriptives of every function in Traditional society. Coomaraswamy's original source for this view is Plato, whose lexicon is clear. "'Demiurge' and 'technician' are the ordinary Greek words for 'artist' (*artifex*) and under these heading Plato includes not only poets, painters, and musicians, but also archers, weavers, embroiderers, potters, carpenters, sculptors, farmers, doctors, hunters, and above all those whose art is government, only making a distinction between creation (δημιουργία) and mere labor (χειρουργία), art (τέχνη) and artless industry (ἄτεχνος τριβή)."[34] Plato's "distinction" was purely philosophical, but this same distinction is used by Coomaraswamy in an actual sense, and is precisely one among those features that separate the Traditional Western culture from the modern.

Of all the aspects that separate modern and Traditional culture in the West, the loss of art and vocation and the gain of reproduction and industry are those for which one needs the least amount of substantiation from Guénon and Coomaraswamy. This modern "gain" has brought with it the almost complete eradication of any play element from the modern workplace and the vast majority of employment in Western societies. The impersonal and insensitive milieu of industrial production-line, clerical, and similar forms of tedious work was deplored by Coomaraswamy and Guénon. In a harsh indictment of production-line industrialism—specifically its effects on workers—Coomaraswamy declares:

> That "industry without art is brutality" is hardly flattering to those whose admiration of the industrial system is equal to their interest in it. Aristotle defines as "slaves" those who have nothing but their bodies to offer (*Politics* 1.5.1254b). It is on the work of such "slaves," or literally "prostitutes," that the industrial system of production for profit ultimately rests. Their political freedom does not make of assembly-line workers and other "base mechanics" what Plato means by "free men."[35]

To be clear, there are really two parts involved in the modern and Traditional attitudes: the artist (or worker) and the artifact (or product). In the Traditional conception, as we have seen, the artist/craftsman was wholly involved in his activity, and for him it was a means of Self-expression and Self-realization: his work was primarily endosomatic. The artifact he produced, the results of his activity, always had imbued in them both beauty and utility, and expressed in the tangible realm or design some reflection of an intangible, and most often metaphysical or mythological, principle. It is, of course, true both craftsmen and artists exist in modern culture. Insofar as such craftsmen are wholly consumed by their craft and view it not as "work" but as a sacred means of Self-realization, they could be considered Traditional in method. The artist, however, is another matter. To Coomaraswamy, the modern Western artist whose artistic philosophy is exclusively aesthetic and whose purpose is "art for art's sake" is a perfect reflection of the modern society in which he lives: a self-indulgent, narcissistic, ostensibly "different" person whose work reflects either his own conscious or unconscious narcissism and too often the chaos, meaninglessness, and despair inherent in the modern worldview.[36] In Coomaraswamy's view, the modern "artist, no longer a member of society but a parasite upon it, 'has become the pekinese of the rich.'" Traditional Western artists, like Eric Gill and Nicholas Roerich, can exist in modernity, but they are in a small minority.

The loss of universally participative art and craftsmanship as one's vocation has been replaced in modernity by technology, whose mass-production assembly-line methods produce little else than cost-effective items whose main purpose is either strictly function or strictly decoration. Any beauty or aesthetic appeal in them is, compared to Traditional art and craft, purely facsimile. The process is artistic reproduction in the purest sense. The labor to produce these items is work qua "necessary evil," literal drudgery. Coomaraswamy wrote that

> The craftsman, under normal conditions, likes nothing better than to talk about his work. We cannot but regard as abnormal the condition of the chain-belt worker who would rather talk about anything but his work; his deep interest is not in the work, in the doing of which he is little more than an irresponsible instrument of the "manufacturer" for profit, but in racing, baseball, films, or other means of entertainment or diversion.[37]

The modern worker, whether assembly-line, clerical, retail, stockroom, bureaucratic, or any of the overspecialized and hyperroutine allied occupations concomitant to mass industrialization, almost without exception fits Coomaraswamy's description. His work is impersonal, tedious, often exosomatic—so that the actual results of his repetitious activity are intangible—and his presence on the job is frequently irrelevant, since he can usually be replaced in a day, unlike the vanishing specie of "skilled worker" (modernity's lesser equivalent to the craftsman). "In fact," wrote Guénon, " the worker as such really has no 'name,' because he is nothing, in his work, except a simple numerical 'unit' without qualities of his own who could be replaced by any and all other equivalent 'units'—that is to say, by any other worker without any change whatsoever in what is produced in this work."[38]

## LOSS OF METAPHYSICS, GAIN OF MATERIALISM

At this point, the loss of which we speak is not, like the other losses, a characteristic of culture or a cultural form, but rather the motive element, the life force of Traditional culture without which a culture cannot be considered Traditional. Without wishing to cover the same ground in the examination of the distinction between modern and natural (or Traditional) metaphysics in preceding sections, it will be useful as a reminder to restate simply that the distinction hinges upon the method employed for the examination of first principles. Logic, reason, and dialectic for the modern philosophers who specialize in metaphysics form the method, versus intellectual intuition (*gnosis, jñāna*) for the Traditional metaphysicists. The Traditionalists accept the former method for conceptual thought, but view it as inapplicable for metaphysics; the moderns eschew intellection altogether as a legitimate tool for metaphysical inquiry, and view it—ironically—as rationally unintelligible.

This loss of natural metaphysics, of first principles—of quality— is therefore one loss to which the other losses can be ultimately traced, since the loss of the remaining contingent cultural elements follows inevitably in its wake. In the Traditional view, the loss of first principles so apparent pursuant to the decline of the culture, the Tradition, of medieval Christendom is sufficiently obvious so as to be empirical, and thus without need of copious evidential citations, proofs, and so on. In other words, the cultural and intellectual chaos and unprincipled scientism of modernity are evidence enough, symptom enough of the pandemic malaise. "All these symptoms," wrote Coomaraswamy, "point to a deep-seated sickness: primarily, the diagnosis must be that of ignorance. By that, of course, we do not mean an ignorance of the facts, with which our minds are cluttered, but an ignorance of the principles to which all operations can be reduced, and must be reduced if they are to be understood."[39] Similar quotes are found on practically every other page in Guénon's writings on modernity.

It is left now to examine the "gain" of modernity resulting from the loss of first principles. In short, the sacred and metaphysical worldview of Traditional Western culture was replaced by one that is empirical and materialistic. It is basically quantitative; its structure is mechanistic; its sacred and irrefutable shibboleth is science, the alleged inviolability and infallibility of which leads by extrapolation to scientism. Modern Western technologic culture, now in fact becoming planetary, holds the ideals of value and validity, but has inverted the Traditional ideal. Value is now quantitative and equates to money (How much is it or he worth?), and validity equates to statistics (What statistical evidence "proves" or supports the hypothesis?). "Somehow, one feels that quantitative appraisal is foreign, degrading and violating to the higher values and one should desist from it."[40] So wrote physicist Henry Margenau in *Ethics and Science* (Princeton, 1964). On the following page, Margenau is forced to conclude that "The vulgarization of intangibles, if that is the true description of tendencies that aim to express the value of intangibles in terms of currency—and I think it is—goes on with increased vigor in our public life." In modernity, anything "valuable" is costly, expensive; anything "valid" is statistically incontrovertible, the most valid, of course, being "100%." Only data that are quantifiable are susceptible to statistization, and only empirical data are quantifiable. Therefore, only the empirical is "valid" in modernity. This attitude again recalls Coomaraswamy's repetition of A. B. Keith's infamous quote, "such knowledge as is not empirical is meaningless," and prompted Guénon to remark that in modernity "no one is concerned about the *quality* of the knowledge which is accumulated, but only about its *quantity*."[41] To use Huston Smith's words, "The scientific gauge is quantity; space, size, and strength of forces can all be reckoned numerically. The comparable 'yardstick' in the traditional hierarchy was quality."[42] The "gain" of modernity equates to having hebetated the quality, the metaphysics, the music of life. This last metaphor fits into a description made by William James in *The Sentiment of Rationality* that distills and encapsulates the problem perfectly. James wrote that "A Beethoven string quartet is truly, as someone has said, a scraping of horses' tails on cats' bowels, and may be exhaustively described in such terms; but the application of this description in no way precludes the simultaneous applicability of an entirely different description."

This gain of modernity—its quantitative, secular, empirical, progressive scientism—is in a way the equivalent of an "essential property" of the modern Western culture in the Traditional view. But it *translates* into cultural forms; it has a manifested counterpart in the daily activity of the modern individual and of the operations of Western societies. Its final translation into form is primarily the phenomenon of machinery—our technologic Western world is mechanized "to the teeth." If the modern secular mass man can be said to have any faith at all, it is faith in his machinery—elaborate and sophisticated as it is— and in technology to keep producing better and faster machinery. From the Traditional view, this "faith" is a tragedy, for though modern man believes in his technology and machinery and believes them to be ultimately the panacea for the world's ills, he too seldom recognizes that his technology and machinery are a double-edged sword, so that the power and sophistication of the productive and healing genre is correspondingly equal to the consumptive and destructive genre.

With unparalleled pride do the modern faithful point to the life-saving vaccines of medical science and to the lunar and space-exploration missions—the latter being invested with a sort of chiliastic hope for the future. Unfortunately, they typically fail to realize that, despite the altruism of motive, natural contagious disease is eventually replaced by the stress and degradation of overpopulation and finally famine, and that what modern man has to offer extraterrestrial space is colonization of Earth's present "civilization," exploitation of other celestial bodies (e.g., mining), and orbiting industries, to say nothing of orbiting particle-beam weapons of unfathomable destructive capability. These are seen as the large achievements, the high points of technology and machinery. Yet, even they do not compete with the cumulative totality of the innumerable machines and appliances that fill the daily lives of the modern Western person. Between the limitless assortment of electric machines (industrial tools, appliances, computers, audio-visual equipment, etc.) and internal combustion machines (mowers, blowers, trimmers, chain saws, motorized bikes and other vehicles, etc.), the entire labor and mundane life of modern man—the mass man of the statistical average mean—in Western societies vacillates. According to Guénon:

From the interior of such a world it may seem that the "ordinary life" has only hereafter to roll on without trouble and without unforeseen accidents, in the manner of the movements of a perfectly regulated "mechanism"; is not modern man, after having "mechanized" the entire world around him, aspiring similarly to "mechanize" himself to the best of

his ability, in all the modes of activity which yet remain
open to his narrowly limited nature?[43]

In the Traditional view, the effects of this mechanistic culture are omi-
nous, and left unchecked, are strictly Orwellian. "What the modern
world has applied all its energies to, even when it pretends to do science
in its own way, is in reality nothing but the development of industry and
its 'machine-ism'; and in thereby wanting to dominate matter and mould
it to their own uses, men have succeeded only in making themselves its
slaves."[44] By a gradual but inevitable process, resulting from the advance
of the modern worldview, man is becoming an appendage to the
machine, literally inverting the original concept of *machine* (from the
Greek root μῆχος, *mēchos*, a "contrivance" by man for his own use).
Somewhat homologous to the metaphysical percept of a substance being
the reflection of its essence, the stupefacient development of technology
and machinery in modernity is but a reflection of its quantitative worldview, summed up by Guénon in his observation that

> In fact it is only a question of producing the very most pos-
> sible; there is little concern for quality, it is quantity which is
> alone important; we return once more to the same conclu-
> sion which we have already made with regard to other
> fields: modern civilization can truly be described as a quan-
> titative civilization, which is but another way of saying that
> it is a material civilization.[45]

LOSS OF INTEGRITY, GAIN OF DIVERSITY

There is far more to the word *integrity* than the moral quality with
which it is endowed by current colloquial usage. Its first or preferred
definition is "the quality or state of being complete; unbroken condition, wholeness; entirety." The two combined—moral uprightness and
wholeness—form in the Traditional perspective one of the central qualities or conditions of a Traditional culture. It should be implicit within
the definition of integrity that one speaks of all levels: metaphysical,
moral, and cultural. Since in a Traditional culture a cultural form does
not exist without a metaphysical referent, the loss of wholeness or
integrity applies to all these spheres: metaphysical unity, moral integrity, cultural homogeneity. With the loss of metaphysical unity came

atrophy, though not complete extinction, of deductive reason, since the deductive method presupposes an a priori, ingenerate whole, or general principle. This is closely related to the Neoplatonic metaphysical "working out" of *epistrophe* or "principle of the return" used by Plotinus and Proclus, and by which they perceived the reversion of all substantive phenomena back to the essential archetypes or ideas from which they emanate. The deduction of the specific from the general, the part from the whole, assumes there is a whole to begin with—an assumption that modern scientism must by necessity deny, it being antithetical to the inductive methods of modern scientism.

An examination of what has been lost with regard to integrity was partially completed in the preceding Part in the section "The Principle of Fusion in Traditional Culture" and again with more specificity in the corresponding portions of "Mediaeval Christendom (1100–1400)." What has been gained—namely, "fission"—in modernity is what will now occupy our attention. This gain is diversification, fragmentation, heterogeneity, "pluralism" and its twin relativism, in both the worldview and subsequently in the culture. Without one cohering principle in which all subsists, without *le grand système* as Eliade says, a sort of philosophical and cultural anarchy is "loosed upon the world," and confusion reigns. The secular, empirical scientism has for its chief analytical tool the keen edge of Ockham's razor, and for its chief analytical method inductive reason; this latter being built upon the cornerstone of peripatetic logic and pure ratiocination. When, by induction, a general principle is reached in relation to social or cultural (human) phenomena, it is often limited and sometimes curious in the extreme; too often, however, only a chaos of unrelated facts results from these methods.

One must at this point be careful not to overgeneralize about the inductive method, since it has its necessary and positive uses. As applied to the physical sciences, induction is an accurate method, as seen in the marvelous achievements of forensics, wherein whole and complete pictures of people and events can be recreated from infinitesimal bits of evidence and data. However, as applied to the human realm, as in the social sciences, it can lead to ludicrous conclusions. As an example, we return to the discussion of the theory that held wide currency among social scientists in the early twentieth century that shamanism was essentially psychopathic—this from viewing partial shamanic behavior and disallowing the connection to the a priori and holistic cosmological or mythological worldview in which the shaman was operating. Durkheim's view of religion as basically the composite of mass collective representations is equally inductive and, in the Traditional view, equally specious as the shamanism qua psychopathology induction.

Among the more obvious effects of the "gain"— diversification, fission, incoherence, and so on—of modernity is specialization or, more accurately, overspecialization. Overspecialization is sometimes lamented by the proponents of modernity as undesirable and infectious, but they are those who do not stop to think that it is only a symptom of a malaise that is far more extensive—in our terms, the "gain" of modernity under discussion here. Overspecialization has reached such crucial proportions that one now hears of specialists whose function is to keep track of specialists. Specialization is perhaps the most condemning feature of the overcomplexity, chaos, and total relativism of "our differentiated and fragmented culture," to use Robert Bellah's words, and it has spread to every field. "A scholar regretfully finds himself," writes Eliade, "becoming a specialist in *one* religion or even in a particular period or single aspect of that religion."[46] Guénon asserts that "In fact 'specialization,' so promulgated by certain sociologists under the name of 'division of labor,' has not only imposed itself upon scholars, but also upon technicians and similarly upon laborers, and, for the latter, all intelligent work has been rendered impossible by it."[47]

Specialization, in effect, cannot be separated from its cause, which, in Carl Jung's words, is the result of an exchange: a modern "world which has sold its soul for a mass of disconnected facts," describes the current condition. There are no unanimously acknowledged and informing first principles to which to relate this ever-increasing number of facts, no "grand systems," whether metaphysical, cosmological, or theological. Modern Western culture has divorced itself from the only Tradition. Modern man is suffering from what Alvin Toffler terms "information overload," and the result is an ever-increasing specialization to keep track of the incessant accretion of disconnected facts and details, since they are viewed as all important by the quantitative standard and adding to the "general storehouse of man's knowledge." No datum must be lost; thus modern man must divide the labor (specialize) in order to preserve all the data. "Moreover, to the extent that we have 'overspecialized,'" wrote Coomaraswamy, "and do not understand one another, we are 'idiots'— etymologically 'peculiar individuals,' and *so* peculiar as to be excluded from whole continents of the normally human universe of discourse."[48] Rampant fission, fragmentation, and complexification continue to grow unchecked, with no end in sight, to the point where "increasing knowledge is pushing anarchically toward all-pervading plurality." Durand continues this thought by establishing a formula that applies to this problem, and that might well suit the need for an epitaph for the demise of modern intellectuality. "The vision of the academic's universe is fragmented at the level of his knowledge."[49] Among the best insights into the problem of overspecialization is found simply stated by a Castilian *refran* Manzanedo gave in his paper on the perennial truths in proverbs: "Más sabe el loco en su casa, que el sabio en la ajena."

# 14

## Cultural Effects of Modernity

The "gains" of modernity just discussed must be classified as ideologic or attitudinal. These gains, which ultimately replaced the metaphysical losses of medieval Christendom, are not essential in the strict sense of the word, relating to essence as a metaphysical percept, but are more accurately attitudes of a purely mental or conceptual order. Moreover, these gains are not strictly philosophic or even ideologic; in the present context, however, the wider sense of what today has come to mean ideologic is somehow appropriate, therefore we describe these gains as ideologic and/or attitudinal. But the gains were the subject of examination in the preceding chapter; our intended subject of examination for the present is the *effects* or contingent application of these gains upon or within modern culture. These effects manifest in the modern Western culture as forms, hence they are cultural realities and secondary to the ideologic gains, though inseparable from them. These cultural forms or effects are more proliferous than the attitudes of which they are reflections, since one attitude—secularism, for example—may manifest in a variety of cultural forms: humanism, divorce of sacrality and government, desuetude of cultural initiatory rites (and other rites of passage), and so on. For this reason it is necessary to discriminate among all the cultural forms indicative of modern Western culture, and choose from them those which now epitomize the fundamental character of modern Western, and now worldwide, culture.

That Guénon and Coomaraswamy had singled out and commented upon the "gains"—the attitudes of secularism, valuelessness, technologization, materialism, and fragmentation—we have just seen. That they commented upon several of the effects of these attitudes half a century past, we will see presently. Yet, neither of them foresaw the almost incredulous scale that the exponential growth of these effects would come to reach in half a century, and for this reason more current critics of modernity must be conscripted for the purpose of updating the critique. This in no way minimizes the role of Coomaraswamy, Guénon, or others of the Traditional school, nor does it imply there is any fundamental difference or unrelatedness in their observations of the 1930s and 1940s and those of the critics of the 1990s. The thrust of the criticism is the same, then as now; the difference lies in more evidential details and a greater magnitude of seriousness that the intervening half century has brought.

The update will be drawn principally from North American sources, since North America was the *paradigme extraordinaire* for modern Western culture for both Guénon and Coomaraswamy. It was the gradual divorce from the first principles of Tradition in medieval Europe that created the modern situation, but from the Traditional view the putative gains (and their effects) bequeathed from the demise of these first principles are nowhere more apparent than in North America. Furthermore, most industrialized nations like America and Canada whose basic cultures were imported from the various imperialist European countries over the past five centuries after overwhelming the local or indigenous cultures—nations like Australia, Argentina, South Africa, and so on— in addition to the industrialized European nations themselves, can be considered the various subcultures of a greater modern Western culture, the characteristic forms of which will now be examined.

## A MONTAGE OF ROTTEN BASES

"The bases of modern civilization are to such a degree rotten to the core that it has been forgotten even by the learned that man ever attempted to live otherwise than by bread alone."[50] Some of the rotten bases of which Coomaraswamy wrote in 1943 were already fully rotten; others were in seminal stages of putrescence. In the intervening decades from then to the present, an exacerbation of these latter rotting bases (cultural forms) of modern civilization has occurred so that neither Coomaraswamy nor Guénon could have commented upon the extreme degree of putrescence to which their exponential growth had accelerated them only half a century later. Certain of these degenerative cultural forms so obvious to current observers are too inchoate in the writings of Coomaraswamy and Guénon to separate and classify in distinct categories, as has been done with the other cultural forms that follow. They will therefore be treated as a complex, a whole, an inextricable set of cumulatively superimposed cultural forms that comprise a montage of—in the Traditional view—putrescent modernity, and to which Coomaraswamy and Guénon handed down a blanket indictment implicit in their total and combined works.

To a culture so firmly committed to and rooted in material abundance and quantitative (economic) considerations, the greatest devastation the modern West faces is first scarcity and ultimately depletion of natural resources—specifically minerals and nonrenewable fuels. "The root of economic scarcity lies not only in the finitude of these resources, but also in the irrevocable entropic degradation."[51] Clearly, Coomaraswamy and Guénon did not frame the problem in as concise a manner as "entropic degradation"—the "entropy law." But owing to their criticism of industrialization, consumerism, and unchecked materialism that have been evinced already, it follows by logical necessity that as it is conceived today, the question of entropy as applied to economics and ecology—and thus to culture—would have occupied a significant place in their writings had they written today. Indeed, had Coomaraswamy ever fulfilled his intention to write an essay on "the bugbear of world trade," we may have had more citations to use in support of this contention. Though they may now have been conversant with the second law of thermodynamics or "entropy law," Guénon and Coomaraswamy would have agreed with Theodore Roszak's statement, "We are living through the most rapid and massive extermination of life-forms and cultural traditions in history,"[52] and also with the notion of the exponentiality of the extermination mentioned. Guénon, as we have seen, held to a strict interpretation of the periodicity of the *yuga* system as it related to both civilizations and universes. The dynamics of this system require that the last quarter of the cycle manifests "an increase in the speed of events," which is not necessarily an exponential increase, but certainly the exponentiality of entropy would fall under the general rubric of "increase." Guénon wrote that

> The increase in the speed of events, as the end of the cycle begins to approach, can be compared to the acceleration that exists during the fall of heavy bodies; the course of humanity at present closely resembles this [movement] of a mobile [body] running down a slope going ever faster as it gets closer to the bottom.[53]

Hand in hand with the problem of entropy is that of urbanization (or ultraurbanization), the prodigious growth of cities and megalopolises around the earth. The exponential increase in the human species (overpopulation) and, hence, in urban populations, is the principal fuel that feeds the problem of entropy. Large cities provide venues for the aggregation of high-entropic activity. In the modern world, the perception is that *Stadtluft macht frei*; the reality is that most large urban areas cannot support themselves by relying on their immediate surroundings for raw materials and resources. They must be supported through high-entropy life-support systems—for example, electric energy generation and delivery, gas pipelines, water pumping, filtration, and delivery pipelines, diverse and energy-hungry cartage methods for the importation of food and material goods, and so forth.

In its extensive form, the entropy law places material limits to the specific mode of life of humanity as a whole, and particularly to the urban mode. "Because the importance of these limitations has come into plain view only recently and because the entropic abundance of the last two hundred years or so is rapidly approaching its end, we must reassess and remodel our approach to economic, political, and social evolution."[54] In the chapter on "Le chaos social" in *La crise du monde moderne*, Guénon speaks of the "ever-increasing encroachment of the State and the growing complexity of social institutions" as being due to an increasing "density" of population in modernity analogous to a density in principle. He links multiplicity with density, "a density increasingly greater, and this tendency [toward density] is that which marks the direction in which human activity, accordingly, has been developing since the modern era."[55] Thus, entropy and ultraurbanization, as more or less reciprocal end results of the tendency toward ultimate materialism (or what Guénon most often referred to as "solidification"), are two of the cultural forms (effects) of modernity. On a mass culturewide level we are beginning to have second thoughts about our accepted views on progress, evolution, and production of things of solely technologic or material value. A few advanced thinkers, like Guénon and Coomaraswamy, stood practically alone half a century ago as erudite and articulate critics, broadcasting their caveat amidst ridicule that was the reciprocation from their progressive peers. They appeared then as the quintessence of reactionism, saying then what Roszak can now say with what is approaching a consensus of agreement: "The fact to hold firmly in mind is that, spiritually and ecologically, urban industrialism is indeed a dinosaur whose days are numbered—a culture that is flirting with extinction."[56]

Entropy and urbanization do not exist in isolation, however. While they may be considered unconscious or passive forms of modern culture, they nonetheless engender conscious or active cultural expressions with which they are inseparable: namely, modern art and nihilism. With regard to the latter, it may be said that, unlike existentialism, which does have a systematic formulation, there exists no systematic formulation for nihilism. It is rather an amorphous, spontaneous, and direct response of despair and surrender to the cultural *Angst* and confusion of an exclusively mechanistic, materialistic, secular world. It might be fairly said that modern nihilism is the next logical step after the existential view of life; an extension of the latter, as it were. An element of nihilism has crept into pure existentialism, and that combination now forms what could be described as a general worldview for modern Western culture. This nihilistic element can be related to what Mircea Eliade refers to as the "pessimism" of modern man, who cannot escape the "terror of history." The weight of the burden of despair and hopelessness also grows exponentially, and the person of good faith grows increasingly weary and despondent under its oppression. More true each day is Coomaraswamy's observation that the "Outstanding characteristics of our world in a state of chaos are disorder, uncertainty, sentimentality, and despair."[57] Meaninglessness is inevitable as long as existentialism and nihilism are the central features of the collective worldview of modernity. In the Traditional view, there can be by definition no meaning as long as existence precedes essence, since an ultimate telelogical or cosmological meaning cannot be rationally induced but only intuitionally grasped from the a priori first principles. The cosmos does not find meaning in the individual; the individual finds his or her meaning in the cosmos, just as the part finds its meaning in the whole. Thus, existentialism can be seen as the exact *inversion* of Traditional metaphysics; nihilism can be seen as a pathologic permutation of existentialism. In existentialism the body may have a soul, even a spirit, whereas in the Traditional conception, it is the Spirit that first has a soul and then a body.

Guénon treats the concept of inversion in modernity in two chapters of *Le règne de la quantité et les signes des temps*, "Le renversement des symboles" and "La grande parodie ou la spiritualité à rebours." Guénon's treatment does not specifically concern existentialism as the inversion of Traditional philosophy, but rather the principial inversions made in modernity between the quantitative and qualitative, which is an effective parallel. Existentialism cannot be extricated from modern scientism; both are primarily empirical and quantitative. Huston Smith observes that in modernity "Existentialism does its best to give man purchase in a world built for the examination of things . . . so in the main philosophy, too, accepts the working premises of science."[58] The consequence of this, insofar as existentialism harbors within it the assumptions of scientism, is that "The universe of scientism is a world devoid of consciousness and purposefulness."[59]

If there can be said to be a *telos* in the worldview of the secular existentialist, it would be the living of a comfortable life with the aspiration of more leisure time. But once the vacuity and ennui of prolonged leisure are discovered, the situation worsens, and pessimism appears. Without Tradition and vocation (which is the true complement to leisure), and with a growing suspicion of the actual apotropaic and curative impuissance of science and technology for the cultural malaise; without meaning and direction, and with the stress of global chaos and the threat of autoannihilation, the existentialism of the modern worldview begins to assimilate nihilism. But among its differences from existentialism, nihilism finds expression more in the "arts" than in philosophical disquisitions—that is, in literature, visual or plastic arts, and music.

That modern art was among the most salient characteristics or rotting bases of our current civilization in the view of Guénon and especially Coomaraswamy can be made evident by innumerable citations. That nihilism is expressed in specific schools or trends of modern art—such as Dada and Punk—is evident by the declared "ideology" of these trends or schools, though it must be noted that whether or not one allows for such a "school," strains of nihilism are evident in much of the art of the modern world, such as in the poetry of Dorothy Parker, for example.

Irrespective of the degree to which nihilism plays a part in the "message" of modern art, it is rather the commerciality and meaninglessness of modern art as a comprehensive genre that is seen as a rotting base or cultural effect by those of the Traditional perspective. Guénon, who spoke less on art than Coomaraswamy, reasserts that "We have frequently said that the 'profane' conception of the . . . arts, such as is now current in the West, is a very modern one and implies a degeneration with respect to a previous state in which [it] had an altogether different character."[60] As to Coomaraswamy, his writings are filled with incessant remonstrations on modern art enough to fill not only John Hatfield's dissertation mentioned earlier and seven chapters on modern versus Traditional conceptions of art in Roger Lipsey's biography, but several tomes more. A few select and representative quotes on modern art qua degenerate cultural form are apposite here, though. Coomaraswamy writes that

> Symptomatic abnormalities in our collegiate point of view include the assumption that art is essentially an aesthetic, that is, sensational and emotional, behaviour, a passion suffered rather than an act performed; our dominating interest in style, and indifference to the truth and meaning of works of art; the importance we attach to the artist's personality; the notion that the artist is a special kind of man, rather than that every man is a special kind of artist; the distinction we make between fine art and applied art; and the idea that the nature to which art must be true is, not Creative Nature, but our own immediate environment, and more especially, ourselves.[61]

Elsewhere he writes, "Our abstract art is not an iconography of transcendental forms, but the realistic picture of a disintegrated mentality"; "If modern art cannot be explained in terms of the same [perennial] philosophy, it may be because it has no ends beyond itself, because it is too 'fine' to be 'applied' and too 'significant' to mean anything"; "Insofar as modern art is devoid of content and truth, the modern artist is no better than the manufacturer"; "And as regards contemporary art, it has been recognized again and again that its private character and the indifference of its subject matter have so effectively separated the art from real living, the artist from the man, that we hardly nowadays expect to meet with the workman who is both an artist *and* a man."[62] More quotes would serve no purpose. The Traditional views implicit—and explicit—in the writings of Coomaraswamy and Guénon suggest that the despair or nihilism of modern thought expressed in the arts of modern culture stem from and are in reciprocal relationship with the entropic and hypermetabolic pace of a degenerate, unprincipaled, ultraurbanized society of the modern West, and growing worldwide. These elements or forms, superimposed upon each other, comprise a montage of the "rotten bases of modern civilization," accompanied by certain others whose examination now follows.

## MASS NEUROSIS

"Neurosis is intimately bound up with the problem of our time and really represents an unsuccessful attempt on the part of the individual to solve the general problem in his own person.[63] So wrote Carl Jung in 1943, and from that date his criticisms of the psychology of modernity—such as its neurotic character—never fundamentally changed. Regardless of the fact that Jung saw himself as an empiricist, and in no sense a metaphysicist;[64] regardless of the fact that Guénon likened Jung to a false prophet; regardless of the fact that Coomaraswamy viewed Jung as Jung viewed himself, but nonetheless used his works and ideas in his own writings;[65] Jung was in certain ways close to the Traditional perspective of the antithetical contrast between the medieval and modern cultures of the West and his appreciation of archaic and Eastern traditions. Among the greatest points of agreement between Jung and the Traditional writers was a depreciation of modernity, specifically of the modern worldview. To Jung, it was a neurotic worldview, and Jung's was a diagnosis based on years of research and clinical experience. "About a third of my cases," he wrote, "are suffering from no clinically definable neurosis, but from the senselessness and emptiness of their lives. It seems to me, however, that this can well be described as the general neurosis of our time."[66]

Jung was not alone among psychologists in his deprecation of modernity as an incubator for neurosis (or now psychosis, evidenced by such phenomena as global terrorism, mass genocide, and ethnic cleansing, or the Jonestown, Guyana, and Waco, Texas, mass suicides). Those of the Jungian school would obviously share similar attitudes, but Jung's contemporaries and later original psychologists held varying but homologous views of the psychopathology of the modern mentality. Beyond the extremes to which R. D. Laing resorted in his vindication of madness over the ostensible sanity of society, more sober and considered psychologists like Rank, Rogers, and Maslow—and others, like Assagioli and Progoff—expressed criticisms of the unchecked materialism, empirical secularism, and competitive pressures of the frenetic modern society. Eliade cites the reported and lugubrious observation of an anonymous British psychoanalyst concerning the life condition of modern man: "We are born mad; then we acquire morality and become stupid and unhappy; then we die."[67] To Jung, the neurosis of modernity is in seeking mass, external, quantitative answers for a problem whose only solution is to be found through individual, internal, and qualitative or depth-psychological means. His extensive use of ancient religious and philosophical belief systems that stressed interiorization as examples of or parallels to his own psychological system was simply to establish precedents or antecedents—a necessity for one who depreciated the loss of symbolic continuity in modernity and viewed this loss as a contributive factor to its pervasive problems. Thus, Heraclitus, Pythagoras, and the ancient Greeks, the Hellenistic Gnostic sects and leaders (especially Basilides), Augustine, Pseudo-Dionysius and the Christianity of the High Middle Ages, and the theosophic systems of Renaissance alchemists were for Jung the linear high peaks on the graph of history of Western civilization with respect to the truth expressed in the Socratic axiom, "Man, Know Thyself."

For the modern man, this axiom means "Know Thy Body and Mind," which is neither the Self of Jung's individuated person nor the Self of Tradition. This existential and empirical divorce from the spiritual Self, from the belief in its reality, is the basic and underlying cause of the mass neurosis in the Jungian view. The mass neurosis itself is the effect within the culture of modernity. This mass effect on a culture-wide scale is really the collectivity of modern individuals, of whose neurosis Jung paints a portrait in two short vignettes and whose edges fade into the surrounding mass of similar individuals:

> Let us suppose that our patient is . . . a flesh-and-blood man of our own day, who has the misfortune to be a typical representative of our modern European culture. . . . He suffers most of all from the disease of knowing everything better; there is nothing that he cannot classify and put in the correct pigeonhole. As to his psyche, it is essentially his *own* invention, his *own* will, and it obeys *his* reason exclusively; and if it should happen that it does not do so, if he should nevertheless have psychic symptoms, such as anxiety states, obsessional ideas, and so on, then it is a clinically identifiable disease with a thoroughly plausible, scientific name.[68]

This is Jung's modern "common man," or woman, the statistically average and equal participant in the mass. His real situation in the schizomorphic culture of modernity is described by Jung in these terms:

> To be sure, we say that this is the century of the common man, that he is the lord of the earth, the air, the water, and

that on his decision hangs the historical fate of nations. This proud picture of human grandeur is unfortunately an illusion and is counterbalanced by a reality that is very different. In this reality man is the slave and victim of the machines that have conquered space and time for him; he is intimidated and endangered by the might of the military technology which is supposed to safeguard his physical existence; his spiritual and moral freedom, though guaranteed with limits in one half of his world, is threatened with chaotic disorientation, and in the other half is abolished altogether.[69]

Jung's solution to the problems of modernity is too complex and detailed to consider here at length since it involves the whole of his analytical psychology. Simply stated, the two "halves" just referred to in the second quotation must be brought into mutual and harmonious reciprocity by the process of individuation, working under the laws of the compensation theory and *enantiodromia*. But as we are concerned here solely with the effects of modernism (as a mental construct comprised of the "gains" of modernity) and not their amelioration, it must be concluded that in Jung's view, similar in content to that of Guénon and Coomaraswamy, the symptomatic effects are diagnosed in socio-psychoanalytic terms. "As our time is characterized by fragmentation, confusion, and perplexity, this fact is also expressed in the psychology of the individual, appearing in spontaneous fantasy images, dreams, and the products of active imagination."[70] It is this individual, in Jung's titular phrase, who is "modern man in search of a soul"; this due to his having "sold his soul for a mass of disconnected facts."

   To repeat, Jung was not alone among psychologists in his depreciation of modernity, but for others, like Rogers and Maslow, this attitude was not surprising. What is surprising and significant is that today's Freudians are observing an ineradicable neurosis of modern times, notwithstanding a Freudian dogma concerning the triumph of science over metaphysical principles. In a book entitled *Madness and Modernity*, the prominent Freudian scholar C. R. Badcock discusses the problem in his chapter, "The Psychopathology of Present-Day Life." There he states that

In short, it is not that classical neuroses no longer exist, or that psychopathology has fundamentally changed—how could it?—but that such neuroses are perhaps acted-out and externalized [in modernity] as interpersonal conflicts rather than intrapsychic ones. In this respect the incidence of neurosis seems inversely proportional to social disorder.[71]

It is one thing for Traditionalists and those close to their views to criticize modernity. It is quite another for Freudians, who have typically upheld the doctrines of empiricism and progressivism, to begin to question seriously the societal fruits of such doctrines.

## TERMINOLOGICAL AND EDUCATIONAL CONFUSION

Earlier in chapter 3 we had occasion to take note of the deprecation by Guénon and Coomaraswamy of the misuse of language. The latter, in fact, devoted an essay to the problem titled "Does 'Socrates Is Old' Imply That 'Socrates is'?" In that essay and in their writings generally, the focus of their criticisms centered around the idea that words are symbols that, used in metaphysical discourse, participate in kind with their referents. Furthermore, they believed the order and stability of a culture's grammatical and syntactical structures for its language equate to or reflect commensurably in its inclusive social structure. Relativism, misuse, abuse, and indifference toward terms and grammatical order were, in their view, reflected in kind in the order of the culture as a whole. These criticisms are, of course, not peculiar to the Traditional view. Similar concerns are shared by the so-called ordinary language school, whose more renowned proponents, like Bertrand Russell and Ludwig Wittgenstein, devoted much of their energies to the structure and meaning of language, though their efforts were applied more to epistemological and purely philosophical questions involved in the use of language. The effort of Alfred Korzybski, through his non-Aristotelian system of "general semantics," is another attempt at bringing clarity (or sanity) into science and exclusive reason insofar as they are particularly characteristic of modern culture. In a somewhat limited sense these views approximate the views of the Traditional school, with the exception of the metaphysical "participation" aspect.

Guénon was the most adamant and concise spokesman for the Traditional perspective of the degeneration of language and the overall terminological confusion. He writes, regarding this issue, that "The falsification of everything is, as we have said, one of the characteristic traits of our epoch," and that, moreover,

That which perhaps shows it best is what might be called the falsification of language; that is, the abuse of certain words diverted from their true meanings, and abuse of this sort is imposed by a constant suggestion on the part of those who, in one way or another, exercise any kind of influence on the public mentality. It is something more than solely this degeneration to which we have made allusion earlier, and by which many words have come to lose the qualitative sense which they had originally, keeping only one which is totally quantitative; it is more a case of a "diversion" by which words are applied to things that they do not in any way fit and to which they are sometimes even opposed in their normal meaning. It is this, above all else, which is an obvious symptom of the intellectual confusion that reigns in the present world.[72]

Terminological confusion does not exist in isolation, however. In the Traditional view, it may be the effect of philosophical atrophy since medieval times when scholastics chose words carefully due to their being charged with metaphysical meaning insofar as they were in reciprocal influence with their referents. The terminological confusion inevitably spills over into other realms, and most evidently in the realm of education and scholarship. Coomaraswamy's essays, "*Manas*," "Recollection: Indian and Platonic," and "Measures of Fire," are in some ways critiques of modern scholastic methods and presumptions. The first of these is more extensively treated in the appendix on methodology.

In the Traditional perception, and particularly in Coomaraswamy's promulgation of it, the problem of modern education lies in the fact that not only is there widespread terminological confusion among scholars, translators, and teachers, but the notion prevails that education is the conveyance of facts and dissemination of theories, where the *actual* process of education cannot be separated from Plato's conception of *anamnesis* (ἀνάμνησίς). The purpose of education is thus to prepare and train the mind for the recollection of the knowledge inherent in it. He writes that "The technique of education is, therefore, always formally destructive and iconoclastic; it is not the conveyance of information but the education of a latent knowledge."[73] Having lost sight of this, and suffering from an extensive terminological confusion, "There is little or nothing in a modern American education," he writes, "to qualify a man for converse with a Tibetan or Indian peasant—not to mention a scholar; all we *can* do together is 'eat, drink, and be merry.'"[74] The preparatory and collegiate institutions of education, in the Traditional view are little more than vocational schools in modernity, equipped to stuff a plethora of disconnected facts into the minds of students and prepare them for a salaried career. According to Guénon:

> Moreover, one might ask whether it is not more a matter of "learning" than of truly "understanding," that is to say whether memory has not been substituted for intelligence in the totally verbal and "bookish" conception of contemporary education, where only the accumulation of rudimentary and heterogeneous notions is sought, and where quality is sacrificed entirely to quantity.[75]

Modern educators and education specialists are now echoing certain of the criticisms of Coomaraswamy and Guénon about the state of education in modernity. Most noticeable among these is Professor Allan Bloom whose widely acclaimed book, *The Closing of the American Mind* (New York, 1987), discusses the issue, to quote from the epigraph, of "How Higher Education Has Failed Democracy and Impoverished the Souls of Today's Students." In a section of the book called "The Decomposition of the University," Professor Bloom laments the overspecialization of learning, and states that "The relations between natural science, social science, and humanities are purely administrative and have no substantial intellectual content."[76] Though not a Traditionalist, Bloom nonetheless summarizes the problem of modern higher education in words that are strikingly parallel to the Traditional view:

> To repeat, the crisis of liberal education is a reflection of a crisis at the peaks of learning, an incoherence and incompatibility among the first principles with which we interpret the world, an intellectual crisis of the greatest magnitude, which constitutes the crisis of our civilization.[77]

## SOCIOLATRY

"The modern man has lost all the metaphysical certainties of his mediaeval brother, and set up in their place the ideals of material security, general welfare and humaneness."[78] Among the most pronounced effects of modernity is the worship of the social collectivity and the view of the "mass," the "people," as the ultimate determinant of all action and purpose, as in the case of Marxism and Durkheimian sociology and their respective epigones of later generations. This worship contains three sacrosanct dogmas, viewed in the Traditional perspective as equality, democracy, and individualism. Equality is a basic assumption in the U.S. Constitution (and Declaration of Independence) and the Communist Manifesto alike, considered inviolable in both. Democracy, insofar as it is "government by the people" as its etymology implies, and not erroneously juxtaposed to "communism" as is the mental habit in capitalist countries, is also endemic to most modern industrial societies. As we shall presently see, individualism is a Janus-like creature, manifesting in two distinct ways in modern culture and related to the notions of liberty and equality in its bipartition. In both ways of its manifestation, individualism—and no less equality and democracy—are intimately involved with the overriding sociolatry of our time in which the position of the existential mass or collectivity of humanity is, by a process of inversion from its metaphysical relation to the One, placed at the top of the spectrum of things important and not infrequently apotheosized. In Jung's words, "All mass movements, as one might expect, slip with the greatest ease down an inclined plane made up of large numbers. Where the many are, there is security; what the many believe must of course be true; what the many want must be worth striving for, and necessary, and therefore good."[79]

Guénon and Coomaraswamy dealt primarily on a metaphysical basis, writing from the standpoint of first principles. In the Traditional view, hierarchy supersedes equality; theocracy supersedes democracy; and unity or unanimity supersedes individualism. Though most of the updating commentators who have been cited more or less approximate Guénon and Coomaraswamy in many of their views of modernity, the ideals of equality, democracy, and individualism are too cherished for most to reject; these commentators probably have not encountered the metaphysical rationale, if not necessity, for doing so.

Regarding the modern notion of equality and no less of democracy, Guénon offers the most devastating critique by any of the Traditional metaphysicists. He writes:

"Democratic" and "egalitarian" conceptions tend, from a purely social point of view, to effect precisely the same thing, since for them all individuals are equivalent to one another; what is carried with this absurd supposition is (the notion) that everyone is equally capable of doing whatever. This equality is a thing for which nature offers not a single example, for the same reasons we have indicated, since it would imply nothing but a complete similitude between individuals; it is evident that in the name of this putative "equality" which is one of the perverted "ideals" so cherished to the modern world, individuals are being effectively rendered as nearly alike to one another as nature will permit, and this primarily by an attempt to impose a uniform education upon everyone.[80]

Such unequivocal pronouncements by Guénon are enough to send most modern sociolaters into paroxysms, regardless of their content of truth, so cherished is the notion of equality in the modern mentality. One cannot fail to notice the irony that criticisms of the Traditional view, considered hopelessly reactionary and atavistic by modern sociologists,[81] often proceed from a milieu which is itself the most conspicuous example of the truth of actual inequality—the hierarchically arranged university system, the tenured faculties of which are chosen from the "top" scholars in their respective fields. At this point, however, after the distasteful but potent medicine has been administered by Guénon, Coomaraswamy steps in with a mediational salve to ease the irritation caused by Guénon's bluntness. As the American Declaration of Independence rightly states, "all men are created equal," the adjective *equal* modifying the noun *men*. What this does not say is that "all men are created equal*ly*," a difference that too few stop to consider. The fact is, as Coomaraswamy points out, "all men are not created equally" (the adverb *equally* modifying the verb form *are created*), as is quite obvious from the empirical standpoint.

In the same way, when it is asserted that "all men are born equal," of what "men" are we speaking? The statement is evidently untrue of all "outer men," for we see that they are both physically and mentally differently endowed and that natural aptitudes have to be considered even in nominally egalitarian societies. A predication of equality is only absolutely true of *all inner men*; true of the men themselves, but not of their personalities.[82]

Of course, from an empirical, existential secular standpoint, "inner men" (*sanctus spiritus, ātman*) do not exist. Thus, equality must be forcibly predicated either to what Coomaraswamy refers to as the "personality," or to the abstract, quantitative notion of a "personhood"; predications both he and Guénon reject. Without a higher worldview, without an understanding of the natural metaphysical hierarchy, the modern person has nothing to replace the notion of equality once it is shown to be fallacious. The modern therefore clings to it as an ideal, rationalizing that the overt differences between people are wholly explained by the differences in their early environment, genetic composition, or other such reductions.

Guénon again harpoons the ideal of democracy from the Traditional perspective, using the barb of natural metaphysics as his spearhead. "The most decisive argument against 'democracy,' can be summarized in several words: the superior cannot emanate from the inferior, because the 'greater' cannot be derived from the 'lesser'; this is an absolute mathematical certitude, against which nothing can prevail."[83] Coomaraswamy's "mediations" come in the form of comparisons between Traditional cultures of "spiritual authority and temporal power," to use Guénon's titular construction: "It is very far from true that in traditional societies the individual is regimented: it is only in democracies, soviets, and dictatorships that a way of life is imposed upon the individual from without."[84] A workable democracy presupposes some degree of participation in the affairs of government by *all* the citizens, which is in fact far from the reality of most modern democracies, where steadily fewer people are taking responsibility even to vote—as in the case of America, for example, where in the past six presidential elections barely half the eligible voters took part. A democracy further presupposes the same degree of aptitude, of intelligence, of investigating the issues, of familiarizing oneself with nominees for office, and so on, which is again far from the actuality, wherein it is shown statistically that voters are more easily swayed by public relations gimmicks, style, presentation, sound bites, appearance, and the like. The "superior cannot emanate from the inferior," as Guénon wrote, and so once again the modern ideal of democracy is belied by the actuality of democracy, and what emanates from the people is but a reflection of their opinions, stylistic tastes, their emotional reactions, which numerically overwhelm the studied and judicious voting element in society. Thus, the ideal of democracy translates into the actuality of ochlocracy. As Roszak notes, "It is just this propensity for massification that has led observers like De Tocqueville to see in the democratic ideal a serious danger of cultural homogenization, a world flattened into dull, despotic, equalitarian uniformity."[85]

Finally, Guénon strikes at individualism. The opening lines of his chapter entitled "L'individualisme" in *La crise du monde moderne* begin with these words: "What we mean by 'individualism' is the negation of all superior principles to the individuality and, consequently, the reduction of civilization in all its domains to the purely human elements alone."[86] Guénon continues to describe what he means by individualism, which is akin to the existentialism just discussed: the denial of intellectual intuition and the repudiation of any higher or essential elements in humans, the exaltation of reason, and the logical outcomes of naturalism and relativism (pragmatism), confining all to the sensible order. The cultural effects of individualism in modernity, as we mentioned, are twofold, Janus-like.

In libertarian societies, individualism is anti-State and related to the liberty to be unique, free, to express oneself according to one's true nature, to pursue one's avocation. This, in the Traditional view, is an illusion, a chimera, since the process of market massification and uniformity (as opposed to unanimity) is hard at work using this very notion to sell or provide everyone with precisely the same items. The valorization of "doing one's own thing" is nothing less than conformity in one way or another to the mass social current: being a sports fan, an uncritical admirer of science, a lover of machines, a follower of fashion, a worshipper of celebrity, a pursuer of leisure. One's own thing is more often than not a specialization of one of these cultural forms, a specialization that is ultimately subsumed by the cultural and conforming current of the mass. In such an individualism, the higher unifying principles are totally disparate, while the contingent forms are by and large uniform.

In radical socialist societies, individualism is pro-State and an ideal implicit in the declared goals of massification. "Social antheaps" is Coomaraswamy's term for this form of culture. Every individual is presumed to be quantitatively equal to all the rest, and his individualism is hypostatized into the mass, the collective whole, in which he finds his natural station and thus his individualism, regardless of the actuality that in all such systems "some people are more equal than others," to use Orwell's phrase.

In both types of system there is rigorous conformity, massification, leveling, professed equality, uniformity, under which conditions the libertarian exercises his rights to be an "individual," and the proletariat asserts his collective authority over the decadent bourgoise and transmutes his oppressed status to become an "individual" in the mono-level mass. Both have little to do with true individuality, in the Traditional perspective, since that is related to what Henry Corbin calls the "real event"—the personality's knowledge of and synthesis with the higher Self, the Inner Man, or the hierogamy of sygyzys (*yoga*). "For the real event," writes Corbin, "exactly implies a break with the collective, a reunion with the transcendent 'dimension' which puts each individual person on guard against the attractions of the collective, that is to say against every impulse to make what is spiritual a social matter."[87] In the Traditional view, therefore, sociolatry is among the more fatal effects of modernity in its repudiation of hierarchy and everything metaphysical—sacred and/or "religious" in the Traditional sense—and its apotheosis of the average mean of the mass as the basic criterion of all ethics, value, and so on, regardless of the incessant flux and relativity of that average mean. "It has often been asserted by rationalists," declared Coomaraswamy, "that religion has been 'the opium of the people'; however that may be, it is quite certain that the modern shibboleths of 'race,' 'equality,' democracy,' and notably, 'progress,' are the people's drugs, and that they are deliberately administered as such by politicians and advertisers."[88]

## POLLUTION: GEOGRAPHIC AND CULTURAL

Pollution as an effect of high-entropy modern culture is well enough known and documented to be hackneyed. Even Coomaraswamy wrote of the impending and inevitable disaster that "There can be no possible doubt that what men now understand by 'civilization' is an essentially vicious and destructive force, or that what is now called 'progress' is both suicidal and murderous."[89] That this destructive force is inextricably linked to overpopulation is equally as obvious—an overbreeding that has doubled itself in a lesser amount of time than the previous doubling and conjures up the image of an uncontrolled planetary population having stripped bare the Earth's resources and literally suffocating in its own waste. Given the present exponential growth rate of the human population, the time is not far off. That overpopulation is inextricably linked to the commensurably rapid depletion of natural resources is also obvious. The obviousness of these effects of the worldview and lifestyle of modern industrial societies does not preclude the necessity of their discussion here, but though these effects are among the most readily observable and quantifiable of all so far discussed, our responsibility here is not to indulge in easily accessible percentages and tonnages. It is rather not to shirk from simply noting the obvious and the overstated—widespread pollution—as perhaps the most visible effect or form of industrialized modern Western culture.

Our purpose is in clarifying the Traditional view, which perceives global pollution as an inevitable effect of modernity: most evident is the physical pollution of the planet—geographic pollution. The air over large urban areas and megalopolitan complexes the world over is typically brownish and thick with different gases and particulants; television news meteorologists announce the danger level index for ozone and other pollutant buildup in certain seasons to warn those with respiratory problems to minimize breathing the air outside. Rivers and lakes are still prime targets for industrial and municipal dumping of every conceivable kind of toxic waste substance to the point that of the Great Lakes of the American Midwest, Lake Erie was pronounced "dead" by ecologists, and the ludicrous image of a river catching fire has its basis in fact. Both shallow and deep water aquifers are now the victims of chemical waste seepage, and those that are not thoughtlessly depleted are often contaminated by wastes from industrial runoff or agricultural pesticides. By emitting fluorocarbons, SST jet traffic, aerosol sprays, and refrigerators continue to destroy the upper levels of the stratosphere—the so-called ozone layer that protects the earth from damaging ultraviolet rays. The earth itself is being ravaged and denuded by myopic city planners, farmers, developers, and industrialists whose landfills, sewerage dumping, strip mining, deforestation, effluent discharges, stack emissions, asphaltization, chemical fertilizers, and herbicides/pesticides combine to create a possibly irremediable global cataclysm. The potential destruction from catastrophes or from the accumulated wastes of nuclear power plants is unspeakable, as Chernobyl silently testifies. Noise, temperature, and litter are less crucial but equally symptomatic pollution phenomena in the modern world. While the first-world nations are beginning to address certain of these problems, the ecological damage being done in third-world nations remains unabated and more than offsets the formers' remedial measures. "The problem the biosphere confronts," writes Roszak, "is the *convergence* of all urban-industrial economies as they thicken and coagulate into a single planetwide system everywhere devoted to maximum productivity and the unbridled assertion of human dominance."[90]

The form of pollution of primary concern to Coomaraswamy and Guénon is what can be termed "cultural" pollution (and/or culturocide), wherein by military conquest, economic domination ("neocolonialism"), or any other form of imposed hegemony or imperialism, the quantitative industrialized cultures of the modern West have corrupted or destroyed Traditional cultures. This is more than a passive passing of traditional society, but more actually an active campaign that proceeds "by subjugating a people; by taking from them what to them is most precious, namely their own culture; by coercing them to adopt mores and institutions of a foreign people; by forcing them into the most odious work in order that they should acquire things which for them are perfectly useless."[91] This destruction is both intentional and unintentional. Of the first kind, Coomaraswamy states that "It would not be too much to say that our educational activities abroad (a word that must be taken to include the American Indian reservations) are motivated by an intention to destroy existing cultures."[92] This is the intentional culturocide, and different in intention from the destruction of

> The modern traveler—"thy name be legion"—proposing to visit some "lost paradise" such as Bali, [who] often asks whether or not it has yet been "spoiled." It makes a naive, and even tragic confession. For this man does not reflect that he is condemning himself; that what his question asks is whether or not the sources of equilibrium and grace in the other civilizations have yet been poisoned by contact with men like himself and the culture of which he is a product.[93]

First by a process of colonization and forced domination, then by a process of attrition, one by one the various indigenous cultures with which the modern West has come into contact since the Renaissance have gradually disintegrated, in the strict sense of the word. Time and again, "the fact that we have destroyed the vocational and artistic foundations of whatever traditional cultures our touch has infected," as Coomaraswamy once wrote, has left the planet with fewer and fewer pristine and coherent Traditional cultures. They have either been forced to relinquish or have gradually abandoned their Traditional ways, based on a qualitative mythological or metaphysical worldview, and literally "bought in" to the illusion of material progress.

Or consider the poor countries that sell themselves to the international tourist industry in pursuit of those symbols of wealth and progress the West has taught them to covet: luxurious airports, high-rise hotels, six-lane motorways. Their people wind up as bellhops and souvenir sellers, desk clerks and entertainers, and their proudest traditions soon degenerate into crude caricatures. But the balance sheet may show a marvellous increase in foreign exchange earnings.[94]

For these countries, these cultures, the pollution is twofold and nearly instantaneous. The visible pollution from the new motorways and factories built respectively to expedite the high-entropy transit crucial to industrialism and to exploit cheap local labor is the outer signal of pollution of a more devastating kind in the Traditional view: the trade of meaning, value, wholeness, sacrality, and quality of life for meaninglessness, relativism, fragmentation, secularism, and quantity.

# 15

## The "Solution" to the Vicissitudes of Modernity

The immediate future did not look encouraging for Guénon and Coomaraswamy, whose concerns for ecological destruction by pollutants were less than their concern for the prognosis of humanity's survival with the new and sinister agent of thermonuclear weaponry. Each man had lived just long enough to see modern humanity's inpropitious first steps—Hiroshima and Nagasaki—toward possible oblivion. Huston Smith, as a current expositor of the Traditional view, similarly has little to be encouraged about with regard to the immediate future: "But with the ecological crisis, energy depletion, the population explosion, and the proliferation of nuclear weapons, to say nothing of the interlocking, depersonalized bureaucratization of life, the short-range future . . . looks bleak."[95]

This picture of modernity is gloomy indeed. Yet, from the Traditional perspective, it is a logical (though not final) outcome of the materialist crescendo of progress in the West that began with the "rupture of Tradition" in the late Middle Ages, and is by no means exaggerated. Guénon once remarked that "We have in no way contested the existence of 'material progress,' but only its importance: we contend that it is not worth the loss of intellectuality, and that in order to be of any other opinion, one must be completely ignorant of true intellectuality."[96] In saying material progress is not worth the loss of intellectuality, Guénon might for once have understated his thesis—certainly Coomaraswamy would have thought so, as do other latter-day commentators:

Having banished God from society, the high-entropy, materialist value system attempts to provide a heaven on earth. In so doing we have placed man and woman at the center of the universe, and defined the ultimate purpose of our existence as the satisfaction of all possible material wants, however frivolous. We have reduced "reality" to that which can be measured, quantified, tested. We have denied the qualitative, the spiritual, the metaphysical. We have entered into a pervasive dualism—our minds separated from our bodies, our bodies divorced from the "surrounding" world. We have gloried in the concepts of material progress, efficiency, and specialization above all other values. In the process, we have destroyed family, community, tradition. We have left behind all absolutes, except for our absolute faith in our ability to overcome all limits to our physical activity.[97]

The *contrast* is now complete: the Traditional culture of medieval Christendom on the one hand; the secular, quantitative, and material culture of Western modernity on the other. "The commonly accepted formula of the existence of a gulf dividing Europe from Asia," wrote Coomaraswamy, "is thus fallacious in the sense that while there is a division, the dividing line is traceable not between Europe and Asia normatively considered but between [Traditional] mediaeval Europe and Asia, on the one hand, and modern Europe on the other."[98] In modern Europe, and in modernity considered as a whole, the first principles of the Tradition, of natural metaphysics, are replaced by all the combined effects of their loss that have occupied our concern in the preceding chapter. The great question that now confronts us is whether there is a solution to the vicissitudes of modernity. How are we to extricate ourselves from this malaise and from the impending and growing threat of self-destruction? In what follows, our attention will be directed toward solutions offered first by the modern mentality itself, and second by the Tradition. We will then extrapolate from the Traditional worldview and offer several ideas or theses regarding possibilities of the future based on certain new trends of thought in modern culture. Our extrapolation will, however, be loyal to the Traditional perspective that it has been our chief occupation to elucidate throughout, and these new trends of thought in modern Western culture are trends in which one finds similarities to the Traditional worldview as expressed in the writings of Guénon and Coomaraswamy.

## TECHNOLOGIC SOTERIOLOGY: THE GREAT CHIMERA

As is by now clear, the observation that the modern world is in a state of tension, confusion, and malaise is not made by Traditionalists alone. A variety of individuals of different philosophic and ideologic perspectives observe the same or similar vicissitudes as do the Traditional writers,[99] though less often pointing to the fundamental causes of the vicissitudes but usually to the effects alone. Among this variety of individuals are those who, like Frazer and Freud writing decades ago, hold a naive but enthusiastic hope of salvation for humanity via science, technology, and the inexorable momentum of progress. In their view, science (more accurately "scientism") had come to replace religion, and faith was diverted from God to technology to answer the exigencies of earthly woes. Even Durkheim, writing in 1915, observed that "Today it is generally sufficient that they [new concepts] bear the stamp of science to receive a sort of privileged credit, because we have faith in science. But this faith does not differ essentially from religious faith."[100] At present, this faith does not differ essentially from that which Durkheim observed in his day. If anything, the faith or religion of modernity—scientism, temporally linear progressivism, and advanced technology—has only spread further around the globe and gathered more converts. "Anything that looks technological goes down without difficulty with modern man."[101] It is by this faith and the absence of any viable alternatives, in the Traditional view, that modern man is impelled to seek amelioration for the degenerating conditions in which he finds himself; his implicit faith in science and technology allows him little choice than to see in them the solution to the modern malaise. What technology and scientism have done for the modern world, especially in regard to nuclear weapons, should in Guénon's words, "be sufficient to smash the pacifist dreams of certain admirers of modern 'progress'; but the dreamers and the 'idealists' are incorrigible, and their naivete seems to know no limits."[102]

Just as an unquestioning and ineradicable faith seems to preclude the Christian evangelist from an objective analysis of the questions concerning inerrancy of the Bible and the historicity of Jesus, the unquestioning faith of modernity's average neoteric in scientism and technology seems to preclude an ability to foresee the negative effects of technologic inventions or cumulative achievements designed to fulfill his soteriological hopes. One day, the neoteric assures himself, medical science and research will make the world free of carcinomas, apoplexy, and heart failure, as they have done intermittently in the West with smallpox, diphtheria, cholera, and other diseases.[103] In his naive optimism he fails to see all the effects of these achievements, where, for example, death from such infectious diseases is in part replaced by death from starvation, of famine created by overpopulation. Agri-science will come to modernity's rescue to feed the additional hungry of Asia, Africa, and South America (and their multiplying progeny) who would otherwise have fallen victim to the disease, but who were saved by vaccines. To do this, however, more chemical fertilizers and more herbicides and pesticides will be required not simply to sustain but increase the requisite level of production. The greater demands that such food production will put on oil production for growing and ship-ping under high-entropy methods are not a real threat to the neoteric soteriologist. More natural resources (nonrenewable or otherwise) can be consumed, and more nuclear energy can be produced to offset the greater demands that more people and their daily needs require. The negative effects of spent fuel from this nuclear energy can simply be buried—out of sight, out of mind—regardless of its lethal toxicity and areally destructive potential for tens of thousands of years.

This soteriologist, whose modern religion is scientism, notwith-standing his correlated faith in dispassionate objectivity, seems ever to overlook the "Chinese finger puzzle" syndrome inevitably conjoined to his high-entropy technologic solutions. Finally, among the most highly entropic of his quantitative soteriological visions is the ultimate of space colonization. Implicit in this argument is the notion that if condi-tions get too overcrowded or polluted on earth—that is, if the entropic effects of technology make life unlivable on earth—then humanity has at its disposal an escape hatch: the colonization of space stations and/or nearby planets. To the neoteric, this is an ultimate soteriology—a ster-ile, hygenic, cybernetic culture, living in the far reaches of space, a metamorphic creature that, like the Phoenix, has left the ashes of the old for the expanse of the new. To the Traditionalist, this would be the ulti-mate pollution, an extraterrestrial pollution, in which fragmented, quantitative, secular humanity would spread its psychic—and no doubt actual—wastes into the course of the planets and the realm of the stars. Coomaraswamy, whose earlier quote lamented the pollution of Bali, would probably have been devastated by the realization of such a pros-pect.

Regardless of the form that new technologic inventions take, the attitude that attributes to them a soteriological character is the true destructive agent, the inventions being only a reflection of this attitude. Both attitude and inventions combined, in the old mode of high-entropy and exclusively quantitative methods, is the ironic admixture that, far from solving its problems, is taking modern humanity on a collision course with autoannihilation through one or more of the means delineated above. This was, in fact, Guénon's prediction:

> As the danger of inventions, even those that are not designed to play a fatal role for humanity but that nevertheless cause many catastrophes—not to mention the unsuspected troubles they create in the terrestrial environment—as this danger, we say, will doubtless continue to grow to proportions difficult to determine, it is permissible to think without too much improbability that (as we have already stated previously) it is perhaps by this method that the modern world will achieve its own destruction if it is incapable of stopping this process while there is still enough time.[104]

Science and technology, in a word, are a double-edged sword, cutting with one edge into positive achievements, and with the other edge on the backswing into negative effects. They thus offer no general panacea for the vicissitudes of modernity. "Our technological achievements are great," as Needleman writes, "but we see they have not brought understanding."[105] Relied upon as ends in themselves or ultimate solutions for the ills that face the conditions of being human and living life on earth in modernity, the inventions of technology and the reductions of scientism are continually mitigated by the fact that the positive achievements are always counterbalanced by equal or sometimes greater negative effects. Jung saw signs of the realization of this percept: "Material security, even, has gone by the board, for the modern man begins to see that every step in material 'progress' adds so much force to the threat of a more stupendous catastrophe."[106]

The basic reduction of progress and scientism is the theory that science and technology will eventually banish all material—and social—evils of humanity; this reduction is the faith. Scientism, the faith of the neoteric, is now increasingly coming under attack by those who perceive the foibles of its presumptions, and who see it as the great chimera of modernity. In something of a coup of irony, the great profession of faith by Freud in his *The Future of an Illusion* has come full circle. The modern high-entropy environment is one wholly based on faith in scientism, quantity, technologization, and is the most potential

medium for autoannihilation; unless the human race begins to reinte-
grate first principles of Tradition into its worldview, the course to irremediable destruction is set. Freud's allegation of *religion* as primordial
superstition is now being replaced by the opposite view, stated here by
Roszak: "Indeed, Reason, material Progress, the scientific world view
have revealed themselves in numerous respects as simply a higher
superstition, based on dubious but well-concealed assumptions about
man and nature."[107]

## THE TRADITIONAL SOLUTION

The natural opponents and critics of the Traditional perspective—
namely, the "true believer" neurotic neoteric whose faith is secular scientism (and the accompanying ideologic *impedementa*)—will assume
all the fulminations of the Traditionalists about the vicissitudes of
modernity are little else than a reactionary nostalgia for some medieval
oligarchic *illud tempus*. This neoteric would assume further that, unable
to cope with the real technologic and engineering challenges created by
the desire for satisfaction of all material wants (as opposed to needs), or
unable to adjust to democratic or socialist massification, Traditionalists
prefer to turn back the clock to a bogus image of medieval life they consider as paradisiacally *in illo tempore*.

Such assumptions, if made, could not be further from the truth.
The issue is not a Traditional nostalgia versus a modern neophilia.
"Thus a turning backward [*a rebours*]," writes Gilbert Durand, "of the
Huysmans type is insufficient: by setting up a 'reactionary' mythology
as opposed to the mythology of progress such a return would still be
playing the game of history."[108] Once accused precisely of this "nostalgia" by Richard Florsheim in a review of Coomaraswamy's "Is Art a
Superstition or a Way of Life?" Coomaraswamy rebutted in a "Post-
script" to that essay, stating that "I have nowhere said that I wished to
'return to the Middle Ages.'"[109] Elsewhere he wrote, in answer to the
question he posed ("How can this world be given back its meaning?"):
"Not, of course by a return to the outward forms of the Middle Ages nor,
on the other hand, by assimilation to any surviving, Oriental or other,
pattern of life."[110] Guénon, due possibly to his reluctance to intricate
himself in the interminable swordplay of polemics, never really discussed the allegation that the Traditional perspective tacitly calls for a
sort of "*illud tempus* revisited." On the other hand, he never mentions

the accusation being made. It is nonetheless clear from the entirety of Guénon's oeuvre that there is not the slightest intention on his part to exhort modernity to return to or assimilate en masse either the complete worldview or the outer forms of any Traditional culture of times past or present.

A return to the classical period of past Traditional cultures—even if such a thing were possible—is therefore *not* the Traditional solution to the vicissitudes of modernity. We will presently address the question of what it is. But before reproducing the statements made by Guénon, Coomaraswamy, and others regarding the actual solution to modernity's problem, it is first necessary to understand from the Traditional view the role played by the process of periodicity in this question. Using developed Hindu metaphysical terminology, from the highest perspective of cosmic duration and *manvantāra/mahāpralaya*, it is in the unremitting spin of the cycle that all problems and all solutions are to be found, and this is no less applicable to what Guénon believed to be the end of the present cycle, in whose last quadrant—the Kali yuga— we now find ourselves. In the section on periodicity in chapter 8, we reproduced sufficient statements from both Guénon and Coomaraswamy to establish their belief in the effects of cyclic motion.

Basically, spiritual evolution moves in a cyclic, helical spiral through the interplay of opposite polarities, and this Traditional view is the perspective of temporal (historical) dynamic of which Hegelian historical dialectic is a rough approximation. Indissoluably infused with this helico-cyclic approach to evolution are the two processes of *enantiodromia* and the compensation theory (which Guénon calls "reinstatement"), which operate in tandem; that is, the germ or seed of the "thesis" dyad is present in the "antithesis" dyad, to borrow Hegel's terms, and that while one dyad is in manifestation, its partner begins to grow after the nadir of its cyclic spin is reached and will eventually equal and then supersede it until it reaches its zenith (at which point its partner is at its nadir), and so on. The seeds for spring are dropped in autumn, its polar opposite in the annual cycle. By the law of *enantiodromia*, there is always a mutual reciprocity between the "opposite polarities": one contracts while the other expands, and vice versa, but neither is ever entirely obliterated.

Needless to say, the cultural forms these periodic expansions take are always different, and even further complicated by varying magnitudes of the cycles involved (in fact, there are cycles within cycles), but they are always a sort of opposite reflex to the preceding one, and thus follow a pattern. William I. Thompson, in discussing the "four ages" thesis found in various mythologies of archaic peoples, describes this dynamic:

> But as entropy reaches its limit in chaos, there is a reversal in the cycle, a cosmic form is generated out of the only ground large enough for it, namely chaos. Chaos creates the fertile decay in which the seeds left over from the previous age of gods spring to life to create a new cosmic myth and a new age of gods. We spiral back into the past in a future on a higher plane.[111]

In the Traditional view, this dynamic is incessant, and the spin of the cycle is irreversible. There can be, therefore, no question of "returning to the Middle Ages," any more than there can be a reversal of the evolutionary cycle, which spins in only one direction. Because it is inseparable from the notion of periodicity, the Traditional solution differs dramatically from the modern technologic solutions, based on science and temporally linear progressivism.

One all-important and overriding question arises regarding the current position of the present on the cycle in relation to the nadir, which most in the Traditional school believe to be just ahead. This question can be framed in several ways, but its basic interrogative is the same: What awaits us, humanity as a whole, when the nadir of the present cycle is reached, as it inevitably will be? To this question, no one has an answer. Traditionalists and many others agree, however, that modernity is in a liminal transitional phase, something similar perhaps to the great apocalyptic and millenarian sentiments that accompanied the momentous cultural paradigm shifts in epochs past. Essentially, the response of Coomaraswamy and Guénon to this question is that it depends, that it is (or will be) a matter of degree.

The impending cyclic nadir could be no more than a planetary discomfiture, as the world has felt with economic and political uncertainty since World War I. It could be a more drastic depression in which a greater number of people suffer famine, disease, and more regional conflicts, with a greater tension due to the potential for global involvement. It could be a catastrophe on a planetary scale where world commerce suffers a complete breakdown and nations become bankrupt in a planetary economic depression, resulting in mass famine, total disruption of business, government, the ascent of societal anarchy and individual competition for survival, possibly compounded by another "conventional" war of global magnitude. Finally, it could be near-total extinction, the quickest method of which would be an internecine thermonuclear Armageddon wherein detonation of numerous atomic and hydrogen warheads would irradiate the entire range of the planet's atmospheric strata beyond the limit of human survival. While the possible scenarios are numerous and the degree of the nadir's effect is speculative, the fact that there will nonetheless be *some* continuity between the end of this modern phase and the beginning of the next is not a matter of speculation. From the Traditional perspective, this continuity is unequivocal, as Guénon states:

> Whatever is to be the manner in which the change that constitutes what can be called the passage from one world to another is accomplished, moreover whether it is a question of greater or smaller cycles—this change, even though it may have the appearance of a complete rupture, can never imply an absolute discontinuity, for there is a causal chain which links all cycles to one another.[112]

Guénon even has a name for the survival of certain elements in one cycle which form the essential foundation for the following cycle: He refers to it as "reinstatement," which is basically the same as what we have referred to as the *enantiodromia*/compensation theory duplex process that so captivated Carl Jung. Guénon asserts that "by the 'reinstatement' which operates at the final moment, this end will itself immediately become the beginning of another *Manvantāra*."[113]

In the light of this, we can say the Traditional view of periodicity and "reinstatement" probably precludes the *total* annihilation of humanity on the earth, though it does not preclude a survival of small groups in remote areas somehow spared the fatal effects of the destructive force, or those stashed in special repositories by their respective bellicose societies to become the stock for repopulation. We can further state, inferentially, that no one in the Traditional school actually expects this sort of instantaneous six-week annihilation, because of what they explicitly affirmed as the solution to the vicissitudes of modernity. Given their beliefs in periodicity; given their belief in reinstatement; and given their belief in some sort of ensuing cataclysmic event or depletion, the hopes of Guénon and Coomaraswamy for a germinal but gradual cure for the modern malaise were placed in the first principles of Tradition, and in the spiritual elite whose function is to intuit and in turn disseminate them.

It was not a return to the outward forms or particular worldview of Gothic Christendom—or any other extant world religion—that Coomaraswamy and Guénon espoused, but rather a return to the first principles found in that worldview. They espoused a return to those first principles which, in the Traditional view, are immemorial and universal (*perennis et universalis*). These first principles are Ariadne's thread, given to the confused Theseus humanity to help guide him out of the labyrinth of modernity. Their solution was to make quantity once again secondary to quality, which arrangement they saw as natural according to the principle of hierarchy; to controvert the unnatural inversion of quantity over quality that they saw as the hallmark of the modern worldview. "What possibility of regeneration, if any," asks Coomaraswamy, "can be envisaged for the West? The possibility exists only in the event of a return to first principles and to the normal ways of living that proceed from the application of first principles to contingent circumstances."[114] Today, the same question is even more applicable to the quantitative planetary culture as a whole. In the view of both Guénon and Coomaraswamy, the East of the 1930s and 1940 still had more to give than the West in terms of sharing the first principles of living traditions. Guénon wrote that "This boon of contact with the traditions whose spirits still subsist today is itself the sole means of reviving that which is susceptible of being revived; it is this, as we have already asserted so frequently, that is one of the greatest services which the East is able to render to the West."[115] Neither Guénon nor Coomaraswamy negated the idea that, as Durand states, "the West bears its remedy within its own Western tradition." They rather concentrated on an "agreement of first principles" between East and West, which each mentions repeatedly. Guénon, in fact, devotes two chapters in *Orient et Occident* to the idea of "agreement": "L'accord sur les principes" and "Entente et non fusion."

Suggesting there is continuity between the two phases, the old and the new; indicating new seeds exist in the humus of the waning quantitative and high-entropy culture of modernity, William I. Thompson writes that "Western civilization is drawing to a close in an age of apocalyptic turmoil in which the old species, collectivizing mankind with machines, and the new species, unifying it with consciousness, are in collusion with one another to end what we know as human nature."[116] A cultural reassimilation and return to an agreement upon the first principles of Tradition—the philosophia perennis or theosophia—this is the Traditional solution to the vicissitudes of modernity. That things will get worse before they get better may well be, but of the continuity, survival, and ultimate fruition of these principles and of higher consciousness, there is little doubt in the eyes of the Traditionalists. The final word of advice Guénon gives in the last paragraph of the sobering *La crise du monde moderne* is this: "There is, therefore, no place for despair; even if there were no hope of achieving a concrete result before the modern world was eclipsed after some catastrophe, this would still not be a viable reason for refraining to embark upon a work whose real import extends far beyond the present era."[117] To those embarking upon this work, Guénon bequeaths this motto: *Vincit omnia veritas* ("truth conquers all").

PLANETIZATION: CONSCIOUSNESS AND CULTURE

Certainly the concept of planetization is not new to the last half of the twentieth century. The League of Nations, for example, was established in 1920; it was succeeded by the formation of the United Nations in 1945. Strictly speaking, neither organization promoted explicitly the idea of a complete planetization of consciousness or culture in the sense that that idea has gained currency in more recent times, but the idea was inherent in these organizations in seminal form from the beginning. From the 1970s, however, more and more literature has been published that deals with the theme of planetization, directly and specifically.[118] R. Buckminster Fuller's "spaceship earth" and Marshall McLuhan's "global village" have become household terms. Pierre Teilhard de Chardin, whose heterodox thought is something of an enigmatic complex and whose theses we thus employ guardedly, was renowned for his views on planetization, especially as expressed in his books *Building the Earth* and *The Future of Man*. Historiography has become ever more global in its perspective since the explorations of the Renaissance European powers, and most especially since the advent of the twentieth century, a fact which Mircea Eliade notes: "Today history is becoming truly universal for the first time, and so culture is in the process of becoming planetary."[119] And outside the scope of those who deal exclusively with planetization in a spiritual or consciousness context, international economic, political, and military observers have had to take into consideration a de facto intricacy or "geopolitical" dimension of the planet in their strategic forecasts as never before.

What must be necessarily precedent to a planetization of culture is a planetization of consciousness, for without the latter the former cannot occur. According to proponents of planetization, the peoples of the earth must begin to think, as is now gradually happening, in terms of global or planetary wholeness. Planet, Earth, Globe, or Terra must replace "country" or "nation" in the consciousness of the earth's inhabitants. Wholeness must replace fragmentation in consciousness before an actualization of planetary culture is possible. To effect such a change in consciousness takes generations and does not occur overnight. Where, one might ask, does Tradition in Guénon's and Coomaraswamy's terms fit into this? William I. Thompson makes the connection: "As the old civilization of the industrial nation-states is falling apart, it is also falling into new forms of a very old consciousness. Within this consciousness an ancient vision of reality is taking us into another dimension in which we can find our bearings once again to make the transition from civilization to planetization."[120]

One should be clear, however, that neither Coomaraswamy nor Guénon were advocates of planetization of culture, nor did they expend any effort to discuss the idea. Moreover, we do not independently advocate this doctrine, but simply observe an historic and inexorable momentum and by simple extrapolation posit with Thompson and others what—with the passage of another three to five centuries—appears to be an inevitability. Even the distinguished historian Arnold Toynbee, as related by Huston Smith, believed that historians two thousand years from now will regard the twentieth century as the one in which mankind took its first steps toward the building of a world civilization.

Among the ironies of this paradigm shift to planetization is one entirely consistent with the "reinstatement" process. It is in the most recent scientific theories (as opposed to scientism) that one finds the fundamental postulates of the ensuing planetary culture and consciousness. Pure science (*scientia*), and not scientific reductionism, is gradually beginning to corroborate the Traditional perspective of holism. Einstein's famous unified field theory and later David Bohm's implicate order have kept alive the notion of universal interconnection for generations of physicists, and by the law of correspondence, this universal macrocosmic principle must apply equally to lesser organisms, which is precisely what the "Gaia hypothesis" proposes for the microcosm of the planet Earth. The new holistic views currently found in pure science in addition to theses only recently gaining wide recognition—for example, the second law of thermodynamics or "entropy law"—are ironically becoming profoundly subversive to the older mechanistic, analytic, fragmented worldview that has dominated modernity since its rupture with Tradition—in Guénon's opinion—or since the Enlightenment in the more accepted consensus.

This collaboration between the newer scientific theories and first principles does not, incidentally, stand the Traditional view of science on its head. Pure science has never been the enemy of Tradition; only scientism, which carries with it a blind soteriological faith in technology and a repudiation of the nonempirical based solely on sciolistic reductionism.[121] Coomaraswamy—the Doctor of Geology, let it not be forgotten—once wrote that "Natural scientist and metaphysician—one and the same can be both; there need be no betrayal of either scientific objectivity on the one hand or of principles on the other."[122] Science can thus be seen to play a dual role in the paradigm shift from "civilization to planetization." Ironically, it destroys the scientism of modernity; genuinely, it substantiates the necessity of planetization by establishing the probity of integrity and reciprocity in person/planet/cosmos as it gradually aligns itself with Tradition in the world of the twenty-first century.

In the application of planetary consciousness to planetary culture, this latter role of science is indispensable. Robert Ellwood writes that "Planetization means the process of coming together—often in only superficial ways—of the peoples of this earth. Today, in ways that would have been unimaginable to our forefathers, we have through the electronic media instantaneous awareness of the farthest reaches of the globe and through supersonic jets relatively easy access to them."[123] Jet travel and other of these means of planetization of culture are high entropy, and thus no solution to planetary disunity. But while it is naive to have a blind faith in what has been described as technologic soteriology, one cannot discount the possibility that nonentropy alternatives to such methods of planetization will eventually be developed by scientific, technologic means. Once science is conjoined with and integrated into a worldview based on first principles where, in Coomaraswamy's words, the "natural scientist and metaphysician" can be "one and the same," a natural screening process for efficient, nonentropy technology with minimum negative side effects will necessarily occur. The nature and characteristics of this single planetary culture will be explored momentarily. It remains to be stated that whatever shape it may take, science and technology—devoid of the faith and reductionism that accompany them in modernity, and subservient to first principles—will doubtless play a major part in its creation and maintenance. Indeed, the seeds of this avant-garde pure science—that is, theories that presuppose a wholeness of things—are already becoming manifest.

The scientific ideal is applicable only to contingent realms, and must collaborate with a metaphysical and a priori worldview based on order, harmony, value, and integrity if planetization of a Traditional culture is to occur. Coomaraswamy hints at precisely this kind of collaboration in writing, "it is no new discovery of modern positivism that *I* 'is merely a name for a series of atomic events'; this is a traditional doctrine, integral to the Philosophia Perennis, and of unknown antiquity."[124] Thus, to counter the effects—the vicissitudes—of modernity, the natural spin of the cycle with its inherent process of reinstatement, in confederation with the reapplication of first principles, the integral theories of pure science, and the vision of a planetary consciousness, may yet revolve to a shift in consciousness or worldview that becomes the only salvation from annihilation.

### A TRADITIONAL PLANETARY CULTURE:
### *NOVUS ORDO SECLORUM*

Exactly what the era beyond modernity will bring is unclear. It would be something more than redundant to begin listing detailed characteristics of any one scenario in this new era as if it were already manifest; it is entirely speculative at this point. But a *projection of trends* into the future, based on the visible degeneration (rotten bases) of modernity on the one hand and the visible seeds and sprouts presently occurring and indicative of the reinstatement process on the other hand, is not so entirely speculative. Quite obviously, it is not yet a fait accompli, but one thing is for certain: the trend toward a planetization of consciousness and culture has actively begun. Skeptics and critics of this theory may point out that, if anything, future trends based on recent world events seem to indicate a pandemic ethnocentrism and xenophobia, parochialism and tribalism, and group solipsism. But when, we ask, has this *not* been the case in recorded history when conditions were uncertain or when foreign cultures interacted? Moreover, when in world history has there ever been such an effort expended in planetization of thought; in international cooperation as exemplified by the United Nations; in unanimity of and conformity brought about by world trade, science, technology; in networks of satellite data gathering and telecommunications; and in educational and artistic exchanges as there is now? International organizations whose *sole* purpose is the promulgation of planetary consciousness now exist, and internationally constituted spiritual communities proliferate.[125]

Conferences and councils of the world's learned religious leaders gather with more frequency to discuss ecumenical cooperation and to find a common ground of spiritual aspiration for a new planetary culture; numerous institutes, like Harvard's Center for the Study of World Religions and the International Cooperation Council, were established for these reasons. In a report on the Petersham Meeting, one observer concluded that "If the rapidly emerging world culture has no spiritual base to sanction its ethic and give it a transcendent vision, it can only lead to darkest despair for a self-destroying race."[126] Similar statements—and beliefs—emanated from the second Parliament of World Religions in 1993. Mircea Eliade suggests the discipline of the history of religions as the method best suited to achieve this spiritual base: "The history of religions can play an essential role in this effort toward *planétisation* of culture; it can contribute to the elaboration of a universal type of culture."[127]

With such efforts and such methods, it remains only for the first principles of Tradition, of natural metaphysics, to be reinstated—reintegrated into the emerging worldview—for there to be a Traditional planetary culture with similar features to those of medieval Traditional cultures described by Guénon and Coomaraswamy, as they relate to wholeness, sacrality, and so on, within the spheres of social structure, art and crafts, the metaphysical system, vocation, and fusion of culture. The reintegration of certain of these principles is already apparent, as we have noted, in the newer theories of *pure* science. Moreover, the fundmental metaphysical axioms of both Eastern religions and Western esoteric schools have become popularized thanks to the Traditionalist writings and the modern Theosophical movement.

The combination of these several forces moves us inexorably toward reintegration, wholeness, and planetization, but it is today no less a race between the force of integration, of which the seeds just mentioned are indicative, and the force of disintegration, in which we are currently enmeshed and traveling downward at alarming speed. "We live in a crucial time, for the decisions we make about the future of humanity and the earth are irrevocable; humanity as a species must either become integral and whole, or undergo painful diminishment. There are no other options."[128] The critical nadir, in the Traditional view, lies immediately ahead, and the race is to that point. Just past the nadir, and beginning the upswing, whether that be decades or centuries from now, the likelihood of a Traditional planetary culture will be far more determinable than at present. Based on contemporary trends and consistent with the morphology of Traditional culture, we can turn our attention to an examination of what the world may be like when—or if—in Coomaraswamy's words, it "has been given back its meaning."

First, a brief mention of what a Traditional planetary culture will not be. Earlier we discussed the objections of both Guénon and Coomaraswamy to what Coomaraswamy referred to as a "sort of religious Esperanto," their rejection of the notion of "the development of a single universally acceptable syncretic faith embodying all that is 'best in every faith.'" But because the basis of a planetary culture if it is to be a new Traditional culture must be a spiritually oriented planetary consciousness, and because this latter must contain sacred principles inherent in, common to, and representative of the world's major religions, the unavoidable conclusion is that the first principles of natural metaphysics that alone satisfy these prerequisites must play a primary role that at first sight may appear to be such a "universally acceptable syncretic faith." One might well ask how this apparent contradiction can be reconciled. Guénon supplies the answer, part of which was quoted earlier:

> The knowledge of principles is strictly the same for all men who possess it, for the mental differences can only affect that which belongs to the individual, and therefore contingent, order, and they do not approximate the domain of pure metaphysics; undoubtedly, each man will express in his own way that which he has understood to the measure that he is able to express it, but the man who has truly understood will always be able, behind the diversity of expressions, to recognize the one truth, and thus this inevitable diversity will never be a cause of disagreement.[129]

Guénon speaks, in this quote, of an "inevitable diversity" of expressions of the one truth, or of the primordial Tradition, as was then found in the cultures of certain Islamic societies, in Tibet, in parts of India and China, and in surviving tribal societies. Yet, neither he nor Coomaraswamy had the opportunity of living another half century to observe both the rapid planetization occurring in consciousness and in the material culture, and the corresponding decline of the remaining Traditional societies.

Though their emphases differed, Coomaraswamy and Guénon each insisted on participation and regular initiation in a *living* Tradition in order to understand and assimilate the first principles and the concomitant esoteric teachings. Similarly, they each rejected the notion of an eclectic "religious Esperanto" comprised of first principles borrowed from and expressed in the idioms of the various Traditional systems. However, they both died before it could be stated unequivocally that upon the face of the earth one can no longer find any thoroughly Traditional cultures, and that all that remains of the former survive in isolated pockets of remote, rural areas. A given tradition may have been "living" enough for Guénon that these principles of the Tradition survive only in orthodox remnants of established religions, or in various orders and secret societies in which initiation is regular under the aegis of a qualified teacher, notwithstanding that these orthodox remnants or orders exist in the midst of heterogeneous modern culture with all its degredation and inversion. For Coomaraswamy, however, the culture was primary, and initiation was a right of all people—not just the spiritual elite—by virtue of practicing a vocation integral to a social order and culture wholly informed by the first principles of natural metaphysics: a "living" Tradtional culture.

If planetization is an inevitable fact, then eventually—possibly within the next few centuries—there will be only one culture remaining on earth. How we value this future occurrence is not at issue here. The point is whether, at some future time, this planetary culture will contain in a wholly new form a unanimous religious or spiritual expression based on the first principles and consequently become a *living* Traditional culture, as so many have done in the past. The indicia of gestation for this occurrence are already apparent, though it remains unclear whether these indications are only prepatory for the advent of a new *avatara*, or whether the unprecedented outpouring of the philosophia perennis or theosophia—the Tradition—in the late nineteenth and twentieth centuries was the progenitor of a new, orthodox planetary living Tradition. If the latter is the case, then based on their lives' work, Guénon and Coomaraswamy would have been key contributors to any future planetary Traditional culture—a subtle irony in light of their position on "religious Esperanto."

One must always keep in mind that the living Traditions so cherished by Guénon and Coomaraswamy were similarly subject to the law of periodicity. The Traditional Hindu culture that Coomaraswamy loved did not exist in 2000 B.C., and except for isolated regions in India, does not exist today. The Islamic tradition adopted by Guénon did not exist in 500 C.E., and with the possible exception of certain regions of the Middle East, does not exist today as a cultural reality. The same can be said for the various Traditional cultures that resulted from the flowering of the highest expressions of the metaphysics of Christianity, of Judaism, of Buddhism, and of Taoism. Each of these cultural manifestations of the Tradition had a beginning and an end, just as will a new planetary living Traditional culture. Until that time arrives, there will still be those who, in the interim, seek truth. Where they will find it is first, *within*, and second, predominantly in the legacy of those who have written on the first principles of the Tradition since the late nineteenth century, as well as in those small initiatic orders beyond the scrutiny of the public.

Planetization has already begun—both technologic and conceptual—as we have seen. But the vision of a planetary culture based on the precepts of Traditional culture as outlined by Guénon and Coomaraswamy is a new entry into the field of futurism. The developed metaphysics contains elements of both the new pure science and crosscultural expressions of first principles in the manner in which Coomaraswamy elucidated the philosophia perennis: "All that I have tried to show is that the axioms of this philosophy by whomever enunciated, can often be explained and clarified or emphasized by a correlation with the parallel texts of other traditions [and now pure science]."[130] By definition, the social structure of the Traditional planetary culture must be hierarchical, and of this Tradition refers only to a spiritual elite determined solely by virtue of ability, whose function it will be to relay, as it were, the higher metaphysical principles and the doctrine that unfolds from them.

Presumably this will be the role of the advanced scientists/metaphysicists ("one and the same can be both") and/or religionists and students of philosophy—like Guénon, for example—who concentrate on these subjects. "[T]here are at present, in the Western world, certain indications of a movement which still remain imprecise, but which can and must, under normal conditions, lead to the reestablishment of an intellectual elite, unless some cataclysm intervenes too rapidly to permit its development."[131] They, like the Brahmins of classical Indian culture, might act as the priestly caste, and presumably the Dumézilian system would operate beyond modernity as it did before the concept (and actuality) of hierarchy was temporarily destroyed by the socialist and egalitarian sentiments of modernity, with politicians and business people occupying their respective places. The art of this future, unlike modern art, might reflect the higher sacred principles and would apply equally to crafts, which even now are becoming more popular and widely practiced. Employment might become more humanized, less drudgerous, and would consequently be considered more a vocation than a necessary evil. This would in turn affect the notions of work and play; the worker may no longer seek leisure as the ultimate good, but seek to realize and express his or her true nature through a vocation, which might serve as both an initiatory and integrative element in the culture as a whole.

Finally, and most important, every person in a Traditional planetary culture might see the unity, the sacrality, the oneness of life, owing to its universal acceptance as a scientific fact. All might hold, consequently, the principle of the universal brotherhood of humanity, and perceive the homology of person/planet/universe and the reciprocity of these phenomena in the wholeness of the system. And there will inevitably be anomalies and exceptions in this Traditional planetary culture, just as Traditionalists and Traditional ideals are anomalies in the modern, quantitative secular culture, for those anomalies may represent the tiny seed elements of a newer regeneration as this new Traditional planetary culture in turn runs its cyclic course in the millennia to come. In any event, a future planetary Traditional culture must be new and congruent with its time, but most importantly it must be *unanimous*—accepted and participated in by all—for without this unanimity it could not be considered Traditional.

No explicit evidence or documentation exists for this scenario in the writings of Guénon, Coomaraswamy, or any of the other writers in and allied to the Traditional school. We have tried, however, to express in graphic terms a dormant and unexpressed vision that inheres in every page of those writings of Guénon and Coomaraswamy that concerned periodicity and cultural renewal. The world can only be given back its meaning "by a return to first principles." This being done, all else must follow ineluctably in their wake, for this is the unalterable modus operandi of all becoming in manifestation according to Traditional metaphysics. Guénon, Coomaraswamy, and the Tradition they promulgated are today still barely audible voices within the din of modernity. They strove to isolate the word Tradition from the milieu of modern academia, and sought to imbue it with a meaning parallel to philosophia perennis and theosophia. They saw this Tradition in the symbolism, mythology and folklore of archaic and holistic cultures, and in the episteme that characterized them. Though not systematically, they outlined the rudimentary constituents of these qualitative cultures, which they called Traditional, and continuously contrasted them to the quantitative Western culture of modernity, which they regarded as a "monstrosity." They explicitly saw the impendence of a "dark hour" through which humanity in modernity will have to pass, though their prognostications of what lay on the other side of this cyclic nadir were not explicit.

All of these combined do not comprise the totality of their Traditional worldview, but they do represent the essential thrust of their thinking. In a superlatively succinct formulation, Gabriel Asfar wrote that "Guénon's God is . . . the Universal Principle; his faith, Knowledge; his revelation, Tradition; his sacrament, Initiation."[132] Those familiar with the writings—and the heart and mind—of Coomaraswamy would accept that this description approximates him as well. Whether explaining past Traditional cultures, or describing the difficult journey of the seeker in modernity, or even speculating on the nature of a new planetary Traditional culture (which they never did), both Coomaraswamy and Guénon would have bid us understand this: first come the truth and the way, then follows the life.

# NOTES TO PART IV

1. Coomaraswamy, *BK*, p. 1.

2. These are five of the top ten international corporations, according to the criterion of "Revenues" as listed in *Fortune Magazine* 132, No. 3 (1995):F–1.

3. See Robert Hughes, *Shock of the New*, chapter 4, entitled "Trouble in Utopia," which concerns the hegemony of these boxy glass-steel-concrete buildings, the paucity of their style or art, and what the author describes as "the glorious failure of modern architecture."

4. Guénon, *OEO*, p. 39.

5. Bellah, *Beyond Belief*, p. 66. Guénon makes a similar observation about these two early sociologists: In *OEO* he states that "even among the partisans of progress, there were those who could not refrain from asserting some rather grave reservations: Auguste Compte, who had begun by being a disciple of Saint-Simon, admitted a progress indefinite in duration but not in extent; for him, the march of humanity could be represented by a curve with an asymptote which it approaches indefinitely but never reaches" (p. 30).

6. Lipsey considers the influence of Ruskin and Morris on Coomaraswamy significant enough to devote two chapters of *CLW* to it. Chapter 6 is "The Appreciation of Indian Art in Britain from Ruskin to Roger Fry," and chapter 17 is "Coomaraswamy and William Morris: The Filiation."

7. In this work, therefore, modernity will refer to a "fixed" chronological time (the nineteenth and twentieth centuries). The examination is undertaken because, in Bellah's words, "Modernization, whatever else it involves, is always a moral and religious problem." op. cit., p. 64.

8. Roszak, *Person/Planet*, p. xxiii.

9. Urban, *Language and Reality*, p. 721.

10. Coomaraswamy, *SPM*, p. 297.

11. Coomaraswamy, *BK*, p. 6. Quoted earlier in the context of "quality and quantity," Coomaraswamy's description bears repeating insofar as it relates to the "standard of living": "Our boasted standard of living is qualitatively beneath contempt, however quantitatively magnificent."

12. Guénon, *OEO*, p. 40.

13. Rifkin, *Entropy: A New World View*, p. 238.

14. Guénon, *OEO*, p. 163.

15. Guénon, *Crise*, p. 97. Cf. Thompson, *Passages about Earth*, p. 154: "We have to accept that we now live in a time when the esoteric traditions of Christianity are dead, and the esoteric traditions of Western science are fast dying, so that the whole light of the civilization that came out of Christian Europe is flickering toward a new age of darkness. We now live in a culture in which the mystical science . . . has been reduced to the university departments of social science, in a culture in which the Christianity of Columba, Aidan, and Cuthbert has been reduced to the soporific pieties of a bureaucracy of sanctimonious clerks."

16. These three "metaphysical catastrophes," in précis are (1) the Church's establishment of temporal hegemony and the replacement of Avicenna's philosophy (of which Henry Corbin has written so extensively) by that of Averröes in the thirteenth century; (2) the objectivism—ranging from Galileo to Descartes—which emerged from sixteenth-century reform movements giving official status to the sacred/profane dualism; and (3) the development of nineteenth-century "historicism," the "hypostasizing of history," by which man, "having sacrificed everything to 'history,' found himself more alienated than ever" (p. 4).

17. Guénon, *Règne*, p. 259.

18. Guénon, *Crise*, p. 151.

19. In order, these excerpts are drawn from Eliade, *The Myth of the Eternal Return*, p. 28; Jung, *Psychology and Religion*, p. 102; and Smith *Forgotten Truth*, p. 6.

20. Shils, *Tradition, p. 285*.

21. Roszak, *The Making of a Counter Culture*, p. xiv.

22. Marty, "The Spirit's Holy Errand: The Search for a Spiritual Style in Secular America," p. 105.

23. Smith, op. cit., p. 16. Guénon employs the same term: "When one sees an exclusively material science present itself as the only science possible, when men have become habituated to accept as an unquestionable truth that no valid knowledge can exist apart from . . . the superstition of this science, which is more properly [termed] 'scientism,' how can men be anything else in practice but materialists?" (*Crise*, p. 132).

24. Roszak, "Ethics, Ecstasy, and the Study of New Religions," in *Understanding the New Religions*, p. 53.

25. Coomaraswamy, *BK*, p. 41.

26. Jung, *Psychology and Religion*, p. 41.

27. Eliade, *The Quest*, p. 67.

28. Urban, *Beyond Realism and Idealism*, p. 256. This statement brings to mind the best-seller by William J. Bennett, *The Book of Virtues* (New York, 1993). Though his diagnosis of society's ills is fundamentally right and his heart is in the right place, Bennett's effort is much too little, much too late.

29. Durand, *On the Disfiguration of the Image of Man in the West*, p. 22.

30. Urban, *Language and Reality*, p. 693.

31. Coomaraswamy, *BK*, p. 6.

32. Smith, op. cit., p. 16.

33. Guénon, *Règne*, p. 196. Thus the value of the individual in modernity is equal to his worth as a "numerical unit," and relative to the manufacture of which he is a part. This is a "horizontalization" of both value and people, and opposite to the axiological principles of Tradition, whose hierarchy remains vertical. This is essentially a celestial orientation, not a horizontal massification of value, whose vertical dimension alone bestows value. Henry Corbin insists that "A presence lacking a vertical dimension is reduced to seeking the meaning of history by arbitrarily imposing the [ergo, *relative*] terms of reference, powerless to grasp forms in the upward direction, powerless to sense the upward impulse of the pointed arch, but expert at superimposing absurd parallelepipeds" (*Man of Light in Iranian Sufism*, p. 3).

34. Coomaraswamy, *FSFT*, pp. 11–12.

35. Coomaraswamy, *SPTAS*, p. 29. Theodore Roszak echoes Coomaraswamy's pronouncement: "The all-important fact is: In premodern society there is no such thing as 'unskilled' labor; there are no workers who exist simply as the routinized adjuncts of machines or assembly lines; there is no one, below the level of the privileged orders, whose life's work is a scam or a boondoggle" (*Person/Planet*, p. 224).

36. Coomaraswamy, in a beautifully perceptive passage, condemns these artists, their art, and the disjointed view of labor that inheres in such a pompous *Kunsttheorie*: "We [moderns] have convinced ourselves that art is a thing too good for this world, labor too brutal an activity to be mentioned in

the same breath with art; that the artist is one not much less than a prophet, the workman not much more than an animal. Thus a perverted idealism and an amazing insensibility exist side by side; neither condition could, in fact, exist without the other" (*SPTAS*, p. 125).

37. Coomaraswamy, BUGB-B, p. 152.

38. Guénon, *Règne*, p. 92.

39. Coomaraswamy, *FSFT*, p. 248.

40. Henry Margenau, *Ethics and Science* (Princeton, N.J.: Van Nostrand, 1964), pp. 117, 118.

41. Guénon, *OEO*, p. 170.

42. Smith, op. cit., p. 2.

43. Guénon, *Règne*, p. 161.

44. Guénon, *Crise*, p. 138. Defining the actual effects of overmechanization, Guénon's description is judged the next logical step in the sequence by Thompson who speculates on the final effects of cyberculture: "We are not free to drop the culture of technology and move on to something else, because now the culture is trying to grow on its own terms by adapting *us* to *it*. The mechanists wish to alter human nature to make the vestigial ape in man fit for life in a technological society" (*Passages About Earth*, p. 143). With respect to this and to scientific progress generally, see the section on "Scientific Progress" in Eliot Deutsch, ed., *Culture and Modernity: East-West Philosophic Perspectives* (Honolulu: University of Hawaii Press, 1991).

45. Ibid., p. 138.

46. Eliade, *The Quest*, p. 1.

47. Guénon, *Crise*, p. 138.

48. Coomaraswamy, *SPM*, p. 417.

49. Durand, op. cit., p. 10. In one salient and astonishing corroborative example of the now institutional confusion and specialist-complexification of academia—if not society at large—the Associated Press ran a story on May 17, 1996 describing the following series of events. Dr. Alan Sokal, a physicist and professor of physics at New York University, wrote an intentionally unintelligible, incomprehensible article—pedantic gibberish—entitled "Transgressing the Boundaries: Toward a Transformative Hermeneutics of Quantum Gravity" and submitted it for publication in the reputable journal *Social Text,* published at Duke University. It was reviewed by editors there and published (volume 14, Nos, 1 & 2, 1996: 217–52). Dr. Sokal then pub-

lished a "confession" of sorts in the journal *Lingua Franca* 6, No. 4 (May–June 1996), titled "A Physicist Experiments with Cultural Studies," pointing out the ludicrous if not sad state of affairs in academia where such an event could occur. From a Traditional point of view, this is simply a logical outcome of a growing trend. The pernicious aspect to it is precisely the argument used by the swindlers in the parable of the Emperor's Clothes—that is, if we do not accept as true the theory being sold, or if we do not understand it (even if, a fortiori, it is not understandable), we will nonetheless agree for fear that others will think we are not clever. Thus, for these reasons, opportunities abound in modernity for the unscrupulous.

50. Coomaraswamy, *BK*, p. 6.

51. Nicholas Georgescu-Roegen in *Entropy: A New World View*, p. 267.

52. Roszak, *Person/Planet*, p. 274.

53. Guénon, *Règne*, p. 64.

54. Georgescu-Roegen in loc. cit., p. 269. Urbanophiles are quick to point out that cities have been with us since Babylon, and possibly further back; moreover, that classical Traditional cultures always had cities. But Roszak, like Murray Bookchin, sees *modern* cities as a different species: "The industrial city *is* something new under the sun. It is not, like the cities of the non-European past, simply a ceremonial center, or market place, or seat of government. It may be all of these, but it is primarily a center of production; it expands the social wealth" (*Person/Planet*, p. 248). In *The Limits of the City* (pp. 3, 137), Murray Bookchin expresses his anxiety about modern cities: "Given its grotesquely distorted form, it is questionable whether the city is any longer the proper arena for social and cultural development." Bookchin's remedy? "To restore urbanity as a meaningful terrain for sociation, culture, and community, the megalopolis must be ruthlessly dissolved and replaced by new decentralized ecocommunities, each carefully tailored to the natural ecosystem in which it is located."

55. Guénon, *Crise*, pp. 123–24.

56. Roszak, *Person/Planet*, p. 236. This thesis on the extinction of urban-industrialism is not dissimilar from the Tofflers' conception of the "Second Wave," which they see as soon ending. Unfortunately, their "Third Wave" appears to contain little more than knowledge that, while not bad in itself, without *wisdom* (which is altogether different) leaves humanity no better off than before. See Alvin and Heidi Toffler, *Creating a New Civilization: The Politics of the Third Wave* (Atlanta, Ga.: Turner, 1995).

57. Coomaraswamy, *FSFT*, p. 247.

58. Smith, op. cit., p. 7.

59. Needleman, *A Sense of the Cosmos*, p. 138.

60. Guénon, "Initiation and the Crafts," p. 163.

61. Coomaraswamy, *FSFT*, p. 247.

62. Coomaraswamy, and taken, in order, from *FSFT*, p. 248; *SPTAS*, p. 43; *SPTAS*, p. 70; *SPTAS*, p. 341.

63. Jung, *Two Essays on Analytical Psychology*, p. 20.

64. Jung's insistence upon his being an empiricist (presumably to valorize his theories of the unconscious) and not a metaphysicist, appears frequently throughout his oeuvre in various places. To cite a few examples: In *Psychology and Religion*, published as the 1937 Terry Lectures at Yale University, he states on pp. 1 and 2, "I restrict myself to the observation of phenomena and I refrain from any application of metaphysical or philosophical considerations." See also note 12 of "Flying Saucers: a Modern Myth" where he defends himself against accusations of being "metaphysical" and/or "psychologizing metaphysics": "I am an empiricist, who keeps within the boundaries set for him by the theory of knowledge" (*Civilization in Transition*, p. 328n.).

65. See Coomaraswamy, note 9 of "Primitive Mentality" in *FSFT*, p. 233: "C. G. Jung is put out of [metaphysical] count by his interpretation of symbols as psychological phenomena, and avowed and deliberate exclusion of all metaphysical significance."

66. Jung, *Modern Man in Search of a Soul*, p. 61.

67. Quoted in Eliade, *Occultism, Witchcraft, and Cultural Fashion*, p. 32.

68. Jung, *Civilization in Transition*, p. 143.

69. Ibid., pp. 267–68.

70. Ibid., p. 242.

71. Badcock, *Madness and Modernity*, pp. 129–30.

72. Guénon, *Règne*, p. 277. Coomaraswamy was the paragon of precise usage of English. Eaton remarks that his uncompromising precision in using words " . . . seems to belong more to the region of mathematics than to that of prose." *The Richest Vein,* p. 200.

73. Coomaraswamy, *SPM*, p. 10.

74. Ibid., p. 418.

75. Guénon, *Crise*, p. 113. Both men adhered to the concept of an institution of higher learning as akin to the Islamic *madrasa* or the late medieval European university where pneumatology, metaphysics, axiology, and theology dominated the curriculum but also offered rhetoric and law. In such a system, physical sciences and engineering would be relegated to purely vocational institutions. Cf. Lipsey, *CLW*, p. 272.

76. Bloom, *The Closing of the American Mind*, p. 350.

77. Ibid., p. 346.

78. Jung, *Modern Man in Search of a Soul*, p. 204.

79. Jung, *Civilization in Transition*, p. 277.

80. Guénon, *Règne*, p. 74.

81. Cammann, in "Remembering Again," *Parabola* 4:2 (1978), says, as a supporter of Coomaraswamy's thought, that "Many of his contemporaries felt that Coomaraswamy's dislike of modern culture was not only exaggerated, but excessively reactionary; and this, too, gained him many enemies. His views on such things were often very sensible, but he tended to overstate his case, instead of persuading his opponents to understand his way of thinking" (p. 86). In this same article Cammann makes only passing mention of Guénon, but if this observation applies to Coomaraswamy it must apply doubly to Guénon who, contrasted to Coomaraswamy on this reactionism, makes Coomaraswamy seem downright conciliatory. As to the modern sociological commentators, the criticisms and analyses are often as keen. See, for example, Edward A. Tiryakian, ed., *The Global Crisis: Sociological Analyses and Responses* (Leiden: E. J. Brill, 1984).

82. Coomaraswamy, BUGB-D, p. 151.

83. Guénon, *Crise*, p. 117.

84. Coomaraswamy, *FSFT*, p. 219. Cf. Coomaraswamy, *SPTAS*, p. 120: "An immanent [Traditional] culture . . . endows every individual with an outward grace, a typological perfection, such as only the rarest beings can achieve by their own effort (this kind of perfection does not belong to genius); whereas democracy, which requires of every man to save his own soul, actually condems each to an exhibition of his own irregularity and imperfection."

85. Roszak, *Person/Planet*, p. 68. A pronounced difference exists between the perception that democracy cannot work because it is flawed *ab initio* (i.e., a fundamentally unworkable theory), and the perception that

democracy is workable but only where a majority participates in a reasoned and civil fashion. The first view comports with Traditional metaphysics and the principle of hierarchy; the second with that of Jean Bethke Elshtain, whose *Democracy on Trial* (New York: Basic Books, 1995) illustrates a serious infirmity in modern American democracy. Traditionalists would hold that Professor Elshtain's book simply corroborates the probity of the former perception.

86. Guénon, *Crise*, p. 90.

87. Corbin, *The Man of Light in Iranian Sufism*, p. 10. On the nature of individuality, which constitutes a basal dogma in the modern worldview, see Coomaraswamy's Traditional definition in BUGB-D, p. 149: "'My' individuality or psychophysical constitution is not . . . an end in itself either for me or for others, but always a means, garment, vehicle or tool to be made good use of for as and for so long as it is 'mine'; it is not an absolute, but only a relative value, personal insofar as it can be utilized as means to the attainment of man's last end of liberation . . . and social in its adaptation to the fulfilment of this, that, or the other specialized function."

88. Coomaraswamy, *SPM*, p. 416. We would add to this list of the "people's drugs" the more recent epiphenomenon of sociolatry that may best be termed "celebriolatry," or the mindless worship of celebrities in modernity. The causes of this phenomenon are manifold, from the planetary envelopment by film, television, and other forms of electronic and printed media to the absence of any true (mythic) hero figures in the modern psyche and worldview. It has reached such proportions today that entertainers, artists, sports figures, and occasionally politicians, are accorded a status by the populace bordering on omniscience solely by virtue of their celebrity, and whose views on all variety of issues are preferred by the mass to noncelebrities of far greater understanding and intelligence with respect to those same issues. The phenomenon is not unlike a secular *darśana* of the sensible, material realm.

89. Coomaraswamy, *BK*, p. 16n.

90. Roszak, *Person/Planet*, p. 33 (italics mine). No one industrial nation can be held entirely responsible for planetary pollution, and so jingoists rationalize that *their* particular nation is thus beyond reproach—the fault lies elsewhere. But the convergence of wastes of such nations *is* apocalyptic in scale.

91. Guénon, *Crise*, p. 145.

92. Coomaraswamy, *BK*, p. 31.

93. Ibid., p. 1.

94. Roszak, Introduction to E. F. Schumacher's *Small is Beautiful*, p. 7.

95. Smith, op. cit., p. 124. Cf. Martin Lings: "Today the situation is considerably worse and considerably better. It is worse because human beings have degenerated still further. . . . It is better because there is no euphoria at all. The edifice of the modern world is falling into ruin. Great cracks are appearing everywhere through which it can be penetrated as it could not be before." *Sophia* 1, No. 1 (1995): 22–23. See Lings's 1987 treatise on the subject, *The Eleventh Hour: The Spiritual Crisis of the Modern World in the Light of Tradition and Prophecy.*

96. Guénon, *OEO*, p. 36.

97. Rifkin, op. cit., p. 205.

98. Coomaraswamy, *SPM*, p. 246.

99. Of the hundreds of titles that could be included in a survey of present and future conditions of malaise and degeneration attributable to modernism, the following (in addition to those used and/or cited in the text) represent a quality and inclusive selection of sociologists, historians, anthropologists, religionists, economists, philosophers. In one way, they can be seen as unwitting witnesses for the prosecution, as unintentional substantiators of the indictments made by Coomaraswamy and Guénon against modernity. This list includes *The Limits to Growth*, D. H. Meadows et al. (New York: Universe Books, 1972); *Mankind at the Turning Point*, Mihajlo Messarovic (New York: Dutton, 1974); *Future Shock*, Alvin Toffler (New York: Random House, 1970); *Creating a New Civilization: The Politics of the Third Wave*, Alvin Toffler and Heidi Toffler (Atlanta, Ga.: Turner, 1995); *An Inquiry into the Human Prospect*, Robert Heilbroner (New York: W. W. Norton, 1974); *An Inquiry into the Human Prospect: Looked at Again for the 1990s*, Robert Heilbroner (New York: W. W. Norton, 1991); *Visions of the Future*, Robert Heilbroner (New York: Oxford University Press, 1995); *Culture of Narcissism: American Life in an Age of Diminishing Expectations*, Christopher Lasch (New York: W. W. Norton, 1978); *The Empty Raincoat: Making Sense of the Future*, Charles B. Handy (London: Hutchinson, 1994); *The Evolution of the Future*, Frank W. Elwell (New York: Praeger, 1991); *Doomsday: The Science of Catastrophe*, Fred Warshofsky (New York: Pocket Books, 1979); *The Future of Technological Civilization*, Victor Ferkiss (New York: Braziller, 1974); *Social Limits to Growth*, Fred Hirsh (Cambridge, Mass.: Harvard University Press, 1978); *The Passing of the Modern Age*, John Lukas (New York: Harper & Row, 1970); *The Spiritual Crisis of Man*, Paul Brunton (New York: Samuel Weiser, 1970); *The Coming of Post Industrial Society*, Daniel Bell (New York: Basic, 1973); *Overload: The New Human Condition*, Leopold Bellak (New York: Human Sciences Press, 1975); *Overskill: The Decline of*

*Technology in Modern Civilization*, Eugene Schwartz (Chicago: Quadrangle, 1971); *Our Cultural Agony*, Vincint Vycinas (Hague: Martinus Nijhoff, 1973); and *Vital Signs 1996: The Trends That Are Shaping Our Future*, Lester Brown, Christopher Flavin, and Hal Kane. Worldwatch Institute (New York: W. W. Norton, 1996).

100. Emile Durkheim, *The Elementary Forms of the Religious Life* (New York: Free Press, 1965), p. 486.

101. Jung, *Civilization in Transition*, p. 329.

102. Guénon, *Crise*, p. 141.

103. There is a popular theory circulated by certain nutritionists and natural foods advocates that the degenerative diseases just mentioned are in themselves effects of the poor eating habits and lifestyle of modern people; that these effects grow worse, or more pervasive, each year. The scientific proof of this theory is hotly disputed in a variety of health, nutrition, and medical journals and symposia too numerous to list. Though little definitive can be said scientifically (except as to the intake of saturated fats) most of the testimonial evidence supports the theory; moreover, the force of the cultural perception should not be underestimated, for it is now increasingly *accepted* as true.

104. Guénon, *Crise*, p. 144.

105. Needleman, op. cit., p. 1.

106. Jung, *Modern Man in Search of a Soul*, p. 204.

107. Roszak, *The Making of a Counter Culture*, p. 146.

108. Durand, op. cit., p. 6.

109. Coomaraswamy, *COTPA*, p. 87.

110. Coomaraswamy, *BK*, p. 10. Wilbur Urban, who must be seen as one who proposes the "Traditional solution," is also squarely against "a return to *philosophia perennis* in any of its specific ancient forms. It is doubtless tempting to try to reinstate such ancient forms literally ... but this is surely to try to turn back the clock" (*Beyond Realism and Idealism*, p. 261).

111. Thompson, *Passages About Earth*, p. 121.

112. Guénon, *Crise*, p. 171.

113. Guénon, *Règne*, p. 368.

114. Coomaraswamy, *BK*, p. 62. Again, Wilbur Urban is in consonance with the Traditionalists: "The arrest of spiritual initiative is an out-

standing fact of our modern culture." This is due, in his view, to the "estrangement" of modern culture from "the great stream of traditional philosophy"—philosophia perennis. The solution is, in Urban's words, a "reuniting of our thought" with that great stream, and this is currently recognized by a few. "It is gradually coming home to many minds that our cultural and spiritual values are indeed bound up with a fundamental metaphysical structure and that estrangement from these ways of thinking means estrangement from the values themselves" (*Beyond Realism and Idealism*, p. 240).

115. Guénon, *Crise*, p. 45.

116. Thompson, *At the Edge of History*, p. 229.

117. Guénon, *Crise*, p. 183.

118. Examples of these works are Dane Rudhyar's *The Planetarization of Consciousness* (New York, 1977), David Spangler's *Toward a Planetary Vision* (Findhorn, 1977), William I. Thompson's *Passages About Earth: An Exploration of the New Planetary Culture* (New York, 1973), Donald Keys's *Earth at Omega: Passage to Planetization* (Boston, 1982), and Theodore Roszak's *Person/Planet* (New York, 1979). There are earlier books on the concept of planetization; namely, Dane Rudhyar's *Modern Man's Conflicts: The Creative Challenge of a Global Society* (New York, 1948). And there are other books—works by authors other than the "circle" of Traditional or closely allied authors used in this work—which have dealt with planetization and which have been influential: one notable example is W. Warren Wagar's *The City of Man* (Boston, 1963).

119. Eliade, *The Quest*, p. 69.

120. Thompson, *Passages About Earth*, p. 145.

121. It cannot be repeated enough that the Traditional view is not "antiscientific." "Render therefore unto Caesar the things which are Caesar's," as Matthew 22:21 states. For the sensible world of matter, the empirical and scientific laws and paradigms are sound and indisputable. It is the *reductionism* of scientism that engendered the polemics of the Traditionalists; that sort of smug repudiation of all things spiritual or metaphysical, by A. B. Keith, for instance, to which science and empirical methods have no accessibility whatsoever. One *cannot* render unto Caesar the things that are God's. In Coomaraswamy's words, "The weakness of the scientific position is, not that empirical facts are devoid of interest or utility, but that these facts are thought of as a refutation of the intellectual doctrine" (*FSFT*, p. 231).

122. Coomaraswamy, *BK*, p. 109. Cf. Roszak, *Person/Planet*, pp. 49–53, his excellent nine-point appraisal of "Science Beyond Reductionism."

123. Robert Ellwood, "Races, Cultures, and Religions in the Evolution of Consciousness," pp. 37–39.

124. Coomaraswamy, *SPM*, p. 410.

125. Planetary Citizens, World Peacemakers, the Institute for World Order, and the Stockholm International Peace Research Institute, among others, expend most of their energies working toward the manifestation of the concept of planetization. Examples of the spiritual communities are Auroville, Chinook, Community of Taizé, and the Lama Foundation, and these comprise the renowned ones: smaller and less known ones are numerous.

126. M. Basil Pennington, "Spirituality for a World Culture," *America*. September 3, 1977, pp. 100–03.

127. Eliade, *The Quest*, p. 69. Cf. Dane Rudhyar, *The Planetarization of Consciousness*, p. 309: "Likewise in religion, underneath the different dogmas loudly proclaimed by priests and moralists, there is one vast millennial effort, circuitous though it may be, toward the planetarization of consciousness and the ultimate achievement of the plenitude of man." Robert Ellwood stops short of discussing "planetization" of culture and religion per se, but makes some interesting predictions in *The History and Future of Faith: Religion Past, Present and to Come* (New York: Crossroad, 1988).

128. Keys, "Personal Transformation and Planetary Service," p. 22.

129. Guénon, *OEO*, p. 167.

130. Coomaraswamy, *SPM*, p. 165.

131. Guénon, *Crise*, p. 178. Cf. Marilyn Gustin who, elaborating on Guénon's premise, states that "Guénon's studies of symbol have the potential for restoring a 'sacred viewpoint' to the world, to the universe, to humankind itself," and further that "Guénon's work could greatly aid such a change toward a profound and broad integration and synthesis." "The Nature, Role and Interpretation of Symbol in the Thought of René Guénon," pp. 223–24.

132. Asfar, "René Guénon: A Chapter of French Symbolist Thought in the 20th Century," p. 322.

# APPENDIX A

*Definitions*

Tradition can be traced to two Latin roots: (1) the verb infinitive *dāre* (to give, deliver), and (2) the prefix *trans* (across, over), forming in combination the thought "to give or deliver over," to "hand over."[1] When applied to cultures or societies in which generations and even centuries are included in the process of handing over, the added element of continuity is introduced into the meaning, and tradition assimilates its ancestor-to-posterity connotation. Thus, the ingredients of relatively prolonged time (Edward Shils's "minimum" for tradition is three generations) of that which is being handed over, and of its actual transmission, combine to form the meaning of a word used in various ways not only in English but in its exact French, German, and Spanish cognates: the word tradition. The three main areas of human endeavor—cultural, theological, and artistic—to which the term tradition typically applies are outlined in the definition given in the *Oxford English Dictionary*:

> 1. Opinion or belief or custom handed down, handing down of these, from ancestors to posterity esp. orally or by practice. 2. (theol.) Doctrine etc. supposed to have divine authority but not committed to writing. 3. Artistic or literary principles based on accumulated experience or continuous usage.[2]

Related to the colloquial and vernacular usage of the word tradition as indicated by the *OED*, the word is used within the specific contexts of certain fields or disciplines, especially in the fields of religion, social sciences, and the arts.[3] Though the meaning of tradition in these disciplines is specifically relative to the field in which it is used and is somewhat different in each, its meaning remains broad when compared to its use in the writings of Guénon and Coomaraswamy. While the particularized metaphysical usage of Guénon and Coomaraswamy is generally radically different from those of the broader vernacular and specific field usages, there do exist areas in which meanings overlap, in addition to parallel elements within the comprehensive definition.

From the standpoint of definition, and of general treatment of the phenomenon, the term, and usages of the term tradition, the work of David Gross serves as a useful counterpoint both to Shils' social sciences perspective and to our specialized usage. In *The Past in Ruins: Tradition and the Critique of Modernity*, (Amherst, 1992) Gross presents a very balanced overview of tradition, and covers a variety of disciplines and cultural forms in his analysis of it. His first chapter is "The Meaning of Tradition," which outlines—as we have sought briefly to do here—the corridors of tradition in the various departments of life. Of particular interest is his thesis that in order for any tradition to be considered authentic, it must contain three elements, the second of which is that it contain "a certain amount of spiritual or moral prestige."[4]

*Social Sciences*

In recent years, sociologists and anthropologists have concerned themselves, among a plethora of other problems, with the question of tradition and especially with the mutual influence and reciprocal effects resulting from the collision of modern lifestyles and worldviews with those of traditional cultures; the principal collision between "modernity and tradition." Whole works have been directed at the examination of the problem; their titles even reflect the themes. Five notable examples of many possible ones are Daniel Lerner's *The Passing of Traditional Society*, Milton Singer's *When a Great Tradition Modernizes*, Shmuel Eisenstadt's *Tradition, Change, and Modernity*, Lloyd and Susanne Rudolph's *The Modernity of Tradition*, and Jessie Lutz and Salah El-Shakhs's *Tradition and Modernity: The Role of Traditionalism in the Modernization Process*. "Yet, in scrutinizing the literature of the social and cultural sciences," writes Edward Shils, "one sees that there has been very little analysis of the properties of tradition. The substantive content of traditions has been much studied, but not their *traditionality*."[5]

Though Eisenstadt's work, Shils's own book *Tradition*, and other more recent attempts at a corrective to this observation have been made, judging from the overall lack of definition or treatment of "traditionality," social scientists still continue to assume their audiences understand the full implications of their use of the term tradition, much like similar assumptions made about the terms *culture* and *modernity*.[6] That problems of definition regarding tradition are acute, Shils points out in a paper published prior to his book—also titled simply "Tradition": "One possibility is that despite the frequency of its use the term [tradition] means nothing at all. Another is that it means so many different things which are so different that there is no point to group them or to analyze them together."[7] Despite the difficulty in determining what constitutes the full or complete definition of tradition within the social sciences, one step toward narrowing its meaning can be safely made: it is usually used in contradistinction to the notion of modernity or "the present." Eisenstadt very concisely elucidates the dichotomy of these two types of society—traditional and modern—within the literature of the social sciences:

> There, a "traditional" society has often been depicted as a static one with but little differentiation or specialization, together with a low level of urbanization, and of literacy, whereas a "modern" society has been viewed as one with a very high level of differentiation, or urbanization, literacy, and exposure to mass media of communication. In the political realm, traditional society has been depicted as based on a "traditional" elite ruling by some mandate of heaven, and modern society has been viewed as based on wide participation of masses which do not accept any traditional legitimation of the rulers and which hold these rulers accountable in terms of secular values and efficiency. Above all, traditional society was by definition bound by the cultural horizons set by its tradition, while a modern society is culturally dynamic and oriented to change and innovation.[8]

Given this conventional perspective of the traditional versus modern society dichotomy with its implied valuation—the perspective that represented the *consensus omnium* of the social sciences milieux during the era in which Guénon and Coomaraswamy wrote—the inevitable conclusion to be drawn is that, again in Eisenstadt's words, "tradition was seen as the power or entity that had to be broken to assure the emergence and growth of modern and developing economic, political, and

social forces."⁹ Gross terms this view the "emancipatory" response to
tradition, which sees tradition as a sort of bondage that impedes creativity. But, as Eisenstadt and a growing number of social scientists point
out, perceptions are changing with regard to this dichotomous paradigm, which in turn necessarily indicates a shift in the meaning or definition of tradition within the social sciences. Again, titles are indicative:
highly representative of the new approach are papers by Richard Bendix, "Tradition and Modernity Reconsidered"; Rajni Kothari, "Tradition and Modernity Revisited"; and Joseph R. Gusfield, "Tradition and
Modernity: Misplaced Polarities in the Study of Social Change."¹⁰

Gusfield, for example, creates an actual taxonomy of fallacies in
the assumptions social scientists made regarding the traditional-modern polarity. His paper outlines seven fallacious assumptions, from the
idea that currently developing societies had previously been static
societies to the idea that traditional and modern forms are *always* in
conflict. Kothari pits the proponents of what he refers to as "universalist modernization" and "relativist modernization" against each other.
The former idealizes modernity and the process of modernization,
while the latter idealizes tradition; in terms of respective disciplines he
views Marxian sociologists as exemplars of universalist modernization and cultural anthropologists as exemplars of relativist modernization. He concludes that "In spite of great differences in attitude and
basic philosophy, both these approaches are characterized by a divorce
from reality."¹¹

With regard to recent perspectives of the modernity-tradition
polarity among social scientists, the consensus is that the polarity is factitious. This is among the basic theses of the Rudolphs' *The Modernity
of Tradition*. So many different strata of complexity occur in the confluence of modern and traditional modes of cultural dynamics that their
simple bifurcation is an insufficient model to explain the tensions found
in rapidly and/or radically changing cultures. The type and speed of the
modernization is a variable; the length of time that has transpired since
its inception is a variable; the natural environment in which it occurs is
a variable; and most important with respect to both our discussion and
the changes manifest in a given culture, the nature and adaptability of
the particular traditions themselves are variables.

Doubtless more variables could be listed; what is germane to the
question at hand is how the desuetude of the conventional modern-traditional contradistinction has affected the definition or usage of tradi-

tion within the social sciences. Kothari uses the term *reintegration* as indicative of the comprehensive sweep toward the revised notion of tradition in the social sciences; that is, tradition is an ineradicable and vital necessity in the ongoing process of establishing new and harmonious modes of cultural activity and function. And in this reintegral dynamic, tradition is no longer the "power or entity that had to be broken" to assure the success of modernity, as Shils so well explains. Neither is it the sacrosanct power or entity whose perception requires unequivocal and thoughtless obedience, nor the outmoded phenomenon whose very existence should at all costs be minimized by "enlightened" moderns. Tradition, in short, no longer means simply the antithesis of modernity within the social science disciplines. Dying is the attitude, as the Rudolphs express it that "Useless and valueless, tradition has been relegated to a historical trash heap. Modernity will be realized when tradition has been destroyed and superseded."[12]

The term has regained much of its original meaning more closely correlating to the dictionary definition already given—with the added notion that the presence of tradition in modernizing cultures is necessary for integrated cohesion and proper function. Among the most useful accounts within today's discourse on tradition in this regard is the view of Hans-Georg Gadamer that texts are or can be instruments of tradition, and that true dialogue with a text is one way of assimilating, through the text's language, the time and place of its origin.[13] The reliance of texts for cohesion in society and within the various disciplines under consideration here is a major element for survival of tradition. Tradition's current meaning in the social sciences seems to correlate closely with another field where tradition is used with a slightly specialized meaning and where reliance on texts is paramount: the field of religious studies.

## *Religious Studies*

Use of the term tradition in religious studies[14] is both older and in a way more specific than in the field of social science. It has been a leitmotif in religions, like Islam and Judaism, where the *Ḥadīth* and both *Talmuds*, the latter even being partially comprised of earlier *Aggadah* and *Halacha*, form central and legitimating doctrines of the faiths. Hinduism might be said to have a tradition found in some of the Vedic hymns, particularly those concerned with ritual, and in the *Upaniṣads*. The cosmogonic and theogonic myths of the *Vedas* and the theophanic and hierophanic myths of the *Purāṇas* place them in a category close to but still different from the percept of tradition as it is used here. In Buddhism, much if not all of the *tripiṭaka* is attributed to the Buddha, most especially the *sūtrapiṭaka*, and since it initially passed via oral transmission from one generation to the next until it was committed to script, one might reasonably argue that the entire Buddhist canonical corpus in all three major divisions (Theravāda, Mahāyāna, and Vajrayāna) could be viewed as tradition. To use another example from Buddhist literature to illustrate the distinction between myth and tradition, one could categorize the canonical *tripiṭaka* as tradition, and the *jātakas* as folklore or myth. This should not be interpreted to mean that folklore and myths are not *plein de sens*, that they do not have significance— didactic or otherwise—for the religious within Eastern and/or tribal religions, but only that myth and tradition as used here convey significance or meaning differently. Finally, certain Christian texts can be placed under the rubric of tradition as well. The earliest of the synoptic gospels (Mark) is dated by Biblical scholars at around 70 C.E. Here, these Christian texts include the gospels, the deutero-Pauline epistles, and other pseudepigrapha of the New Testament (and the large corpus of apocrypha[15] separated from canon by the thin membrane of conciliar decrees from Nicea onward), as contrasted to the genuine apostolic letters and the later theological commentaries.

To distinguish between tradition and myth at all within the sphere of religious studies, one must generalize and say that the former is recollection of principles or events transmitted either orally or scripturally and passed to a more select group (sacerdotal and religious professionals and/or specialists) within the religious community while the latter in its functional state is usually orally transmitted and directed toward a more widespread or popular element within a culture. The two are not exclusive, and there exists areas of overlapping as in the case of Muhammad's *mi'rāj* or ascent to heaven that, though it is only very briefly mentioned in the Qur'ān (Sūra XVII;1), is among the prominent *Ḥadīth* and figures significantly in Islamic theology.[16]

To distinguish between tradition and revelation within religious studies is somewhat more difficult than distinguishing between tradition and myth. Revelation, in our context, differs from tradition only in that it is theophanic as opposed to immemorially recollected; again, the two are by no means exclusive. A helpful parallel for clarifying this distinction are the Sanskrit terms *smṛti* (remembered, recalled) for tradition, and *śruti* (hearing) for revelation. Historically, of course, we know Moses probably did not write the Pentateuch containing the direct revelation of the Decalogue, nor did Muhammad write down his visions and communications with Gabriel; both were recorded decades and even centuries later (at least the oldest texts available so indicate). Despite questions about the historicity of these revelations, they are *regarded* as revelations, so the relevant point to this discussion in terms of the distinction between tradition and revelation is that in the cases of Moses, Muhammad, and for that matter, Joseph Smith, a *claim of revelation* is made that includes the communication between mortal man and a deity or deific figure. Once revealed, however, the content, irrespective of its etiology, is still "handed over" from ancestors to posterity.

Within religious studies, the term tradition can almost stand as a replacement for religion itself when referring to a particular religion; it has historically had a broad meaning that is no less evident in current usage. N. P. Williams, who wrote the article on tradition in Hastings's *Encyclopaedia of Religion and Ethics*, corroborates this observation by declaring:

> Most religious systems claim to bear within themselves a deposit, consisting of ceremonial, myth, dogma, or ethics, or of some of these elements, revealed by some ultimate divine or quasidivine authority, and meant to be handed down to posterity by a succession of duly qualified trustees.[17]

There would appear to be little else in a religion, according to Williams's definition, which tradition does not cover. And if we compare historically the broad religious studies' usage of tradition to that of the social sciences, we find it is as old—if not older—than the actual developed disciplines of the social sciences, as attested to by J. L. Jacobi's 1847 publication of *Die kirchliche Lehre von der Tradition und heiligen Schrift*.

One contemporary example of a historian of theology who uses tradition with a similarly broad meaning is Jaroslav Pelikan. In his five-volume history of Christian doctrine entitled *The Christian Tradition*, he gives a more expanded and detailed definition of tradition than Williams, at least as it manifests in the current thought of scholars of religion. Pelikan states, relative to the ahistorical flavor often attached to tradition:

There is a sense in which the very notion of tradition seems inconsistent with the idea of history as movement and change. For tradition is thought to be ancient, hallowed by age, unchanged since it was first established once upon a time. It does not have a history, since history implies the appearance, at a certain point in time, of that which had not been there before.[18]

Pelikan refines and expands his observations on tradition in his book *The Vindication of Tradition* (New Haven, 1984). Though he uses Christianity as his paradigm, Pelikan's conclusions can by extrapolation be applied to most major religions undergoing significant change in modernity.

This perennial and immemorial attribute of tradition in the view of religious scholars closely resembles one attribute of tradition in the sense of Guénon and Coomaraswamy. In addition to this immemoriality, theologians and historians of religion include a sacrality, ahistoricity, and functional aspect to their meaning of tradition. It is thus a usage of the term that is limited to the field of religious studies, and in this it shares another similarity to the social sciences. Beyond sharing a definition that conforms and applies itself to the needs of their respective fields, scholars of religion and social scientists also share a rather large latitude in what can be included in their definitions of tradition, plus a relatively close proximity to the colloquial or vernacular usage of the term. One very good example of how the use of the term between these disciplines coincides appears in the papers published as *Ancient Traditions: Shamanism in Central Asia and the Americas* (Boulder, 1994). These similarities, however, are in contradistinction to the usage of the term tradition by Guénon and Coomaraswamy, with the single qualification that there is some overlapping of meaning and parallel elements of definition, as has been stated.

*Alternate Usages*

Beyond religious studies and social sciences, the term tradition also has a particularized meaning within the arts, as was indicated by the *OED* definition given above. Especially within literature and drama, tradition has played an important role and has had renowned proponents. For example, in an essay entitled "Tradition and the Individual Talent" published in 1919, T. S. Eliot advises his readers that a twentieth-century poet cannot write well unless he is thoroughly apprised of the poetry and poetic traditions of the past. Influenced by Eliot, the literary critic Frank Raymond Leavis continued this theme in *Revaluation: Tradition and Development in English Poetry* (London, 1936). Leavis, who saw the literary critic's purpose as assessing literature according to the moral position of the author, and who rejected the "anaemic and shoddy" attempts of writers trying to reformulate or even ignore traditional literary genres, applied these criteria to the novel in his major book *The Great Tradition* (New York, 1948). Here again, as in the other fields under discussion, the term tradition approximates the vernacular and colloquial usages in significant ways while still retaining those particular meanings peculiar to the field—in the case of the arts, modality of expression, media, content, purpose, and so on. However, tradition in the arts retains too exclusive a meaning to be profitably compared to its counterparts in religious studies and the social sciences. Regardless of the fact that Coomaraswamy was an acclaimed historian of the arts, a comparison of tradition in the arts and Tradition in the metaphysics of Guénon and Coomaraswamy shows even more divergence in meaning than a comparison of its usage by the metaphysicists and either the social scientists or the religionists.

Having considered these three main usages, at this point, mention must be made of Edward Shils's treatment of the theme of tradition in his book simply titled *Tradition* (Chicago, 1981). Shils' essential thesis is that the modern world has been too hasty in its pandemic abandonment of tradition; that it is a quite necessary and inextricable component of human life; that not all traditions should be accepted or perpetuated *in toto*, but neither should they be so rejected. Understandably, Coomaraswamy and Guénon are not mentioned, nor is the notion of *the* Tradition. Yet, there is a certain similitude in spirit between Shils's work and the worldview of Guénon and Coomaraswamy, though the latter Tradition must nonetheless be treated as a special and particularized usage for, as Shils himself states in his introduction, "In many usages of the term 'tradition' there are implicit delimitations of the substantive content of tradition."

One last account of a form of tradition—"traditionalism"—must be made as part of the process of examining tradition in the writings of Guénon and Coomaraswamy, since it is a source of confusion. Their perspective of the term *traditionalism* is explained in Part 1, note 21, and accompanying text. In the modern perspective, according to philosopher George Boas, "Traditionalism was a philosophy of history and political program developed by the Counter revolutionists in France. It was ultramontane in politics and antiindividualist in epistemology and ethics."[19] The use of traditionalism in its nonphilosophic sense by Kothari has been noted above; Pelikan also uses the term in its nonphilosophic sense: "Tradition is the living faith of the dead; traditionalism is the dead faith of the living."[20] Both scholars—social scientist and religionist—conscripted the term *traditionalism*, and applied it in a new special meaning within their respective fields. Certainly there is nothing sacrosanct in the term that precludes its adoption in another sense; it would have been to the advantage of their readers, however, to have noted the philosophic usage to avoid confusion.

# APPENDIX B

## CULTURE

Like the terms *modernity* and *tradition,* the term *culture* is susceptible to an almost limitless variety of definitions. Indeed, one sees culture used in various different (and ill-defined) ways by scholars and
ethnographers who simply assume their readers know exactly which
brand of usage or nuance they are employing. The best indication of the
ubiquity and difficulty of the problem is a classic work that treats this
subject directly, in addition to giving some historical background and
apposite etymological information concerning the terms *culture* and
*civilization*: A. L. Kroeber and Clyde Kluckhohn's *Culture: A Critical
Review of Concepts and Definitions.*

Kroeber and Kluckhohn were anthropologists, and it is in the field
of anthropology the term has its greatest currency, though that does not
necessarily mean this wide currency indicates anything like a consensus
of the primary constituents of what forms a culture. A review of the various
expositions by contributing anthropologists in *Culture and the Anthropological Tradition* (Lanham, 1990) will corroborate this assertion. "Culture" is used as widely by other branches of the social sciences, not
excepting psychology, which in fact exacerbates the definitional problem.
Clifford Geertz, in *The Interpretation of Cultures,* deprecates the tendency
among the various reductionistic approaches to examining and/or trying
to define unequivocally the phenomenon of culture—that is, "turning culture into folklore and collecting it, turning it into traits and counting it,
turning it into institutions and classifying it, turning it into structures and
toying with it."[21] Geertz takes what he calls a "semiotic" approach, and
in more a confession than an assertion, gives us his definition:

> Believing with Max Weber, that man is an animal sus-
> pended in webs of significance he himself has spun, I take
> culture to be those webs, and the analysis of it to be there-
> fore not an experimental science in search of law but an
> interpretive one in search of meaning.[22]

329

Thus, within the social sciences, the definitions range from the objective to the subjective, from dissociated analysis to participative empathy, and all degrees in between.

Running parallel to the social science usages are those within the humanities, especially those by historians. One book that well represents this general area—written in a sequential fashion based on the chronology of the scholars examined—is Karl Weintraub's *Visions of Culture* (Chicago, 1966). Weintraub traces the perspectives and usages of the phenomenon of culture from Voltaire to Ortega y Gasset, and includes Guizot, Burckhardt, Lamprecht, and Huizinga between them. Of them all, however, Huizinga was most instrumental in the establishment of what today has come to be called the "history of culture." This latter is based not exclusively, but rather primarily, on the "supralogical" elements in culture that can be traced to the "playing and dreaming man," whose collective hopes, fears, wishes, aspirations, dalliance, and imagination—that is, the *spirit* of a culture—are equally if not more determinant of culture than material (economic and geographic) elements.

This view allows legal commentators like Stephen Carter, for example, reflecting on the constitutionally institutionalized secularism of America in modernity, to refer to *The Culture of Disbelief* (New York, 1993). Not inconsistent with Huizinga's vision, but located somewhere on the edge of these multifarious views of culture, is an intriguing and fundamentally accurate one by a professor of communication—Herbert Schiller—who posits that, using the tools of mass marketing, large corporations increasingly create culture to forward their own interests. In *Culture, Inc.: The Corporate Takeover of Public Expression* (New York, 1989), Schiller describes the effect particularly of growth "cultural industries"—for example, publishing, recording, television, film, sports, and so on—whose "symbolic outputs" are in fact "elements of corporate expression."[23] Carter, Schiller, and other, later historians of culture, like Theodore Roszak and William Irwin Thompson, knowingly or not have followed Huizinga's thought— Roszak makes a classic pronouncement of Huizinga's definition of and approach to culture:

> And yet that elusive conception called "the spirit of the times" continues to nag at the mind and demand recognition, since it seems to be the only way available in which

one can make even provisional sense of the world one lives in. It would surely be convenient if these perversely ecto-plasmic *Zeitgeists* were card-carrying movements, with a headquarters, an executive board, and a file of office mani-festoes. But of course they aren't. One is therefore forced to take hold of them with a certain trepidation, allowing excep-tions to slip through the sieve of one's generalizations . . . but hoping always that more that is solid and valuable will finally remain behind what filters away.[24]

Captive by the basic presumptions and goals of science— whether conscious or subliminal—the ardent social scientist strives to make a definitive or an exact statement or theory regarding the true nature of culture. Not so encumbered by such presumptions, cultural historians tend to minimize the archaeologist's shards and hunting/cooking implements—the materially deterministic elements of culture—and concentrate on the intangible spirit of culture. Each defines the term in a way most consistent with his or her methods and findings. Ultimately, however, regardless of any attempts to have it otherwise, the *totality* of culture is not susceptible to exactitude—though parts of it may be—and one must rest content with that fact and proceed from there. From this it follows, as well, that there is not nor can there be an exact definition of cultures: ultimately, one must define it for oneself consistent with one's purposes or choose among the existing definitions.

Guénon and Coomaraswamy defined culture themselves, or rather what they said about it in their writings can be compiled to form a definition; neither of them ever addressed the definition of culture directly in a monograph or book chapter. Two points should be made clear at this time, however, before proceeding to passages in their works. First, both Guénon and Coomaraswamy used the French-ori-ented term *civilization* for what most contemporary English or German observers mean by "culture"; second, while there can be said to be a common Traditional usage of the term *civilization* (one to which both Guénon and Coomaraswamy subscribed), the two men meant different things by the term *culture*.

In *An Introduction to the Study of the Hindu Doctrines*, Guénon is content "to describe a civilization as the product and expression of a certain mental outlook common to a more or less widespread group of men."[25] In "Civilisation et Progrès" in *Orient et Occident*, Guénon launches into a historical survey of the word *civilization*, and concludes, "Thus the word 'civilization' has no more than a century and a half of existence."[26] Two pages later, Guénon admits the inexactitude and complexity in defining the term *civilization*, yet does not attempt any further definition, and leaves it to the reader:

> Thus we say unhesitatingly that there exist multiple and diverse "civilizations"; it would be rather difficult to define exactly this complex amalgam of elements of different orders which constitutes what is referred to as a civilization, but nevertheless everyone knows well enough what is to be understood by it."

It is clear that to Guénon's mind there was little connection between the terms *civilization* and *culture*. In a blunt and unequivocal statement concerning the substance and effects of modern education, Guénon claims:

> It is here that one can see as clearly as possible the confusion with profane instruction, described by the term "culture" which has become today one of the most habitual designations; that ["culture"] is something which has not the slightest relation to traditional teaching nor with the aptitude for receiving it; and furthermore, as the so-called elevation of the "level of the average mean" has as an inevitable counterpart the dissolution of the intellectual elite, it can be said with certainty that this "culture" represents exactly the opposite of a preparation for that which is under consideration [i.e., traditional teaching].[27]

Whether Guénon was still influenced by the attitude, as Kroeber and Kluckhohn claim, that "In the French of the nineteenth century, *civilisation* is ordinarily used where German would use *Kultur*,[28] we cannot say. What is clear is that Guénon's use of civilization equates to Coomaraswamy's use and to what in today's usage would be culture; further, he eschewed all use of culture qua civilization.

Coomaraswamy most often referred to Traditional "civilization" in the same sense as Guénon and in the sense that most contemporary commentators would refer to Traditional "cultures," though he did use it in the contemporary sense as well. Coomaraswamy employed culture far more than did Guénon, who disparaged its use. And he also meant something different by culture. To Guénon, culture seemed to be an institutional affectation; to Coomaraswamy, culture seemed to be true refinement, though of course he recognized people often only approximated true culture and were thus refined or "aristocratic" only in a bogus or cosmetic way. But, insofar as the whole of one or all of the hierarchic orders in a developed Traditional culture subscribed to a particular refined code of behavior, they were cultured, and thus could be designated *a* culture in the true sense. Coomaraswamy claims, for example, that "Ch'an-Zen represents all and more than we now mean by the word 'culture': an active principle pervading every aspect of human life, becoming now the chivalry of the warrior, now the grace of the lover, now the habit of the craftsman."[29] Elsewhere, he refers to culture as "an ideal quality and a good form that can be realized by all men irrespective of condition"; as "an impartial knowledge of style"; and claims that "Acts of self-renunciation are required of all those who aspire to 'culture'."[30] There was thus in Coomaraswamy's writing something of a double entendre for culture: one synonymous to civilization and approximating the normative current usage, and one— unlike Guénon's usage—relating to a true refinement of one's nature.

Consonant with the Buddha's prescription, we chose to follow the middle way in the usage of culture throughout this work. It is not used exclusive of material determinants; there is, without question, some probity in the theses of Marvin Harris and his "cultural materialism." But we have concentrated on what Huizinga called cultural *forms*, and these only in relation to informing principles of culture. The emphasis, therefore, is on the informing principles of which the forms are contingent effects, and to some degree of the effects or forms themselves. We agree with Roszak when he states, "It is always a problem in the study of popular culture to discriminate the running tides of change from the froth that rides the waves."[31] It is admittedly inexact, it is "supralogical," it concerns the "spirit" involved, much of which is inextricable from the informing principles of any given culture. But it is the component of culture we have chosen to emphasize, and when combined *with* the material aspects, forms a totality—and the most adequate definition—of culture.

# APPENDIX C

## ONTOLOGY

It is obvious the question of ontology cannot be either fully or adequately treated in an appendix to any work. The purpose of this brief appendix, therefore, is simply to make a conscious and an intentional *bifurcation* of ontology into two distinct and opposite perspectives. By invoking this bifurcation there is no intention to suggest there is not a range of differing perspectives that may be found in between those of the opposite extremes. But, neither is our purpose to embark on a disquisition of the various intermediate degrees of these polar extremes. It is, in a way, almost a paradox that as among the four topic areas treated in the appendices, that of ontology is at once the most subtle and complex, yet lends itself most readily to a lucid bifurcation of opposite extremes. The question of ontology is easier to comprehend initially in this simplified bifurcated mode—we will let the nuance and permutations of interplay between these extremes be left to specialists in other works devoted specifically to that subject.

Following the line of reasoning and thought in the Tradition of Guénon and Coomaraswamy throughout, the two perspectives of reality and the nature of being that we now propose are: (1) the integrated complex of the empirical, material, quantitative, rational, and analytical, as opposed to (2) the integrated complex of the nonempirical, nonmaterial, qualitative, suprarational, and synthetic. Such an exposition of ontological perspectives is, indeed, liable to the criticism of being simplistic, but we have explained the reasons for expositing the problem in such a way, and further assert that everyone can be placed in one or the other category according to the *predominance* of his or her collective views. Obviously, no person can be said to be 100 percent imbued with such views, nor is anyone exactly split between them so that he or she cannot be placed on one side or the other. Thus everyone can be categorized in this special sense as falling within the "scientific" or "supernormal" parameters (the shortened epithets of the two opposite perspectives as outlined above in *1* and *2*, respectively).

The opposition of these two ontological perspectives can be seen in a variety of manifestations. Of the first or "scientific" perspective (empirical, material, quantitative, rational, analytic), it can be said that a preponderance of what may be called the normative modern Western worldview is comprised of this complex. This complex or perspective forms the basis of the whole technologic and industrial system of the West, and is growing worldwide. Furthermore, it is basically secular and "value free," and generally repudiates the "supernormal" perspective. Moreover, the methods employed by the scientific research and academic communities are largely inseparable from this ontological perspective, as outlined in the discussion on the inextricability of methodology and ontology in Appendix D.

Of the second or "supernormal" perspective (nonempirical, nonmaterial, qualitative, suprarational, synthetic), it can be said that a minority of what Ellwood calls the "alternative reality tradition,"[32] is extant in the modern world, most often belittled, repudiated, and in some instances persecuted. This supernormal ontological perspective would accept the veracity of first principles of metaphysics—the intelligible realm of ideation, the occult arts, paranormal phenomena, the experiences of religious mystics, feats of the siddhi yogis, and so on—though it may not rank them all equally. When these latter do not fall under the protective aegis of established and popularly accepted religions, such as the miracles of which one reads in *Acts*, for example, their promulgators are viewed as fraudulent or disturbed, or both, and are usually ostracized or forced into a sociologically marginal status, if not persecuted outright. Among academicians, those who overtly profess and articulate a supernormal ontology within their disciplines fall on the ontological scale somewhere between rare and nonexistent, though indications are that this may be changing (e.g., the contributors to Robert K. Forman's *The Problem of Pure Consciousness* [New York, 1990]).

The way in which these two ontological perspectives interact is simple. Those who hold to the supernormal perspective conditionally accept the scientific perspective (and method) for the world of physical phenomena. But insofar as the scientific gratuitously and wholly rejects the supernormal ontology as viable, the supernormal perspective then views the scientific as reductionist. On the other hand, those who hold exclusively to the scientific perspective of reality more often than not view the supernormal perspective as illusory, delusory, hallucinogenic, or otherwise pathological. The more magnanimous and intellectually honest of those who hold the scientific view simply withhold judgment, but too many are like A. B. Keith, for whom "such knowledge as is not empirical is meaningless to us and should not be described as knowledge."[33] Of these types Coomaraswamy wrote, "the modern man is a disintegrated personality, no longer the child of heaven and earth, but altogether of earth."[34] This modern man has thus "fallen to the level of that empiricism of which Plato was so contemptuous, and to that of those Greeks whom Plutarch ridiculed because they could no longer distinguish Apollo from Helios, the reality from the phenomenon."[35] In Guénon's view, the scientific method was primarily inductive, and its ontology subsequently "inverted": both were working from the bottom up, as it were, rather than—in the Traditional mode—from the top down.

Without digressing into a detailed discussion of epistemology, it is necessary at least to mention a difference in modes of apperception of the two perspectives. The scientific mode relies primarily on the senses in the observation and measurement of data; concomitantly, these empirical data are interpreted by logic and reason. Again, the supernormal perspective agrees with this process up to that point. It differs in that it relies on the additional faculty of intellectual intuition and on other forms of extrasensory perception as taught in other branches of the alternative reality tradition. The realities perceived by these latter modes are completely imperceptible by the sensory mode and so are empirically nondemonstrable. They are inextricable from and therefore comprise part of the supernormal ontology. Moreover, the interpretation or expression of these realities often employs a simultaneous affirmation of ostensible contradictions, which violates the Aristotelian principle of noncontradiction upon which Western logic—and the scientific ontology—rests.

Methodology, modes of apperception (or epistemology), and the things that are perceived and assimilated by these, therefore, determine one's ontological view. The dichotomy has been pronounced and at times volatile in the modern West, especially as there appears to be at present a significant cultural paradigm shift away from the exclusively mechanistic, materialistic scientific perspective and toward the supernormal one (as was noted in the advances of thought in particle physics, for example, in earlier contexts). Still, a pronounced bifurcation in basic ontologies currently exists in the modern West.

This bifurcation is no better exemplified than by the examples of people who resisted the dominant or normative ontology in favor of an alternative reality—people like Coomaraswamy, Guénon, Jung, Blavatsky, Urban, and similar Traditionalists and/or theosophists. Jung, in fact, writes of this ontological bifurcation within the cadre of religious experience, though it could as easily apply to metaphysical or esoteric (paranormal) experience: "Religious experience is absolute. It is indisputable. You can say that you have never had such an experience, and your opponent will say: 'Sorry, I have.' And there your discussion will come to an end."[36]

Jung states in this form of dialogue what is more succinctly stated in the adage, "For those who believe in God, no explanation is necessary. For those who do not believe in God, no explanation is possible." These later expressions point precisely to the bifurcation of ontological perspectives to which Paul referred two millennia ago in his first letter to the Corinthians: the unspiritual person "believeth not in the things of the Spirit of God; for they are foolishness unto him; neither can he know them, because they are *spiritually discerned*." (2:14, emphasis added). Those who hold the scientific perspective eventually reach an ontological chasm whose breadth they cannot leap, where the other side not only accommodates but valorizes the reality of the supernormal.

# APPENDIX D

## Methodology (or Ethnomethodology)

Those whose ontological views are either parallel to or, to varying degrees, approximate the Tradition of Guénon and Coomaraswamy (e.g., theosophists, esotericists, and parapsychologists), subscribe to a picture of reality and the nature of being that is at odds with the dominant view currently held by the populace and by the scientific and academic communities as well. This difference of worldview inevitably entails a difference in the methods by which subjects of a metaphysical, esoteric, or theosophical nature are or can be examined and/or assimilated, especially as the methods appropriate to a genuine understanding of these latter are contrasted with the normative methods employed by the social sciences and by academicians generally.

Antoine Faivre has shown that esotericism can in fact be studied using empirical methods, but the results are basically taxonomies of past and present trends of Western esoteric thought and their influences, together with historic treatments of renowned esotericists and their surviving treatises. While we acknowledge that this can serve a useful pedagogic purpose, we maintain with Coomaraswamy that it is more useful from the standpoint of *understanding* to study esotericism by its own terms—from the "inside," as it were—since it is both a semantic and metaphysical inversion to attempt a phenomenology of noumena.

In recent decades, and still subject to the hegemony of analytical methods used since the "eighteenth-century rationalists" of the post-Enlightenment period, it has been the standard modus operandi of researchers to investigate a given subject or issue using essentially empirical tools such as measurement, logic, and induction, irrespective of the fact that the subject or issue under scrutiny was nonmaterial in nature. In fact, these quantitative, empirical methods, representative of a purely modern scientific ontology, still comprise the basic approach taken by social scientists today to the investigation of other cultural and ontological modalities. Ontology and methodology are, for these reasons, interdependent and codeterminant.

In response to the abuses and often ludicrous conclusions reached in recent decades by quantitative, empirically oriented methods employed by researchers in the social sciences (under which rubric we place psychology) investigating esoteric and related cultural and ontological realities, more current theses or theories have been forwarded that try to deal more appropriately with the problem. In terms of definitive theories per se, the genetrix can be traced to Harold Garfinkel's ethnomethodology. In *Studies in Ethnomethodology* (1967), Garfinkel speaks of discovering the formal properties of sociological phenomena "from within," arguing that "The formal properties obtain their guarantees from no other source, and in no other way." The most renowned application of this method (and, perhaps, the most contested) was achieved by Carlos Castaneda in his works on the shamanism and psychotropic dimensions of Don Juan and the Yaquis of northern Mexico; Castaneda worked with Garfinkel at UCLA, in fact.

The most direct application of ethnomethodology to what Robert Ellwood calls the "alternative reality tradition"[37] (i.e., metaphysics, esotericism, theosophy, parapsychology, etc.) was achieved by Trent Eglin in an essay titled "Introduction to a Hermeneutics of the Occult: Alchemy."[38] Eglin writes:

> In any case, approaches to the documents of the Occult Sciences, and to the documents of religions, treat of them as formulations . . . deficient in observation, logic, sense, completeness, cogency, etc.; that is, as the products of methodologically untrained minds, products for which the victories of science and analysis stand as correctives.

The results of these reductive, empirical, quantitative "approaches" (methods) into the realm of the nonquantitative alternative reality tradition are, in Eglin's view, obscurative: "That these representatives of the analytic sciences have obscured the salient and, indeed, remarkable features of the Occult Sciences becomes clear on a careful reading of their own research 'confessions.'"

Ethnomethodology, as applied by Eglin, stands as a corrective to this problem since different cultural or ontological modalities must be assessed by their own criteria—esoteric, religious, or otherwise. Whether ethnomethodology was only a blip on the radar screen of late twentieth-century anthropology, or social science in general, remains to be seen. What is important, regardless of the term used to describe it, is that such modalities must be seen and examined from within for any sense to be made of them; one must, as it were, assimilate the constituents of such a modality in order to perceive, assess, evaluate, or understand it properly. As Eliade notes:

> Obviously such [intercultural] 'encounters' will become culturally creative only when the scholar has passed beyond the stage of pure erudition—in other words, when, after having collected, described, and classified his documents, he has also made an effort to understand them *on their own plane of reference.*[39]

While Garfinkel acknowledges influence from Edmund Husserl, Talcott Parsons, and Alfred Schutz, and Castaneda and Eglin acknowledge influence from Garfinkel, this development of methodological—or ethnomethodological—form has nonetheless evolved from perspicacious yet extra-Traditional thinkers. Prior to all of these, with the exception of Husserl, is Coomaraswamy himself, whose method in the research and explication of the Tradition is substantially "ethnomethodological," though it was never so designated by him. John Hatfield, in an unpublished doctoral dissertation on Coomaraswamy's method, states, "According to Coomaraswamy, the student or critic must be able to identify with the culture he is studying, and he must be able to interpret also, not just historically, tracing stylistic changes, but iconographically, seeking the ultimate referent of the symbol."[40] Taking one further step, Hatfield distills the method into a concise sentence: "The student's method will be adequate to his subject matter only to the extent that he accepts this ideal as a personal goal."[41]

Passages abound in Coomaraswamy's oeuvre—unlike Guénon's on this particular point—which relate to methodology, and even in some cases specifically to phenomenology. The most concise and truly representative of them all, however, is found in his essay on *"Manas"* where he states:

> We maintain, accordingly, that it is an indispensable condition of true scholarship to "believe in order to understand" (*crede ut intelligas*), and to "understand in order to believe"

(*intellige ut credas*), not, indeed, as distinct and consecutive acts of the will and the intellect, but as the single activity of both.[42]

It must be remembered that to Coomaraswamy—and Guénon—the intellect was comprised of more than the mental process of discursive ratiocination, which forms the basis of the analytic and scientific methods: the greater intellect also contains the intuition, by which faculty alone the nonempirical realities can be realized. To "believe in order to understand" thus meant the general acceptance of the ontological probity of the nonempirical—the Tradition in this instance. Lipsey adds another perspective to the methodology of the Tradition:

> It is a working hypothesis, supported perhaps privately by intuition, but for the purposes of public discussion only by long comparative study. It encourages specialized study of the details of distinct artistic and literary traditions while suggesting that specialized insights can be linked together in a common "universe of discourse."[43]

Finally, Coomaraswamy encapsulates both the foundation of the Traditional methodology (or ethnomethodology) and the difference that separates it from the empirical (nominalist) method:

> All tradition proposes means dispositive to absolute experience. Whoever does not care to employ these means is in no position to deny that the proposed procedure can lead, as asserted, to a principle that is precisely *aniruktam*, no thing and no where, at the same time that it is the source of all things everywhere. What is most repugnant to the nominalist is the fact that granted a possibility of absolute experience, no rational demonstration could be offered in the classroom, no "experimental control" is possible.[44]

Following not only the ethnomethodological precedents of Garfinkel et al., but a fortiori, those of the expositors of Tradition themselves, we have employed two different but interrelated methods.

The first method is historical and is of two types. The first type sets the personae and events in their times and places. This initial chronological and descriptive historical method is applied when it is needed for clarification and understanding, such as in the assertion that from the historic viewpoint, as against the initiatic, the Traditional school of the twentieth century begins from the coequal and contemporaneous efforts of Coomaraswamy and Guénon. The chronologic, descriptive historical data are not presented in one separate section *in toto*; rather, they are incorporated into the general presentation of the work as they are required. The second type is a cultural historical one, following the lead of Johan Huizinga, and is used in order to explain both the spirit that infused the milieu in which Coomaraswamy and Guénon wrote and taught, contributing to the creation of the following they attained, and the nature of Traditional culture. Huizinga often wrote for the "senses" of readers, in order to relay a graphic or sensate picture of the time and place he chose as his subject. We have altered this form somewhat, and have employed more of the feeling and even mental elements involved, since we are culturally close enough to the milieu of Guénon and Coomaraswamy so as not to need a detailed cultural history of the time. With respect to the milieu of Coomaraswamy and Guénon, the feelings of disputation, polemics, resentment of arrogant repudiations of Tradition, intellectual competition, and simple misunderstanding are those upon which we have tried to focus.

The second method is ethnomethodological. In other words, we have presumed the probity and integrity of Tradition and have approached its first principles and their application to culture from that standpoint. This was done because we agree with Garfinkel, Eglin, and no less with Coomaraswamy, that an empirical or a phenomenological approach to the "alternative reality tradition," however much it may reveal about its locations and influences in the world of thought, cannot of itself lead to any true understanding of its essential content.

# NOTES TO APPENDICES

1. *The Oxford Dictionary of English Etymology*, ed. C. T. Onions (Oxford: Clarendon, 1966), p. 935.

2. *The Concise Oxford Dictionary*, ed. J. B. Sykes. 6th ed. (Oxford: Clarendon, 1976), p. 1229.

3. The history of culture, which should be mentioned in conjunction with these fields, is purposely excluded for the reason that the history of culture is as yet only a perspective; not a "field" in the normal sense. An interesting treatise might one day be written comparing the concept of tradition with what Johan Huizinga terms "cultural ideals."

4. Gross, *The Past in Ruins: Tradition and the Critique of Modernity*, p. 10.

5. Shils, "Tradition," p. 124.

6. *Culture* and *modernity* are two more terms used repeatedly in social sciences and other fields of scholarship in notoriously vague ways. The meanings of each cover too broad a spectrum and represent too many multivalencies to be left to the assumptions of readers. For the meanings of these terms here, see Appendix B regarding "culture." With regard to "modernity," we must agree with Zwi Werblowsky's shrewd observation in *Beyond Tradition and Modernity*: "In fact, sooner or later historians will have to make up their minds whether to use the term modernity as a movable indicator of temporal or cultural location or as a fixed chronological term" (p. 18). The same can be said of the newer terms *postmodern* and *postmodernity*, most generally regarded as a construction of philosophers to describe conceptual relativism and a reevaluation of prior ("modern") assumptions in the wake of and since the posthumous publication of Ludwig Wittgenstein's *On Certainty* in 1969. Like modernity, postmodernity is also used in notoriously vague ways, depending on whether the field of discourse is theology, architecture, art criticism, or philosophy and, depending again on the field, whether one might have encountered the term in the early 1960s. As both modernity and postmodernity are not Traditional, we make no distinction between them. Modernity has often been used to describe the trend of thought beginning as far back as the post-Enlightenment period; consequently, one must ask what will be "modern" in the twenty-third century. In this work, therefore, modernity will refer to a "fixed chronological" time—the nineteenth and twentieth centuries.

7. Shils, "Tradition," p. 124.

8. Eisenstadt, *Tradition, Change, and Modernity*, p. 261.

9. Ibid., p. 13. See Shils, *Tradition*, the subsection of the introduction titled "The Blindness of the Social Sciences to Tradition," where he facetiously remarks, "Realistic social scientists do not mention tradition" (p. 7).

10. These papers are found, respectively, in *Comparative Studies in Society and History*, 1966–67 (9: 292–346); *Government and Opposition*, 1968 (3: 273–93); and *The American Journal of Sociology*, 1973 (79: 351–62).

11. Kothari, "Tradition and Modernity Revisited," pp. 277, 279. It must be pointed out that the use of the word *traditionalism* is less than careful in this instance; the author should have noted the fact that "traditionalism" is a particular philosophical perspective that refers to a politicohistorical view held among some postrevolutionary French thinkers in the first half of the nineteenth century. See below, note 19.

12. Rudolphs, *The Modernity of Tradition*, p. 3.

13. Notwithstanding Gadamer's heavy emphasis on language as the medium of tradition, if not a constituent element of tradition, his contribution is nonetheless instructive. Where it may differ with the Traditional view is in the latter's symbolic and semiotic understanding of language especially in hieratic texts. While tempting, space and time prevent any further analysis with Gadamer's theses and what Guénon described as "The Language of the Birds." See Hans-Georg Gadamer, *Truth and Method* (New York: Crossroad, 1965).

14. "Religious studies" is deliberately broad, since we wish to group theology and the history of religions into one category. Further, we are not unaware of the debate at present as to exactly what constitutes the history of religions—that is, the methodological problem for one thing, and for another, the true translation of what some consider to be the German oxymoron *Religionwissenschaft*. For our purposes, the history of religions will include the anthropology, sociology, philosophy, "science," and all other "ofs" of religion.

15. The reference to Christian apocrypha refers not only to the fifteen or so apocryphal books normally placed in the back of modern English Bibles, but refers more specifically to the numerous apocryphal opuscula found in Edgar Hennecke's two-volume edition of *Neutestamentliche Apokryphen* (Tubingen: J. C. B. Mohr, 1959).

16. The correlation of this *ḥadīth* (found in the *Masabih as-Sunna* of al-Baghawi) to myth is to be found in the common myth motifs of celestial

ascension, which Mircea Eliade has shown repeatedly. See sections 32–34 of *Patterns in Comparative Religions,* which treat respectively Ascension Myths, Ascension Rites, and Ascension Symbolism. Cf. Henry Corbin, *The Man of Light in Iranian Sufism,* chapter 3, "Midnight Sun and Celestial Pole."

17. N. P. Williams, "Tradition" in Hastings's *Encyclopedia of Religion and Ethics* (New York: Scribner's, 1908–27). Reprinted 1955. See also, the brief annotated bibliography on "tradition" by Paul Valliere in vol. 15, *The Encyclopedia of Religion,* Mircea Eliade, Editor-in-Chief (New York: Macmillan, 1987).

18. Pelikan, *The Christian Tradition,* vol. 1, p. 7.

19. George Boas, "Traditionalism" in *Encyclopedia of Philosophy* (New York: Collier Macmillan, 1967).

20. Pelikan, op. cit., p. 9.

21. Clifford Geertz, *The Interpretation of Cultures* (New York: Basic, 1973), p. 29. Culture no doubt can be studied and/or defined by the classic empirical, analytical approach of reducing it to its constituent parts (assuming this is possible). As Professor Geertz appears to do, T. S. Eliot perceived the element of *synergy* at work in culture: "But just as a man is something more than an assemblage of the various constituent parts of his body, so a culture is more than the assemblage of its arts, customs, and religious beliefs. These things all act upon each other, and fully to understand one you have to understand all." *Notes Towards the Definition of Culture* (New York: Harcourt, Brace Jovanovich, 1968), p. 198.

22. Ibid., p. 5.

23. Schiller, *Culture, Inc.: The Corporate Takeover of Public Expression,* p. 44.

24. Roszak, *The Making of a Counter Culture,* p. xi.

25. Guénon, *An Introduction to the Study of the Hindu Doctrines,* p. 89.

26. Guénon, *Orient et Occident,* p. 23.

27. Guénon, *Règne,* p. 116.

28. A. L. Kroeber and Clyde Kluckhohn, *Culture: A Critical Review of Concepts and Definitions* (New York: Random House, 1952), p. 17. See also, Marshall Sahlins' incisive treatment of these two terms on pages 10–14 of *How "Natives" Think: About Captain Cook, for Example* (Chicago: University of Chicago Press, 1995). Sahlins laments that the term "culture" has

today "escaped anthropological control," and observes that "'Culture,' it seems, is in the twilight of its career, and anthropology with it" (p. 14).

29. Coomaraswamy, *The Transformation of Nature in Art*, p. 42.

30. In order, from Coomaraswamy's *BK*, p. 21; *SPTAS*, p. 103; and *SPTAS*, p. 226.

31. Roszak, *Person/Planet*, p. xxix.

32. Ellwood, *Religious and Spiritual Groups in Modern America*, pp. 42–87. Cf. Renée Weber, "The Reluctant Tradition," p. 100: "The term 'esoteric' is itself more than a word; in the context of this essay it is *an alternative ontology*, a way of conceiving Being that differs from exoteric disciplines."

33. Coomaraswamy, *BK*, p. 55. See above, page 24, for Keith's citation.

34. Coomaraswamy, *SPTAS*, p. 175.

35. Coomaraswamy, *SPM*, p. 169.

36. Jung, *Psychology and Religion*, p. 113.

37. Ellwood, *Religious and Spiritual Groups in Modern America*, pp. 42–87.

38. Trent Eglin, "Introduction to a Hermeneutics of the Occult: Alchemy," in *On the Margin of the Visible*, ed. Edward Tiryakian (New York: Wiley, 1974).

39. Eliade, *The Quest*, p. 4. Professor Faivre approaches describing this process in the third of his four fundamental elements of "esotericism considered as a form of thought," which he refers to as "Imagination and Meditations." *Access to Western Esotericism*, pp. 12–13.

40. Hatfield, "The Structure and Meaning of Religious Objects," p. 38.

41. Ibid., p. 23.

42. Coomaraswamy, *SPM*, p. 219

43. Lipsey, *CLW*, pp. 275–76.

44. Coomaraswamy, *SPM*, p. 261 n.

# BIBLIOGRAPHY

Arnold, Wilhelm, and Hermann Zeltner. *Tradition und Kritik.* Festschrift für Rudolf Zocher. Stuttgart-Bad Cannstatt: Friedrich Fromann Verlag, 1967.

Asfar, Gabriel. "René Guénon: A Chapter of French Symbolist Thought in the Twentieth Century." Ph.D. dissertation, Princeton University, 1972.

Badcock, C. R. *Madness and Modernity.* Oxford: Basil Blackwell, 1983.

Bagchee, Moni. *Ananda Coomaraswamy: A Study.* Varanasi: Bharata Manisha, 1977.

Banton, Michael, ed. *Anthropological Approaches to the Study of Religion.* A.S.A. Monographs 3. London: Tavistock Publications, 1966.

Barzun, Jacques. "Cultural History as a Synthesis." In *The Varieties of History.* Ed. Fritz Stern. New York: World Publishing Company (Meridian Books), 1956.

Bednarowski, Mary F. *New Religions and the Theological Imagination in America.* Bloomington: Indiana University Press, 1989.

Bellah, Robert N. *Beyond Belief: Essays on Religion in a Post-Traditional World.* Berkeley: University of California Press, 1991.

———. *The Broken Covenant: American Civil Religion in Time of Trial.* 2d ed. Chicago: University of Chicago Press, 1992.

Bendix, Reinhard. "Tradition and Modernity Reconsidered." *Comparative Studies in Society and History* 9 (1966–1967): 292–346.

Bennett, William J. *The Book of Virtues.* New York: Simon & Schuster, 1993.

Blavatsky, Helena P. *The Key to Theosophy.* Adyar: Theosophical Publishing House, 1933.

———. *Practical Occultism.* Adyar: Theosophical Publishing House, 1948.

———. *The Secret Doctrine.* Vols. I and II. de Zirkoff ed. Adyar: Theosophical Publishing House, 1978.

Bloom, Allan. *The Closing of the American Mind.* New York: Simon & Schuster, 1987.

Boas, Franz. *The Mind of Primitive Man*. New York: Macmillan, 1938.

Boas, George. "Traditionalism." In *Encyclopedia of Philosophy*, vol. 8. Ed. Paul Edwards. New York: Collier Macmillan, 1967

Bookchin, Murray. *The Limits of the City*. New York: Harper & Row, 1974.

―――. *The Modern Crisis*. 2d ed. New York: Black Rose Books, 1987.

Burckhardt, Titus. *Mirror of the Intellect: Essays on Traditional Science and Sacred Art*. Cambridge: Quinta Essentia, 1987.

Cammann, Schuyler. "Remembering Again: The Life and Work of Ananda Coomaraswamy." *Parabola* 3, No. 2 (1978): 84–91.

Campbell, Bruce A. *Ancient Wisdom Revisited: A History of the Theosophical Movement*. Berkeley: University of California Press, 1980.

Campbell, Joseph, ed. *Man and Time: Papers from the Eranos Yearbooks*. Bollingen Series 30. Princeton, N.J.: Princeton University Press, 1973.

―――. *The Masks of God: Primitive Mythology*. Rev. ed. New York: Penguin, 1984.

―――, ed. *The Mysteries: Papers from the Eranos Yearbooks*. Bollingen Series 30. Princeton, N.J.: Princeton University Press, 1978.

Carter, Stephen L. *The Culture of Disbelief*. New York: Basic, 1993.

Cassirer, Ernst. *The Philosophy of Symbolic Forms. Vol. II. Mythical Thought*. New Haven, Conn.: Yale University Press, 1955.

Chacornac, Paul. *La vie simple de René Guénon*. Paris: Éditions Traditionnelles, 1982.

Collins, James. *Three Paths in Philosophy*. Chicago: Henry Regency, 1962.

Congar, Yves M.J. *Tradition and Traditions: An Historical and a Theological Essay*. New York: Macmillan, 1967.

Coomaraswamy, Ananda K. *Am I My Brother's Keeper?* Freeport, N.Y.: Books for Libraries Press. 1967.

―――. *Buddha and the Gospel of Buddhism*. New Hyde Park, N.Y.: University Books, 1969.

―――. *The Bugbear of Literacy*. Middlesex, U.K.: Perennial Books, Ltd., 1979.

―――. *Christian and Oriental Philosophy of Art*. New York: Dover, 1956.

———. *Coomaraswamiana.* Ed. S. Durai Raja Singam. Singapore: Kwok Yoke Weng, 1960.

———. "The Darker Side of Dawn." *Smithsonian Miscellaneous Collection* 94, No. 1 (1935): 1–18.

———. *Figures of Speech or Figures of Thought.* Second Series. London: Luzac, 1946.

———. *Hinduism and Buddhism.* Westport, Conn.: Greenwood, 1971.

———. *Selected Letters.* Ed. Alvin Moore, Jr., and Rama P. Coomaraswamy. New Delhi: Oxford University Press, 1988.

———. *Selected Papers: Metaphysics.* Ed. Roger Lipsey. Bollingen Series 89. Princeton, N.J.: Princeton University Press, 1977.

———. *Selected Papers: Traditional Art and Symbolism.* Ed. Roger Lipsey. Bollingen Series 89. Princeton, N.J.: Princeton University Press, 1977.

———. "Sir Gawain and the Green Knight: Indra and Namuci." *Speculum* 19, No. 1 (1944): 104–25.

———. *Sources of Wisdom.* Selected Essays. Colombo, Sri Lanka: Ministry of Cultural Affairs, 1981.

———. *Spiritual Authority and Temporal Power in the Indian Theory of Government.* New Haven, Conn.: Yale University Press, 1942.

———. *Time and Eternity.* Ascona: Artibus Asiae, 1947.

———. *The Transformation of Nature in Art.* New York: Dover, 1956.

———. *What Is Civilisation?* Oxford: Oxford University Press, 1989.

Coomaraswamy, Rama P., ed. *Ananda K. Coomaraswamy Bibliography/ Index.* Berwick-upon-Tweed: Prologos Books, 1988.

Corbin, Henry. *Creative Imagination in the Sufism of Ibn 'Arabī.* Bollingen Series 91. Princeton, N.J.: Princton University Press, 1969.

———. *The Man of Light in Iranian Sufism.* Boulder, Colo., and London, England: Shambhala, 1978.

———. *Spiritual Body and Celestial Earth.* Bollingen Series 91:2. Princeton, N.J.: Princeton University Press, 1977.

de Santillana, Giorgio, and Hertha von Dechend. *Hamlet's Mill.* Boston: David R. Godine, 1977.

Diamond, Stanley. *In Search of the Primitive.* New Brunswick, N.J.: Transaction, 1974.

————, ed. *Primitive Views of the World*. New York: Columbia University Press, 1964.

Duby, Georges. *The Three Orders: Feudal Society Imagined*. Chicago: University of Chicago Press, 1980.

Dudley, Gilford, III. *Religion on Trial: Mircea Eliade and His Critics*. Philadelphia: Temple University Press, 1977.

Dumont, Louis. *Homo Hierarchius: The Caste System and Its Implications*. Chicago: University of Chicago Press, 1970.

Dundes, Alan., ed. *Sacred Narrative: Readings in the Theory of Myth*. Berkeley: University of California Press, 1984.

Durand, Gilbert. *On the Disfiguration of the Image of Man in the West*. Ipswich: Golgoonza, 1977.

Durkhein, Emile. *The Elementary Forms of the Religious Life*. New York: Free Press, 1970.

Eaton, Gai. *The Richest Vein*. Ghent, N.Y.: Sophia Perennis et Universalis, 1995.

Eisenstadt, Shmuel N. *Tradition, Change, and Modernity*. New York: Wiley, 1973.

Eliade, Mircea. *A History of Religious Ideas*. Vols. I–III. Chicago: University of Chicago Press, 1978–85.

————. *Myth and Reality*. New York: Harper & Row, 1963.

————. *The Myth of the Eternal Return; or, Cosmos and History*. Bollingen Series 47. Princeton, N.J.: Princeton University Press, 1974.

————. *Myths, Dreams, and Mysteries*. New York: Harper & Row, 1975.

————. *Occultism, Witchcraft, and Cultural Fashions*. Chicago: University of Chicago Press, 1976.

————. *Patterns in Comparative Religion*. A Meridian Book. New York: World, 1963.

————. *The Quest: History and Meaning in Religion*. Chicago: University of Chicago Press, 1969.

————. *Shamanism: Archaic Techniques of Ecstasy*. Bollingen Series 76. Princeton, N.J.: Princeton University Press, 1972.

————. "Some Notes on Theosophia Perennis: Ananda K. Coomaraswamy and Henry Corbin." *History of Religions* 19, No. 2 (1979): 167–76.

———. *Yoga: Immortality and Freedom.* Bollingen Series 56. Princeton, N.J.: Princeton University Press, 1970.

Eliot, T. S. "Tradition and the Individual Talent," in *Selected Prose of T. S. Eliot.* Frank Kermode, ed. New York: Harcourt, Brace, Jovanovich, 1975.

Ellwood, Robert S., Jr. *Alternative Altars: Unconventional and Eastern Spirituality in America.* Chicago: University of Chicago Press, 1979.

———. "Races, Cultures, and Religions in the Evolution of Consciousness. *The American Theosophist* 69, No. 2 (1981): 37–39.

———. *Religious and Spiritual Groups in Modern America.* Englewood Cliffs, N.J.: Prentice-Hall, 1973.

Elshtain, Jean Bethke. *Democracy on Trial.* New York: Basic Books, 1995.

Evans, C. de B. *Meister Eckhart by Franz Pfeiffer.* Vols. I and II. London: Watkins, 1924–1931.

Faivre, Antoine. *Access to Western Esotericism.* Albany: State University of New York Press, 1994.

Fernando, Ranjit, ed. *The Unanimous Tradition.* Colombo: Sri Lanka Institute of Traditional Studies, 1991.

Foucault, Michel. *The Order of Things: An Archeology of the Human Sciences.* New York: Vintage, 1994.

Frazer, James G. *The Golden Bough.* Abr. ed. New York: Macmillan, 1963.

Freud, Sigmund. *The Future of an Illusion.* New York: W. W. Norton, 1961.

———. *Moses and Monotheism.* A Vintage Book. New York: Random House, 1967.

———. *Totem and Taboo.* New York: W. W. Norton, 1950.

Fuller, R. Buckminster. *Critical Path.* New York: St. Martin's, 1981.

Garfinkel, Harold. *Studies in Ethnomethodology.* Englewood Cliffs, N.J.: Prentice-Hall, 1967.

Geertz, Clifford. *The Interpretation of Cultures.* New York: Basic, 1973.

Gide, André. *Journal (1942–1949).* Paris: Librarie Gallimard, 1950.

Godwin. Joscelyn. *The Theosophical Enlightenment.* Albany: State University of New York Press, 1994.

Gombrich, Ernst. *In Search of Cultural History.* Oxford: Oxford University Press, 1969.

Gomes, Michael. *Theosophy in the Nineteenth Century: An Annotated Bibliography.* New York: Garland, 1994.

Gross, David. *The Past in Ruins: Tradition and the Critique of Modernity.* Amherst: University of Massachusetts Press, 1992.

Guénon, René. *Aperçus sur l'ésotérisme chrétien.* Paris: Éditions Traditionnelles, 1977.

———. *Aperçus sur l'initiation.* Paris: Éditions Traditionnelles, 1980.

———. *Formes traditionnelles et cycles cosmiques.* Paris: Éditions Gallimard, 1970.

———. *Fundamental Symbols: The Universal Language of Sacred Science.* Cambridge: Quinta Essentia, 1995.

———. "Initiation and the Crafts." *Journal of the Indian Society of Oriental Art* 6, No. 3 (1938): 163–68.

———. *Introduction to the Study of the Hindu Doctrines.* London: Luzac, 1945.

———. *La crise du monde moderne.* Paris: Éditions Gallimard, 1946.

———. *La grande triade.* Paris: Éditions Gallimard, 1957.

———. *Le règne de la quantité et les signes des temps.* Paris: Éditions Gallimard, 1945.

———. *Le symbolisme de la croix.* Paris: Éditions Véga, 1957.

———. *Le Théosophisme: histoire d'une pseudo-religion.* Paris: Éditions Traditionnelles, 1975.

———. *Les états multiple de l'être.* Paris: Éditions Véga, 1980.

———. *Man and His Becoming According to the Vedānta.* London: Luzac, 1945.

———. *Melanges par René Guénon.* Paris: Éditions Gallimard, 1976.

———. *Orient et Occident.* Paris: Payot, 1924.

———. *Saint Bernard.* Paris: Éditions Traditionnelles, 1977.

———. "Some Remarks on the Doctrine of Cosmic Cycles." *Journal of the Indian Society of Oriental Art* 6, No. 1 (1938): 6–28.

Gusfield, Joseph R. "Tradition and Modernity: Misplaced Polarities in the Study of Social Change." *American Journal of Sociology* 79, No. 5 (1974): 351–62.

Gustin, Marilyn J. "The Nature, Role and Interpretation of Symbol in the Thought of René Guénon." Ph.D. dissertation, Graduate Theological Union (Berkeley), 1987.

Häberlin, Paul. *Philosophia Perennis: Eine Zusammenfassung.* Berlin: Spring-Verlag, 1952.

Haskins, Charles H. *The Renaissance of the 12th Century.* A Meridian Book. New York: World, 1957.

Hatfield, John T. "The Structure and Meaning of Religious Objects: A Study in the Methodology of the History of Religions Based upon the Thought of Ananda Kentish Coomaraswamy." Ph.D. dissertation, Claremont Graduate School, 1964.

Herskovits, Melville J. *Cultural Relativism: Perspectives in Cultural Pluralism.* A Vintage Book. New York: Random House, 1972.

Hobsbawm, Eric, and Terence Ranger, eds. *The Invention of Tradition.* Cambridge: Cambridge University Press, 1983.

Hofstadter, Douglas R. *Gödel, Escher, Bach: An Eternal Golden Braid.* A Vintage Book. New York: Random House, 1980.

Huizinga, Johan. *Homo Ludens: A Study of the Play Element in Culture.* Boston: Beacon, 1955.

―――. *Men and Ideas.* A Meridian Book. New York: World, 1966.

―――. *The Waning of the Middle Ages.* Doubleday/Anchor Book. New York: Doubleday, 1954.

Huxley, Aldous. *The Perennial Philosophy.* Harper Colophon Books. New York: Harper & Row, 1970.

Jaspers, Karl. *The Perennial Scope of Philosophy.* New York: Philosophical Library, 1949.

Jensen, Adolf E. *Myth and Cult Among Primitive Peoples.* Chicago: University of Chicago Press, 1963.

Judah, J. Stillson. *History and Philosophy of the Metaphysical Movements in America.* Philadelphia: Westminster, 1967.

Jung, Carl G. *Aion: Researches into the Phenomenology of the Self.* Bollingen Series 20. Princeton, N.J.: Princeton University Press, 1979.

―――. *Civilization in Transition.* Bollingen Series 20. Princeton, N.J.: Princeton University Press, 1970.

―――. *The Integration of the Personality.* New York: Farrar and Rinehart, 1939.

————. *Memories, Dreams, Reflections.* 2d ed. New York: Vintage-Random House, 1989.

————. *Modern Man in Search of a Soul.* A Harvest/HBJ Book. New York: Harcourt Brace Jovanovich, 1933.

————. *Mysterium Coniunctionis.* Bollingen Series 20. Princeton, N.J.: Princeton University Press, 1977.

————. *Psychology and Religion.* New Haven, Conn.: Yale University Press, 1978.

————. *Psychology and the Occult.* Bollingen Series 20. Princeton, N.J.: Princeton University Press, 1977.

————. *Two Essays on Analytical Psychology.* Bollingen Series 20. Princeton, N.J.: Princeton University Press, 1972.

Kelley, Carl. F. *Meister Eckhart on Divine Knowledge.* New Haven, Conn.: Yale University Press, 1977.

Kothari, Rajni. "Tradition and Modernity Revisited." *Government and Opposition* 3, No. 3 (1968): 273–93.

Kroeber, A. L., and Clyde Kluckhohn. *Culture: A Critical Review of Concepts and Definitions.* A Vintage Book. New York: Random House, 1952.

Kuhn, Alvin B. *Theosophy: A Modern Revival of Ancient Wisdom.* New York: Henry Holt, 1930.

Laurant, Jean-Pierre. *Le sens caché dans l' oeuvre de René Guénon.* Paris: Éditions L'Age D'Homme, 1975.

Le Goff, Jacques. *Medieval Civilization, 400–1500.* Oxford: Basil Blackwell, 1988.

————. *Time, Work and Culture in the Middle Ages.* Chicago: University of Chicago Press, 1980.

Leeming, David A., ed. *The World of Myth.* New York: Oxford University Press, 1990.

Leitgeber, Boleslaw. *East and West in Man's Perennial Quest.* Calcutta: Writers Workshop, 1978.

Lerner, Daniel. *The Passing of Traditional Society.* Glencoe, Ill.: Free Press, 1958.

LeShan, Lawrence. *Toward a General Theory of the Paranormal.* Parapsychological Monographs No. 9. New York: Parapsychology Foundation, 1969.

Lévy-Bruhl, Lucien. *How Natives Think*. New York: Arno, 1979.

———. *Primitive Mentality*. London: George Allen & Unwin, 1923.

Lévi-Strauss, Claude. *The Savage Mind*. Chicago: University of Chicago Press, 1966.

———. *Structural Anthropology*. New York: Basic, 1963.

Lings, Martin. *The Eleventh Hour: The Spiritual Crisis of the Modern World in the Light of Tradition and Prophecy*. Cambridge: Quinta Essentia, 1987.

———. "René Guénon." *Sophia* 1, No. 1 (1995): 21–37.

Lipsey, Roger. *Coomaraswamy: His Life and Work*. Bollingen Series 89. Princeton, N.J.: Princeton University Press, 1977.

———. "The Two Selves: Coomaraswamy As Man and Metaphysician." *Studies in Comparative Religion* 6, No. 4 (1972): 199–211.

Livingston, Ray. *The Traditional Theory of Literature*. Minneapolis: University of Minnesota Press, 1962.

Lovejoy, Arthur O. *The Great Chain of Being*. Cambridge, Mass.: Harvard University Press, 1978.

Lutz, Jessie G., and Salah El-Shakhs. *Tradition and Modernity: The Role of Traditionalism in the Modernization Process*. Washington, D.C.: University Press of America, 1982.

Maibre, Jean, ed. *Julius Evola: Le visionnaire foudroye*. Paris: Éditions Copernic, 1977.

Malinowski, Bronislaw. *Myth in Primitive Psychology*. London: Kegan, Paul, Trench, Trubner, 1926.

Manzanedo, Marcos. "Los Refranes y las 'Filosofía Perenne.'" *Revista de Filosofía* 22, No. 83 (1962): 423–465.

Maritain, Jacques. *Art and Scholasticism*. New York: Scribner's, 1962.

Marty, Martin E. "The Spirit's Holy Errand: The Search for a Spiritual Style in Secular America." *Daedalus* 96, No. 1 (1967): 99–115.

———. *Pilgrims in Their Own Land*. Boston: Little, Brown, 1984.

McInerny, Ralph. ed. *Modernity and Religion*. South Bend, Ind.: University of Notre Dame Press, 1992.

Mead, G. R. S. *The Doctrine of the Subtle Body in Western Tradition*. Wheaton, Ill.: Theosophical Publishing House, 1967.

————. *Fragments of a Faith Forgotten.* New Hyde Park, N.Y.: University Books, 1960.

Mead, Margaret, ed. *Cultural Patterns and Technical Change.* New York: New American Library, 1955.

Merkur, Dan. *Gnosis: An Esoteric Tradition of Mystical Visions and Unions.* Albany: State University of New York Press, 1993.

Meroz, Lucien. *René Guénon ou la sagesse initiatique.* Paris: Plon, 1962.

Meyer, Marc A., ed. *The Culture of Christendom.* London: Hambledon, 1993.

Miller, Timothy, ed. *America's Alternative Religions.* Albany: State University of New York Press, 1995.

Müller, F. Max. *Theosophy or Psychological Religion.* Collected Writings, Vol. IV. New York and London: Longmans, Green, 1903.

Naravane, Vishwanath S. *Ananda K. Coomaraswamy.* Boston: Twayne, 1977.

Nasr, Seyyed Hossein. "Contemporary Man, Between the Rim and the Axis." *Studies in Comparative Religion* 7, No. 2 (1973): 113–126.

————, ed. *The Essential Writings of Frithjof Schuon.* Rockport, Mass.: Element, 1986.

————. *Knowledge and the Sacred.* Albany: State University of New York Press, 1989.

————. "Progress and Evolution: A Reappraisal from the Traditional Perspective." *Parabola* 6, No. 2 (1981): 44–51.

————. *Sufi Essays.* Albany: State University of New York Press, 1991.

Nasr, Seyyed Hossein, and Katherine O'Brien, eds. *In Quest of the Sacred: The Modern World in the Light of Tradition.* Oakton, Va.: Foundation for Traditional Studies, 1994.

Nasr, Seyyed Hossein, and William Stoddart, eds. *Religion of the Heart.* Washington, D.C.: Foundation for Traditional Studies, 1991.

Needleman, Jacob. *A Sense of the Cosmos: The Encounter of Modern Science and Ancient Truth.* New York: E. P. Dutton, 1976.

————. *Consciousness and Tradition.* New York: Crossroads/Continuum, 1982.

————, ed. *The New Religions.* New York: E. P. Dutton, 1977.

Needleman, Jacob, and George Baker, eds. *Understanding the New Religions.* New York: Seabury, 1978.

Needleman, Jacob, and Dennis Lewis, eds. *Sacred Tradition and Present Need.* New York: Viking, 1975.

Needleman, Jacob, and Antoine Faivre, eds. *Modern Esoteric Spirituality.* New York: Crossroad, 1992.

Norman, Dorothy. *The Hero: Myth/Image/Symbol.* New York: World, 1969.

Northbourne, Lord. "The Survival of Civilization." *Studies in Comparative Religion* 7, No.2 (1973): 21–30.

Obeyesekere, Gananath. *The Work of Culture.* Chicago: University of Chicago Press, 1990.

O'Flaherty, Wendy D., ed. *Karma and Rebirth in Classcial Indian Traditions.* Berkeley: University of California Press, 1980.

Olcott, Henry S. *Old Diary Leaves.* Vols. I–VI. Adyar: Theosophical Publishing House, 1974–1975.

Oldmeadow, Harry. "Mircea Eliade and Carl Jung: 'Priests without Surplices'?—Reflections on the Place of Myth, Religion, and Science in Their Work." *Studies in Western Traditions,* Occasional Papers No. 1. Bendigo: La Trobe University, 1995.

Olney, James. *The Rhizome and the Flower: The Perennial Philosophy—Yeats and Jung.* Berkeley: University of California Press, 1980.

Pagels, Elaine. "Gnostic Texts Revive Ancient Controversies." The *Center Magazine* 13, No. 5 (1980): 53–64.

Pallis, Marco. "A Fateful Meeting of Minds: A. K. Coomaraswamy and R. Guénon." *Studies in Comparative Religion* 12, Nos. 3, 4 (1978): 176–88.

Panofsky, Erwin. *Gothic Architecture and Scholasticism.* A Meridian Book. New York: New American Library, 1976.

Pelikan, Jaroslav. *The Christian Tradition.* Vols. I–V. Chicago: University of Chicago, 1971–1989.

———. *The Vindication of Tradition.* New Haven, Conn.: Yale University Press, 1984.

Pennington, M. Basil. "Spirituality for a World Culture." *America.* (September 3, 1977): 100–03.

Perry, Whitall N. "The Bollingen Coomaraswamy Papers and Biography." *Studies in Comparative Religion* 11, No. 4 (1977): 205–21.

———. "Coomaraswamy—The Man, Myth, and History." *Studies in Comparative Religion* 11, No. 3 (1977): 159–65.

————. *The Widening Breach: Evolutionism in the Mirror of Cosmology.* Cambridge: Quinta Essentia, 1995.

Poortman, J.J. *Philosophy, Theosophy, Parapsychology: Some Essays on Diverse Subjects.* Leiden: A. W. Sythoff, 1965.

————. *Vehicles of Consciousness.* Vols. I-IV. Utrecht: The Theosophical Society in the Netherlands, 1978.

Quinn, William W., Jr. "Ananda K. Coomaraswamy on the Philosophia Perennis." *Re-Vision* 2, No. 2 (1979): 18–27.

————. "Mass Man, Mass Society, Individual Solution." *Quadrant: Journal of the C.G. Jung Society* 15, No. 2 (1982): 41–54.

————. "Meister Eckhart and the Sacred Tradition—Some Axial Theses." *The Liberal Catholic* 50, No. 1 (1981): 19–27.

————. "Metaphysics in Traditional Cultures: The North American Indian Case." *The American Theosophist* 73, No. 10 (1985): 354–61.

Radhakrishnan, Sarvepalli, ed. *History of Philosophy Eastern and Western.* Vol. II. London: George Allen & Unwin, 1953.

Radin, Paul. *Primitive Man as Philosopher.* New York and London: D. Appleton, 1927.

Rennie, Bryan S. *Reconstructing Eliade: Making Sense of Religion.* Albany: State University of New York Press, 1996.

Rifkin, Jeremy. *Entropy: A New World View.* New York: Viking, 1980.

Roszak, Theodore. *The Making of a Counter Culture.* Anchor Book. New York: Doubleday, 1969.

————. *Person/Planet.* Anchor Book. New York: Doubleday, 1979.

Rudhyar, Dane. *The Planetarization of Consciousness.* New York: ASI, 1977.

Rudolph, Lloyd I., and Susanne H. Rudolph. *The Modernity of Tradition.* Chicago: University of Chicago Press, 1967.

Ryan, James H. *An Introduction to Philosophy.* New York: Macmillan, 1924.

Sahlins, Marshall. *How "Natives" Think: About Captain Cook, for Example.* Chicago: University of Chicago Press, 1995.

————. *Stone Age Economics.* Chicago: Aldine/Atherton, 1972.

Schiller, Herbert I. *Culture, Inc.: The Corporate Takeover of Public Expression.* New York: Oxford University Press, 1989.

Schmitt, Charles B. "Perennial Philosophy: From Agostino Steuco to Leibniz." *Journal of the History of Ideas* 27, No. 4 (1966): 505–32.

Schumacher, E. F. *Small Is Beautiful: Economics as if People Mattered.* Perennial Library. New York: Harper & Row, 1975.

Schuon, Frithjof. *Gnosis: Divine Wisdom.* London: John Murray, 1959.

———. *Islam and the Perennial Philosophy.* World of Islam, 1976.

———. *Logic and Transcendence.* London: Perennial, 1984.

———. *Stations of Wisdom.* Bloomington, Ind.: World Wisdom, 1995.

———. *Survey of Metaphysics and Esotericism.* Bloomington, Ind.: World Wisdom, 1986.

———. *The Transcendent Unity of Religions.* A Quest Book. Wheaton, Ill.: Theosophical Publishing House, 1984.

Seaman, Gary, and Jane S. Day, eds. *Ancient Traditions: Shamanism in Central Asia and the Americas.* Boulder: University of Colorado Press, 1994.

Sérant, Paul. *René Guénon.* Paris: Éditions du Vieux Colombier, 1953.

Shils, Edward. "Tradition." *Comparative Studies in Society and History* 13, No. 2 (1971): 122–59.

———. *Tradition.* Chicago: University of Chicago Press, 1981.

Singam, S. Durai Raja. *Ananda Coomarawamy: Remembering and Remembering Again and Again.* Kuala Lumpur: Khee Meng, 1974.

———. *Ananda Coomaraswamy, the Bridge Builder: A Study of a Scholar-Colossus.* Kuala Lumpur: Khee Meng, 1977.

Singer, Milton. *When a Great Tradition Modernizes.* New York: Harper & Row, 1976.

Smith, Huston. *Beyond the Post-Modern Mind.* A Quest Book. Wheaton, Ill.: Theosophical Publishing House, 1984.

———. "The Coming World Civilization." *Centerboard* 2, No. 2 (1984): 8–13.

———. *Forgotten Truth: The Primordial Tradition.* New York: Harper & Row, 1976.

———. "The Meaning of Tradition." *Parabola* 1, No. 1 (1977): 80–91.

Snodgrass, Adrian. *Architecture, Time and Eternity: Studies in the Stellar and Temporal Symbolism of Traditional Buildings*. 2 vols. New Delhi: Aditya Prakashan, 1990.

Spangler, David. *Towards a Planetary Vision*. Forres, Scotland: Findhorn Foundation, 1977.

Steuchus, Augustinus. *De Perenni Philosophia*. New York: Johnson Reprint, 1972.

Thomas, Sharon. "Coomaraswamy: A Vision of Unity." *The Theosophist* 99, No. 3 (1977): 84–86.

Thompson, William Irwin. *At the Edge of History: Speculations on the Transformation of Culture*. Harper Colophon Book. New York: Harper & Row, 1972.

———. *Passages About Earth: An Exploration of the New Planetary Culture*. Perennial Library. New York: Harper & Row, 1974.

Tiryakian, Edward A., ed. *On the Margin of the Visible: Sociology, the Esoteric, and the Occult*. New York: Wiley, 1974.

Toffler, Alvin, and Heidi Toffler. *Creating a New Civilization: The Politics of the Third Wave*. Atlanta: Turner Publications, Inc., 1995.

Tourniac, Jean. *Propos sur René Guénon*. Paris: Dervy, 1973.

Tylor, Edward B. *The Origins of Culture*. Gloucester, Mass.: Peter Smith, 1970.

Urban, Wilbur M. *Beyond Realism and Idealism*. London: George Allen & Unwin, 1949.

———. *The Intelligible World: Metaphysics and Value*. New York: Macmillan, 1929.

———. *Language and Reality*. New York: Macmillan, 1939.

von Rintelen, Fritz-Joachim, ed. *Philosophia Perennis*. Vols. I and II. Festgabe Josef Geyser. Regensburg: Druck und Verlag von Josef Habbel, 1930.

Waterfield, Robin. *René Guénon and the Future of the West*. Oxford: Crucible, 1987.

Webb, James. *The Harmonious Circle*. New York: Putnam's, 1980.

Weber, Renée. "The Reluctant Tradition." *Main Currents in Modern Thought* 31, No. 4 (1975): 99–106.

Weintraub, Karl J. *Visions of Culture*. Chicago: University of Chicago Press, 1966.

Werblosky, R. J. Zwi. *Beyond Tradition and Modernity*. London: Athlone, 1976.

Wetmore, James. "Tradition's Tide: An Interview with Gerard Casey." *Parabola* 21, No. 2, 1996: 44–51.

Wilbur, Ken. "Physics, Mysticism, and the New Holographic Paradigm." *Re-Vision* 2, No. 2 (1979): 43–55.

———. *The Spectrum of Consciousness*. A Quest Book. Wheaton, Ill.: Theosophical Publishing House, 1977.

Wilder, Alexander. *New Platonism and Alchemy*. Albany: Weed, Parsons, 1869.

Wilhelm, Richard, trans. *The Secret of the Golden Flower: A Chinese Book of Life*. A Harvest Book. New York: Harcourt, Brace & World, 1962.

Williams, N. P. "Tradition." In *Encyclopedia of Relgion and Ethics*. Vol. 12. Ed. James Hastings. New York: Scribner's, 1908–1927. Reprinted 1955.

Winthrop, Robert H., ed. *Culture and the Anthropological Tradition: Essays in Honor of Robert F. Spencer*. Lanham, Md.: University Press of America, 1990.

Woodhouse, Mark B. "The Perennial Wisdom and Moral Philosophy." *The American Theosophist* 72, No. 10 (1984): 327–343.

Xenos, Nicholas. *Scarcity and Modernity*. New York: Routledge, 1989.

Yates, Frances A. *Giordano Bruno and the Hermetic Tradition*. A Vintage Book. New York: Random House, 1969.

———. *The Rosicrucian Enlightenment*. Boulder, Colo.: Shambhala, 1978.

# INDEX

365

*Index* 367

Cappadocian Fathers, 100
Carolingian era, 210
cartels, international, 238
Carter, Stephen, 249, 330
Casey, Gerard, 230
Cassirer, Ernst, 172
Castaneda, Carlos, 340
caste system, Hindu, 227
Catholicism, 11
causality, absolute and relative, 137; in relation to *karma*, 136
cause, as karma, 135
*celebriolatry* as element of modernity, 314
*Celestial Hierarchy, The*, 214
Celtic cultures, 201
Center for the Study of World Religions, 301
Centre International de Recherche Spirituelle Comparée, 101
cerebral hemispheres, 134
Ceylon, 9–11,
Ceylon Reform Society, 108–109
Chacornac, Paul, 56
chakravarti principle, 191
change of cultures, as inevitable, 201
Chastellain, 213
chauvinistic perspective of primitive culture, 164–170
Chinese Taoism, 20
Christ, 200; quaternity of, 49
Christian apocrypha, 324, 346
*Christian Tradition, The*, 214, 325
Christianity, 181, 304
civilization, and culture, 331; as culture, 226
Clement of Alexandria, 100
*Closing of the American Mind, The*, 277
*Collations on the Hexaemeron*, 214
Co-Masonic Order, 107
*coincidentia oppositorum*, 46, 48, 131–135 passim, 224
collective unconscious, 213
Collége Rollin, and Guénon, 11,
*Commentarium I Sententiarum*, 153
*Commentary on the Sentences*, 214

Communist Manifesto, 278
comparative metaphysics, 152
compensation theory, 131, 274, 295
complements, conjunction of contraries and, 47; union of, 48
complexification, in modernity, 263, 310
complexio oppositorum, 43–53
Compte, Auguste, 240, 307
computerization, 237
*Confessions,* of Augustine, 143
continuity, between end of modernity and next phase, 295
contraries, as irreconcilable, 48
Coomaraswamy, Ananda K., 3, 338; and ethnomethodology, 341–342; and modern Theosophy, 108; as scientist, 299; biographical data 9–11; biographies of, 56; collected works of, 38; carried on extended correspondence, 36; criticism of, 313; defines "secularization," 251; influence of on others, 38; lists Traditional cultures, 180; not advocate of planetization, 298; objections to academic philosophy, 70; on art and vocation, 255; on arts and crafts in medieval Christendom, 215; on Christian missionaries, 251; on equality, 279; on folk and primitive mythology, 200; on culture, 331–333; on education and scholarship, 276; on folklore, 82; on hierarchical arrangement of Traditional culture, 182; on *karma*, 136; on mass production, 256; on meaninglessness, 269; on modern art, 270–271; on mythology, 165; on periodicity, 127; on return to first principles, 296; on return to the Middle Ages, 292; on sin, 229; on specialization, 262; on synthesis of opposites, 132; on the Absolute, 120; on the greater mysteries, 203; on Traditional arts, 185; precision of language, 312; published in *The Theosophist*, 150; style of elucidating Tradition, 13
Coomaraswamy, Doña Luisa, 56
Coomaraswamy, Rama P., 55, 60

*Discarded Image, The*, 242
*disputatio*, 207
dissimilarity between primitive and
developed Traditional cultures, 205
diversification, in modernity, 261
divison of labor, Durkheim vs. Traditional, 231
*Doctrine of the Subtle Body*, 140
Doki, Egypt, and Guénon, 12
Dominate, 189
Dominicans, medieval, 207
Dostoevski, Feodor, 144
Doutté, Edmond, 17
Dravidian culture, 201
dualism, as false conception, 50
duality, 131–135 passim
Duby, Georges, 214
Dudley, Gilford, 51, 225
dukes of Burgundy, 215
Dumézil, Georges, 47, 183, 214
Dumont, Louis, 47, 227
Duns Scotus, 100, 211
*duo sunt in homine*, of Aquinas, 133
Durand, Gilbert, 33, 248, 263, 292
Durkheim, Emile, 26, 262, 289
Durkheimian sociology, 278

Eastern religions, popularized, 301
Eaton, Gai, 312
Eckhart, Meister, 100, 181, 204, 211, 212, 218
Eckhartshausen, 96
ecological damage, 283
Edison, Thomas A., 107
education, Traditional system of, 50–51
educational confusion, of modernity, 274–275
Eek, Sven, 150
effect, as karma, 135
effluent discharges, 283
Eglin, Trent, 340
Egypt, 12, 201
Einstein, Alfred, 298
Eisenstadt, Shmuel, 320
*Eleventh Hour, The*, 240, 315
El-Shakhs, Salah, 320

Elshtain, Jean B., 314
Eliade, Mircea, 36, 42, 101, 114, 123, 130, 140, 154, 173, 190, 208–209, 249, 269, 297, 341; on secularization; 251; on specialization, 262; as bridge between Tradition and history of religions, 175; on planetization, 301; on the terror of history, 269
Eliot, T. S., 42, 326; on culture, 347
Elkin, A. P., 171
Ellwood, Robert, 99, 103, 149, 299, 340
Emerson, Ralph Waldo, 192
empirical data, as validity in modernity, 258
empiricism, 80
*enantiodromia*, 194, 274, 293, 295; definition of, 131
*Encyclopedia Britannica*, 92
*Encyclopedia of Religions and Ethics*, 91, 94, 325
England, as forum of Traditional thought, 33–34; medieval, 210
English, W. A., 108
Enlightenment, 241, 299
enlightenment, spiritual, 134
Enneads, 96
*ens perfectissimum*, 134
*Entmythologisierung*, 249
entropic degradation, 267
entropy law, 267, 299
epistemology, 79; and science of neurology, 134
*epistrophe*, 261
equality, 279; of substance in modernity, 278
Eranos conferences, 101, 147
*Eranos Jahrbuch*, 101
eschatology, 80
Esoteric School of Theosophy, 106
esotericism, empirical study of, 339, 340
esotericists, 339
*Essays in National Idealism*, 109
*Essential Unity of All Religions, The*, 122
*Essential Writings of Frithjof Schuon*, xvi, 143
eternal now, 123

eternity, 123; and aeviternity, 124–125
*Ethics and Science*, 258
ethnic cleansing, 272
ethnocentrism, 165–167, 300
ethnomethodology, defined, 339–341
*Études Traditionnelles*, 18, 33, 38, 57
euhemerism, in mythology, 230
Evola, Julius, 39–40; on Guénon, 61
evolution, 128, 130; and involution, 130;
    of Darwin confused with Theosophi-
    cal teaching, 130
evolutionary cycle, 293
evolutionism, 154–155; as informing
    chauvinistic perspective, 164–165;
    attitude of relating to primitives, 162
exegesis, 26; and hierarchy, 24; levels of, 21
existentialism, 268–271; as inversion of
    Traditional metaphysics, 269
*Exploring Mysticism: A Methodological
    Essay*, 224
*extasis*, and view of oneness, 138
extraterrestrial pollution, 290
Exxon Corporation, 238

Fabian Society, 113
Faculté des Sciences Hermétique, 111
famine, 290
fascism, 80
Faivre, Antoine, 5, 33, 100, 147, 339
*fanā'*, 182, 204
Ficino, Marsilio, 71, 77, 100
first principles, xiii, 14, 84, 257, 295–296;
    a return to, 52, 306; as common to
    philosophia perennis, Tradition, and
    Theosophy, 116; as nucleus of primor-
    dial perennial Tradition, 115; loss of,
    257, in modern West, 247 passim; of
    philosophia perennis, 75; of
    *philosophia perennis* and Tradition,
    115–142 passim; of Tradition, 297,
    304
*First Principles*, 115
Flammarion, Camille, 107
Flanders, medieval, 210
Flaxman, John, 96
flood myth, 127

Florsheim, Richard, 292
Fludd, Robert, 100
fluorocarbons, 283
folk and aristocratic elements, within
    developed Traditional culture, 205
folk cultures, within developed Tradi-
    tional culture and primitive, 199
folk wisdom, 81
*Forgotten Truth: The Primordial Tradi-
    tion*, 18, 41, 154
Forman, Robert K. C., 224, 336
*Formation of a Persecuting Society:
    Power and Deviance in Western
    Europe, 950–1250, The*, 210
*Formes traditionnelles et cycles
    cosmique*, 127
forums of the Traditional perspective,
    31–39
forum of Traditional thought, only one
    universal, 37
Foucher, Simon, 77
Foundation for Traditional Studies, 36
*Future of an Illusion, The*, 291
fragmentation, in modernity, 261
France, as forum of Traditional thought,
    32–33; Gide in, 39; medieval, 210
Franciscans, medieval, 207
Frazer, Sir James G., 165, 166, 289
Free-Thinkers, 113
Freud, Sigmund, 26, 166, 167, 169; and
    evolutionism, 165, 289, 291
Freudians, questioning moderity, 274
Fröebe-Kapteyn, Olga, 147
Fry, Roger, 109
Fuller, Buckminster, 239, 248, 297
fusion, in medieval Christendom, 219–
    221; principle of, 261, in Traditional
    culture, 189–192 passim
*Future of Man, The*, 297

Gabriel, 325
Gaia hypothesis, 299
Gadamer, Hans-Georg, 323, 346
Garfinkel, Harold, 340
Geertz, Clifford, 103, 329
genocide, 237